INDUSTRIAL GEOGRAPHY

INDUSTRIAL GEOGRAPHY

H. D. WATTS

Copublished in the United States with
John Wiley & Sons, Inc., New York

Longman Scientific & Technical
Longman Group UK Limited
Longman House, Burnt Mill, Harlow
Essex CM20 2JE, England
and Associated companies throughout the world

Copublished in the United States with
John Wiley & Sons, Inc., 605 Third Avenue, New York, NY 10158

© Longman Group UK Limited 1987

First published 1987

British Library Cataloguing in Publication Data

Watts, H. D.
Industrial geography
1. Industries — Location 2. Geography,
Economic
I. Title
338.09   HC79.D5
ISBN 0-582-30135-1

Library of Congress Cataloging-in-Publication Data

Watts, H. D.
Industrial geography.

Bibliography: p.
Includes index.
1. Industry — Location. 2. Industrialization.
I. Title.
HD58.W33   1987   338.6'042   86-10677

ISBN 0-470-20784-1 (Wiley, USA only).

Set in Linotron 202 10/12 pt Baskerville
Produced by Longman Group (FE) Limited
Printed in Hong Kong

For Lydia

CONTENTS

PREFACE

We are all aware of the changing nature of manufacturing industry. As sunrise industries emerge in landscaped science parks, so the demolition of the smokestacks of the nineteenth century signifies the passing of an older industrial age. While the patterns of change are rather more complex than this stereotyped picture suggests, there is little doubt that they have been accompanied by marked shifts in the geography of industrial activity. Derelict factories and cleared sites are characteristic of some areas while in other areas the skyline is broken by the steel frameworks of new factories under construction. Such changes in the geography of industrial activity receive little attention in existing overviews of industrial geography and the principal stimulus for this book was that as a research worker and as a teacher of industrial geography I found that there was no text which reflected the topics which interested me and my students. This is, then, a book designed for readers interested in trying to understand changes in regional patterns of industrial activity. It is aimed particularly at students who wish to specialise in industrial geography to an extent greater than is usually provided by introductory courses in human geography.

As a book, it is distinctive in three ways. First, in its focus upon industrial change; second, in its recognition of the roles of different industrial organisations; and third in its concern with the births, deaths and migrations of industrial establishments. Part IV of the book breaks with tradition by examining the geographies of these different elements rather than, as is more common, providing sketches of industrial change in specific industries and regions. The discussion adopts an eclectic approach and, like much contemporary industrial geography, it is essentially empirical in outlook and draws most of its examples from North America and Britain. Although industrial geography is a well-established speciality in geography it is one that is developing very rapidly. Much remains for a newcomer to explore and almost every chapter provides an indication of gaps in our understanding of the changing geography of industrial activity. This is not a technical manual but a few technical aspects are outlined in the appendices.

In many ways this is a 'multi-author' work and my most obvious debt is to other industrial geographers in North America, Europe and Australasia whose ideas have been borrowed, consciously or not, to form the basis of the chapters of the book. I am indebted particularly to Roger Hayter (Simon Fraser University), Michael Healey (Coventry Polytechnic) and Howard Stafford (University of Cincinnati) for critical comments on various drafts and, indeed, to the more general stimulus they have provided in making me think carefully about some of the problems faced by industrial geography. Thanks are also due to Paul Coles of the Cartographic Unit in the Department of Geography at the University of Sheffield who converted my rough sketches into the finished maps and diagrams, to Mary Green who typed up the initial drafts and to Audrey Rixham and Helen Owen who have prepared the final version for publication. Finally, a big thank you for everything to Suzanne and Lydia.

Recently, Michelin has announced 2,000 redundancies in Britain and Rank-Hovis-McDougall is to cut 1,200 jobs as part of a long-running programme of reorganisation. Changes in the geography of industrial activity are very much part of the contemporary scene.

Doug Watts
Sheffield
St. Swithin's Day,
1985

ACKNOWLEDGEMENTS

We are grateful to the following for permission to reproduce copyright material:

Alexandrine Press for fig 6.3 from fig 2 p 15 (A Saxenian 1983); Edward Arnold Ltd for extracts, fig 14.4 & table 14.5 from fig 1, table 3 (H D Watts & H A Stafford 1986); the Association of American Geographers for figs 2.4 from figs 2.3, 2.4 (J E McConnell 1980), 4.5 from fig 3 p 219 (J R Borchert 1978), 9.1(1) from p 346 (C Harris 1954) & table 1.4 from table 2 p 190 (A J Scott 1982); the Association of American Geographers and the author, M I Logan for fig 8.2b from fig 3 p 456 (M I Logan 1966); the editor, *Australian Geographical Studies* for fig 4.6 from fig 2 p 55 (P Sheard 1983); University of Birmingham for table 12.6 from tables 5.6, 5.7 pp 56–57 (P M Townroe 1971); the authors' agents on behalf of the authors, B Bluestone and B Harrison for table 14.3 from table A2 (part) p 273 (B Bluestone & B Harrison 1982); Cambridge University Press for figs 6.2b from fig 3 p 249 (R P Oakey, A Thwaites & P Nash 1980), III.1 from fig 1 p 302 (A G Hoare 1973), 11.3a & table 11.1 from fig 1 & table 6 pp 225,7 (P N O'Farrell & R Crouchley 1984), 11.3b & 11.4a from figs 4, 6 pp 195,7 (A Gould & D Keeble 1984), 12.1b from fig 10 p 210 (D Spooner 1972), 12.3 from figs 4,5 p 299 (M B Green & R G Cromley 1984), fig 12.4, from figs 2.9, 2.10, pp 57, 58, (M Chisholm & G Manners 1971), 15.2 from fig 1 p 94 (B Moore & J Rhodes 1973), table 3.4 from table 4 p 148 (R Norton & J Rees 1979); Centre for Urban Policy Research, New Brunswick for fig 3.2 from exhibit 9 (G W Sternleib & J W Hughes 1975); Clark University, *Economic Geography* for fig 5.1 from fig 1, p 96 (D M Smith 1966), fig 9.4b from figs 2, 3 p 48 (J P Osleeb & R G Cromley 1978), Table III.2 from Table 2, p 130 (R. Peet 1983); Croom Helm Ltd for figs 1.1 from fig 13.2 p 288 (R Peet 1982), 12.1c, 4.2 from figs 7.4, 8.5 pp 179, 198 (H D Watts 1980b), table 4.2 from table 2.1 p 8 (D J Storey 1982); the editor, *Economica* for table 6.2 from table 1 pp 28–30 (B Lyons 1980); the editor, *Environment & Planning* for fig III.3b from fig 5 p 950, table 3.5 from tables pp 949/50 (D Keeble 1980); the Geographical Association for fig 6.1a from fig 1 p 158 (R P Oakey 1984b); the editor, *Geography* for fig 9.2 from fig 2 p 14 (H D Watts 1974); the editor, *Geojournal* for fig 13.2 from figs 1, 4 pp 137, 140 (M J Healey 1984); Gower Press for table 11.2 from table 8.17 (M Cross 1981); Wm Heinemann Ltd for fig 11.4b, tables 1.3, 8.1 from fig 6.2, tables 2.5, 5.1 pp 120, 23, 107 (S Fothergill & G Gudgin 1982), table 2.5 from table 4.2 p 80 (F Blackaby 1978); the Controller of Her Majesty's Stationery Office for fig 15.1a (Trade & Industry 1978), tables 13.3, 15.1, 15.2 (Pounce 1981 HMSO), 15.1b (British Business 1984 HMSO); Institute of British Geographers for figs 5.5 from fig 5 p 105 (H D Watts 1971), IV.1 from fig 7 p 80 (Lloyd & Mason 1978); Lloyds Bank for fig 9.1(3) from p 11 (C Clark 1966); Longman Group UK Ltd for Oliver & Boyd Ltd for fig 8.2a (Bale 1981); Longman

Group UK Ltd for fig 4.3 (M J Healey & H D Watts 1975); University of Lund for fig 5.4 from fig 11 p 92 (A Pred 1967); Macmillan Accounts & Administration Ltd for figs 5.3 (D Pocock & R Hudson 1978), 7.1a (P Toyne 1974), table 10.3 (D J Storey 1983b); Methuen Ltd for fig III.3a from fig 5.1b p 96 (D Keeble 1976); New Zealand Geographical Society for fig 5.2 from fig 1 p 68 (P J McDermott 1973); the author, P A Nickson for table 2.6 from table 4.6 p 73 (F Gaffikin & A Nickson 1984); Pergamon Press Ltd for table 12.2 from table 4.5 p 149 (M Sant 1975b); Prentice-Hall Inc for tables 12.4, 14.4 adapted from tables 3.20, 3.21, 5.1 pp 150, 237 (R W Schmenner 1982); the editor, *Journal of Regional Science* for fig 9.4a from figs 11.12 p 238 (E Leamer 1968); Regional Science Association for table 12.3 adapted from table 3 (part) pp 70–71

(B M Moriarty 1983); Saxon House Publishers for fig 9.1(2), table 13.1 from fig 2.2, table 9.7 (G Gudgin 1978), table 5.1 from table 6.2 p 165 (P Townroe 1979); the editor, *Scottish Journal of Political Economy* for table 14.2 (Henderson 1980); the Librarian, Treasury & Cabinet Office Library for table 1.7 from table 3.16 p 39 (A Macey 1982); John Wiley & Sons Ltd for figs 2.1 from fig 7.2 p 270 (G Steed 1981), 2.2, 2.3 from figs 10.6 (part), 10.5 (part) pp 387, 384 (G T Bloomfield 1981), 6.5 from fig 1.2 p 49 (G Norcliffe 1975), 8.1 from fig 11.2 p 266 (D M Smith 1981), 12.1a from fig 7.4 p 201 (J Rees 1974), table 12.5 from table 6.1 p 174 (H A Stafford 1974), table 2.1 from table 1.4 p 18 (F E Hamilton & G Linge 1981); V H Winston & Sons Inc for fig 6.1b from fig 1 p 59 (R. A. Erickson and T. R. Leinbach 1979).

1

THE GEOGRAPHY OF
INDUSTRIAL CHANGE

The central task of contemporary industrial geography is to describe and explain changes in the spatial pattern of industrial activity. It is a task which provides a distinctive focus for industrial geography and one which distinguishes it from the closely related fields of industrial economics and industrial sociology. The emphasis in industrial geography is on explaining where and why changes in the location of industrial activity have taken place and on trying to understand why some areas experience industrial growth and other areas experience industrial decline.

The term 'industry' in its widest sense refers to all economic activities. It is used in this way in referring to the fishing industry, the electronics industry or the retailing industry, but industrial geography is not the study of the location of all economic activities and its sphere of interest is usually restricted to what is called *manufacturing industry*. This also includes industries which 'process' mineral, agricultural and forest products.

In geographical studies of industrial activity spatial patterns of change are often measured by increases or decreases in the *employment* opportunities in different areas. Employment change is a particularly appropriate measure to use. It is easier to visualise 50 employees than to visualise 1,000 micro-chips or £5 million output. It helps to express industrial activities in human terms and to stress that they provide employment for our friends and relatives. Industrial change, measured by employment provision, is reflected in lost jobs and unemployment in areas where industrial employment is declining and new jobs and new opportunities in areas where industrial employment is growing.

Manufacturing industries have an important influence upon patterns of urban and regional development but in recent years there has been a fall in the relative importance of manufacturing industry as a supplier of employment opportunities in the developed capitalist economies which are the main concern of this book. The decreasing significance of manufacturing employment in such economies has been called *de-industrialisation* although the exact meaning of the term is open to debate (Blackaby 1978; Bluestone and Harrison 1982). The extent of de-industrialisation is seen in Table 1.1. Although manufacturing activity still accounts for between one-fifth and one-third of the employment in the countries listed, its share fell between 1972 and 1981 in all

Table 1.1 Manufacturing as a proportion of all employment, selected countries, 1972 and 1981

	1972	1981
Australia*	25.5	19.4
Canada	21.8	19.4
West Germany	36.8	33.4
Japan	27.0	24.8
United Kingdom	32.9	28.4
United States	24.3	21.7

(*Source*: *Employment Gazette* Dec. 1983:S15)
* Includes electricity, gas and water.

of them. As a consequence of this fall the important role of manufacturing employment in regional
and urban development has been questioned
(Daniels 1983). While it is possible to envisage
regional and urban growth led by certain types of
service activity (such as tourism) it is still manufacturing industry which forms the basis upon
which many regional economies are built.
Changes in service employment (especially at
regional level) will be a response to changes in
the manufacturing sector in many, if not most,
areas. As Fothergill and Gudgin (1982:47) observe 'for better or worse... the pattern of urban
and regional growth depends... on what hap-
pens to manufacturing employment'.

This introductory chapter illustrates some of
the main trends in the distribution of industrial
activity at the present time. The examples show
quite clearly the differential spatial impact of
manufacturing employment change and indicate
how the rates of employment change vary from
one area to another. These spatial variations
have important social and political consequences
for they underly many of the patterns which
occur in the geography of well-being and the
quality of life. An insight into the reasons underlying the geography of industrial change
makes an important contribution towards understanding some of the problems facing the societies in which we live.

THE CHANGING GEOGRAPHY OF INDUSTRIAL ACTIVITY

Changes in the spatial pattern of industrial activity as measured by changes in employment in
manufacturing activity can be seen at a variety
of spatial scales – international, regional, inter-
urban and intra-urban. Employment trends do
not necessarily reflect trends in industrial output.
Admittedly, employment growth usually reflects
output growth, but employment decline can be
associated with falling, static and even rising
output. A critique of employment as a measure
of industrial activity appears in Appendix I
(pages 229–30).

International patterns

Figure 1.1 illustrates the principal changes in the
international distribution of manufacturing activity between 1965 and 1975 and maps these on
countries which are drawn in proportion to the
number of their manufacturing employees in
1975. The most striking feature is the marked
percentage increases in some newer and smaller
industrial areas. In some areas, especially those
in Africa, the large increases reflect the operation
of the small base value effect which arises when
using percentage growth rates (Appendix I, page
231) but in the *newly industrialising countries* the

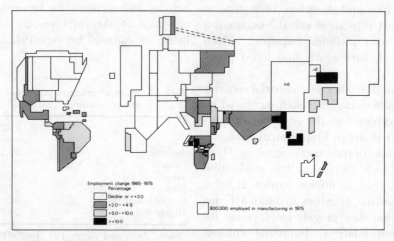

Fig. 1.1 Manufacturing employment change, international patterns, 1965 to 1975 (*Source*: Peet 1982: 288)

rapid increase in employment in manufacturing industry has continued to the present day. More recent data are available only for a limited number of countries but between 1974 and 1983 manufacturing employment in Hong Kong rose by 43 per cent, in Singapore by 41 per cent and in Korea by 77 per cent (International Labour Office, 1984). While industrialisation is characteristic of only selected parts of the developing world (Peet 1982:287–9), limited employment growth or employment decline is characteristic of most parts of the developed world.

A more detailed picture of trends from 1972 to 1982 in some developed countries indicates that while the *relative* importance of manufacturing declined in virtually all of them (Table 1.1) the nature of *absolute* changes in employment levels differed (Fig. 1.2). In the United States manufacturing employment fluctuated between 18 and

21 million paid employees. Canada showed fluctuations between 1.8 and 2.1 million employees and Japanese employment fluctuated between 11 and 12 million. There are slight hints of a downward trend in the Japanese data. A downward trend is displayed in the other three countries and is most striking in the case of West Germany and the United Kingdom. West Germany lost 1.3 million jobs (or 14 per cent) over the ten-year period while the United Kingdom lost 2 million jobs (26 per cent). No less than 1.4 million of the United Kingdom jobs were lost between 1979 and 1982.

Regional changes

Major changes can be traced in the levels of manufacturing employment within these countries. Contrasts in the performance of the differ-

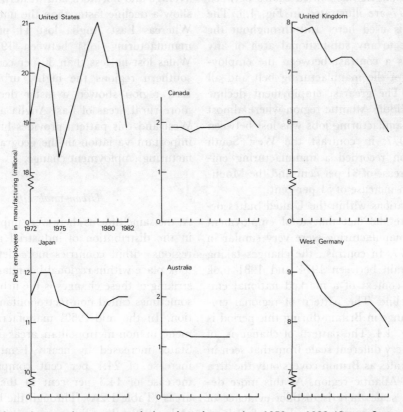

Fig. 1.2 Manufacturing employment trends in selected countries, 1972 to 1982 (*Source*: International Labour Office 1984)

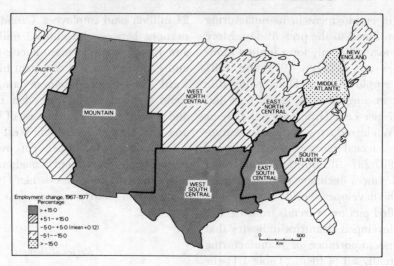

Fig. 1.3 Manufacturing employment change, United States, 1967 to 1977 (*Source*: US Bureau of Census 1984: Table 1341)

ent major regions of the United States between 1967 and 1977 are illustrated in Fig. 1.3. The term region is used here, and throughout the book to refer to any sub-national area of any size. There is a contrast between the employment record of the manufacturing belt and all other areas. The greatest employment decline was in the Middle Atlantic region where almost one in five manufacturing jobs was lost between 1967 and 1977; in contrast the West South Central region recorded a manufacturing employment increase of 31 per cent and the Mountain region an increase of 51 per cent.

These variations within the United States occurred despite the fact that total employment numbers in manufacturing were very similar in 1967 and 1977. In contrast, the changes taking place in Britain between 1974 and 1981 took place in the context of a marked national employment decline. The pattern of regional employment change in Britain during this period is shown in Fig. 1.4. The pattern of change is, of course, at a very different scale from that seen in the United States as Britain covers only the area of the South Atlantic region. At this more detailed spatial scale there is distinct evidence of contrasts between southern regions of Britain which show a decline less than the national

average and northern and western regions which show a decline faster than the national average. Whereas East Anglia lost 11 per cent of its manufacturing jobs between 1974 and 1981 Wales lost no less than 30 per cent. Within the southern regions the highly urbanised South-East region showed a faster decline than the more rural areas of East Anglia and the South-West and this pattern provides hints of another important variation in the geography of manufacturing employment change.

Urban–rural shifts

At the same time as there were important changes in the distribution of industrial activity across regions within countries more detailed changes took place within regional boundaries. The most striking of these changes is the urban–rural shift, sometimes called non-metropolitan industrialisation. In the mid-1960s manufacturing employment in non-metropolitan areas in the United States increased by nearly 1 million jobs, an increase of 24.1 per cent compared with an increase of 14.3 per cent in the metropolitan areas (Table 1.2A). Through the late 1960s and early 1970s this difference was maintained although the rates of percentage change were much

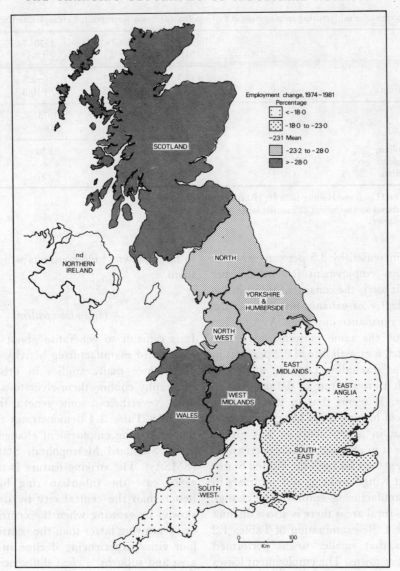

Employment change, 1974~1981
Percentage
< -18·0
-18·0 to -23·0
-23·1 Mean
-23·2 to -28·0
> -28·0

Fig. 1.4 Manufacturing employment change, Britain, 1974 to 1981 (*Source: Employment Gazette* 1975 and 1983)

smaller. One of the most striking features of this non-metropolitan industrialisation was that '52 per cent of the entire 1962–78 increase of 1.8 million workers... (in non-metropolitan areas) ... were added... between March 1962 and March 1967' (Haren and Holling 1979:15–17). Estall (1983) examined the 1970–78 trends in more detail (Table 1.2B). The 50 largest metropolitan areas of the 1970 census recorded a loss

of almost 6 per cent of their manufacturing employment, the remaining metropolitan areas registered a very slight increase while the non-metropolitan areas witnessed an increase of nearly 20 per cent.

Similar urban–rural contrasts can be seen in Britain (Table 1.3) where the better employment record of the rural areas stands out quite clearly. From 1971 to 1975 manufacturing employment

Table 1.2   Changes in manufacturing employment in metropolitan and non-metropolitan areas, United States, 1962–78

(A) 1962–1978*	1962–67 (%)	1967–70 (%)	1970–74 (%)	1974–78 (%)
Metropolitan	+14.3	+0.7	−2.3	−1.3
Non-metropolitan	+24.1	+5.3	+10.8	+1.2
(B) 1969–1978†		1969 (000s)	1973 (000s)	Per cent change
Large metropolitan		10,446	9,836	−5.8
Small metropolitan		4,462	4,586	+2.8
Non-metropolitan		5,248	6,157	+17.3

(*Source*: (A) Based on Haren and Holling 1979:18; (B) Based on Estall 1983:139)
* Using 1977 boundaries and including 225 mostly larger of 278 SMSAs.
† Using 1969 boundaries.

in rural areas increased by 3.5 per cent while in the conurbations employment fell by 2.2 per cent. Of interest too is the consistent trend in the data. As the degree of urbanisation falls so the employment performance improves. As long ago as 1959 to 1966 the same patterns stood out. Over that period, a growth rate of 0.2 per cent in the conurbations (excluding London) was to be contrasted with a growth rate of 6.0 per cent in the rural areas. It seems that in Britain since 1959 employment in rural areas has either grown faster than that in urban areas or has grown while employment in urban areas was decreasing.

Although these data for both the United States and the United Kingdom bring out contrasts in the rate of manufacturing employment change between urban–rural areas there is also a distinct inter-urban effect. Re-examination of Tables 1.2 and 1.3 shows that smaller towns performed better than larger towns. The employment losses

in larger towns hide contrasts which exist *within* them.

Intra-urban patterns

It is difficult to generalise about the changing location of manufacturing activity within urban areas since many studies in urban industrial geography confine themselves to a single urban area. Nevertheless, some general trends are discernible. Table 1.4 demonstrates the pattern of manufacturing employment change in a sample of 17 Standard Metropolitan Statistical Areas (SMSAs). The striking feature is that in almost every case the suburban ring has performed better than the central city by declining more slowly, by growing when the centre is declining or by growing faster than the centre. Among the four cities experiencing decline in both central area and suburbs, a clear difference between the

Table 1.3   Urban and rural employment change, Britain, 1959–75

Area	Per cent per year of manufacturing employment at the start of each period		
	1959–66	1966–71	1971–75
London	−0.7	−3.6	−5.1
Conurbations	+0.2	−1.7	−2.2
Free-standing cities	+1.7	−0.1	−1.3
Industrial towns	+2.8	−0.2	−0.5
County towns	+3.0	+1.1	+0.1
Rural areas	+6.0	+1.9	+3.5

(*Source*: Fothergill and Gudgin 1982:23)

Table 1.4 Intra-urban employment change, selected SMSAs, 1972–77

	Total employees 1977	Central city % change	Suburban ring % change
New York	796.6	−19.5	−2.4
Buffalo	140.3	−12.8	−4.7
Pittsburgh	239.7	−11.2	−8.0
Kansas City	117.8	−0.9	−0.8
Miami	85.1	−19.1	+6.6
Atlanta	128.7	−18.1	+6.1
Chicago	884.3	−15.0	+8.2
Detroit	564.4	−15.0	+10.7
Milwaukee	204.1	−14.0	+20.3
Boston	269.7	−13.7	+4.5
Minneapolis – St Paul	216.9	−10.2	+16.9
Cleveland	265.4	−7.9	+5.0
Cincinnati	160.2	−5.6	+7.2
Dallas – Ft Worth	269.9	+5.1	+28.0
Seattle – Everett	131.9	+11.5	+31.6
Los Angeles – Long Beach	825.5	+12.7	+2.2
Houston	210.1	+36.5	+14.6

(*Source*: Scott 1982:190)

two zones appears in New York, Buffalo and Pittsburgh. In New York a central area decline of −19.5 per cent is to be compared with a suburban ring fall of only −2.4 per cent. At the other end of the spectrum, only two of the sampled cities recorded higher rates of increase in the central area from 1972 to 1977, these were Los Angeles – Long Beach and Houston. The latter's central area growth of 36.5 per cent has to be contrasted with a growth of 14.6 per cent in the suburban ring (Scott 1982).

This series of maps and tables demonstrates quite clearly that employment change has taken place at different rates in different places. As a result of these differing rates of change, some areas experience an increase in their share of total manufacturing employment and other areas experience a decrease in their share of total manufacturing employment. These increases and decreases in the shares of different areas are the *locational changes* which form the main concern of industrial geography. It is rare for locational change to involve the physical movement of a factory from one area to another.

Locational change raises some important and interesting questions for industrial geography. Why have some countries in the developing

world experienced rapid manufacturing employment growth? Why have capitalist countries in the developed world experienced stable or declining manufacturing employment? Why have the southern and western parts of the United States witnessed manufacturing employment growth while the north and east have witnessed employment decline? Why has employment declined faster in northern Britain than in southern Britain? Why have non-metropolitan areas in the United States and Britain experienced industrialisation? Why do manufacturing employment change rates vary between inner and outer city areas?

Unfortunately, it is not possible to examine all these questions here and the discussion is oriented deliberately towards locational change at regional and inter-urban scales with most emphasis placed upon regional differences. This is a reflection of the inherent interest of much industrial geography in the implications of employment change in manufacturing industry for regional and urban development within national economic systems. This discussion thus excludes questions about changes in the international distribution of manufacturing activity except in so far as they have effects on national economic systems. It also pays only limited attention to the analysis of intra-urban industrial patterns since these tend to be associated with the redistribution of jobs within rather than between regions.

DISAGGREGATING EMPLOYMENT CHANGE

Locational change in manufacturing activity arises mainly from changes involving the *plants* (factories) in which production takes place. Plants undertaking similar activities make up *industries*. Although plants are the points at which employment changes are implemented, decisions about such changes are taken by *firms*. Employment change in manufacturing industry is the outcome of decisions made by firms which express themselves in activity levels at particular plants. In a *single-plant firm* the terms plant and firm are synonymous but in the *multi-plant firm*, and especially the multi-regional firm, the experience of the firm as a whole can be very different from the experience of one of its plants.

The changes in the relative importance of different areas described in the last section reflect net changes. *Net change* is the sum of employment changes (both positive and negative) taking place within particular industries, firms or plants

within a particular area. The employment experience of a particular region mirrors the balance between industries expanding and contracting their employment, the balance between firms hiring and laying-off labour and the balance between the employment growth and employment decline associated with particular plants. These balances are not independent of one another since plants are controlled by firms and firms can influence the employment performance of an industry. But industries, firms and plants have their own distinctive geographies of employment change and these geographies raise some further interesting and important questions.

Industries

Some of the variety of industrial activities found within the manufacturing sector are listed in Table 1.5. Although terms such as *heavy industry* and *light industry* are used in everyday discussions careful analysis demands the use of a well-defined terminology. Industries are usually identified by reference to a *Standard Industrial Classification* (SIC) which classifies activities into either *two-digit industries* (Orders) or *three-digit industries* (Minimum List Headings). Although

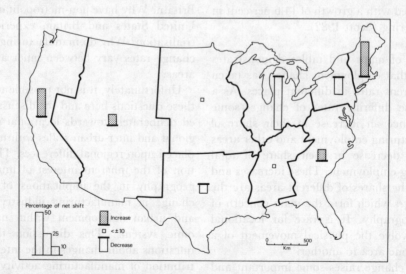

Fig. 1.5 Net shift in employment in the engineering and scientific instruments industry, United States, 1972 to 1981 (*Source*: estimated from US Bureau of Census 1973; US Bureau of Census 1982)

Table 1.5 Classification of industrial activities

United Kingdom, 1968 Standard Industrial Classification*	United States, Standard Industrial Classification
III† Food, drink and tobacco	20† Food and kindred products
IV Coal and petroleum products	21 Tobacco products
V Chemicals and allied industries	22 Textile mill products
VI Metal manufacture	23 Apparel and other textile products
VII Mechanical engineering	24 Lumber and wood products
331‡ Agricultural machinery (except tractors)	25 Furniture and fixtures
332 Metal-working machine tools	26 Paper and allied products
333 Pumps, valves and compressors	27 Printing and publishing
334 Industrial engines	28 Chemicals and allied products
335 Textile machinery and accessories	29 Petroleum and coal products
336 Construction and earth-moving equipment	30 Rubber and miscellaneous plastic products
337 Mechanical handling equipment	31 Leather and leather products
338 Office machinery	32 Stone, clay and glass products
339 Other machinery	33 Primary metal industries
341 Industrial (including process) plant and steelwork	34 Fabricated metal products
342 Ordnance and small arms	35 Machinery, except electrical
349 Other mechanical engineering	36 Electric and electronic equipment
VIII Instrument engineering	361‡ Electric distributing equipment
IX Electrical engineering	362 Electrical industrial apparatus
X Shipbuilding and marine engineering	363 Household appliances
XI Vehicles	364 Electric lighting and wiring equipment
XII Metal goods not elsewhere specified	365 Radio and TV receiving equipment
XIII Textiles	366 Communication equipment
XIV Leather, leather goods and furs	367 Electronic components
XV Clothing and footwear	369 Miscellaneous electrical equipment
XVI Bricks, pottery, glass, cement, etc.	37 Transportation equipment
XVII Timber, furniture, etc.	38 Instruments and related products
XVIII Paper, printing and publishing	39 Miscellaneous manufacturing
XIX Other manufacturing industries	

* Replaced by the 1980 SIC from 1981 onwards. The introduction of the new SIC often precludes comparison of post-1981 data with earlier time periods.
† Orders, two-digit industries
‡ Minimum List Headings, three-digit industries

industrial data sets clearly tie specific employment figures to each industrial category these do not reflect necessarily distinct activities, for activities are allocated to classes with reference to a set of well-defined rules (Appendix I page 236).

Each industry has its own geography of employment change. Figures 1.5 and 1.6 illustrate just some of these patterns in a number of three-digit industries and show the regions which were increasing or decreasing their share of national employment in the selected industries. The technique of shift analysis upon which these maps are based is described in Appendix I (pages 231–2).

In the engineering and scientific instruments

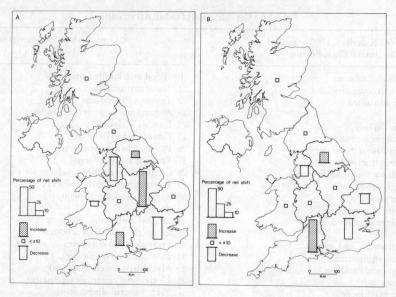

Fig. 1.6 Net shift in employment in two British industries, 1974 to 1981 (A) Hosiery (B) Electronic computers and radio, radar and electronic capital goods industry (*Source*: *Employment Gazette* 1975 and 1983)

industry in the United States employment increased between 1972 and 1981 and almost half the increase in jobs contributed to the net shift between regions (Fig. 1.5). The major changes were associated with net shifts out of the Middle Atlantic and East North Central regions and net shifts into the New England and Pacific regions. Of the net losses 85 per cent were associated with the former two regions which in 1972 accounted for just over half the employment in the industry.

Redistribution of activities was less evident in the British hosiery industry where despite a decline of 36,000 jobs only 4,000 jobs (a net shift of 11 per cent) were involved in changing the relative importance of regions (Fig. 1.6A). The general trend was for the East Midlands to increase its share of the national industry, despite the fact that in 1974 it had almost two-thirds of the British employment in the hosiery industry. The newer British industries shown in Fig. 1.6B recorded an increase of 44,000 jobs between 1974 and 1981 and a net shift, involving 10,000 jobs, of 23 per cent. Over half the losses were associated with the South-East and East Anglia which accounted for two-thirds of the employ-

ment in these industries in 1974 and almost half the gains were in the South-West which saw its share of these industries rise markedly.

Firms

The disaggregation of manufacturing activity on the basis of industrial sector is employed widely in industrial geography. Its widespread use reflects its inherent 'neutrality'. Recently emphasis has been placed upon isolating the patterns of change created by large multi-plant firms. Just two examples illustrate the way in which the geographies of groups of firms or an industrial firm can change.

Figure 1.7 shows the patterns of employment change between the early and late 1970s in 410 major firms in the United States. These firms increased their employment by over 1 million jobs and one-third of these jobs (a net shift of 33 per cent) were linked to changes in the relative importance of different regions. The net losses were shared almost equally between the Middle Atlantic and East North Central regions and all other regions (except New England and South Atlantic) recorded net gains of over 10 per cent.

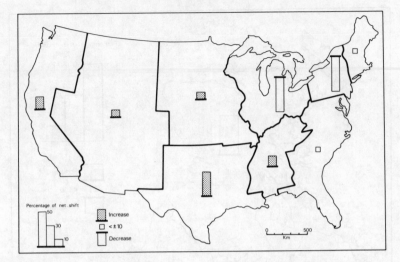

Fig. 1.7 Net shift in employment in 410 major manufacturing firms in the United States, early and late 1970s (*Source*: Schmenner 1982:175)

The most marked shift of activities (one-third of the positive net shifts) was towards the West South Central region (Schmenner 1982:174). In this case, the overall pattern is not very different from manufacturing as a whole.

While Fig. 1.7 shows the experience of a group of predominantly multi-regional firms, Fig. 1.8 shows the experience of one such firm (Cadbury Schweppes). This firm which manufactures chocolates, confectionary, soft drinks and household hygiene products reduced its labour force by 4,000 employees between 1972 and 1984. More interesting is its geographical redistribution of its employment opportunities with a net shift of 57 per cent. The majority of the net losses were associated with its main production region (the West Midlands) which accounted for 45 per cent of the firm's employment in 1972 but only 33 per cent in 1984. The net gains were more evenly distributed with almost 80 per cent going to Scotland, East Anglia and the South-East. Regions like the North-West and Scotland which were showing rapid rates of decline in all manufacturing were showing net gains in their shares of employment in Cadbury Schweppes.

Plants

At plant level, just as net population change is

disaggregated into births, deaths and migration so net manufacturing employment is disaggregated into new plants (births), plant closures (deaths) and the transfer of plants from one area to another (migration). Births include entirely new firms as well as the branch plants of established firms. *Births*, *deaths* and *transfers* affect the employment opportunities in different areas but it is also necessary to add a fourth element for which there is no parallel in population geography. This fourth element records the employment change created by the *in situ* expansion or contraction of plants which were not involved in births, deaths or transfers during the time period being examined. These four elements make up the main *components of change*. Some of the problems of isolating the different components of change are discussed in Appendix I (pages 236–7) but the ways in which different components make different contributions to net changes in specific areas are shown in Table 1.6 and Table 1.7.

Table 1.6 relates to two SMSAs with declining manufacturing employment from 1965 to 1968 (Cleveland and Minneapolis–St Paul) and two with increasing employment (Boston and Phoenix). In both declining centres, the major component contributing to employment decline was plant closures although it was offset to a greater

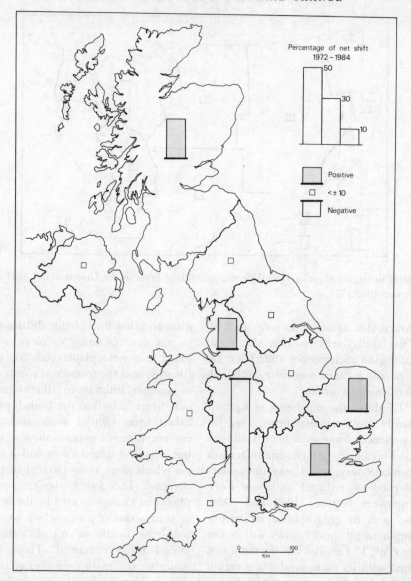

Fig. 1.8 Net shift in employment in Cadbury Schweppes, 1972 to 1984 (*Source*: Cadbury Schweppes)

extent in Minneapolis–St Paul than in Cleveland by births. Net *in situ* change made little difference. Data on *in situ* contractions and *in situ* expansions are not available. In Boston, growing manufacturing employment was achieved by net *in situ* expansion, despite a marked loss of jobs in plant deaths. Only a small number of jobs was created in new plants. The Phoenix data record the smallest percentage loss in employment

through deaths, while net *in situ* growth again dominates, although the 12 per cent increase in employment in new plants makes an important contribution to the rate of change. Overall, there are marked variations in the inter-urban geography of *in situ* change; the contrasts are less marked in births and even less in closures. In the case of closure there are only six percentage points difference between the highest and lowest

Table 1.6 Components of manufacturing employment change, selected SMSAs, United States, 1965–68

SMSA	Closure*	Net *in situ* change†	Births‡	Net change
	% of 1965 employment			
Cleveland	−7.8	+0.5	+2.6	−4.7
Minneapolis – St Paul	−11.2	−0.9	+6.1	−5.9
Boston	−8.0	+10.5	+1.3	+3.8
Phoenix	−5.3	+20.4	+12.1	+27.1
Range (percentage points)	5.9	21.3	10.8	

(*Source*: Based on Struyk and James 1975:41, 58, 75 and 90)

* Includes transfers out.

† Net *in situ* change is employment change arising from *in situ* expansion less employment loss in *in situ* contractions. In this example it also includes transfer within the city.

‡ Includes transfers in.

rate of job loss but over a ten-year period the inter-urban employment losses through closure would range from 18 per cent to 37 per cent.

The experience of different areas is also brought out in the British evidence for the period between 1972 and 1975 (Table 1.7). The principal feature to notice is the dominant role played by *in situ* change, with *in situ* contraction resulting in the loss of between 8.1 per cent and 11.9 per cent of the jobs existing in a region in 1972. This is offset partly by *in situ* increases ranging from 7.2 per cent to 10.5 per cent of

1972 employment. Openings and closures were less significant than either *in situ* contraction or *in situ* expansion. Looking at the overall geography of each component, employment loss through closure was highest in Scotland and lowest in the Northern region, employment gains in openings were highest in East Anglia and lowest in the West Midlands, *in situ* employment contraction was highest in the West Midlands and lowest in Scotland while *in situ* expansion was highest in East Anglia and lowest in the South-East. In contrast to the figures for the United States all

Table 1.7 Components of manufacturing employment change by region, Britain, 1972–75

Region	Closure*	*In situ* contraction	*In situ* expansion	Births†	Net change
	% of 1972 employment				
South-East	−5.6	−11.4	+7.2	+1.5	−8.2
East Anglia	−3.5	−10.9	+10.5	+3.8	−0.2
South-West	−3.7	−10.5	+8.2	+2.0	−4.0
West Midlands	−3.9	−11.9	+9.2	+0.2	−6.4
East Midlands	−3.6	−11.1	+7.8	+2.1	−4.8
Yorkshire & Humberside	−4.2	−8.4	+8.8	+1.1	−2.7
North-West	−4.1	−9.7	+7.8	+0.7	−5.3
North	−2.5	−9.9	+10.0	+1.2	−1.3
Wales	−3.4	−9.1	+9.6	+3.5	+0.6
Scotland	−6.1	−8.1	+10.3	+1.8	−2.1
Range (Percentage points)	3.6	3.8	3.3	3.6	

(*Source*: Macey 1982:39)

* Includes transfers out of region.

† Includes transfers into region.

the components show similar degrees of variation between regions, although the range of three to four percentage points is lower.

These two examples illustrate the extent to which the different components of change can interact with one another to produce net employment changes within an area (Further examples are provided later, pages 205–7). Each component, like each firm and each industry, has its own distinctive geography.

Examination of locational change in industries, firms and plants raises yet more questions to supplement those which arise from net employment change. Why did the instruments industry show a net shift into the New England and Pacific regions? Why did the British hosiery industry show an increased concentration in the East Midlands? Why did some newer British industries show a net shift to the South-West? For what reasons did major manufacturing firms in the United States show a marked shift towards the West South Central region? What led Cadbury Schweppes to reduce its dependence on the West Midland region? Why was employment in births important in Phoenix? Why did so much employment loss through plant deaths occur in Minneapolis–St Paul? Why was the *in situ* contraction of employment so high in the West Midlands of England?

It is, of course, impossible to illustrate more than a few examples of the changing geography of industrial activity but these examples are indicative of the kind of changes which have taken place. In examining the geography of employment change in manufacturing industry the intrinsic variety in the patterns of spatial change is self-evident and each geography poses a number of questions. It is the challenge of answering these questions that provides a stimulus to enquiry in modern industrial geography.

APPROACHES TO INDUSTRIAL GEOGRAPHY

There is no one agreed approach or methodology which is used consistently throughout contemporary industrial geography in trying to answer the kind of questions posed above. Attempts to categorise the variety of approaches and methodologies are made difficult by the fact that many studies, while written predominantly within one approach, contain hints of others. Nevertheless, most studies can be associated with one of three approaches: behavioural, neoclassical, and structural.

Behavioural approaches place emphasis upon the ways in which firms and individuals influence the changing location of industry. They are subdivided into two groups. One group collects data about the attributes of firms and individuals and relates these attributes to their behaviour to infer an explanation for that behaviour. The second group adopts a more direct approach and asks the firm or individual why particular actions were undertaken. The first group relates firm attributes (for example, nationality of ownership) to the changing location of industry, the second focuses upon the factors influencing decisions and the way those decisions are made. In some cases, both groups examine individual firms or small groups of firms, especially where such firms dominate an industry or region.

Neoclassical approaches, derived in part from work in neoclassical economics, see firms, plants and individuals as sufficiently similar in attitudes, intentions and responses to stimuli to allow explanations of changes across industrial sectors or, indeed, across manufacturing as a whole. They assume that changes in employment levels in different areas reflect the responses of a group of plants to inter-area variations in, for example, labour markets or access to suppliers. They would regard the finding that 'low wages encourage employment growth' as an adequate explanation for job creation in a particular region. The neoclassical approach can be taken to include numerical descriptions of industrial change.

Structuralist approaches adopt a more holistic view. For them, the finding that 'low wages encourage employment growth' provides no explanation at all and this approach argues it is necessary to pose the question as to why there are low wages in some areas and not others, and why firms try to exploit low wages. Explanations of locational change are sought in the structure of the capitalist society in which the firm works.

In essence, behavioural studies see explanations for the geography of employment change lying in the behaviour of different types of firm, neoclassical explanations stress the reactions of plants (in aggregate) to external stimuli in the areas in which they operate, while structuralists see explanations lying in the forces operating within the world capitalist system.

In identifying these different approaches it is difficult to suggest 'indicators' which enable particular pieces of work to be allocated to a particular approach. Yet some works written predominantly within one approach can illustrate the differences between the approaches. Compare, for example, Peet's (1983) structuralist analysis of net employment change in the United States with Fothergill and Gudgin's (1982) neoclassical analysis of the urban–rural shift in Britain. A behavioural approach is well illustrated by Krumme's (1981a) work on Volkswagen's decision to invest in the United States and Watts's (1978) study of inter-organisational relations in the United Kingdom brewing industry.

It is perhaps not surprising that there is a vigorous and sometimes acrimonious debate among the proponents of these different approaches. Massey (1984:50) sees much behavioural geography as 'simple description'. Likewise, Taylor (1984:2) describes Peet's (1983) structuralist analysis as 'descriptive monitoring ...shrouded in clouds of Marxist jargon and mystified by language'.

There have been attempts to bring these approaches together. Hay (1979) suggests that it might be possible to accept that two different industrial geographies can coexist. One is a *critical* industrial geography which shows, for example, the extent to which present-day changes in the geography of industrial activity are the outcomes of the capitalist system of production, while the other is a *nomological* industrial geography which searches for explanations of the way in which change in the geography of industrial activity takes place. In contrast, Hamilton and Linge (1983:7) make the suggestion that the different approaches might be integrated within a *systems framework*. Changes analysed through a behavioural approach can be regarded as nesting within changes analysed through the neoclassical approach and, in turn, the neoclassical approaches take place within a capitalist system which can be analysed through a structuralist approach.

Integration is not as easy as the systems approach suggests since the different approaches have different *methodologies* which influence the way in which research is carried out. For example, whereas neoclassical and some behavioural analyses tend to use a *positivist* (or hypothesis testing) methodology to establish general principles, structuralist analyses use a *structuralist* methodology which investigates the processes of change and the structures which create and influence them at a specific point in time. Since society is evolving from capitalism to socialism there can be no general principles of location.

Not only is work in industrial geography characterised by different approaches and different methodologies, it also accepts different modes of analysis. At one extreme are *qualitative* assessments of the opinions of individuals and written sources: these are usually interpreted in a scholarly manner with arguments backed up by lengthy reference lists. At the other end of the scale are *quantitative* assessments written in terse styles and full of tabular material, statistical tests and mathematical symbols. Modes of analysis are related to approaches and methodologies in that neoclassical approaches tend to be quantitative, structuralist approaches tend to be qualitative and behavioural approaches have a balance between the two modes.

Any discussion of contemporary industrial geography cannot ignore the variety of approaches, methodologies and modes of analysis. This introduction to industrial geography adopts an eclectic approach which acknowledges the contributions made by the writers working within the different traditions. There is no formal treatment of traditional industrial location theory. It is assumed readers will have covered this in introductory human geography, and most emphasis in placed upon questions raised by the geography of employment change and the attempts to answer them. Modern industrial geography is problem-oriented with a strong tradition of empirical enquiry.

STRUCTURE

This eclectic approach to industrial geography consists of five main sections. Part I considers the international and historical frameworks within which individual firms operate. Part II examines the firms themselves and the ways in which location decisions are made. Part III describes the specific context within which change takes place. It begins with a consideration of the fundamental decisions as to what to manufacture and then examines the influence on locational change of the availability and cost of labour, capital and land and of variations in accessibility to supplies and markets. These factors operate within a specific political system which through a variety of ways influences the distribution of manufacturing activity. While Part III considers primarily the influence of these elements in relation to *net change*, Part IV takes a more detailed look not at specific industries but at the different *components of change*. It reviews the traditional branch plant location literature but it also includes the first textbook discussions of the geography of job creation through the birth of entirely new firms and the geography of job loss arising through the closure of plants. Part V examines deliberate attempts by the state to modify the geography of employment opportunities and the book concludes with a brief discussion of possible developments in industrial geography in the late 1980s.

Although attention is concentrated upon capitalist and mixed economies it is most important to remember this is not a manual for managers of firms seeking the best location for a new plant, although some material of relevance to this problem is found in Part IV. Nor is it a text which seeks to explain the location of an industry at one point in time: emphasis is placed upon an analysis of the changing location of employment opportunities in manufacturing industry.

Three difficulties are often experienced by newcomers to this field of enquiry. First, objections can be raised about some of the explanations of locational change because those involved in making decisions have never heard of the ideas found in the industrial geography literature. This assertion may be true but individuals are often unaware of the aggregate behaviour to which they contribute.

Second, there may be a feeling that many locational changes reflect the whims and personal foibles of a firm's managers or owners rather than emerging as the result of a careful evaluation of alternative courses of action. Some changes may be the outcome of decisions strongly influenced by personal considerations, others may arise from 'back-of-the-envelope' calculations and yet others from computer-aided mathematical solutions but as this chapter has shown decisions, in aggregate, produce distinctive geographical patterns which suggest that there are important underlying forces which can be used to explain the spatial patterns of employment change.

Third, it can be difficult placing the study of industrial geography within the academic discipline of geography. Ideas are drawn both from geography and a number of related fields – economics, sociology, psychology and management science provide some examples – and occasionally the boundaries between geography and these other fields may become blurred. While geographers may draw on concepts and facts apparently 'belonging' to other disciplines and while it is important to realise that there are no specifically geographical factors or facts other than the coordinates of place which fix a particular pattern of industrial change to a particular area, the specific role of industrial geography, which places it clearly within the field of geography, is its concern to explain changes in the spatial pattern of industrial activity.

—— PART I ——

FRAMEWORKS

Contemporary changes in the geography of industrial activity should not be divorced from either the international framework within which they are set or the historical context in which they operate. Chapter 2 considers the ways in which industries and organisations within national economies are integrated into and influenced by the world industrial system. Chapter 3 illustrates how present-day patterns of industrial change are but the most recent stages in the evolving geography of industrial activity and examines the extent to which inherited industrial structures influence regional patterns of employment change.

2

THE INTERNATIONAL
FRAMEWORK

It is unrealistic to isolate regional employment changes from the global environment in which they occur. Changes in the spatial distribution of world manufacturing activity and associated changes in the world trade in manufactured goods have 'knock-on' effects on regional manufacturing systems. There are two major reasons for these effects. First, many firms find their home markets are threatened by imports from overseas. Second, many firms depend to some considerable extent on their export markets. Increased export activity can help to maintain or expand employment while loss of overseas orders can have a deleterious effect upon a firm's employment levels. However, the world manufacturing system is more than a system of competing firms in separate countries and world manufacturing patterns are increasingly modified and adjusted by the purposive actions of large multinational organisations with production facilities in more than one country.

In this chapter the international setting of changing employment levels in different *industries* precedes a discussion of the way those changes are influenced by the operation of multinational *firms*. The chapter begins by describing the principal features of world trade in manufactured goods and illustrates the degree of export dependence and import penetration in different countries. The dynamic nature of the world industrial system is then examined with reference to the global clothing industry which has seen major changes in its geography over the last decade. The second part of the chapter examines the role of multinational organisations with particular reference to their current interest in reorganising their world-wide operations. The multinational firm is introduced in this chapter both to illustrate the international framework of industrial change and to provide a precursor to the full discussion of firms and their location decisions in Chapters 4 and 5.

WORLD TRADE IN MANUFACTURED
GOODS

The global manufacturing system (outside the planned economies) is dominated by three inter-related sub-systems focused upon North America, Western Europe and the West Pacific. Not surprisingly these are the major sources of exports of manufactured goods. Less expected perhaps is that they are also the major importers of these goods.

The extent to which the developed world dominates trade in manufactured goods is brought out in Table 2.1. No less than 82 per cent of *exports* of manufactured goods originated in the developed world, a figure which rises to 92 per cent if the planned economies are included. Of the remainder, just over 7 per cent is accounted for by the *newly industrialising countries*. Similarly, 86 per cent of imports of manufactured goods in OECD countries come from the developed world. Explanations of this trading pattern lie at the heart of geographical studies of

Table 2.1 Origins of world exports of manufactured goods*

Country or group	1963 (%)	1976 (%)
United States	17.24	13.55
West Germany	15.53	15.81
United Kingdom	11.14	6.59
France	6.99	7.41
Japan	5.98	11.38
Italy	4.73	5.49
Canada	2.61	3.32
Other developed countries†	17.14	18.13
Sub-total: developed countries	81.36	81.68
Spain	0.28	1.07
Portugal	0.30	0.21
Greece	0.04	0.22
Yugoslavia	0.40	0.60
Brazil	0.05	0.41
Mexico	0.17	0.51
Hong Kong	0.76	1.15
South Korea	0.05	1.20
Taiwan	0.16	1.23
Singapore	0.38	0.52
Sub-total: newly industrialising countries	2.59	7.12
India	0.85	0.49
Argentina	0.01	0.17
Other developing countries	1.84	0.89
Sub-total: other developing countries	2.70	1.55
Eastern bloc countries	13.35	9.65
World total	100.00	100.00

(*Source*: Based on Linge and Hamilton 1981:18)
* Standard International Trade Classification 5–8 minus 68 (non-ferrous metals).
† All other OECD countries not listed in table plus South Africa and Israel.

international trade but they are of interest here primarily because of their influence on manufacturing employment trends within the developed countries.

Within a national economy the extent to which its industries are tied into world trading patterns is seen in the extent to which its industries and firms are dependent upon export markets and the degree to which domestic markets are supplied by imports. Loss of home markets to imports and loss of export markets to competitors almost inevitably result in a loss of employment opportunities and the more open an economy is to imports and the more dependent it

is on export markets the greater will be its sensitivity to changes in the international trading system. In Britain, particularly, many of the trends in employment in individual industrial sectors, described in the next chapter, arise from lack of competitiveness in international markets.

Export dependence and import penetration

The extent to which the manufacturing activities in different national economies are dependent on exports varies. Of the goods manufactured in the United Kingdom 29 per cent were exported in 1982 but the dependence on exports was much less marked in the United States where only 13 per cent of manufactured goods were sent to export markets. Canada's dependence lay midway between the two with 21 per cent of such goods being exported. Dependence upon export markets can vary markedly from area to area within a country. This is illustrated dramatically in the Canadian data in Table 2.2. Whereas almost two-thirds (by value) of Newfoundland's manufactured goods are destined for overseas markets as are two-fifths of the manufactured goods originating in British Columbia, in the Prairie provinces of Manitoba and Saskatchewan the proportions fell to between 10 and 12 per cent. This suggests that whereas manufacturing employment trends in the latter provinces can be influenced only slightly by the performance of

Table 2.2 Dependence on export sales, Canadian provinces,* 1974

Province	Manufactured goods sold abroad (%)
Newfoundland	64.6
British Columbia	41.3
New Brunswick	35.1
Nova Scotia	27.6
Ontario	21.7
Canada	21.2
Quebec	14.7
Saskatchewan	11.6
Manitoba	10.2
Prince Edward Island	9.7
Alberta	7.7

(*Source*: Based on Walker 1980a:37)
* Excluding Yukon and North-West Territories.

Table 2.3   Export ratios by industrial sectors, United Kingdom (1982), United States (1981)

United Kingdom Exports as percentage of manufacturers' sales		United States* Export-related employment as a percentage of all employment	
Instrument engineering	63	Machinery, not electrical	22
Mechanical engineering	48	Instruments	19
Vehicles	46	Primary metal	19
Electrical engineering	45	Tobacco	19
Chemicals	41	Chemicals	18
Leather	35	Transportation equipment	18
Textiles	32	Electrical engineering	17
Metal manufacture	27	Fabricated metals	12
Other manufacturing	22	Paper	11
Clothing and footwear	19	Rubber	11
Shipbuilding	18	Textiles	10
Coal and petroleum products	17	Lumber	10
Metals n.e.s.	17	Stone	9
Bricks, pottery and cement	13	Miscellaneous manufacturers	9
Paper and printing	11	Petroleum and coal	7
Timber	7	Food	5
Food and drink	6	Apparel	3
		Furniture	3
All manufacturing	27	Printing	3
		All manufacturing	13

(*Source*: Central Statistical Office (1985) *Annual Abstract of Statistics 1985*; US Bureau of Census (1985) *Statistical Abstract of the United States, 1985*: Table 1355)

* Employment associated with direct exports plus employment at establishments producing components, supplies and parts for use by plants producing for export.

Canadian industries in export markets, in British Columbia and Newfoundland a weak performance in those markets might result in a marked reduction in employment levels.

In part, the degree of regional variation in export dependence is influenced by a region's industrial structure. Some industries show a greater propensity to export than others (Table 2.3). The propensity to export in the United States in 1981 was highest in non-electrical machinery followed by instrument manufacture, primary metal manufacture and tobacco. Very low levels of exports were associated with industries such as food, furniture, apparel and leather goods. Overall, some 1.5 million manufacturing jobs in the United States were related *directly* to employment in exports. Much higher dependence levels are found in United Kingdom industries. Food, timber and paper and printing serve mainly the domestic market as do bricks, pottery and cement. In contrast, in instrument engineering no less than 63 per cent of manufacturers' sales are exported, while exports account for over

40 per cent of sales of mechanical engineering, electrical engineering, vehicles and chemicals.

In turning to a consideration of imports, the sectoral data emphasise the high level of import penetration in the United Kingdom (Table 2.4). Nearly two-thirds of the market for instrument engineering is met by imports as is over two-fifths of the market for electrical engineering, vehicles, textiles and leather goods. Low levels of penetration are characteristic of food and drink and bricks, pottery and cement. More significantly perhaps for changes in employment levels is that the level of import penetration has doubled or almost doubled in electrical engineering, vehicles, textiles and clothing and has risen by 18 percentage points in instrument engineering over the last decade. Similar patterns are shown in the sectoral performance of Canadian industries where, despite tariff protection, imports have been increasing in leather goods, textiles, hosiery and knitted goods, clothing and electrical and electronic products (Walker 1980a:17). The closed nature of the United States economy is

Table 2.4   Import penetration by industrial sector, United Kingdom (1973 and 1982), United States (1974 and 1981)

United Kingdom*			United States†		
	1973	1982		1974	1981
Instrument engineering	46	62	Leather and leather products	20	40
Electrical engineering	27	49	Miscellaneous manufacturers	17	30
Vehicles	23	45	Transportation equipment	13	17
Leather goods	27	45	Apparel and textile products	8	16
Textiles	21	40	Primary metal products	12	16
Mechanical engineering	26	36	Electrical and electronic equipment	10	14
Clothing	18	35	Instruments and related products	8	13
Chemicals	22	33	Lumber and wood products	9	10
Metal manufacture	21	31	Machinery, not electrical	6	9
Timber	29	28	Petroleum refining	16	7
Paper and printing	19	22	Paper and allied products	6	7
Other manufacturing	15	24	Rubber and miscellaneous plastics	5	6
Coal and petroleum	17	17	Textile mill products	5	6
Shipbuilding	56	17	Stone, clay and glass	4	5
Metals not elsewhere specified	10	16	Furniture and fixtures	3	5
Food and drink	19	15	Chemicals and allied products	4	5
Bricks, pottery, glass, cement	7	11	Fabricated metals	3	4
			Food and kindred products	5	4
			Tobacco products	1	2
			Printing and publishing	1	1

(*Source*: Central Statistical Office (1985); US Bureau of Census (1985): Table 1357)
* Imports as a percentage of home demand.
† Ratio of imports to new supply (domestic product shipments plus imports).

seen in that only two industries have import penetration ratios of over 25 per cent. In both Canada and the United Kingdom clothing imports have had an important effect on the domestic clothing industry and even in the United States the import penetration of apparel doubled between 1974 and 1981.

The clothing industry

In many countries in the developed world employment in the clothing industry has been reduced as a result of competition from less developed countries. This effect has been particularly marked because of the concentration of the clothing industry in particular types of area (notably the inner city). In the clothing industry 'competition has probably become more intense and widespread globally...than [in]...almost any other manufacturing industries' (Steed, 1981:265) and the dramatic changes in world clothing over the five-year period 1970–75 are shown in Fig. 2.1. Whereas in 1970 only 38 per cent of clothing exports came from the less deve-

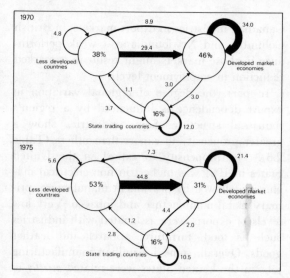

Fig. 2.1 World trade in clothing, per cent of total value 1970 and 1975 (*Source*: Steed 1981:270)

loped countries this had risen to 53 per cent five years later. By 1975 45 per cent of world trade in clothing consisted of flows between the less developed and developed market economies, and in

1973 the United States was receiving major clothing imports from Hong Kong, Taiwan, Japan and South Korea. Not all sectors of the clothing industry in developed economies are open to this competition, particularly where style and fashion changes necessitate a close contact between supplier and markets, but for items which change little from year to year (men's shirts are a good example) a location where labour costs are low is feasible.

The changes in the distribution of the world clothing industry illustrate well the principle of *comparative advantage*. This principle argues that individual countries and, indeed, different parts of a national economic system, enjoy particular advantages for the production of certain goods because of their differing resource endowments. In a manufacturing context most emphasis has been placed upon labour resources with which the less developed countries are well endowed and which provide them with a comparative advantage over the developed world.

In the clothing industry Steed (1981:278) stresses that 'the key spatially variable cost is wages' and that variations in wages are not offset by variations in productivity because potential output per trained employee varies little between countries. Wages are so much lower in the developing countries that in the case of polyester/cotton shirts wage costs in the United States were greater than total production costs in Hong Kong. Differences like this indicate the severe disadvantages of clothing producers in the developed market economies, a disadvantage further emphasised by the lower fabric costs. In the case of Britain and Hong Kong the fabric cost differential was around 37 per cent to the advantage of Hong Kong. Distance offers little protection either on these staple clothing items as the total cost of moving a shirt from Hong Kong to London adds only 14 per cent to the Hong Kong production cost.

With cost differentials of this magnitude it might be expected that in the long run all staple clothing manufacture will disappear from the developed market economies and all developing countries will concentrate upon labour intensive activities such as clothing. That this has not occurred and is unlikely to occur reflects important institutional constraints on international trade in manufactured goods. Much of the world trade in clothing is regulated by the Multi Fibre Arrangement and there have been strong political pressures to protect the domestic clothing industry in developed countries; none more so than the United States where American producers, as a result in part of protection policies, retain about 80 per cent of the domestic market (Steed 1978:42) a much higher proportion than that found in Canada or Britain. Similarly in many developing countries emphasis has been placed upon import substitution as a basis for growth rather than development of those sectors in which the country has a comparative advantage and thus export-led growth based on the clothing sector has not occurred.

Although the industrial decline of some advanced countries is often associated with competition from 'cheap' imports from developing countries, it is important to remember the point made earlier that only 9 per cent of world exports come from these countries. In many ways the clothing industry is atypical; more typical is the British cutlery industry. Its decline is popularly associated with cheap imports from developing countries but in 1983 one-quarter of Britain's scissor imports came from West Germany, one-quarter of the knives from West Germany, France and Switzerland, and one-quarter of the spoons and forks from other parts of the EEC. Very often the competitive performance of different countries in the world market is associated not with production costs *per se* but with questions of marketing, servicing, delivery, reliability and product quality. For most industries, competition comes from other advanced economies and not from the developing world.

Intra-firm trade

Traditional approaches to international trade are based on the concept of comparative advantage and assume that trade takes place exclusively among competing firms or, at a more aggregate level, between competing countries and that market prices (modified by import/export controls and distance) govern the pattern of trade. Yet in many industrial categories trade between countries reflects not competition between firms but decisions by multinational firms to alter intra-firm trading patterns.

Where international trade occurs within firms it takes place at prices determined by the firm which may have little to do with the price of the commodities on the open market. Flows of goods within the firm will be decided in relation to the firm's overall strategy and the products will be sold (transferred) between plants at *transfer prices*. These transfer prices might be designed to help to minimise taxes in particular countries. It is because of the ability of the firm to set its own transfer prices and to decide on the system of trade which is in its own best interests that there is a suspicion that intra-firm trade creates patterns which differ from those developed in response to comparative advantage. Whether this suspicion is justified has yet to be established because research into the internal pricing systems of firms is very difficult because of its sensitive nature.

The role and significance of intra-firm trade is remarkably under-researched and 'few seem as yet to have realised the extent to which . . . intra-firm trading practices have already come to dominate important segments of world trade' (Helleiner 1981:32). Intra-firm trade is made up of two main elements.

1. *Distributional activities*:
   (a) exports by domestic firms for sale without further manufacture overseas;
   (b) imports for sale without further manufacture by domestic subsidiaries of foreign firms.
2. *International production activities*:
   (a) exports by domestic firms to production plants overseas;
   (b) exports by the domestic subsidiaries of foreign firms to production plants overseas;
   (c) imports by domestic firms from production plants overseas;
   (d) imports for sale after further manufacture by the domestic subsidiaries of foreign firms.

It is extremely difficult to allocate particular flows to these two major categories and only 'guesstimates' of their relative importance can be made.

Investigation of exports has shown that 29 per cent of Swedish exports in 1975 and 30 per cent of United Kingdom exports in 1973 were undertaken on an intra-firm basis (Linge and Hamilton 1981:65). In North America export data from a study of 298 United States multinationals indicated that in 1970 20 to 22 per cent of manufactured exports were from United States owned parent companies to their majority-owned foreign affiliates. In all cases a proportion of the exports would have been to overseas operations concerned only with distributional activities. Apart from these occasional snapshots, data on intra-firm exports are sparse and in the United States there have been no data reported on the extent of intra-firm exports since 1970 (Helleiner 1981:17).

Rather more detail is available relating to imports. In Canada, the Gray report (1972:184–5) indicates that in 1969 'reporting subsidiaries' accounted for 40 per cent of all imports, although this proportion fell to between 20 and 25 per cent when the four major automobile manufacturers and other firms in the transport sector were excluded. In the United States an indication of the extent of intra-firm trade as part of the international production system is provided by data from 5,900 majority-owned foreign affiliates of a sample of 282 US firms (Helleiner, 1981:15–27). Majority-owned affiliates are those companies in which the firms hold at least 50 per cent of the voting stock. The data relate to imports of both raw materials and manufactured goods but if attention is confined to imports from Europe, it is likely that these will be dominated by manufactured items produced in United States owned plants in Europe for the North American market. Sales by majority-owned affiliates to the United States as a percentage of total United States imports from Europe over the period 1966–75 were 12 per cent and within this period there was a small rise from 10 to 14 per cent. The proportion of intra-firm transactions in imports from the United Kingdom was 15 per cent. It appears that over one-quarter of world trade in manufactured goods is associated with intra-firm transactions and probably about half of this (about 12 per cent of the total) is associated with transactions which form part of international production activities within the multinational firm.

THE MULTINATIONAL FIRM

Just as industries in specific economies are linked into the world manufacturing system by the international trading system, so too many firms within national economies are part of larger multinational organisations which permit some degree of co-ordination of production activities across national boundaries. Geographical investigations of multinational firms have emphasised the spatial pattern of their manufacturing activities. These studies draw upon ideas and concepts developed in the economics and management literature (Dunning 1981).

Multinationals are firms 'which own or control producing facilities in more than one country' (Dunning 1971:19). More precisely, they are firms which have undertaken *foreign direct investment*. Direct investment is where a firm controls the operations of the plant or plants in which the investment is made and is to be contrasted with purchases of stocks and shares in overseas operations (portfolio investment) which offers no day-to-day control over the firm's activities. In the manufacturing context, investment in a manufacturing plant in another country will mean that the investing firm may influence, for example, the plant's purchasing policy, its product mix, the areas in which it can sell its products and, most importantly, the level of employment in specific plants both overseas and at home.

A firm's foreign investment may be relatively small; many multinationals have investments in only one other country, but at the other extreme there were in the mid-1970s 324 multinationals with affiliates in more than 20 countries. In empirical studies attention is frequently focused on these larger multinationals and the smaller multinationals tend to be forgotten but it is in the very largest multinationals that the distinctive features of multinational firms appear most clearly.

The leading countries in terms of direct foreign investment are shown in Table 2.5. Overseas manufacturing investment by the United States

Table 2.5 Distribution of foreign investment in manufacturing 1971 (percentages)

	UK	Germany*	Japan†	US
Developed countries				
North America			6	
US	16	9	n.a.	—
Others	9	8	n.a.	30
Europe			5‡	
EEC-6	18	31	n.a.	24
Others	2	21	n.a.	20[3]
Australia, NZ, South Africa	33	2	6	7
Total	81	72	17	83
Developing countries				
Asia	n.a.	3	43	2
Latin America	5	15	37	14
Total	19	28	83	17
Estimated total stock ($ millions)	10,251 (book values)	4,602 (transactions)	967 (approvals)	35,632 (book value)

(*Source*: Based on Morgan 1978:79)
* Refers to *all* foreign investment.
† To end March 1971.
‡ Includes developing countries in Europe.

was, in value in 1971, 3.5 times greater than that for the United Kingdom while the United Kingdom's investment was twice as large as West Germany's and very much larger than the Japanese. It is because of the dominance of United States' activity at world scale that it is often United States' firms that dominate direct foreign investment in particular countries. Two phases can be discerned in the overseas operations of the larger firms: expansion and re-organisation.

Expansion

The development of overseas production facilities has been eased by the continued improvement in international communications systems. These improvements were important in three ways.
1. The secure and more rapid transhipment of manufactured goods by container–ship and by air freight operation encouraged all forms of international trade and not only intra-firm transfers within multinational operations.
2. Increases in the speed and frequency of scheduled passenger services reduced the problems of movement of personnel from head office to manufacturing sites in different parts of the globe and aided the control of world-wide operations from a single head-quarters.
3. Equally important were developments in the transmission and storage of information. With the development of computer systems it became much easier to handle and interpret data relating to global manufacturing operations and to communicate that information from one part of the world to another.

Developments like these have reduced the friction of distance and opened up the way for the rapid growth of multinational firms. The spread of production facilities into overseas locations can be related to either or both of marketing and cost considerations. Production overseas is a frequent follow-up to sales overseas while cost considerations can be associated with a concern to minimise the cost of production. Overseas expansion can be interpreted in terms of the product-cycle concept which is explored in Chapter 6.

Market-led expansion

It is important to distinguish between the advantages of extending into overseas markets and the advantages of *production* in those markets. Important factors pushing firms into overseas markets were the need to diversify markets and to continue growth in sectors where further growth in the home market was not permitted either by monopoly legislation or by market saturation (Ch. 3). Among the advantages associated with production overseas are opportunities to transcend tariff barriers, to respond rapidly to local market conditions, to reduce transport costs on the finished products and to obtain a price advantage over other competitors in the market. The presence of production facilities implies a strong commitment to a particular market and, even without a price advantage, may offer an advantage over other foreign firms selling but not producing in the same market. Successful expansion into new production facilities to serve an overseas market will depend on the multinational firm having some advantage over indigenous firms (Hayter 1981). These advantages can include one or more of the following features:
1. New technologies or new products that are not available to firms in the host country;
2. Economies of scale, particularly in providing plants to serve more than the host countries national market;
3. Advanced marketing skills usually associated with extensive and established marketing and distribution systems;
4. Managerial expertise, which might be particularly relevant where new products and technologies are involved;
5. Financial resources to cover start-up costs and possible losses in the early years of operation.

More generally, any problems the plant has to face may be eased by seeking information, expertise and capital from the multinational's headquarters and research and development staff.

Cost-led expansion

For many industries with well-established products wage costs are particularly significant for the mass production of standardised items for world markets. In an intensively competitive situation with firms competing for market share, variations in costs become critical and 'labour has often proved the source of the real difference between costs in the United States and those abroad' (Vernon 1971:74). Therefore production in United States' multinationals has been shifted to low-wage areas overseas; this has been particularly evident in the electronics industries. Once a global production system is established a wide spread of activity allows firms to compare costs in different locations and to switch activities between locations where this is appropriate.

Whether stimulated by the search for new markets or lower costs the very largest multinationals have developed global production systems of which the best developed is that of General Motors (Fig. 2.2).

There are some interesting differences in the corporate geography of firms based in different countries. Firms based in the United States, United Kingdom and West Germany have 70–80 per cent of their investments in developed countries and less than one-third in developing countries (Table 2.5). In contrast, over 80 per cent of Japanese investment is in developing countries. Within the developed countries, the historical influence of the Commonwealth stands out clearly in that one-third of the United Kingdom investment is in Australia, Canada and South Africa. Among United States firms the 30 per cent of investments in North America outside the United States reflects the strong United States dominance in Canada. Overall investment patterns are not, of course, static and over the period 1972 to 1975 British firms tended to invest more in Europe and the United States and the Japanese reduced their emphasis upon investment in developing countries (Morgan 1978:85).

The overall patterns shown in Table 2.5 are in part related to spatial proximity as seen in the spread of United States' operations into Canada and British operations into Europe; in part, related to size of markets as seen in United States' firms moving into Europe and British firms into the United States; in part, associated with tariff barriers; in part associated with differences in production costs as seen in the development of

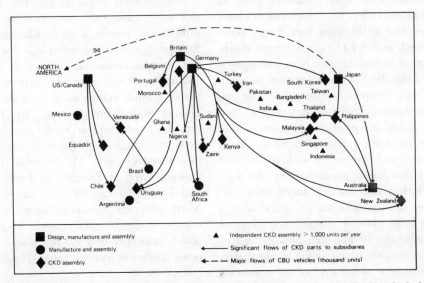

Fig. 2.2 A global production system: General Motors, 1977 (CKD = completely knocked down; CBU = completely built up) (*Source*: Bloomfield 1981:387)

electronic assembly plants in the developing world and partly associated with cultural affinity seen in British investment in English-speaking Commonwealth countries and an early focus of United States investment in Europe, in Eire and the United Kingdom. It has also been suggested that the international spread of multinational corporations reflects a form of oligopolistic reaction in that when a few firms dominate a particular industry they are forced to imitate each other's behaviour in order to retain their market shares. The effect of oligopolistic reaction on the multinational spread of the production facilities is examined in a number of geographical studies (Rees 1978; Gwynne 1979; Laulajainen 1981). Imitation may be important but the initial spread will reflect the forces listed earlier.

Reorganisation

In their expansion phase multinational firms tended to follow a plant by market strategy with plants being located to serve particular national markets, although in the 1970s cost-led locations became more evident. It is cost pressures now that have led firms to integrate and reorganise their multinational production systems. The environments in which the firms operate in the 1980s differ from those of the expansion phase in the 1960s. Trade barriers between countries have been reduced and at the same time larger economic units such as the EEC are now well established. Pressure to reduce costs was put upon a number of firms both by competition between themselves and competition from low-cost imports. In the motor-vehicle industry both United States and European producers began to face stiff competition from Japanese exports. Under such pressures, and sometimes without them, it was realised that larger plants serving the markets of more than one country would offer considerable cost savings. The nature of the savings arising from large plants is discussed in Chapter 6. Making adjustments and fine tuning the corporate system became easier as firms' familiarity and knowledge of a wide range of environments increased and with production plants in several countries comparative data on relative produc-

tion costs became readily available. In this way, a predominantly market-led expansion gave way to cost-led reorganisation.

Yet while the pressures for and the possibility of integrating production plants in different countries increased there were constraints upon the extent to which production systems could be integrated across national boundaries. There is a need to meet with and conform to the political demands and policies of the host countries and there are national variations in taste and style that may best be met, in some instances, by retaining production plants in a particular country.

The firm has to seek a resolution to the conflict between the economic imperative which demands success and long-run survival and the political imperative of adjusting to the demands of host countries. In some firms the economic imperative is uppermost and a policy of full integration is pursued; in others, particularly those reliant on government purchases, national responsiveness is the key strategy to meet local political demands. A third group follow no strategy other than administrative co-ordination of their different activities, allowing national affiliates to develop their own solution to the conflict between the economic and political imperatives.

Among firms pursuing policies of integration, this integration may be global or restricted to integration within a particular area such as Europe. Global integration was the objective of the reorganisation of Honeywell in the early 1970s. Until this time the firm was manufacturing similar information systems in both the United States and Europe. By 1974, at the launch of the firm's series 60 computers, all the production of a single product was concentrated in a single country. The Level 61 machine was manufactured in France, the Level 63 in Italy, and Levels 66 and 68 (the larger systems) in North America. European level integration was evident in the case of Goodyear which developed plants primarily to serve the whole of the European market in rubber tyres (Hood and Young 1982:118–33).

Moves towards integration clearly will have consequences for the levels of employment at individual plants. Reorganisation results in changing product roles, changing market allocations and changing locational networks. Changing product roles are particularly evident in industries where potential economies of scale (Ch. 6) are unrealised. Plants, instead of producing a whole range of products, begin to manufacture only one product or one component. Changing products leads, almost inevitably, to changes in the markets allocated to each plant, thus reorganisation results in a general trend away from individual plants serving local (usually national) markets. It would be surprising if changes like this did not have an influence on level of employment and number of plants in individual corporate systems. Brief examination of the experience of the European operations of two firms illustrates some of the patterns of change associated with European integration by multinational firms.

Ford represents the most far-reaching example of integration within the European motor industry (Bloomfield 1981). Ford Europe was created in 1967 and reflected a desire to spread investment, a shortage of labour near existing plants, the high cost of new model development and the

markets offered by the EEC to which Britain did not belong in 1967. By 1977 Ford was producing five European models (Fiesta, Escort, Capri, Cortina-Taunus and Granada) in a number of assembly plants in the United Kingdom, West Germany, Belgium and Spain; these assembly plants were serviced by a number of component manufacturing plants. The Fiesta, assembled mainly in Spain, includes parts from Belfast (carburettors and distributors), Dagenham (engine castings), Basildon (radiators) and Bordeaux (transmissions and axles). The increasing degree of integration between Ford's European plants between 1970 and 1978 is shown in Fig. 2.3.

The Ford Europe reorganisation did not lead to major plant closures. This is not the case in Singer's reorganisation of its European operations (Hood and Young 1982:42–60). This firm (known mainly for its sewing machines) employed 18,000 workers in Europe in 1973 and had manufacturing plants in France, Germany, Italy, The Netherlands and the United Kingdom. In the domestic sewing machine market each factory concentrated on a specific part of the range while production of industrial sewing

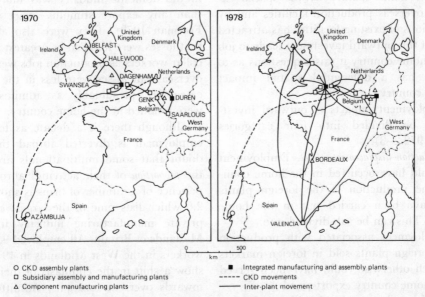

Fig. 2.3 European integration: Ford 1970 and 1978 (*Source*: Bloomfield 1981:384)

machines and needles was divided between Britain and Germany. Under severe pressure of competition, mainly from Japan, major cutbacks in capacity became necessary. The German industrial sewing machine plant was closed in 1976 and production concentrated at the Scottish plant but this too was faced with closure in 1978 as production of all such machines was to be concentrated in the United States. Needle manufacture too was concentrated at one plant in Germany and their manufacture in the United Kingdom ceased. In the domestic sewing machine market moves were made towards many more inter-plant links. 1979 saw further job cuts in Singer's other European and North American plants as the firm began to concentrate its sewing machine production in Third World locations. In this case the multinational firm is deliberately shifting production to the Third World.

Outward investment

While multinationals were in a period of expanding production and employment there was little interest in the effects of overseas expansion on employment in the home country. With the present emphasis upon reorganisation the extent to which multinationals are shifting employment outside their home country by the spatial expansion of overseas production facilities and by reorganisations of existing facilities has attracted attention. If this outward investment leads to job loss in the home country it raises questions as to whether it has a differential spatial impact within that country.

The employment impacts of outward investment can be divided into four categories (Hawkins 1972:2–3).
1. *The production–displacement effect.* Employment that would have occurred in the home country if the production of the foreign plants could have been carried out in the home country. This can be sub-divided into:
   (a) employment associated with production in foreign plants sold in foreign markets which otherwise could have been served by home country exports; and
   (b) employment associated with production

in foreign plants imported into the home country and which could have been produced in the home country.
2. *The export-stimulus effect.* Employment created in home production plants which would not have occurred if the foreign plants had not been set up. This can be sub-divided into:
   (a) employment associated with capital goods exported when the foreign plant is established; and
   (b) employment created due to the marketing advantages which export sales from the home country receive as a result of the local presence of the foreign plant.
3. *The home-office effect.* Employment gains in white-collar occupations in the head office as a result of overseas expansion.
4. *The supporting firm effect.* Employment gains in other domestic firms which supply services associated with the new overseas activities to the investing firm.

It is useful to isolate the influence of these four elements to determine the extent to which multinationals substitute overseas production for domestic exports.

Investigations of a number of industries in the United States in the 1970s indicated that export displacement with a resulting loss of employment in the domestic industry was more significant than any export stimulus effect (Frank and Freeman 1978). They were also able to show that losses were likely to be greatest among blue-collar workers as production jobs were developed overseas but losses were less in the white-collar categories, presumably as administrative jobs were retained in the home country.

Although there is a debate as to how much employment is diverted abroad there is little doubt that some multinationals are increasing the *proportion* of their activities abroad. The experience of a number of firms is shown in Table 2.6 which lists nine of the largest employers in private manufacturing industry in the West Midlands of Britain. All employed 9,000 or more workers in the West Midlands in 1977. All firms show a shift in the emphasis of their operations towards overseas locations. Admittedly, in the case of Cadbury Schweppes the change in em-

Table 2.6 Global workforce of selected West Midland firms, 1978 and 1982

Firm	Main industry	1978	1982
		% of global employment in Britain	
BSR	Electrical engineering	95	44
Guest, Keen and Nettlefold	Motor vehicle components	67	52
General Electric	Electrical engineering	85	76
Delta	Electrical engineering	80	71
Lucas	Motor vehicle components	81	73
Dunlop	Rubber	48	42
Imperial Metal Industries	Metals	80	75
Tube Investments	Metals engineering	86	82
Cadbury Schweppes	Food	62	60

(*Source*: Gaffikin and Nickson 1984:73)

phasis was small but in the most extreme case (BSR) the British share of employment fell from 95 per cent to 44 per cent between 1978 and 1982. These shifts result in part from the industrial structure of the firms' activities in different areas and may also reflect conscious opening up of new markets or resources and it might never have been possible to develop or expand the operations in Britain.

The nature of the diversion of employment from the United Kingdom by United Kingdom multinationals has been explored by Owens (1980) with reference to investment in Eire from 1958 to 1978. The investments could be placed into three categories: those tied to markets or supplies in Eire (32 per cent); unscheduled investments mainly arising from requests to be taken over (28 per cent); and projects diverted to Eire from Britain (40 per cent). While the first two categories may have some implications for employment in the home country (orders or jobs may be switched to Eire at some later stage) the diverted projects are of most interest. In one-third of these cases a British location was considered but in the majority of instances Britain was rejected 'on the basis of some preconceived prejudices about some aspect of the British space economy (e.g. labour relations) or because of a hostile bureaucratic environment' (Owens 1980:55). Many of the new plants in Eire represented a clear loss of employment to the British

economy and in cases where output change in Britain could be related to the development of production in Eire the predominant effect was a run-down or closure of a British plant. These changes resulted from the transfer of products from a British to an Irish plant and the rearrangements of markets served from individual plants resulting in the loss of markets for British plants. The diverted projects led more frequently to spatial adjustments than either of the other categories and were particularly likely to affect directly the output of the British plants of the multinational firm.

While it is feasible to make attempts at quantitative assessments of the effects of overseas investment on home country employment levels such attempts do not provide any indication of the regional distribution of these changes within a national economic system. Tracing these changes down to regional and plant level is very difficult.

Inward investment

Examining the spatial impact of inward investment is a more straightforward task than identifying the regional employment effects of outward investment. As a result, an ever-increasing number of studies examine the impacts of different multinationals in different countries. In these cases, foreign firms have a direct and measurable impact on the location of employment opportunities within a country but as is shown below their control over total manufacturing employment is small but increasing.

Foreign investment in the United States

Details of contemporary trends in employment in plants with headquarters outside the United States are not available but there is a wealth of data on investments by foreign-owned manufacturing firms. These are defined as subsidiaries in which 10 per cent or more of the voting shares are held by foreign firms. These foreign-owned subsidiaries mainly from Britain, Japan, Canada and West Germany, control about 6 per cent of United States employment although recent increases in foreign investment suggest that this proportion is rising (US Department of Commerce 1985, Tables 913 and 1337). The increased investment by foreign firms reflects the increasing size and complexity of firms based outside the United States and the relative prosperity of the large United States market. The total stock of foreign direct investments in the United States' manufacturing sector grew from $13.3 billion in 1970 to $40.8 billion in 1976; an average annual growth rate of over 25 per cent (McConnell 1980).

The data relating to the distribution of these investments refer to all forms of investment and thus include both the establishment of entirely new plants as well as the acquisition of existing United States' firms. Their major disadvantage is that only the *number* of investments is available at state scale and not the actual value of the investments. Figure 2.4 shows the trends from 1974 to 1978 in foreign direct investments in the United States. In the first period (Fig. 2.4A) states that gained new foreign direct investment at rates exceeding the national growth rate were concentrated in the manufacturing belt and its periphery and on the West Coast. A contrast is apparent in Fig. 2.4B. Here eight of the seventeen most rapidly growing states were in the South. Whereas the number of investments in the South grew by 4.37 per cent from 1974 to 1976, a rate *below* the national average of 8.65 per cent, it grew from 1976 to 1978 by 16.29 per

cent, a rate *above* the national average of 13.99 per cent.

This shift to the South did, however, lag behind the shift that was identifiable in manufacturing employment data as a whole before the mid-1970s. The difference might arise from the fact that one set of data relates to employment, the other to investment but if the lag did exist there are a number of interpretations as to why it occurred. It might reflect the development of localised industrial incentive schemes (see Ch. 10), or a change of locational strategy by the foreign firms, or foreign investors' greater experience of North American operations and a resultant willingness to invest outside the major industrial region. However, foreign-based firms have been increasing their investments in high-technology manufacturing (chemicals, machinery and scientific instruments) which have been growing faster outside the traditional manufacturing areas and in many cases they have acquired the facilities of United States' manufactures. It is, therefore, not surprising that the increasing number of acquisitions have a bias towards areas away from the manufacturing belt.

Foreign-owned plants in the UK

These plants in 1981 employed 858,000 workers or around 15 per cent of the manufacturing workforce. The fortunes of nearly 1 million employees are influenced directly by decisions that, in the last resort, are the responsibility of managers overseas. The degree of foreign influence has increased with the growth of multinationals, rising from about 7 per cent in 1963. These data probably underestimate the degree of foreign ownership since they exclude employment in linked plants and they relate only to plants in which more than 50 per cent of the shares are foreign owned. Not surprisingly, United States' firms dominate and account for about three-quarters of the employment with the remainder being divided approximately equally between EEC (excluding the United Kingdom) based multinationals and other countries (mainly Canada and Switzerland). To illustrate the ways in which foreign investment influences employment change in different regions attention is

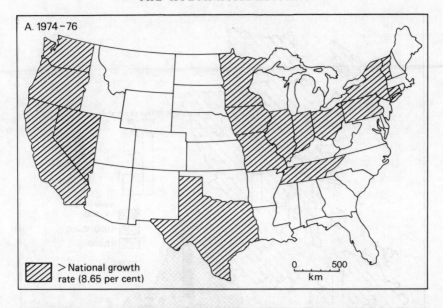

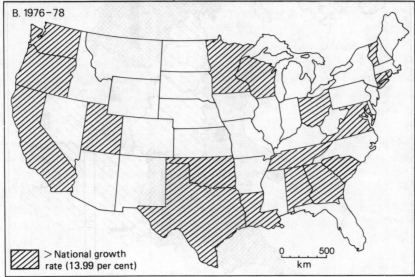

Fig. 2.4 Percentage change in foreign direct investments, United States, 1974 to 1978 (*Source*: McConnell 1980:267)

concentrated upon changes in employment in the United States owned plants at regional scale.

In 1975 United States' firms employed 658,000 employees in the United Kingdom compared with 602,000 some four years earlier (Watts 1982). This increase (which is based only in part on new jobs because it includes acquisition of companies already in operation) was not evenly distributed over all regions (Fig. 2.5). Where firms are acquired it has to be remembered that the employment acquired reflects the pre-existing distribution of a firm's activities and not necessarily a multinational's choice of region. Four major areas stand out as regions which contemporary employment change suggests are least attractive to United States' firms. They fall

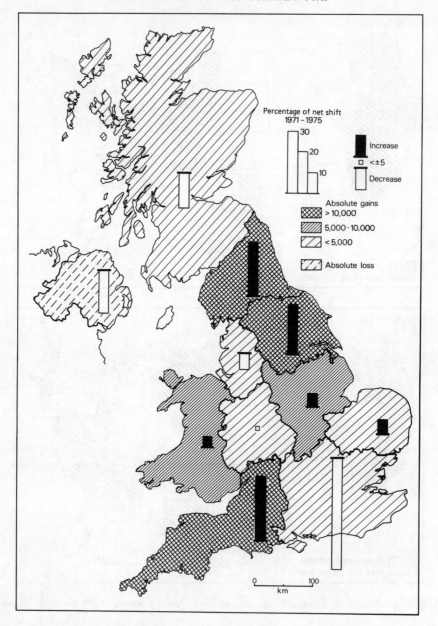

Fig. 2.5 Shifts in employment in United States owned plants in the United Kingdom, 1971 to 1975 (*Source*: Business Statistics Office, unpublished tabulations)

into two groups both characterised by negative net shifts: major industrial regions (North-West and South-East) and two peripheral regions (Scotland and Northern Ireland). The poor record of Scotland might reflect the old age of United States' investment in Scotland while in Northern Ireland it may mirror the area's disturbed political situation. The losses in Northern Ireland represented one-fifth of the employees which existed four years earlier. Major gains were recorded by the Yorkshire and Humberside and Northern regions as well as the South-West, these three regions accounting for three-fifths of the net increase in employment in United States' firms.

These two studies show the distinctive outcomes of foreign investment, yet it is important to recognise that firms based in different countries tend to have different locational preferences. Thus in Britain, European firms have placed more emphasis upon East Anglia than United States' firms (Watts 1980a) while in the United States, British investments are concentrated primarily in the North-East while the Japanese have the greatest range of manufacturing investments on the West Coast (McConnell 1983). It is also shown in Chapter 12 that firms new to Britain select different regions from those preferred by established foreign firms.

CONCLUSION

An international perspective on industrial change has illustrated how industries and firms are tied into the international industrial system. The main factor influencing employment trends in individual sectors is the effectiveness of firms operating within them in holding or increasing their shares of the domestic market and in competing in export markets. In a number of cases, the national employment record is affected by the strategies of both domestic and foreign multinational firms as they switch products and output between regions and countries. Yet in terms of changes in the geography of industrial activity within national economies the international influences interact with the local and national framework which has been evolving over the last 200 years.

3
THE HISTORICAL FRAMEWORK

Contemporary changes in the distribution of employment opportunities are the most recent manifestations of a constantly changing geography of industrial activity. Remnants of past industrial patterns are all around us at the present time and as Smith (1949:xiii), a pioneer of modern industrial geography, argued it is because of the 'dynamic quality of... [industrial] ...geography... [that] ...an historical introduction is essential'. This chapter traces briefly the process of industrialisation and shows how employment in different industries rises and falls over time, how the geography of industrial activity has changed in the past, and how these changes have left a set of industries with distinctive spatial patterns and regions with distinctive industrial mixes. The final part of the chapter examines the influence of a region's inherited industrial structure on its contemporary employment performance.

THE EVOLUTION OF THE MANUFACTURING SYSTEM

The evolution of the manufacturing system in advanced western economies is reflected in a series of long waves or *Kondratieff cycles*. Each cycle lasts about 50 to 60 years and interest in them has grown in recent years since the major recession of the 1980s appears to mirror the recession of the 1930s some 50 years earlier. Each cycle has left a considerable inheritance which can be seen in the present-day distribution

of industrial activity. The first cycle was based on steam power, the second on railways, the third on electricity and the automobile and the fourth on electronics and synthetic materials. Kondratieff argued that one of the main forces underlying these long waves was that during a recession 'an especially large number of important discoveries and inventions...are made which...are usually applied on a large scale, only at the beginning of the next long upswing' (Kondratieff 1978:53). Not everyone accepts the technological push argument for long waves (Rothwell 1982:363), nor indeed the existence of the long waves themselves, but they provide a starting point for a discussion of the spatial evolution of the manufacturing system.

Domestic and factory systems

The first two cycles (based on steam power and railways) saw the emergence of the factory system of production. In Britain before the introduction of factories most manufacturing was undertaken in small workshops adjacent to or within a worker's home. Initially, workers bought their own materials and sold their own products but as society developed, control of industrial activity in many industries passed from workers to merchants. The merchants supplied the materials to the cottage workers, paid them for the finished products and sold those products in the market. This is known as the *domestic system* or sometimes the *putting-out system* since work was put out from a central point to the workers in their homes. The domestic system survived quite extensively in the footwear and hosiery industries in Britain into the second half of the nineteenth century and, indeed, in clothing until the twentieth century but for most industries it was replaced by factory production. It has not, however, completely disappeared and certainly survives, usually employing the female members of low income families particularly in larger cities and often in the clothing trades.

Some local specialisations in Britain can still be traced back to regional concentrations of industry which developed under the domestic system. Notable examples are the wool textile industry of Yorkshire (Gregory 1982), and the footwear industry of the East Midlands (Mounfield 1964–67; Mounfield, Unwin and Guy 1982). In these regions the domestic system was replaced eventually by the factory system; where this did not occur, for example in the textile industries of South-West England and East Anglia, the regional specialities disappeared.

The 'industrial revolution' and the introduction of the *factory system* are normally associated with the last quarter of the eighteenth century in Britain (Mathias 1983). The main features of the factory system were (and are) substantial output of a standardised product, the 'concentration of the processes of manufacture under one roof, the use of specialised machines...the organisation and direction of the labour force by specialised management...(and the adoption)...of mechanical power' (Chapman 1972:17). Its major attraction to the manufacturer was its ability to increase labour productivity, reduce costs and increase profits. In the cotton industry the number of operative hours to spin a 45.3 kg of cotton fell from around 2,000 hours with Crompton's mule (in 1780) to about 135 hours with Robert's automatic mules in 1825.

The factory system was not a discovery of the nineteenth century and large plants had been characteristic of some sugar refiners, brewers and shipbuilders since the early eighteenth century. However, the development of new techniques in the textile industry to which water power and then steam power could be applied accelerated the development of the factory system. The widespread adoption of steam power, particularly after the opening of the Boulton and Watt foundry in 1795; the increased output of iron, following from Darby's discovery of the method of smelting ore with coke rather than charcoal, and the development of the inland waterway system all contributed to the rapid industrialisation of Britain through the growth of the factory system. As the nineteenth century progressed the railway replaced the canal and steel replaced iron and there emerged in Britain an employment structure founded on textiles, clothing and metal-based activities. The main features of Britain's nineteenth-century employment structure were well established by 1841, towards the end of the first Kondratieff cycle and the first year for which there are reliable employment data (Table 3.1). The most striking feature is the dominance of the textile industry which employed more than one in three of all industrial workers, and together with clothing and footwear accounted for just over 60 per cent of industrial employment. Over three-quarters of the employment was in these two industries plus food, drink and tobacco and metal manufacture. The

Table 3.1   Great Britain: industrial structure, 1841*

	Number (000s)	Percentage
Food, drink, tobacco†	244	10.5
Chemicals	25	1.1
Metal manufacture	165	7.1
Mechanical engineering	32	1.4
Instrument engineering	16	0.7
Shipbuilding	27	1.2
Vehicles	39	1.7
Metal goods n.e.s.	81	3.5
Textiles	864	37.0
Leather goods	50	2.2
Clothing and footwear	549	23.5
Bricks, pottery, glass	55	2.4
Timber and furniture	108	4.7
Paper and printing	47	2.0
Other manufacturing industries	18	1.0
All manufacturing industries	2,320	

(*Source*: Lee 1979)
* These data are not comparable with the data in Table 3.2.
† This category also includes a large number of distributors rather than manufacturers of food products.

1841 workforce of 2.3 million had more than trebled by 1911 in association with the second Kondratieff cycle but the same four industries were still dominant and of the same standing in terms of their relative importance to each other although their share of manufacturing employment had dropped to 63 per cent. The main difference was the growth in the importance of metal-using industries. Mechanical engineering's share of employment increased from 1.4 to 7.3 per cent. The four industries plus mechanical engineering and metal goods made up just 75 per cent of the manufacturing workforce in 1911.

Inevitably, the process of industrialisation led to changes in the geography of industrial activity. Overviews of these changes are provided by Perry (1975:52–124) and Darby (1973:302 et seq.) but the main features are summarised in Fig. 3.1 which is based on population estimates for the six major cities of England and Wales. Such estimates are markedly influenced by boundary changes and definitions as to which administrative districts are properly part of a city but they do give a broad indication of shifts in economic activities. In the early years of the eighteenth century the six major towns were London and the provincial cities of Exeter, Bristol, Norwich, York and Newcastle (Darby 1973:381). Only Bristol and London were still in the top six by 1801 and Exeter, Norwich, York and Newcastle had been replaced by Birmingham, Liverpool, Manchester and Leeds. These cities were still small by modern standards; the largest, Liverpool, had a population of 82,000 and the smallest, Leeds, had a population of just 53,000. By 1861 the midland and northern industrial cities were dominant. The five largest English cities outside London by 1861 were Birmingham, Leeds, Liverpool, Manchester and Sheffield a dominance they still retained in 1911. They were much changed from the early nineteenth century; Liverpool's population had reached almost half – a – million by 1861 and nearly three-quarters of a million persons by 1911 (Mitchell and Deane 1962:24–7). In the late nineteenth century these cities and many other urban places developed the characteristics of what Mumford (1961:446) so appropriately called 'Coketown'.

Industrialisation in the course of the first two Kondratieff cycles saw the emergence of the British coalfields and their environs as the major centres of industrial activity, replacing the older long-established towns, with the marked exception of London.

The industrialisation of Britain initially met little competition but from 1850 industrialisation first in mainland Europe (Henderson 1969) and then in North America gathered speed. While manufacturing employment in Britain doubled from 1841 to 1881 and increased by a further 50 per cent between 1881 and 1911, the pace of change in the United States was much more rapid. Here industrial employment doubled from 1849 to 1869, doubled again from 1869 to 1889 and increased by just over 50 per cent in the 14 years between 1899 and 1914. By 1909/1911 industrial employment in the United States was approximately equal to that in Britain.

The United States in 1900 was a major industrial producer (Robertson and Walton 1979) but the experience of industrialisation in the United States was rather different from that in Britain. As Kroos (1974:427) observes 'there was no industrial revolution in the true sense of the word in the United States. The American economy started to industrialise almost from its very beginnings.' Until 1850 increases in industrial employment were associated either with independent craftsmen working in their homes or with production under the putting-out system. From around 1845 there was a move towards increased factory production based on water power, although factory production can be traced back to the 1790s. In 1860 water was still the chief source of power but it was to be rapidly superseded by steam. The relatively undeveloped nature of the economy at this time is reflected in the fact that as late as 1850 the output of iron was one-fifth of that in Great Britain although the populations of the two countries were very similar (Warren 1973).

Industrialisation with iron, steel, and textiles was thus much later in the United States than in Britain. By 1874 pig iron output was still less than that of Britain but by 1895 it was almost 20 per cent greater. United States steel production

Fig. 3.1 Major cities of England and Wales in the eighteenth and nineteenth centuries (*Source*: Mitchell and Deane 1962:24–7)

overtook Britain in 1890 and by 1906 American output was nearly four times as great (Warren, 1973:8). It is difficult to separate the changing distribution of United States' industry during

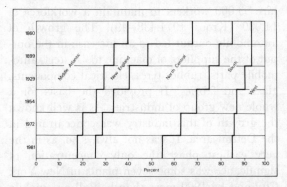

Fig. 3.2 Manufacturing employment change in the United States in the nineteenth and twentieth centuries (*Source*: Based on Sternlieb and Hughes 1975: 115 and US Bureau of Census 1984: Table 1341)

industrialisation from the spread of settlement to the interior and West Coast. This is illustrated in Fig. 3.2 which shows the fall in the share of manufacturing employment in the Middle Atlantic and New England regions between 1860 and 1899.

In both the United States and Britain the nineteenth- and early twentieth-century industries are still in operation though often with changed processes. They are much less important as providers of employment opportunities in both a relative and absolute sense but steel mills and footwear plants remain features of the industrial scene.

Mass production and scientific management

At the end of the nineteenth century industrial structures were little different from those of 25 years earlier (Table 3.1). Textiles were still the dominant industry in the United States with just over 1½ million employees, followed by iron and steel with 1 million employees. Yet the seeds of the new industrial growth of the twentieth century had been set. The basic ideas underlying mass production – notably the use of interchangeable parts in continuous production – and scientific management – aimed at maximising workers' output per unit of time – had been established. By 1919 'just over 80 per cent of all factories with an annual product of over $500 were using electrically powered equipment' (Potter 1974:23). The stage was set for continued growth in the number employed in manufacturing, a growth based initially on the electrical products and automobiles associated with the third Kondratieff cycle. Two indicators of the growth of new industries in the United States in the 1920s illustrate the scope of the change. In 1922 60,000 families had a radio, by 1929 it was 10 million, while the number of registered automobiles rose from 9 million in 1920 to 23 million in 1929. Around 2 million jobs in manufacturing were added to the United States economy between 1909 and 1929. A fall in numbers after the crash of 1929 was offset by an increase in the Second World War to 14 million followed by a steady increase through the 1950s and 1960s

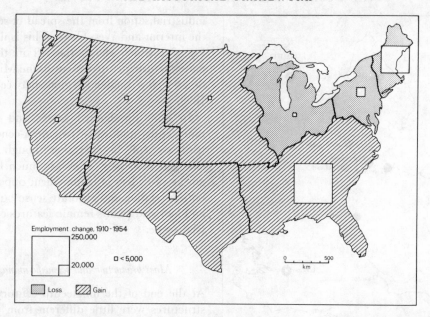

Fig. 3.3 Employment shifts in the United States cotton and cotton goods industry, 1910 to 1954 (*Source*: Perloff, Dunn, Lampard and Muth 1960:158)

adding 1½ million jobs in the 1950s and 3 million in the 1960s. Such growth was, not surprisingly, associated with major changes in the distribution of employment in manufacturing industry. Reference back to Fig. 3.2 shows that whereas the Middle Atlantic and New England areas accounted for about 50 per cent of manufacturing employment in 1899 their share had fallen to one-third by 1954. These overall patterns hide the performance of individual industries both the old established and the new.

Among the geographical changes in the older industries the most dramatic was the shift of the textile industry to the South (Fig. 3.3). Throughout the 1920s the number of wage-earners in the textile industry remained almost constant while the four leading New England cotton textile states lost 74,000 jobs between 1919 and 1929 the four leading southern states gained 75,000 jobs.

The growth of entirely new industries is well typified by the automobile industry. Duryea Brothers in Springfield (Massachusetts) was the first firm to produce more than one automobile of a given design. In 1896 it produced 12 vehicles

(Boas 1961:225). The beginnings of mass production were evident with the start-up of Oldsmobile production in 1901 in Lansing. This was taken further by Ford which split tasks into minute segments and by careful time-and-motion studies reduced the time taken to assemble a vehicle from 12½ hours to 93 minutes! It was in the Ford production line that mass production and scientific management were welded together, but not without cost. In the 1920s Ford had to hire 53,000 workers to maintain a workforce of 14,000 (Kroos 1974:438–49). The growth of automobile output led to an increase in the output of the suppliers of machine tools, steel, automobile parts, rubber tyres, electrical components, glass and fabrics. It provided the basis for a whole new group of industries. As is well known the growth of this industry was concentrated in the Detroit area. It was not always so, as in the very earliest phase the only concentration of significance was some seven plants in New York City and by 1900 more than half all automobile assembly plants were on the North-Eastern seaboard; yet by 1914 Detroit had emerged as the principal centre. Why this should have occurred is a fascinating question for the historical geographer, but in this context it illustrates how the development of a new industry contributed towards a shift of manufacturing away from New England and the eastern manufacturing belt. Such shifts were later emphasised further by the wartime development of defence industries, notably aircraft production, outside the traditional manufacturing areas.

New industries, especially automobiles, were causing changes in Britain too, often accompanied by major changes in the older industries. While output of steel castings of around 9 million tons in 1920 was matched by an output of around 10 million tons in 1938 (Mitchell and Deane 1962:137), output of cotton yarn and cotton piece goods halved between 1912 and 1938 (Pollard 1962:121). This fall in output was paralleled by a fall in employment in cotton textiles from 577,000 in 1907 to 393,000 in 1938. In the woollen industry the fall was less marked. The number of employees fell from 269,000 in 1923 to 216,000 in 1938. The rise of the new industries was dramatic. The number of employees in electrical engineering rose from 174,000 in 1924 to 367,000 in 1937 – thus overtaking the woollen industry and challenging the cotton textile industry as a major source of employment. In the motor vehicle industry the first mass-produced car rolled off the production lines in 1921 and by 1924 the industry was employing 220,000 workers (this figure also includes employment in the aircraft industry). By 1939 the number employed was 380,000.

From the mid-1930s onwards the innovations of the fourth Kondratieff played a role. The petro-chemical industry with its wide range of synthetic materials, notably fibres, plastics and rubber, added yet new elements to the industrial geography of the United States and the United Kingdom. Paralleling these developments were advances in electronics affecting consumer products (seen for example in the manufacture of advanced hi-fi systems), and capital goods such as computers and the complex hardware produced for the military.

Taking an overview of the third and fourth Kondratieff and comparing Britain's industrial structure of 1971 with that of 1911 shows, in a striking fashion, the changes that had taken place. Changes after 1971 are discussed later. The most obvious change between 1911 and 1971 (Table 3.2) is that no single group of industries dominates the structure, the maximum percentage in any one group being 14 per cent in mechanical engineering. The share of clothing and textiles has fallen from 42 per cent to 13 per cent, while the share of industries such as electrical engineering and vehicles has increased from 2 per cent to 10 per cent in the former case and from 3 to 10 per cent in the latter case. The general pattern has been for newer industries to increase their shares (for example, instrument engineering) and for the share of older industries to decrease (for example, leather goods and shipbuilding). Only textiles, clothing and leather showed an absolute fall in employment levels over the 60-year period to 1971.

As in the United States such changes were accompanied by adjustments in the location of employment opportunities. The older industries did not witness such dramatic shifts as the textile industries in North America, but some changes did take place. The steel industry, for example, increased its reliance on home ores and built a large new plant on the East Midlands orefield at Corby. While the nineteenth century saw a drift to the coalfields the new industries were most successful in the South-East and Midlands. Major motor vehicle assembly plants were constructed in Coventry, Birmingham, Oxford, Luton and Dagenham (near London). The latter being a branch of the Ford organisation. The net output of Great Britain attributable to the nineteenth-century industrial regions fell from 50 per cent in 1924 to 38 per cent in 1935. The share of the newer industrial regions rose from 29 to 37 per cent (Pollard 1962:126).

This sketch of over 200 years of change illustrates the essentially dynamic nature of industrial activity. At the present time we are reaching the end of a fourth Kondratieff wave based on electronics and synthetic materials. In 1785 it was difficult to foresee the changes which would follow from the introduction of steam power and the factory system; in 1885 it would have been

Table 3.2 Great Britain: industrial structure, 1911* and 1971

Industry	1911		1971	
	Number (000s)	Percentage	Number (000s)	Percentage
Food, drink, tobacco	334	5.8	738	9.2
Petroleum products	—	—	59	0.7
Chemicals	123	2.1	459	5.6
Metals	360	6.2	551	6.8
Mechanical engineering	516	8.9	1,125	13.9
Instrument engineering	39	0.7	145	1.8
Electrical engineering	101	1.8	844	10.4
Shipbuilding	156	2.7	180	2.2
Vehicles	193	3.3	789	9.8
Metal goods n.e.s.	495	8.6	586	7.3
Textiles	1,298	22.5	591	7.4
Leather goods	90	1.6	53	0.7
Clothing and footwear	1,144	19.9	470	5.8
Bricks, pottery, glass	195	3.4	306	3.8
Timber, furniture	276	4.8	302	3.7
Paper and printing	336	5.8	612	7.5
Other manufacturing industries	106	1.9	323	3.4
All manufacturing industries	5,762		8,133	

(*Source*: Lee 1979)

* These data are not comparable with the data in Table 3.1.

difficult to envisage the changes consequent upon the introduction of electricity and the internal combustion engine; 1985 is another watershed and identifying the industries which will form the basis of a fifth Kondratieff is a topic for debate. What is certain is that their geographical distribution will be welded on to an exceedingly complex spatial industrial system the consequences of which it is difficult to escape at the present time.

THE DIFFERENTIATED SPACE ECONOMY

It is because of the long history of industrialisation discussed in the last section that changes in the distribution of industrial activity take place not on the isotropic plane of traditional industrial location theory but within a *differentiated space economy* in which industries with different spatial patterns combine to give regions with differing industrial structures.

Industries, industrial regions and employment trends

Each industry has a distinctive geographical dis-
tribution and these distributions range along a continuum from widely dispersed to highly concentrated. Two such different patterns are illustrated in Fig. 3.4. In the paper boxes and containers industry (Fig. 3.4A) the most important state (Illinois) accounts for only 8 per cent of the industry's jobs, and the top three states (Illinois plus New York and Ohio) account for only just over one-fifth of the jobs. This pattern contrasts markedly with the motor vehicles and equipment industry (Fig. 3.4B) where the leading state (Michigan) accounts for almost one-third of the nation's jobs in the industry and the top three states (Michigan plus Ohio and Indiana) account for just over half (53 per cent) of the jobs. Even higher levels of concentration are evident in the smaller area of Britain; no less than 70 per cent of the office machinery industry was concentrated in South-East England in 1981 but the highest concentration was probably the pottery industry with 77 per cent of its employment in the West Midlands.

Another way of looking at the distribution of an industry is to compare its distribution with the distribution of manufacturing industry as a

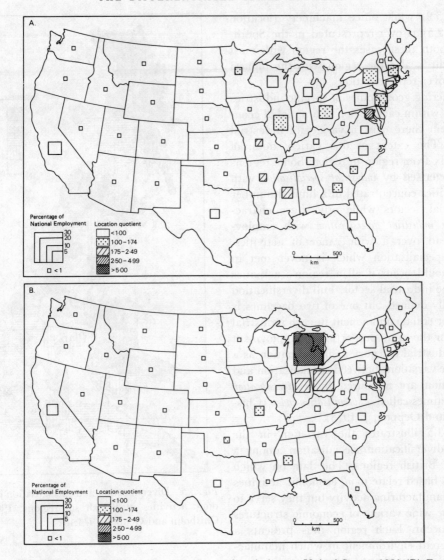

Fig. 3.4 (A) Employment in the paper boxes and container industry, United States, 1981 (B) Employment in the motor vehicles and equipment industry, United States, 1981 (*Source*: US Bureau of Census 1982)

whole. This is undertaken by using a *location quotient* which relates an area's share of a particular industry to its share of all manufacturing. A location quotient of 2.0, for example, suggests an area has twice as much employment in a specified industry than would be expected from its share of all manufacturing employment. Areas with the highest levels of over-representation of an industry are not necessarily those with the highest levels of employment in an industry as reference back to Fig. 3.4 will show.

Over-representation and high levels of employment are characteristic of the motor vehicle industry where Michigan has a quotient of 6.8, Ohio 2.3 and Indiana 2.1. In the paper boxes and containers industry the highest degree of over-representation occurs in Maryland (2.7) which ranks twelfth in terms of state employment in the industry, while the second highest location quotient is associated with Missouri which ranks sixth. In the British data pottery is over-represented in the West Midlands (location quotient, 5.9) while office machinery (location quotient, 2.5) is over-represented in the South-East. In both these cases the region with most employment is also the region with the highest degree of over-representation.

The differing geographies of specific industries mean that within each region of a national economic system there exist a variety of industrial activities. The extent of this variety does, of course, vary from region to region. Some regions are characterised by *industrial specialisation* with most activities concentrated in a limited number of industrial sectors while others are characterised by *industrial diversification* with employment spread over a wide range of activities. Extreme specialisation which is never met in practice would occur if all a region's activities were in one industrial sector. Full diversification is less easily defined but one of two baselines is used, either equal employment in each industrial category, or the same proportion of employment in each industrial category as in the nation as a whole. The variations between specialisation and diversification are measured by a *diversification index*, sometimes called a *specialisation index* (Chisholm, M. and Oeppen, J. 1973).

Figure 3.5 illustrates the variation in the degree of diversification/specialisation among a number of British regions. The data on which this map is based relate to *all* economic activities not only manufacturing activity but they serve to indicate the wide variety of economic structures that can occur. Each region thus presents a rather different environment in which manufacturing employment change takes place.

These few examples make clear that industries have distinctive spatial distributions and regions have distinctive industrial structures. The patterns created by the distribution of industries reflect the evolution of regional and industrial structures over a number of years. In a contemporary context, the key point is that each region inherits a particular industrial structure and that structure can influence the rate of employment change in a region. This influence operates because the employment in different industries may be declining (or growing) nationally at different rates.

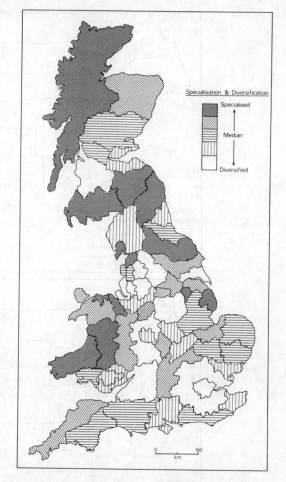

Fig. 3.5 Diversification and specialisation in *all* economic activities in British sub-regions, 1968 (*Source*: Chisholm and Oeppen 1973:48)

The extent of variations in the employment performance of different sectors over the last decade is shown in Table 3.3. All manufacturing employment in the United States rose by 6.5 per cent from 1972 to 1981 but this hides a variation between sectors from +35 per cent to −18 per cent; in Britain from 1971 to 1981 an overall fall of −30 per cent covered declines ranging from −52 per cent to −14 per cent. Clearly the range of experience in the United States is greater than that of Britain but the rankings of the industries are not very different. Direct comparisons are not possible because of detailed differences between the industrial classifications.

Table 3.3 Employment trends in United States' industries (1972–81) and British industries (1971–81)

United States	Percentage change
Employment growth	
Administrative and auxiliary units	+35.2
Instruments and related products	+35.0
Machinery, except electrical	+30.2
Printing and publishing	+20.2
Electric and electronic equipment	+17.9
Rubber and miscellaneous plastic products	+11.8
Petroleum and coal products	+8.6
Chemicals and allied products	+6.6
All manufacturing	+6.5
Paper and allied products	+0.5
Fabricated metal products	+0.1
Employment decline	
Furniture and fixtures	−0.4
Transportation equipment	−1.7
Food and kindred products	−3.7
Stone, clay and glass products	−5.3
Lumber and wood products	−6.1
Primary metal industries	−7.0
Miscellaneous manufacturing	−7.4
Tobacco products	−7.6
Apparel and other textile products	−8.6
Leather and leather products	−6.5
Textile mill products	−17.6

Great Britain

Employment decline (< mean)	
Chemicals	−13.5
Instrument engineering	−15.3
Paper, printing and publishing	−17.8
Electrical engineering	−23.6
Food, drink and tobacco	−24.9
Shipbuilding	−25.0
Timber	−26.3
Other manufacturing industries	−27.3
Vehicles	−27.4
Metals not elsewhere specified	−27.5
All manufacturing	−29.8
Fast employment decline (> mean)	
Mechanical engineering	−32.8
Bricks, pottery, glass and cement	−34.5
Leather and fur	−42.3
Metal manufacture	−43.4
Clothing	−43.9
Textiles	−48.5
Coal and petroleum products	−51.7

(*Source*: Based on US Bureau of Census 1984:768–73; *Department of Employment Gazette* 1972:277–8; *Employment Gazette* 1982:507–9)

The greatest percentage losses in the United States were in textile mill products and leather and leather products. In apparel and other textile products and primary metal industries smaller percentage losses were associated with absolute losses over 75,000 jobs. The two major industries characterised by employment growth were instruments and related products and machinery, except electrical (increases of around 30 per cent), and these were followed by electric and electronic equipment and printing and publishing (with increases of around 20 per cent). Major increases were also associated with the administrative and auxiliary units of larger firms (discussed in the next chapter).

Although coal and petroleum products saw the greatest decline in Britain, they were followed closely by textiles, leather, clothing and metal manufacture, all of which recorded employment declines of over 40 per cent. While vehicles and electrical engineering lost 'only' around one-quarter of their employees, one-quarter of a million jobs disappeared from each industry. The best employment performance (in this context, industries in which employment was declining at the slowest rate) came from chemicals, instrument engineering and paper, printing and publishing.

The reasons for the variations in the employment performance of different sectors raise some fascinating questions which it is not possible to explore in detail but as the previous chapter showed the international competitiveness of an industry's products is particularly important. Since different sectors of national economies have different employment performances and regions have different combinations of industrial activities it is sometimes claimed that a region's employment performance arises from its particular mix of industries. This argument has particular force where the range of variations between industries is large. For example, a region in the United States with most of its employment in textiles and leather in 1972 would show a much worse overall employment trend from 1972 to 1981 than a region whose 1972 employment was concentrated in instruments and non-electrical machinery. Admittedly, regions also inherit industrial characteristics, such as a particular mix of plant sizes or a particular level of foreign ownership, which can influence employment performance but these elements may themselves arise from industrial structures. For example, Chapter 6 shows how different plant sizes are associated with particular industrial sectors. It is the industrial mix which has been seen as a basic influence on industrial change in a region and to examine its effect a technique called *shift–share analysis* is used.

The influence of industrial structure

Shift–share analysis recognises that the overall rate of manufacturing employment change results from the operation of three elements: the national rate of change in manufacturing; the industrial structure of the region; and a residual element which may be intepreted as indicating the locational advantages or disadvantages of a region. Shift–share analysis permits the identification of the relative importance of these three elements.

Shift–share analysis recognises four basic terms. Unfortunately, the terminology does vary slightly between studies and these alternative terms are indicated in parenthesis below.

1. *Regional share* (national change) indicates what would have happened if a region's manufacturing employment had changed at the national rate of change. It describes what would have happened to a region's employment if it had maintained its *share* of national manufacturing employment.
2. *Total shift* is the difference between the employment expected from the regional share and the actual employment.
3. *Structural* (proportional, mix, compositional) *shift*, as its name suggests, measures the structural influence and reflects the mix of industries in a region.
4. *Differential* (regional, competitive) *shift*. This is a residual element some, or all, of which may arise as a result of locational advantages and disadvantages.

In some studies (for example, Danson, Lever and Malcolm 1980) further elements are identified

but they refine rather than change the basic form of the technique. The terms 'shift' and 'share' used to describe the different elements give the technique its name. A detailed discussion of the technique with a worked example is provided in Appendix I (pages 232–6). The main feature to note here is that the size of the structural shift provides an indication of the effect of industrial structure on regional employment change.

Application of the shift–share technique suggests that increasingly industrial structure is playing a relatively unimportant role in the spatial pattern of manufacturing employment change. This conclusion has been reached from analysis of both United States and United Kingdom data. Unfortunately there are relatively few analyses confined to the manufacturing sector as most shift–share analyses examine all economic activities.

Regional shifts

Table 3.4 shows the results of shift–share analysis of the period 1972 to 1976 for nine regions. It was shown in Chapter 1 that during this period the manufacturing belt was losing manufacturing employment while the remainder of the United States was gaining jobs. Analysis of the structural and differential shifts shows that this trend was in fact in the *opposite* direction to that expected from regional industrial structures. If employment change in the two areas had arisen

Table 3.4   Structural and differential shifts in manufacturing employment, United States, 1972–76

Region	Structural shift (000s)	Differential shift (000s)
New England	+5	−34
Mid-Atlantic	+4	−362
EN Central	+49	−138
Manufacturing belt	+58	−534
WN Central	+11	+62
S Atlantic	−59	+247
ES Central	−18	+71
WS Central	−1	+184
Mountain	−1	+25
Pacific	−4	+133
Periphery	−73	+722

(*Source*: Based on Norton and Rees 1979:148)

solely from their industrial structures in 1972 then there would have been an increase of 58,000 jobs in the manufacturing belt and a loss of 73,000 jobs elsewhere. It will be noted that in all regions the employment loss or gain associated with the differential component is very much larger than the employment change associated with the structural component.

Urban-rural shifts

Similar conclusions were derived from a study of the urban–rural shift in manufacturing employment from 1971 to 1976 in the United Kingdom (Keeble 1980). In examining the structural shifts in Table 3.5 it is clear that they made only a small contribution to the overall pattern of change, and in the more detailed county data not shown here over three-quarters of the counties recorded structural shifts of less than plus or minus 2 per cent.

It seems that in these two cases industrial structure is not a major factor explaining the geography of manufacturing employment change. Geographical patterns of industrial change cannot be explained away by 'structural' factors. Explanations based upon industrial structure may have been important in the past but at the present time two factors are reducing their influence. First, industries are becoming increasingly dispersed so that regional industrial structures are becoming similar to one another. As a result regions with a once favourable industrial structure are having that favourability reduced while those with an unfavourable structure are finding their dependence on particular industries with a poor employment record decreasing. Second, the rates of employment change in different industries are converging and if employment changes take place in all industries at the same rate there will be no structural effect at all.

CONCLUSION

This chapter has illustrated how the evolution of the industrial system over the past 200 years has produced particular industrial patterns and different regional industrial structures. These structures play a small role in explaining spatial variations in the rate of employment change; but analysis of industrial structures themselves leaves much of the geography of industrial change unexplained. Analysis of industrial structure inevitably focuses on industries but as was seen in Chapter 1 changes are guided not by industries but by the basic unit of industrial organisation: the firm.

Table 3.5 Structural and differential shifts in manufacturing employment, United Kingdom, 1971–76

	Structural shift (mean %)	Differential shift
Conurbations	−0.5	−2.8
More urbanised counties	+0.2	+3.3
Less urbanised counties	+1.2	+5.6
Rural counties	+0.2	+11.0
All United Kingdom counties	+0.5	+5.8

(*Source*: Keeble 1980:949–50)

PART II

FIRMS

Changes in the geography of employment in manufacturing industry arise from decisions made by firms although these decisions are constrained by the international framework within which the firm operates and by the patterns of industrial activity inherited from the past. Firms too inherit specific corporate spatial structures from their past activities and Chapter 4 outlines the characteristics of the spatial structures created by larger firms and shows how the modern firm operates within a segmented economy. Chapter 5 looks specifically at the way in which decisions are made by firms and the influence of decision making upon geographical patterns of industrial change.

4

THE SEGMENTED ECONOMY

Industrial activity is organised by firms which make decisions about what to produce, how much to produce and how to produce it. These decisions influence both the number of people employed in manufacturing industry within a national economy and the amount of employment in manufacturing activity within the different regions of the economy. Attention has already been drawn to the diversion of jobs overseas by domestic multinationals and to the differential regional impact of employment changes in foreign-owned firms.

The principal function of a firm is to co-ordinate activities to manufacture a product or products. In Penrose's (1980:15) words it is 'an autonomous administrative planning unit, the activities of which are interrelated and are co-ordinated by policies which are framed in the light of their effect on the ... [firm] ... as a whole'. Figure 4.1 illustrates some of the more important

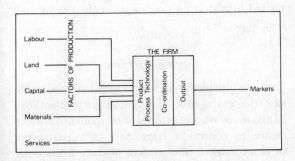

Fig. 4.1   The activities of a firm

co-ordinating activities a firm undertakes in its day-to-day operations. Such co-ordination is to try to ensure that *revenues* (sales) exceed *costs* in order to generate *profits* to permit the long-run survival of the firm. While it is usual to assume that firms seek to earn profits 'there ... is ... no doubt that business executives pursue other motives in addition to profit' (Starbuck 1971:19). These include increasing sales, increasing managerial satisfaction and reducing costs. In any one firm, one of these motives may predominate while in other firms the motives may include aspects of all three. However, since a certain level of profit is necessary for a firm to remain as a viable concern, it is most useful to recognise the creation of profit as the key objective of a firm.

To meet the profit objective (assuming that product, process and output are fixed) a firm has to purchase the appropriate quantities of *materials* and draw upon *services* ranging from those provided by legal and financial organisations to those concerned with the maintenance of machinery and equipment. Co-ordination of the labour inputs is necessary in order to utilise the material and service inputs to manufacture the finished product. It is also important to ensure that finance is available to purchase the materials and services, to pay the labour force, to pay the rent or mortgage on the factory premises and to pay interest on loans. Control over the three *factors of production* – labour, land and capital – is central to a firm's co-ordinating task. In terms of the final output a firm has to co-ordinate plant outputs with warehouse capacity and customer demand. All these activities impose costs upon a firm and since they vary in relative importance between firms each firm has its own distinctive cost structure. Plant, as distinct from firm, cost structures are discussed in Chapter 6.

The co-ordination task becomes more complex if output changes are taken into account. The implications of a proposed cut in output must be traced back to make adjustments in material and service requirements and to adapt the factors of production to meet the new level of demand. Output cuts lead to a reduction in a firm's needs for materials and services, in labour force lay-offs and, possibly, in the disposal of land and other capital assets. Expansion of output may require searches for new suppliers, a need to raise more capital, the hiring of more labour and, possibly, a search for a new site. In a multi-plant firm the co-ordination of activities in one plant often has to be synchronised with changes in other plants in the corporate system.

Although all firms have a co-ordinating role they can differ quite markedly in other ways. For example, Chapter 1 drew attention to the distinction between the multi-plant and single-plant firm while Chapter 2 discussed the significance of multinational firms. Over time the population of firms has become increasingly differentiated. *Atomistic economies* characterised by a myriad of small firms have given way to *segmented economies* characterised by a variety of firms ranging from large multinational organisations to the small back-street workshop. The recognition of the existence of a variety of firm types is very important in any modern study of industrial activity since it is believed different types of firm act in different ways (Massey and Meegan 1982:164). In the 1980s the distinctive roles of large firms, small firms and the interdependencies between them have been stressed increasingly in industrial geography. This chapter traces the emergence of the segmented economy and then examines its present-day significance. Particular emphasis is placed upon the spatial structures of large industrial firms.

EMERGENCE OF A SEGMENTED ECONOMY

Firms grow by either *internal growth* or *external growth*. Internal growth is characterised by gaining new markets or out-competing rival firms in existing markets. External growth is achieved by acquiring other firms. It has already been shown how the establishment of new plants and the acquisition of existing plants both contributed to increases in employment in foreign-owned plants in the United States and Britain. There is considerable debate as to the relative importance of these two modes of growth in contributing to corporate growth.

Internal growth is particularly characteristic of firms whose product markets are growing rapidly. A good example is provided by the development of the Ford organisation in the first half of the twentieth century but since the middle of the nineteenth century various merger waves (periods of high levels of acquisition activity) have contributed to the development and growth of the large firms.

In the United States merger waves occurred between 1898 and 1906, in the 1920s and in the years following the Second World War. In Britain merger peaks occurred in 1880–1910, in the 1920s, and in the late 1950s and 1960s. Figure 4.2 provides two examples of acquisitions being used to create a large firm. Each horizontal line represents an independent brewing firm in Britain in 1951, the vertical lines indicate acquisitions and the principal firms are represented by a bold horizontal line. Merger waves differ in character over time. Whereas early acquisitions were predominantly motivated by a desire to create single-product firms, later mergers were characterised by a desire to create diversified firms and conglomerates.

Single-product firms

The late nineteenth and early twentieth centuries saw the emergence of large single-product organisations whose growth was motivated by a desire to control a large part of a particular product market. The growth of these firms both

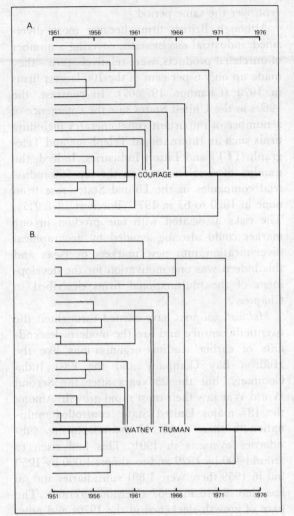

Fig. 4.2 Acquisitions and corporate growth in the British brewing industry, 1951 to 1976 (A) Courage (B) Watney Truman (*Source*: Based on Watts 1980b: 179)

at the turn of the century and later can be associated in many cases with the drive and acumen of particular individuals. Carnegie built up what was to become United States Steel, Rockefeller guided the growth of Standard Oil, while Ford's company still bears his name. In Britain, Lord Nuffield built a fortune based on the Morris car while other firms were developed by Cadbury (in chocolate), Tate (in sugar) and Rank (in flour milling).

In addition to the firms cited above other examples are provided by American Can, International Harvester, the American Sugar Refining Company and the United States Rubber Company and, in Britain, by the United Alkali Company which brought 48 chemical firms together in 1891 and the English Sewing Cotton company which brought 14 competing firms together in 1897. Developments in Britain and the United States were not independent of one another and when American Tobacco entered the British market in 1901 13 British firms in the industry combined to form Imperial Tobacco. The emergence of these large corporate organisations played a key role in creating the segmented economy (Sobel 1972; Hannah 1976).

Diversified firms and conglomerates

The twentieth century saw a gradual change in the nature of large industrial organisations and a move towards more diversified firms. In part, this reflected increasing public opposition to *monopoly power* which arises where a few firms control most of the output of a particular industry. Opposition was particularly strong in the United States where legislation as early as 1890 was designed to limit the growth of monopolies. Notable break-ups of large organisations under the 1890 Sherman Act included the Standard Oil Company of New Jersey and the American Tobacco Company; the former at one point owned or leased 90 per cent of United States' refining capacity, the latter held a monopoly of the cigarette industry. In the United Kingdom opposition to monopoly power was not formalised until the setting up of the Monopolies Commission in 1948. Legislation of this nature encouraged firms to seek out new products if they desired to continue growth based on domestic markets. There are also good economic reasons for diversification, notably spreading corporate interests across a range of activities reduces any adverse effects created by a fall in demand for any one of them. An example of the risks inherent in a single-product firm are the problems created for tobacco companies by the increasing awareness of the health risks associated with cigarette smoking.

An illustration of a diversification strategy is provided by Du Pont which in 1913 had only 3 per cent of its business outside explosives (Chandler 1962:78–91). The explosives business was particularly sensitive to fluctuations in demand partly because of a dependence on government contracts (which could cease at short notice) and on the state of international relations. Since the main business was explosives, a branch of the chemical industry, it was agreed that plans for diversification would concentrate upon processes based on the science of chemistry. Focusing attention on products which had nitro-cellulose as their basic ingredient, artificial leather was selected as the first new line and in 1910 Du Pont acquired Fabrikoid one of the leading firms in the field. This was followed by a decision to move into celluloid products, in this case by building a new plant, but plans were curtailed by the outbreak of the First World War. In the post-war period activities in these two fields were strengthened and the firm also moved into products where the war had created significant shortages. The most important of these was dyestuffs. A third area was varnishes and paints which was joined, from 1919 by the manufacture of rayon. Over a period of about 10 years a single-product firm was transformed into a diversified organisation.

This process of *diversification* among the larger industrial firms has continued to the present day. Measuring this corporate diversification is difficult as such measures are very sensitive to definitions of product. A firm in the food industry can be regarded as a single-product firm producing food or a diversified firm manufacturing perhaps 10 or more different food products. Diversification came rather later in Britain than in the United States but a distinct move away from the single-product firm is evident in the United Kingdom from 1950 to 1970. Whereas 31 per cent of the 100 largest firms were single-product concerns in 1950 this proportion had fallen to 6 per cent in 1970; the percentage of firms producing a wide range of different but related products rose from 21 per cent to 54 per cent over the same period.

Although British firms became more diversified, industrial *conglomerates*, covering a number of unrelated products, were relatively rare – they made up only 6 per cent of the 100 largest firms in 1970 (Channon 1973:67). In contrast, the 1960s in the United States saw the emergence of a number of important conglomerates including firms such as International Telephone and Telegraph (ITT) and Litton Industries. Indeed, the number of conglomerates in the top 500 industrial companies in the United States rose from none in 1920 to 63 in 1971 (Borchert 1978:217). The risks associated with one product in one market could also be avoided by geographical diversification into new markets overseas and this indeed was one motivation for the development of the multinational firms described in Chapter 2.

Multinational firms have existed throughout the twentieth century and are the modern descendants of earlier trading organisations like the Hudson Bay Company and the East India Company, but the 25 years after the Second World War saw their most rapid growth. Among the 187 major United States controlled multinationals there were 47 manufacturing subsidiaries overseas in 1901. This had risen to around 400 by 1929 and to almost 1,000 by 1950 but in 1959 there were 1,891 subsidiaries and no less than 3,646 in 1967 (Vernon 1971:62). The pace of growth slackened in the 1970s and now, as was seen in Chapter 2, a new phase of multinational activities has begun. Geographical expansion has given way to a period of reorganisation. Nevertheless expansion of some multinational firms continues. Examples are provided by West German investment in the United Kingdom where the number of West German owned enterprises rose from 19 to 35 over the period from 1968 to 1975 (Watts 1982:70), the continued overseas expansion of Japanese firms (Dicken 1983), and the development of British investment in North America (McConnell 1983).

The growth of large corporate organisations by either internal or external growth saw an increasing concentration of corporate power in the hands of a relatively few firms. This trend is

Table 4.1   Share of the 100 largest enterprises in manufacturing net output, 1909–70

	United States	United Kingdom
1909	22	16
1924		22
1929	25	
1935	26	24
1947	23	
1949		22
1953		27
1954	30	
1958	30	32
1963	33	37
1967	33	
1968		41
1970	33	41*
1977	25	
1980		39

(*Source*: Prais 1976:4, 213; 1977 (US Bureau of Census 1985); 1980 (Business Statistics Office 1980: PA 1002))

* Estimate low because of increased census coverage of small firms in this year.

illustrated in Table 4.1. Although the shares of the 100 largest enterprises in net output remained at less than 25 per cent from around 1910 to 1950 the level of concentration was consistently higher in the United States. In both countries concentration increased in the two decades between 1950 and 1970. In the United Kingdom this increase was particularly dramatic, the share of net output of the 100 largest enterprises almost doubling between the two decades (Prais 1976:140). In 1970 a 41 per cent share by the *100* largest firms in the United Kingdom was to be contrasted with a 43 per cent share of the *200* firms in the United States. The most recent data (for 1977 and 1980) suggest that the shares of these large firms have begun to fall. Of course these large firms have not replaced small firms they have been superimposed upon them and many small firms survive in manufacturing at the present time, together with the many medium-sized firms which are not included in the top 100.

THE ORGANISATION OF INDUSTRY IN THE 1980S

As a result of the *restructuring* of industrial activity (Hamilton 1984) described above, decisions

about the changing geography of employment opportunities are taken by firms whose characteristics vary markedly from the one-person engineering workshop to organisations the size of General Motors and Ford. Any modern study of industrial geography has to recognise the important differences between such firms primarily because the ways in which large firms react to the environments in which they operate and the ways in which they make decisions differ markedly from those of the small firm. Also, unlike the small firm the larger firm creates its own distinctive geographical patterns and its potential for altering the regional distribution of employment opportunities is so much greater. The large firm can respond quickly to economic change, can shift employment between regions and often adds to or subtracts from its plants large numbers of employees. The small firm may 'muddle along' in changed economic circumstances, is unlikely to move its operations between regions and the closure or opening of a single small firm makes little difference to a regional economy. The typical small firm reacts to the environment in which it operates, the larger firm helps to create that environment. Although discussion often suggests there is a marked dichotomy between large and small firms it is more valuable to consider firms as being arranged along a continuum and the characteristics of the two ends of the spectrum will be reflected in part in firms in the middle-size range. In other words it is now recognised that most advanced capitalist economies are characterised by a *segmented economy* of which the most obvious indication is the distinction between large and small firms.

One of the earliest discussions of the important differences between large and small firms was by Galbraith (1967). He distinguished between the *planning-system firms* and the *market-system firms*: the former represent the larger organisations, the latter the smaller organisations. Similar distinctions were made by Averitt (1968) who recognised centre firms (large) and periphery firms (small) and by Holland (1976) who identified the meso-economic sector of the economy dominated by large firms which had to be contrasted with the micro-economic sector of the economy made up of small firms. Taylor and Thrift (1983) use the terms corporate sector and smaller firms sector. It is Galbraith's terminology which is used here. Of course, this dichotomisation of firm types hides much of the inherent variety in the corporate organisation of industry (Taylor and Thrift 1982a, 1982b).

Market-system firms

These firms take their name from the fact that their behaviour is a response to changes in the market (i.e. demand) for their products and no firm has a large enough part of the market to influence the price of the product. As demand changes so each firm attempts to adapt its behaviour to meet the changed circumstances. In the firm itself it is usual for the owner to play a major role in the conduct of the business so that the person responsible for its day-to-day activities will own a large part of it. Not only will ownership and control reside in the same person but there will be little specialisation of functions within management. Indeed, in the one-person firm the owner will co-ordinate activities and will be production worker, marketing person, sales person and take on all the other multifarious roles that have to be undertaken to run a business successfully. Most market-system firms are small and carry out all their operations on one site. They manufacture a single product or, at most, a group of closely related products.

Table 4.2 The contribution of small firms to employment in manufacturing

Country	Year of data	Employment in small firms*
		% All manufacturing employment
Japan	1970	52
Netherlands	1973	36
West Germany	1970	29
France	1976	25
United States	1972	25
United Kingdom	1976	17

(*Source*: Storey 1982:8)
* 1–99 employees.

Clear identification of market-system firms is not straightforward. The new independent firms discussed in Chapter 11 all belong to the market system and a useful surrogate for market-system firms is the small firm. Even here definitions vary with small in the United States referring normally to firms with less than 100 employees while in Britain small is taken to refer to firms with less than 200 employees. Table 4.2 illustrates the relative importance of market-system firms (small firms) in a variety of countries. Among the countries listed, only in Japan does the percentage of manufacturing employment in small firms exceed 50 per cent, while in the United States it is just less than 25 per cent and in the United Kingdom it is as low as 17 per cent. Indeed, this is the lowest proportion among all countries in the list. With less than a quarter of all employees in small (market-system) firms, it is perhaps not surprising that attention has been turned increasingly to the role of the larger planning-system firms in contributing to the changing geography of industrial activity.

Planning-system firms

The most characteristic geographical feature of a planning-system firm is that it is a diversified multi-plant concern often with multi-regional and multinational operations. These characteristics are well illustrated by the 1984 geography of Cadbury Schweppes shown in Fig. 4.3. Cadbury Schweppes is about 27th in size by turnover among firms operating primarily in manufacturing industry in the United Kingdom and it employs 22,900 workers in Britain. These represent 60 per cent of its world-wide labour force which helps to stress the extent to which the largest planning-system firms are embedded into world-wide corporate production systems. Figure 4.3 illustrates clearly its multi-regional, multi-plant system. The firm, it will be recalled from Chapter 1, is known primarily for its chocolate and drink activities and it is, like many planning-system firms, organised on a multi-divisional basis. The principal divisions engaged in manufacturing are confectionery, drinks, tea and foods, and health and hygiene. The product

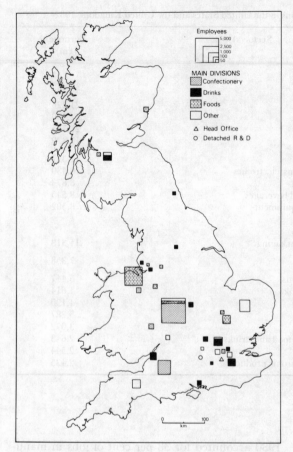

Fig. 4.3 Corporate spatial structure: Cadbury Schweppes, 1984 (*Source*: Healey and Watts 1987:152)

range is wide varying from Cadbury's Milk Tray chocolates to disinfectant, from Chivers Old English Marmalade to aerosols, and from Schweppes Tonic Water to Parazone bleach. Like many planning-system firms it has a distinct core region in which much of its employment is concentrated, in this case the West Midlands. A particularly striking feature of the spatial arrangement of the firm's activities is that some research and development (R & D) activities (in Reading) are detached from production sites as are its head office activities which are located in central London.

The multi-locational multi-product nature of firms like Cadbury Schweppes gives them considerable flexibility. They have the ability to evaluate readily and select between sites both within and outside the corporate system and to create a flexible production system such that production activities can be switched between plants, regions or nations both to overcome adverse circumstances in particular areas and to exploit quickly new opportunities as they arise. This flexibility is further enhanced by the diversified product-mix of many large firms. Such diversification permits effective comparisons of the returns from different activities and thus encourages redeployment of assets from one activity to another.

The contrast with the single-product single-plant market-system firm could not be more marked. There are other differences too which can affect the way in which planning-system firms respond to the forces creating locational change. Unlike market-system firms, planning-system firms are not pushed and pulled by market forces but they choose to plan certain courses of action. They can manipulate and create demand by advertising expenditure, they often operate in *oligopolistic* (few firm) *environments* where they influence and are influenced by each other's behaviour (see pages 122–3) and when dealing with these firms the image of a firm at the mercy of its environment has to be replaced by that of a firm which takes purposive actions to modify its environment. Their very size gives them power to negotiate with governments but, equally, their very size encourages governments to try to intervene in the firm's affairs. In these firms too, ownership is no longer related closely to control. Ownership resides in the shareholders or stockholders who, save in exceptional circumstances, have little direct control over the operations of the firm. Control is exercised by professionals who have the skills and training necessary to co-ordinate the activities of a large organisation. Control by professionals rather than owners may reduce personal commitment to place and this lack of commitment may be enhanced by the spatial concentration of decision makers in head offices distant from the plants affected by their decisions.

Table 4.3 provides some examples of the very largest firms in the United States and United

Table 4.3 The ten largest (non-oil) manufacturing firms in the United States and the United Kingdom, 1982

Company	Sector(s)	Turnover (£m)
A. *United States*		
General Motors*	Motor vehicles	39,232
Ford Motors*	Motor vehicles	24,226
IBM*	Computer systems	22,460
Du Pont*	Chemicals	21,785
General Electric*	Electrical products	17,320
United States Steel*	Steel	12,357
ITT*	Telecommunications/electronics	10,430
United Technologies	Aircraft equipment	8,873
Reynolds Industries	Tobacco, foods and beverages	8,545
Western Electric	Communication equipment	8,502
B. *United Kingdom*		
BAT Industries*	Tobacco, paper, packaging	11,318
ICI	Chemicals	7,358
Unilever†	Foods and detergents	5,447
Imperial	Tobacco, food, drink	4,614
General Electric	Electrical products	4,190
Ford	Motor vehicles	3,287
British Leyland	Motor vehicles	3,072
Allied-Lyons	Brewing and other food and drinks	2,643
Rothmans International	Tobacco	2,544
Thorn EMI	Electrical and electronic products	2,435

(*Source*: Allen 1983)
* Among the world's top 30 industrial firms.
† Excludes Unilever NV operations based in the Netherlands.

Kingdom economies. Seven of the United States' firms are among the 30 largest firms in the world and all are multinational, multi-locational concerns. Some are widely known and operate under their own name throughout the world (Ford, IBM), others operate under the names of their subsidiaries; General Motors, for example, operates as Vauxhall within Britain. Their size is daunting and their decisions, together with those of other large planning-system firms, have a major effect on the geography of employment change.

The dominance of the large planning-system firms in terms of output was described earlier. The dominance is no less striking in terms of employment. The largest 100 firms in the United States in 1977 accounted for 33 per cent of employment in manufacturing, the largest 200 for 44 per cent, that is 8.6 million jobs. In the United Kingdom, the largest 100 firms were slightly less dominant but they nevertheless in

1980 accounted for 38 per cent of jobs in manufacturing. More strikingly, 29 firms with over 20,000 employees operated just over 2,000 plants with an average of about 784 employees per plant. These very large and dispersed production systems create their own spatial structures.

Locational hierarchies

To create a system capable of administering their diversified operations planning-system firms create their own *organisational structures*. Most typical of the larger firms is the multi-divisional structure illustrated in the *organisation chart* in Fig. 4.4. In this example, the organisational hierarchy consists of a head office, three divisions, a research and development (R & D) unit, and a number of departments within each division. Each division has its own *sub-corporate head office*. Divisions usually deal with a group of products or related products (see, for example, Cadbury Schweppes) but in many cases one

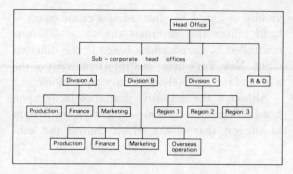

Fig. 4.4 Multi-divisional organisational structures

division is concerned with all a firm's overseas operations. In Fig. 4.4 three different ways of departmentalising divisional operations are illustrated. Division A has functional departments. Division B has some functional departments plus a separate department for overseas operations and Division C has created departments based on geographical areas.

Not only does each planning-system firm have a distinctive organisational structure, it is now becoming clear that 'each type of business organisation has a particular *establishment structure* that is laid out over space' (Taylor and Thrift 1983:458). In the small market-system firm with only one plant all types of activity are concentrated upon one site, in the larger planning-system firms specific sites can concentrate upon specific activities. Apart from head office sites, sub-corporate head office sites and R & D sites, Luttrell (1962) suggests branch plants of the different divisions may perform different functions. Some will duplicate the work of the parent plant, some will manufacture components for the parent plant or parent firm's product, while others will manufacture an entirely different product from the parent plant. Massey (1984) has recently suggested the term *cloning structure* for multi-plant firms with an establishment structure of plants making the same product and *part-process-structure* for firms with branch plants making only components of the firm's main product.

Critical to an understanding of the implications of the different organisational structures is the recognition that these structures can influ- ence the flow of information within the firm – a theme taken up in Chapter 5 – but of equal interest is the distribution of control within the corporate hierarchy. The level at which decisions are taken can influence, for example, the spatial allocation of investment within a firm – a topic explored in Chapter 8 – and is related, in part, to a firm's establishment structure. Part-process plants are almost inevitably tied closely to the corporate system but there is potential to give cloned plants a high degree of autonomy. While organisational and establishment structures can influence patterns of change within multi-plant firms they also create their own spatial structures.

The inter-meshing of organisational and establishment structures produces a *locational hierarchy* within planning-system firms. This is defined as a spatial separation of a firm's activities between, for example, 'research, development and initial production on the one hand and fully finalised mass production on the other' (Massey and Meegan 1979:207). More pragmatically, it specifies that high-level functions in a firm locate in one area; low-level functions locate in other areas: this is seen clearly in the case of Cadbury Schweppes (Fig. 4.3) where both head office and R & D sites are in South-East England and the main production sites are elsewhere. This separation arises partly from the different needs of the different functions which can be related to the arguments about the product-cycle discussed in Chapter 6 and partly to firms seeking out different types of labour in different areas discussed in Chapter 7.

The locational hierarchy in planning-system firms is illustrated by the distinctive geographies of their white-collar workers. In comparison with all manufacturing employment white-collar jobs in head offices, sub-corporate head offices and R & D establishments are concentrated in a limited number of areas.

Studies of the location of the head offices of the largest 'n' corporations all tend to depict a marked concentration of control activities in a limited number of urban centres. The United Kingdom pattern shows a very high degree of centralisation; 74 per cent of the head offices of the 100 largest (by turnover) manufacturing firms are in South-East England, the majority in London (Healey and Watts 1987). The largest concentration of the head offices of the 500 largest United States' manufacturing corporations in 1972 (New York) had about 30 per cent of the total (Pred 1977:113). The concentration of control functions in particular cities is illustrated

vividly in Fig. 4.5A. Instead of a crude count of head offices this describes the value of assets controlled by corporations based in the different cities. New York firms control 41 per cent of the assets of the top 500 industrial corporations.

Although the majority of studies focus upon head offices there is some evidence from Britain to suggest that offices which control the sub-

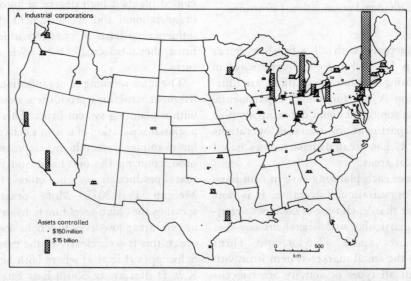

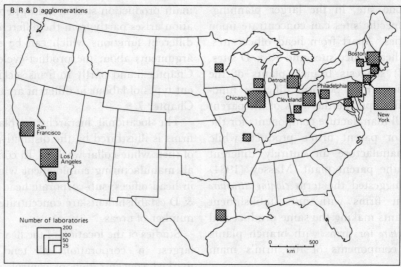

Fig. 4.5 (A) Head offices of the largest 500 industrial corporations, United States, 1971 (B) R & D laboratories of major R & D performing firms, United States, 1977: includes only centres with 16 or more laboratories (*Sources*: (A) Borchert 1978: 219 (B) Based on Malecki 1979: 312)

sidiaries or divisions of the larger firms may also be concentrated in specific regions. Gudgin, Crum and Bailey (1979:152–6) estimated that an over-representation of white-collar jobs in South-East England was due partly to the 50,000 jobs in corporate head offices but also to no less than 70,000 jobs associated with the sub-corporate offices. A further 20,000 jobs were associated with R & D units. Descriptions of the spatial concentrations of control functions provide only a crude guide to the locations of control for, as is shown in Chapter 8, variations in the degree of plant autonomy are quite marked.

Research and development activities are more widely dispersed than head office activities. In 1980 47 per cent of research establishments in private sector industrial firms in Great Britain were in South-East England (Healey and Watts 1987), while the New York–Newark–Jersey city area, although having the greatest concentration of laboratories among major R & D performing firms, accounted for only 17 per cent of the laboratories located in the principal R & D areas (Malecki 1979). The overall distribution of the R & D agglomerations and their size is shown in Fig. 4.5B. Two major concentrations are in California (the Los Angeles and San Francisco areas), and these centres, together with whose based upon New York, Chicago, Philadelphia and Boston account for over half the laboratories located in major centres.

The locational hierarchy concept also argues that the skilled and unskilled manual workers are found at different locations within the hierarchy. The limited evidence for this is discussed later in Chapter 6 but Massey (1984:79) has argued recently that this kind of spatial separation is 'relatively rare and typical only of certain kinds of "advanced" sectors of production'.

Market-system and planning-system interdependencies

The most striking form of interdependency lies in the flows of materials between the market-system and planning-system firms. In the British chemical industry an example is provided by a firm buying all its inputs and selling all its outputs to one large chemical company while in the en-gineering industry a components manufacturer can sell virtually all its output to one large firm (Johnson and Cathcart 1979:270–1). A study of 52 firms supplying the 30 largest manufacturing enterprises in Sweden discovered that on average the firms were selling 36 per cent of their output to their major customer (Fredriksson and Lindmark 1979:168). Such sales patterns are particularly characteristic of subcontractors to planning-system firms.

Four forms of subcontracting relationships are recognised:
1. Subcontractors receive material from the larger firm;
2. Subcontractors provide their own materials;
3. Subcontractors receive some materials but not others;
4. Subcontractors lease material from larger firms.

Not only may the subcontractors depend upon the contractors for their markets and supplies the contractors can increase their hold through credit and other financial arrangements.

One of the most extensive of subcontracting systems can be found in the Japanese motor industry (Sheard 1983) which goes part of the way to explaining the preponderance of small firms in Japan. Figure 4.6 depicts the main features of this system and the different layers of subcontractors. Labour-intensive and low-value operations are transferred to smaller firms. Thus in 1978 the value added per worker in firms employing 1,000 or more workers was $A 37,051, while in those firms with 10–19 workers it was $A 14,185 and in workshops with 1–3 workers it was only $A 7,891. The existence of these clearly delineated subcontracting layers is an important feature of the Japanese motor vehicle industry with the first layer comprising the firms with which the assembly plant has direct transactions. On average the production system of only one assembly firm consists of 171 first layer, 4,700 second layer and 31,600 third layer subcontractors.

While this is perhaps an extreme example of the interdependencies fostered by subcontracting it also illustrates the extent to which market-system firms can be intertwined with the firms

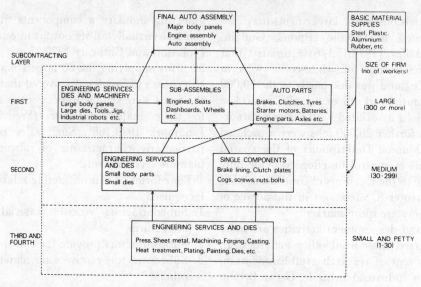

Fig. 4.6 Japanese auto-production system: layers of subcontractors (*Source*: Sheard 1983:55)

operating in the planning system. The dependence of market-system firms is particularly marked. A survey of more than 2,000 subcontractors across a range of industries in Japan in 1976 showed that on average more than half of a subcontractor's sales went to its major market (Sheard 1983:52). The 'distance' between the characteristic market-system firm and the characteristic planning-system firm is large and despite the existence of these interdependencies, movement between these two segments of the economy is small. Where movement does take place the planning-system firm acquires a successful firm within the market system (Taylor and Thrift 1982a, 1982b). The Du Pont acquisition of Fabrikoid provides an historical example of this process.

CONCLUSION

Firms exist to co-ordinate the activities that are necessary to manufacture a particular product or products. As an essential part of that co-ordinating role they work to ensure revenues exceed costs to generate profits. The last 200 years have seen a move away from the atomistic economy made up of a myriad of small firms towards economies dominated increasingly by diversified

firms and conglomerates. At the present time there exists a segmented economy with a continuum of firm sizes from the very large planning-system firm to the usually very small market-system firm. The latter still operates to some extent in an atomistic economy but for many market-system firms this is an illusion because of a dependence on sales to or purchases from the larger planning-system firms.

These large planning-system firms impose their own spatial structures on a national economy and their multi-locational structures give firms the flexibility to switch activities (and the employment associated with them) between different geographical areas. What is more, because of the spatial separation of control activities from production activities, these firms may have only a limited commitment to some of the places within which they operate.

The dichotomisation of firms creates an artificial break in a continuum of firm types but it is a useful framework within which to work although it does have at least two major disadvantages. First, it tends to hide the wide variety of firms which lie between the archetypal market-system and planning-system firms. Some market-system firms may be run by managers, some planning-system firms may still be under strong family control; likewise other market-system firms will be multi-plant concerns while other planning-system firms may be single-plant organisations. Nevertheless, as long as the potential variety of firm types is recognised the distinction between market-system and planning-system firms is a useful one. Second, and perhaps most important, the dichotomy tends to play down the role of the medium-sized firm. After all, the largest 100 firms plus small firms account for about 55 per cent of employment in manufacturing in the United Kingdom and 50 per cent in the United States. Medium-sized firms provide 45–50 per cent of jobs in manufacturing and clearly have an important role in influencing the geography of employment change in manufacturing industry.

The organisational and establishment structures together with the locational hierarchies of planning-system firms can influence where locational changes are implemented. This operates in two ways. The locational hierarchy helps to create a spatial division of labour (Ch. 7) which

may influence the locational behaviour of all firms, but the existence of the hierarchy also means that within a particular larger firm each plant has to be seen within the corporate context in which it operates; a point which is very evident in the discussion of branch plants, *in situ* change and closures in Part IV. This corporate context is particularly important at the present time since most advanced western economies are dominated by multi-locational planning-system firms. It is a dominance which is probably underestimated by the figures given earlier which related only to the very largest firms. While all large firms fall within the planning system, the planning system also includes those firms which are relatively large within the industrial sector in which they operate and even quite small firms can be included within the planning system if they have a large share of a very small market. Further, many market-system firms, because of their dependence on planning-system firms for either supplies or markets are, in reality, controlled by that system.

5

THE LOCATION
DECISION

It will be recalled from Chapter 1 that locational change arises from different rates of employment change in different geographical areas and that net employment change in an area reflects employment changes at specific manufacturing plants. Decisions to open or close plants or to expand or contract employment at plants are made by either planning-system or market-system firms and are called location decisions since they are decisions which, in the final analysis, have implications for the employment opportunities in specific locations. At one time the term 'location decision' was restricted to decisions by existing firms to establish a plant at a new site. Occasionally, the term location decision is still used in this very restricted sense but as Estall and Buchanan (1980:17) observed location decisions include 'many more... [decisions] ...than...those on where to locate a new plant'.

Location decisions, are, in essence, investment or disinvestment decisions and industrial geography is concerned with the employment consequences which arise from them. Although these decisions have important consequences for employment levels in particular areas it should not be assumed that 'location' always plays a key role in the decision process; in many cases it may have no role at all. Location may be important where, for example, a firm has to decide whether to close a TV assembly plant in an inner city or a seaside town or when a location has to be selected for a branch plant. In contrast, location has a negligible role where a firm decides to close

all its plants making a particular product or where a firm decides to make major investments in its largest plant. Nevertheless, the one thing all location decisions have in common is that they change the spatial pattern of employment opportunities.

Setting out to examine location decisions may suggest that all such decisions are the result of careful deliberation. It might be true that in some planning-system firms the management teams evaluate carefully which plant to close, which section should take most of the lay-offs and which is the best location for a new plant. Similarly, the owners of some market-system firms may carefully review the options open to them before expanding or contracting their workforce. Yet, in many cases, the decisions may be made in a more informal way. New products can be developed because of a 'business hunch'; plants can be closed because it is felt 'obvious' that a certain plant should close. In the market system new firms are set up near an owner's home because that location is the most convenient. Likewise some plants can grow because, fortuitously, there are associated with a growing market, while others may decline because, equally fortuitously, they manufacture a product the demand for which is falling. Despite the rather arbitrary nature of these decisions, in aggregate they produce the distinctive patterns of change illustrated in Chapter 1. These patterns suggest that some of the general principles underlying location decisions are worth exploring. Most research into location decisions has focused upon the branch plant location decision and this is considered fully in Chapter 12, but there are a number of factors influencing the outcome of all location decisions and it is these which are considered in this chapter.

OPTIMISERS AND SATISFICERS

The decision maker in traditional discussions of industrial geography is 'economic man', an *optimiser* who desires to maximise the profits received from manufacturing activities. Other non-profit objectives were discussed briefly in the introduction to the previous chapter. The profit maximiser

is assumed to have knowledge of all the relevant aspects of his environment which, if not absolutely complete, is at least impressively clear and voluminous. He is assumed also to have a well-organised and stable system of preferences, and a skill in computation that enables him to calculate, for the alternative courses of action that are available to him which of these will permit him to reach the highest attainable point on his preference scale (Simon 1955:99).

Expressing these ideas in geographical terms, a firm seeking to maximise profits and considering a change in the nature, scale and location of its activities must assemble a remarkably impressive range of information. It has, for example, to calculate the cost of assembling materials to and distributing products from its existing site or sites and to or from all potential sites; to estimate labour costs at potential sites, to assess the availability of services and to predict the actions of all other firms and, with all this information, attempt to select that form of locational change which will maximise profits. This calculation can also include, as *psychic income*, any non-pecuniary satisfactions managers receive; for example, the sense of satisfaction received from living in a residentially attractive area (Greenhut 1956). In practice, firms find precise accounting of these current costs and revenues a difficult task; selecting an appropriate time frame and projecting for the future engenders intense debate and alternative scenarios result. The psychic income although real is even more difficult to specify and measure.

Not surprisingly, it has been argued that firms are not run by omniscient 'economic people' but by *satisficers* who are 'choosing organism(s) of limited knowledge and ability' (Simon 1955:114). Firms attempt to make satisfactory decisions in the light of information available to them and their ability to use that information, but clearly a major constraint is that (except in the very short term) they are unable to operate at a loss.

Although the characteristics of areas do not always play an important part in where locational change is implemented location can influence profit in two ways. Production costs can vary from place to place, such variations being described by a *cost-surface* (page 76), and revenues can vary from place to place, a variation normally described by the *market potential surface* (Ch. 9). Where either or both of revenues and costs vary from place to place, space plays a critical role in identifying an area or areas within which a particular plant can operate at a profit. A cross-section through hypothetical cost and revenue surfaces is shown in Fig. 5.1 where X–Y represents a geographic region in which, for a plant of a given size, total costs (TC) vary in space with minimum cost at A and total revenues (TR) vary in space with a maximum at B. Traditional theory would assume that all new capacity would be added at O – the *optimum location* where profits are maximised. Yet, at every point between M_a and M_b a plant could

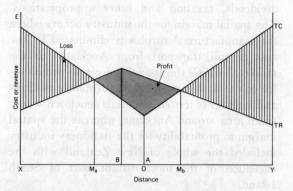

Fig. 5.1 Optimum location and spatial margins to profitability (*Source*: Smith 1966: 96)

earn some profit. M_a and M_b represent what Rawstron (1958) called the *spatial margin to profitability*.

The areas enclosed by the spatial margin to profitability are not necessarily contiguous. They may, for example, enclose all cities over a certain size or enclose an area of a particular size around a number of seaports. The actual size of the areas enclosed by the spatial margins to profitability is dictated by the slopes of the cost and revenue lines. Where the gradients of the lines are steep, the more restricted will be the areas within the spatial margins to profitability and the shallower the gradient the larger the areas that are encompassed by the margins. Since costs and revenues vary between industries different industries will have different spatial margins and, less widely recognised, plants of different size in the same industry may well have differing spatial margins to profitability because they too have different costs (Ch. 6). Of course, the positions of the margins will change over time in response to changes in the cost and revenue curves.

McDermott (1973) examined the spatial margins to profitability for a number of industries in New Zealand. The spatial margin to profitability for the leather goods industry enclosed the whole country but smaller areas were features of the other four industries shown in Fig. 5.2. The horizontal axis shows distance from the optimum location (Auckland), the vertical axis shows the surplus available to manufacturers per ton of output prior to the payment of dividends, taxation and other appropriations. The spatial margin for the industry occurs where the manufacturers' surplus is eliminated by the cost of rail transport from Auckland to the market. In 1969 the spatial margin to profitability of the basic metal industry (mainly castings and forgings of ferrous materials) enclosed a very small area around Auckland whereas the spatial margin to profitability for the stationery industry included the whole of New Zealand with the exception of the most distant part of South Island.

Critics of the spatial margin to profitability concept have argued that since it encloses such

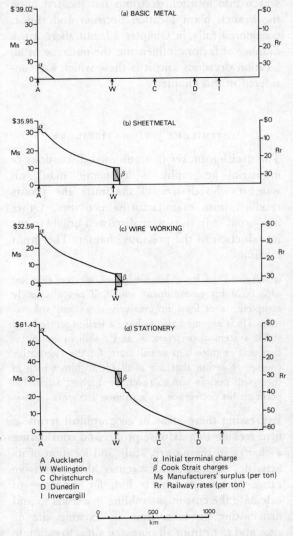

A Auckland
W Wellington
C Christchurch
D Dunedin
I Invercargill

α Initial terminal charge
β Cook Strait charges
Ms Manufacturers' surplus (per ton)
Rr Railway rates (per ton)

0   500   1000
km

Fig. 5.2 Spatial margins to profitability in four New Zealand industries, 1969 (*Source*: McDermott 1973:68)

large areas in many industries it is of no relevance in explaining spatial patterns of industrial change. This is a fundamental misconception and arises from an undue emphasis upon the actual *margins* rather than upon variations in the level of profit within them. Certain areas may be more profitable than other areas for certain industries and plants and this might influence location within the margins. Optimising firms might be expected to implement changes near to an optimum site, while satisficing firms would tend to operate anywhere within the spatial margins to profitability. In these decisions in which space plays a key role and, indeed, in all location decisions the differences between firms will reflect, in part, the information available to them and their ability to use it.

Information

Each firm will have a particular stock of knowledge about the firm and the environment in which it operates. This is built up from private information (obtained through person-to-person contacts and from personal experience of place) and from public information (obtained, for example, from government sources, books, radio and TV). The nature and variety of this information will reflect people's patterns of daily contact with others, their access to public information and the extent and variety of their travel experience. Since information is collected over time the information available to any one individual may vary with age and education (Pred 1967:32–40). This information will also include subjective impressions of the attractiveness of different places.

To this stock of basic information is added the information collected to cope with a particular problem. The key point to note here is that the collection of information takes time and this imposes a cost on the firm. Thus the quality and quantity of information available will reflect both the time available to the firm for the collection of information and the amount of resources it is prepared to spend on searching for information. In general, an optimising firm seeking the best solution to a problem will spend more time and money collecting information than will a satisficing firm seeking only a satisfactory solution. General information relating to the attributes of areas is more widely available than at any time in the past. No longer is it necessary to search for data as both local and national government departments have information readily available and, more important, free of charge. Further, firms are bombarded with publicity material attempting to raise their awareness of and information about different places (Burgess 1982). The nature of publicly available material based on case studies in the United States is shown in Table 5.1 and the details of a typical 'promotion pack' are described in Chapter 15.

Table 5.1 Public sources of locational information

	Source							
	General Community information*	Prevailing economic structure (competition)	Market growth & potential	Labour characteristics & costs	Transportation freight rates, schedules	Energy & power supplies & costs	Taxes local & state	Housing
Federal/national govt. agencies, departments	1			1		1	1	
State/local development agencies	1	1		1	1	1	1	1
Municipal officials	1			1		1	1	1
Banks	1		1					
Chambers of commerce	1			1			1	
Agricultural/industrial/ commercial associations	1	1						
Unions				1				
Real-estate firms			1					1
Local newspapers	1							1
Specialised journals		1		1		1	1	
Transportation agencies					1			
Utilities	1					1		

(*Source*: Compiled by P. E. Lloyd and P. Dicken in 1972 and cited in Townroe 1979:165)
* Includes general amenities, educational facilities, community attitudes, political climate.

In the planning-system firms the information will not only reflect the views of all the individuals contributing to the decision process but the nature of the firm itself may influence the nature and scope of the information available. These multi-regional firms through the greater geographical scope of their operations will have a familiarity with more areas than the single-plant firm, and indeed this contributes to their flexibility noted in the last chapter. Yet how this information is filtered through the firm may depend upon its organisational structure. Figure 4.4 illustrated different forms of departmentalisation within divisions and while Division C may be very much aware of the characteristics of its different areas but have a limited perception of the overall production system of the firm, Division A will have a clear view of its overall production system but may be less aware of regional variations. Equally important to the basis of divisionalisation and departmentalisation is the allocation of power within the structure. A highly centralised firm can be unaware of subtle variations in capabilities of different plants and regions; in contrast a firm whose individual units have a high degree of autonomy may fail to integrate all the information that is available within it.

The significance of organisational structures is seen in those firms which change from one structure to another. In the British brewing industry the organisational structures at one time were based on divisions operating within specific geographical areas. The main problem of this form of structure was that it was difficult for the firm to assess, or indeed develop, a strategy for all its production sites. Expansion plans were formulated in the light of each area's production needs with little regard to the overall needs of the firm. In at least three major companies the late 1960s saw a change in structure to one which concentrated control of production into a single production division and in each case the new division undertook major reviews of production facilities which, for the first time, were seen as a whole. These new frameworks led to policies to expand certain sites and to abandon production at others with marked implications for the changing geography of employment opportunities (Watts 1980b:226–36).

Despite the wider availability of information it is possible that changes are implemented as a result of perceptions of plants and areas and not as a result of objective measures of their attributes. The objective facts about the environment or environments in which the firm operates or plans to operate can be less important than the *perceived* environment. Attention has already been drawn (Ch. 2) to the diversion of jobs to Eire as a result of the perceived 'hostile bureaucratic environment' in Britain and Chapter 10 will show how certain urban administrations are perceived as unhelpful. More generally, in the absence of accurate cost data, firms may rely on their general perceptions of the suitability of areas for industrial activity. One such attempt to map these perceived environments is shown in Fig. 5.3 which indicates that firms do value different regions in different ways. Whether location decisions are based upon objective measures or upon the perceived attributes of plants and areas they will be influenced by the ability to utilise the available information.

Ability

Either using an established stock of knowledge or an established stock plus specially collected information the firm then has to decide upon its course of action. Although there may be a debate over what are 'good' or 'bad' decisions, good and bad decisions will be made reflecting the firm's ability to use information, that is its decision-making ability.

Perhaps the most obvious reason for variations in this ability lies in the intelligence and education of those running the firm. The not unreasonable assumption may be made that, in general, firms run by highly intelligent highly educated individuals will tend to make better decisions in the light of information available to them than firms run by less educated persons. Further, optimisers may evaluate data more carefully than satisficers who only have to see whether a proposed course of action meets their minimum requirements. These requirements will, of course,

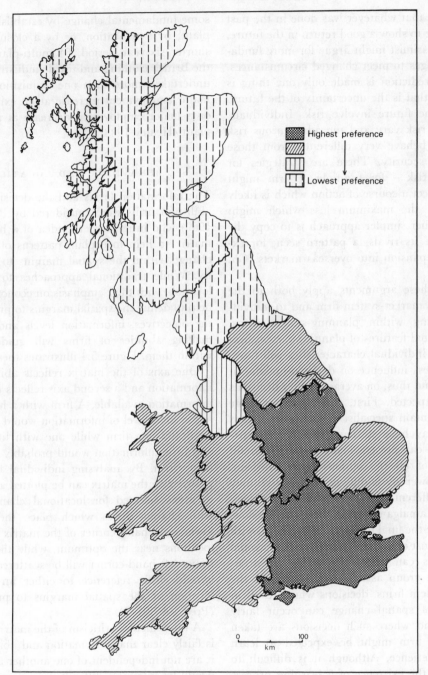

Highest preference

Lowest preference

0   100
km

Fig. 5.3 Space preferences of businesspeople, Britain, 1974 (*Source*: Based on Pocock and Hudson 1978:118)

vary between firms whose aspiration levels will be influenced by past experience.

Since any assessment of the outcome of a change requires some prediction of future con-

ditions an element of uncertainty is involved. Assessments of the future will also be influenced by whether the individuals involved are optimists or pessimists. In some firms an optimist might argue that whatever was done in the past will continue to show a good return in the future, while the pessimist might argue for more fundamental changes to meet changed circumstances. Whatever prediction is made only one thing is certain and that is the uncertainty of the future. Plans for the future involve risk. Individuals' attitudes to risk vary and the adventurous risk takers may behave very differently from those who prefer security. There are strategies for minimising risk – for example, a firm might decide to select a course of action which is likely to minimise the maximum loss which might occur. A rather simpler approach is to copy the behaviour of its rivals, a pattern seen, for example, in expansion into overseas markets (Ch. 2).

Most of these arguments apply both to the owner of the market-system firm and to individuals operating within planning-system firms. Four additional features of planning-system firm suggest that individual characteristics will have, in general, less influence on decision-making in these firms and thus, on average, better decisions might be expected. First, the ability of large firms to maintain specialist departments means that they may have strategic planning departments which can present managers with careful evaluations of all the options open to them. Second, at lower levels different individuals may deal with different aspects of a particular decision and the amalgamation of these subdecisions may enhance the final decision itself. Third, with all but the most dominant personalities, personal idiosyncracies can be overruled by the arguments of the group as a whole. Fourth, in the planning-system firms, decisions which result in some kind of spatial change can occur fairly frequently and where such decisions are taken frequently a firm might be expected to learn from its experience. Although it is difficult to demonstrate the existence of a learning process the repetitive nature of location decisions in planning-system firms is seen in a survey by Hamilton (1978) of 1,486 British multi-locational firms in the period 1960–72. All firms had altered the relative importance of, or functions of, existing units and only 14 per cent had not made

some fundamental change by establishing a new plant, by a relocation, or by a closure. Over a shorter six-year period, 64 multi-plant firms in the British clothing and textile industry had each undertaken more than one acquisition, closure, major employment increase at an existing plant or a major employment decrease at an existing plant (Healey 1983:331).

BEHAVIOUR AND LOCATION

The information levels and the decision-making ability of firms were considered by Pred (1967, 1969) who introduced the idea of a behavioural matrix to help to explain patterns of locational change within the spatial margins to profitability. While traditional approaches to industrial location, with their emphasis on economic forces, help to define the spatial margins to profitability, the objectives, information levels and decision-making abilities of firms will guide location within them. Figure 5.4 illustrates these points.

One axis of the matrix reflects ability to use information and a second axis reflects the level of information available. A firm with a high ability and a high level of information would tend to be an optimising firm while one with little ability and little information would probably be a satisficing firm. By analysing individual firms their position on the matrix can be plotted and related to areas selected for locational change. Firms with characteristics which place them in the lower right-hand corner of the matrix will select locations near the optimum, while those in the upper left-hand corner will be scattered randomly with little reference to either an optimum location or the spatial margins to profitability (Pred 1967:91–5).

A fundamental criticism of the matrix is that it is fairly clear that information and ability to use it are not independent of one another and that it would be extremely difficult to operationalise the matrix. Admittedly, Pred recognises that only crude and arbitrary measures could be used to measure the information levels and abilities of different firms. It is perhaps significant that there is no published work which operationalises the matrix and relates it to spatial patterns of

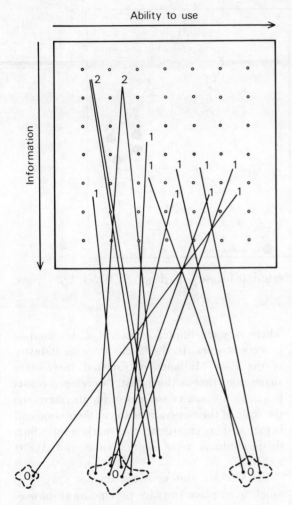

Ability to use

Information

Fig. 5.4 The behavioural matrix (*Source*: Pred 1967: 92)

change, but it is possible to examine the influence of variations in information available and ability to use it.

An interesting example of the effects of variations in information and ability can be drawn from the British sugar industry. Two major firms involved in setting up the industry were the Anglo-Dutch group expanding its sugar interests from a strong basis in the sugar industry in the Netherlands and the Anglo-Scottish group which was attempting to diversify its interests by moving parts of its activities from engineering to sugar manufacture. The plants constructed by

the two groups are shown in Fig. 5.5. All the plants were constructed within a five-year period and used similar technologies but the contrast in the geographical patterns of the plants of the two firms could not be much greater. Examination of the records of the two groups shows that the Anglo-Scottish group, drawing upon evidence from the French sugar industry, was convinced that small plants were viable and that, therefore, the plants could be spread widely over the arable area. Its abilities to assess the information collected were limited severely by the group's lack of experience in the sugar industry. In contrast, the Anglo-Dutch group drew on its experience in the Dutch sugar industry. It built much larger plants (Dutch plants at this time were significantly larger than French ones) and, partly because of their larger size all four plants were concentrated in the principal area of East Anglia. A few years after the establishment of the plants the Anglo-Dutch group was reporting profits on its British plants. The less well-informed and less able Anglo-Scottish group recorded a loss on the sugar industry part of its business (Watts 1971). Differences then can occur in the way in which an industry grows as a result of the different organisations involved in its operations.

Although considerable attention has been concentrated upon the ways in which decisions are made and stress has been placed upon the satisficing behaviour of firms it can, nevertheless, be argued that in the longer term it is the profit-maximising firms that survive.

A firm making only a small profit runs the risk that during a recession a profit will turn into a loss and this provides a marked incentive to maximise profits. If it is found relatively easy to increase profits a firm's aspirations will rise and what were previously accepted as reasonable profit levels will be seen as unacceptable. Further, a firm seen to be making a small profit when others are doing well may experience a loss of customer confidence, an adverse effect on the supply of capital, and a threat of takeover. In the larger planning-system firms the individual departments of the firm may be judged by various guidelines which in aggregate result in profit maximisation by the firm as a whole. Overall, it

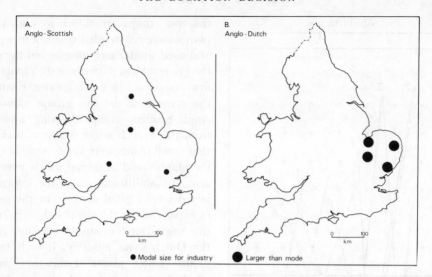

Fig. 5.5 Information, ability and new plant location: beet-sugar industry, England and Wales, 1928 (*Source*: Based on Watts 1971:105)

is likely that the aggressive profit maximising firm will force less successful firms out of business.

If this is so, locational changes ought to reflect industries and firms moving towards optimal location patterns. This was suggested 30 years ago by Tiebout (1957:84) who argued that 'if enough firms set up and the economic system gets to pick and choose, it would not be surprising if reality yields results consistent with optimal decisions'. This reflects the survival of successful firms which have carefully identified the most appropriate course of action to enable them to survive, together with those firms which, by chance, find themselves in an appropriate location. The former consciously *adapt* themselves to their environment; the latter are *adopted* by it. Pred too (1969:103) suggested that over time 'an industrial actor population diagonally marches through the behavioural matrix'. At phase one of an industry's development most firms would have little ability or information while, at a later phase increasing experience of the industry would enhance both the information levels and abilities of the firms. Such a tendency would be reinforced since over time an industry's profit levels fall and it has to pay closer attention to minimising costs and maximising revenues.

There is some limited evidence of this kind of process at work. In the broiler-growing industry of the East Midlands of England there were suggestions that as the industry developed plants began to use nearer sources of inputs, increased the scale of their operations to cut their costs and began to cluster around the markets to which their products were sent (White and Watts 1977).

Yet if costs and revenues do not vary very much from place to place psychic incomes may play an important role in optimising calculations. While in some firms non-pecuniary attributes may offset less than optimal profits where optimal profits are not particularly dependent on location these non-pecuniary factors may play a part in location decisions. Certainly, as will be seen in Chapter 12, branch plant locations are affected by community attitudes but most interest recently has been in the influence of environmentally attractive or residentially attractive areas upon locational change. This factor may have an influence both upon the managers or owners of firms and upon the ability of a firm to attract professional and scientific staff. What is, or is not, residentially attractive varies from person to person but each national space economy has within it areas which are perceived as offering the most attractive environments. Gould and White (1968) show from a study of school children (!) that there are peak levels of attractiveness in the South and West of Britain while in North America typical impressions of the West Coast environment are provided by the quotation below relating to Santa Clara County (the Silicon Valley discussed in the next chapter).

It's a particularly pleasant place to live and work – a beautiful landscape of hills and plains, a bounteous garden of nature where fruit trees and wild flowers bloom even in February...Few places on earth so agreeably mix hedonistic delights with the excitement of urbanity...it enjoys mild winters, fog-free summers and a balmy spring and fall. Outdoor sports and recreation are year-round attractions...The area boasts 4,000 PhDs...There are also at least 12,000 horses, some kept by those PhDs right on their home acreages, which are often within minutes of work. And within an hour's drive are the shops, restaurants, and cultural offerings of San Francisco (Bylinksy, cited in Saxenian 1983:14).

Certainly some branch plant location decisions (Table 12.1) are influenced by a need to find areas attractive for managerial and scientific employees and studies of net change in Britain (see pages 136–8) do show that at some points in time net employment growth is associated significantly with residentially attractive areas. Similarly, Wheat (1973) attributes much of the southern and western movement in the United States to the climatic characteristics of those areas. Yet, as will be shown in Chapters 7 and 8 residentially attractive areas are often associated with particular types of labour and with particular types of site and separating out the roles of these different influences is particularly difficult.

CONCLUSION

Firms make location decisions which lead to changes in the employment levels at specific plants, to the opening of new plants and the closure of old ones. The actual location decisions may be less than optimal, because of deficiencies in a firm's information and/or because of limitations to its ability to use the information it has. The deficiencies may be more evident in the market-system firms but even in planning-system firms the variations in information and ability between firms influence patterns of industrial change. Yet whether these influences are of fundamental importance is open to debate. Some would argue that in the longer term the optimising firms force the satisficers out of business and thus the intricacies of the decision-making process are of little relevance in understanding changes in the geography of industrial activity.

Yet it is only by studying decisions and decision-makers that industrial geography gets to grips with the fact that geography of employment opportunities is moulded not simply by firms but by the individuals who run them. To ignore these individuals would omit an important influence on industrial change as they, through their firms, decide what to make, how to make it and, most importantly, where it will be made.

PART III

THE CONTEXT OF CHANGE

Each manufacturing plant operates in a specific local or regional context and the characteristics of that context can influence its employment performance. The local environment may be less important to plants of planning-system firms than to those of market-system firms since ties to the local area may be replaced by links with other parts of the firm but the planning-system firm has greater potential than market-system firms to exploit the differences between different areas. Local and regional environments can influence the take-up of new products and processes – one of the main themes of Chapter 6 –

and each environment can have its own labour, land and capital markets (Chs 7 and 8). Each region has differing degrees of accessibility to supplies of materials and services and to markets (Ch. 9) and may be influenced in different ways by the policies of national and local governments (Ch. 10). It is first necessary, in a preamble, to discuss some general points about the relationships between regional characteristics and regional employment performance before beginning a discussion of a firm's fundamental decision of what to make and how to make it.

An underlying assumption in much of industrial geography is that differences in regional environments influence regional patterns of employment change. At the simplest level, regions may be classified by regional typology variables. For example, employment change can be related to the degree of urbanisation (rurality) or the degree of peripherality (centrality). Similarly employment change might be related to variations in the size of towns or regions. Analyses using regional typology variables provide a useful first step towards understanding the geography of employment change but it is essential to probe into the mechanisms underlying them.

A firm's response to a regional environment depends upon either or both of the potential the environment offers for earning revenues and the costs it will impose. Rates of employment change can be related to the comparative advantages (Ch. 2) of different regions. While this is a widely accepted form of analysis, it does need to be viewed cautiously and care must be taken not to extend the argument to see an area's characteristics as the essential causes of the spatial pattern of industrial change nor to blame an area for a poor performance. Many regional characteristics arise from the earlier behaviour of industrial firms which created the particular mix of industries and jobs in a region (Chs. 3 and 4).

It will be recalled from the last chapter that regional variations in costs create cost surfaces and that regional variations in revenue are described by market potential surfaces. Examples of these surfaces are provided later. Figures 8.1, 8.2 and 9.1A provide examples of cost surfaces and Fig. 9.1B provides an example of a market potential surface. In examining cost surfaces it is evident that the different elements imposing costs on a firm vary at different spatial scales. Whereas land costs usually vary markedly within a city, labour costs may be relatively uniform within it. Similarly, whereas labour costs can vary regionally interest rates on loans may show little spatial variation. Regional variations in labour costs mean that there are only small differences between adjacent areas (except where the state intervenes) whereas land and rent costs can vary markedly over very short distances. It is partly because of these variations in the nature of cost surfaces that explanations of changes in the geography of employment in manufacturing, like many geographies, are extremely sensitive to scale considerations.

Locational changes can be studied at a number of different scales, the examples in Chapter 1 illustrated net changes at national, regional, urban–rural and intra-urban scales. These changes can be associated with different influences at different scales. For example, land prices might influence locational change within a city whereas labour costs may not. Attractive residential regions may encourage the growth of new industries in a region but they will not indicate why one small town within an environmentally attractive region has seen growth of these industries while another has not. Similarly employment in manufacturing industry may grow rapidly *in* a certain region mainly because of government regional policies but it does not follow that variations *within* the region reflects government assistance. The significance of the scale factor was stressed by Stafford (1972) who argued that firms identified potential regions by assessing demand factors (markets) but towns within the regions which met the demand criteria were selected primarily with reference to cost factors (land and labour). Different associations at different scales do not always occur as, to take the most extreme case, a particular commodity available at only one point within a country can determine the region, sub-region and site selected by a firm using that commodity.

Failure to recognise these scale differences can lead to confusing statements. For example, examine the sentence 'the beet-sugar factory at York grew rapidly because the sugar-beet acreage in Britain was increasing'. The problem here is that the pattern of change at a point (York) is explained by changes in an area (Britain). There were many other plants in Britain that could have been expanded. Similarly, to argue that an oil refinery was located in the Philadelphia area because Philadelphia is on the Delaware River confuses a point location with a linear phenomenon. There will be many other places on navigable rivers which do not have oil refineries! Increasing beet acreage or access to a waterway may be *necessary* conditions for the particular form of change but they are not *sufficient* to explain the changes taking place at a point. While one set of variables may explain why beet-sugar processing factories are set up in areas growing sugar beet another set of variables may explain their locations within those areas.

Recognition of these scale differences leads to a rejection, or at least modification of the concepts of *material oriented*, *market oriented* and *footloose* industries. Traditionally it was argued that material oriented industries would grow most rapidly near their materials; market oriented industries would grow most rapidly where their markets were growing and the footloose industries would not be influenced strongly by access to either materials or markets. However, an in-

dustry might well be market oriented at regional scale, material oriented at sub-regional scale and footloose in choosing between urban areas in a sub-region. If terms such as material oriented, market oriented and footloose are used they have to be accompanied by a scale statement such as 'this industry is market oriented at the sub-regional scale' (Massey 1975:94).

In some specialised cases, locational change can be associated with accessibility to a particular point, for example an inter-state access point or a seaport, and in these cases the spatial extent of the area in which a plant benefits from accessibility to that point can vary. These variations reflect the *sphere of influence* of the location factor. Three possible spheres of influence are shown in Fig. III.1. The diagrams illustrate the proportion of plants whose managers or owners thought that they had benefited from proximity to the variable being considered. In (a) plants in proximity to a particular facility do see it as a particular benefit; in (b) proximity brings benefits but these benefits are available over a larger area; while in (c) proximity is less beneficial, advantages increase with distance from the particular influence and then begin to fall again. Figure III.1(a) could represent access to major financial institutions, such contacts may involve face-to-face meetings and therefore increased distance from the institutions will markedly increase travel times and impose a cost penalty. Figure III.1(b) could represent the advantages of access to a major concentration of industry with its sources of inputs for a firm and a market for its products. As distance from the concentration increases, so costs of access increase. Figure III.1(c) could relate to accessibility to an international airport. Proximity brings congestion and competition for labour while increased distance to the airport raises costs for executives making use of airport facilities, only in a middle distance zone are benefits maximised (Hoare 1973).

Clearly, the problem of scale cannot be ignored in moving towards an explanation of locational change and the results of particular investigations can be very sensitive to scale effects. Figure III.2A shows an area with four regions and

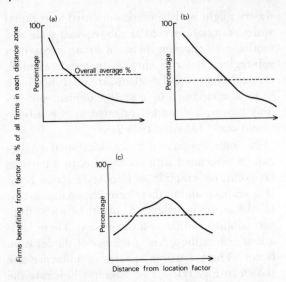

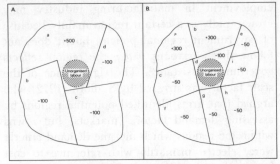

Fig. III.2 Employment change in two hypothetical sub-regional systems (A) Large sub-regions (B) Small sub-regions

Fig. III.1 Spheres of influence of location factors (*Source*: Based on Hoare 1973: 302)

employment growth in electronics occurs in a region with unorganised labour: it could be suggested that the employment growth in electronics is associated in some way with unorganised labour. Figure III.2B shows the same area only this time it is divided into eight regions and areas of growth in electronics employment are not those with unorganised labour. A rather different result arises because smaller areal units are being used in the examination. This is called the *modifiable areal unit* problem and shows analyses using different areas (spatial scales) produce different results. In many cases the areas cannot be selected by the investigator since they are determined by published sources which often relate only to specific administrative areas.

The sensitivity of the results of enquiries into locational change to the scale factor make it essential that care is taken in comparing different studies to ensure that they were undertaken at similar scales and that that scale is specified carefully in any one study. In individual studies more than one scale can be used. For example, a

first stage of an analysis might seek to explain changes in regional employment patterns and then a second stage might consider urban–rural contrasts within the regions, but scale has to be handled consistently within each part of the investigation. It was, in part, because of a desire to avoid some of the problems arising from confusion of scales that this book focuses upon regional contrasts in manufacturing employment change. These regional patterns relate to *either* differences between major regions in the United States *or* differences between states in the United States and between planning regions in the United Kingdom.

Finally, before discussing the context in which changes take place it is important to recall a point made in the discussion of location decisions (Ch. 5). Analysis of the context of change has to depend upon what the investigator is able to measure or describe. There is no guarantee that this is the same as that perceived by managers and owners of industrial plants. It could be argued that the perceptions of variations in cost in place to place are the only costs of importance but there is an extensive body of literature which does show a clear relationship between the geography of employment change and the characteristics of a firm's environment as measured by an outside observer.

6

PRODUCTS AND
PROCESSES

Perhaps two of the most critical decisions facing industrial firms, whether they belong to the market or planning systems are the decisions about the nature and range of products to be manufactured at their plants and the selection of the appropriate process technology with which to produce them. The product or products manufactured by a firm and the technology it uses have an important influence on the materials and services a firm requires and on the relative importance of the different factors of production in the manufacturing process. In turn, the relative proportions may have an influence upon where locational change is implemented. A new technology with new labour skills may suggest a location away from regions where labour unions have been resistant to technical change; equipment requiring more factory space per worker may suggest avoiding congested urban areas. Since in the majority of cases the decisions to manufacture a new product or more of the same product precedes decisions about production technology the first part of the chapter focuses upon products while the second part considers production processes. Of course, in certain instances the product of one industry is the process technology of another industry. A milling machine can be a *product* of a machine tool firm but a new *process technology* to the purchasing firm. In order to clarify the discussion, however, products and processes are, for the most part, treated separately. New products and new processes can play a critical role in regional economic development (Thomas 1975) and in the process of growth and change in individual firms (Thomas 1981).

PRODUCTS

In many studies of employment change in manufacturing industry the product manufactured at a plant is taken as given. Although firms have flexibility to change products this is less obvious at plant level because of the rigidities imposed by plant technologies. Nevertheless, plants can be adapted by firms to manufacture new products as will be seen in Chapter 13. Similarly, new products can be introduced into a region both by the construction of new plants by established firms and by the setting up of new firms. Firms and plants 'generate innovations and imitate the innovations developed by other(s)...to remain competitive regionally, nationally and internationally' (Malecki 1981:72). The development of new products may help to retain or expand a region's employment levels. Essential to an understanding of product innovations is a consideration of the product-cycle concept and its geographical derivative, the filter-down process.

Product-cycles and filtering down

The basic idea underlying the *product-cycle concept* is that any product has a distinctive life-cycle

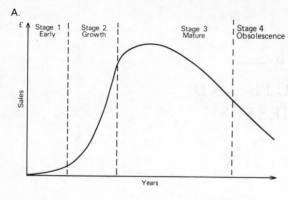

PRODUCT-CYCLE PHASE

REQUIREMENTS	Early	Growth	Mature
MANAGEMENT	2	1	3
SCIENTIFIC–ENGINEERING KNOW-HOW	1	2	3
UNSKILLED LABOUR	3	2	1
EXTERNAL ECONOMIES	1	2	3
CAPITAL	3	1ª	1ª

Fig. 6.1 The product-cycle and production inputs (*Source*: Based on Oakey 1984b:158 and Erickson and Leinbach 1979:59)

made up of four parts, an early stage, a growth stage, a mature stage and then obsolescence. (Fig. 6.1A). A successful firm will generate a stream of new products so that at any time it has a product mix that encompasses all four stages. The product-cycle concept (Thomas 1975:17–22) argues that each stage of a product's development has different requirements, there being particularly marked contrasts between the 'early' and 'mature' stages. These differences are summarised in Fig. 6.1B.

The early stage is particularly associated with high levels of engineering, scientific and technical inputs. Important too at this stage are economies arising from access to scientific and technical information, and to specialist subcontractors. These external economies are discussed fully in Chapter 9. In this early stage capital intensity is low as investment in fixed assets is avoided by large-scale subcontracting. Production runs will be short, consisting of single items or small batches (page 86) and technologies and products will be undergoing constant modification and adaptation which is, of course, why it is so necessary to employ highly skilled workers in this stage of the cycle.

While management skills are required to exploit and develop the market in the early stage they, together with access to capital, take on a critical role in the growth phase of the cycle. The managerial abilities are necessary to plan and organise the growth of production and sales while the capital is necessary both to fund expansion and to increase the capital–labour ratio as investment in capital equipment enables the firm to undertake some of the activities it contracted out in the early stage. Production will be in large batches (see page 86) giving way rapidly to mass production.

It is mass production which is most characteristic of the mature stage. By this stage the production technology is stable and output consists of long production runs of a standardised product. Clearly, major capital investment is necessary to set up the mass production techniques but this is offset by the distinctive labour inputs of this stage: semi-skilled and unskilled labour. This labour undertakes primarily routine tasks which require little training. The increasing dependence on unskilled labour which comes with mass production and standardisation is paralleled by a decreasing dependence on specialist manpower, on access to specialised information and on access to subcontractors. The association of the introduction of mass production technologies with the mature phase of the product's life provides an indication of the difficulty of treating products and processes separately.

This sketch of the main stages of the product-cycle illustrates a typical cycle but, of course, not all products will follow this path in exactly this form and the length of the cycle will vary between products (Oakey 1984a:49). New high technology products may have a life of only a few years whereas that of the railway steam locomotive spanned about 150 years. Nevertheless the output pattern of initial small output levels (the early stage) followed by rapid expansion of output (the growth stage) followed by steady and then slowly declining output is a feature of virtually all products.

The spatial implications of the product-cycle were first examined in an international context and it was argued that the early and growth stages would be associated with production in developed economies with their technical expertise and access to information and subcontracting networks while the mature phase would be located in developing countries for access to low-cost unskilled labour. The motor for this shift being competition between firms forcing them to seek to reduce their production costs in order to retain their competitive strengths. Some aspects of this international spread were discussed in Chapter 2 but the idea was used in an intra-national context by Thompson who introduced the notion of a *filter-down process*.

Although 'the filtering-down process remains rather loosely defined' (Park and Wheeler 1983:20) the most concise definition of it is that provided by Thompson (1973:8–9) himself:

In national perspective industries filter down through the system of cities, from places of greater to lesser industrial sophistication. Most often, the highest skills are needed in the difficult, early stage of mastering a new process, and skill requirements decline steadily as the production process is rationalised and routinised with experience. As the industry slides down the learning curve, the high wage rates of the more industrially sophisticated innovating areas become superfluous. The ageing industry seeks out industrial backwaters where the cheaper labour is now up to the lesser demands of the simplified process.

Thompson, thus saw mature products filtering down the urban system primarily within an intra-regional context but as Howells (1983:164) observes 'the application of filter-down theory has been considerably extended over time from a largely urban–rural intra-regional process to national scale urban hierarchies and, latterly, [to] inter-regional core-periphery differences'.

The empirical evidence relating to the validity of the product-cycle concept and the filter-down process is of two types. One group of studies concentrates on the early stage of the product-cycle and examines the location of product innovations to see, in fact, whether new products are concentrated in specific types of urban places and regions. The second group examines the mature stage in an attempt to trace the filtering-down or diffusion of product innovations from the regions in which they originate.

The early stage

The spatial pattern of corporate research and development (R & D) was described in Chapter 4 and was shown to be linked to particular regions and cities. R & D can be associated with work on both processes and products but most corporate R & D is associated with products. R & D activities are not necessarily associated with production sites so interest arises in where new products are first manufactured. While a strong R & D presence at firm or plant level may enhance a plant's innovativeness it will also be affected by the environment in which a plant is set. Thus external factors such as the location of public research (in universities and government research institutions), the availability of venture capital (Ch. 8) and the presence or absence of specialist producer services (Ch. 9) may all affect a plant's ability to generate and manufacture new products.

That there are regional variations in the introduction of new products is reflected in British data showing innovations between 1965 and 1978 in relation to the number of manufacturing workers in each region (Fig. 6.2A). The data do not distinguish between product and process innovations although they appear to apply primarily to product innovations. East Anglia and the South-West have the best record in terms of the number of manufacturing workers per innovation while Scotland and Wales have the worst. While there was some transfer of innova-

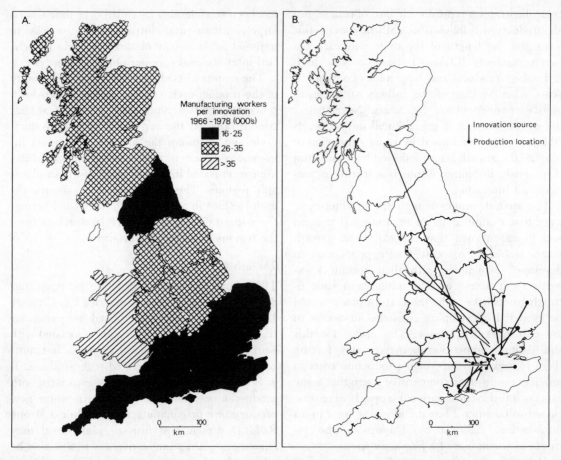

Fig. 6.2 Innovations in Britain, 1965 to 1978 (A) Regional variations (B) Movement of South-Eastern produced innovations to other sites within multi-plant organisations (*Source*: Oakey, Thwaites and Nash 1980 (A) Based on Table 5:243 (B) 249)

tions from development site to first production site the majority were first manufactured in the region within which they were developed but in the case of South-East England (Fig. 6.2B) just over 20 per cent of the innovations spread further than adjacent regions (Oakey, Thwaites and Nash 1980).

Innovativeness does vary between industries and this, in part, explains some elements of the pattern shown in Fig. 6.2 and therefore intra-industry variations in innovation between regions is perhaps more revealing than data relating to manufacturing as a whole. Examination of a group of industries which were highly innovative (metalworking machine tools, scientific and in-

dustrial instruments and radio and electronic components) focused specifically upon products new to plants in the period 1973–77 (Thwaites 1982). The main spatial analysis contrasted Development Area plants (Scotland, Wales and the Northern Region) with those in the South-East and showed a high level of innovation in the South-East. 88 per cent of the plants in the South-East had introduced a new or improved product, a proportion some 15 percentage points higher than that of plants in the Development Areas. Plants in the West Midlands and East Anglia were as highly innovative as those in the South-East whereas in the Northern Region the percentage of plants introducing new and improved products was 26 percentage points below the level recorded in the South-East. The performance of firms in the Northern Region with respect to new and improved products in these industries is in marked contrast to their innovative performance shown in Fig. 6.2A.

Although plants belonging to planning-system (multi-plant) firms were equally innovative throughout Britain a marked regional disparity occurred among market-system (single-plant) firms. Whereas only 55 per cent of such firms in the Development Areas had introduced a new or improved product no less than 85 per cent of the South-Eastern plants had done so. A critical factor in the innovation record of the market system firms was their level of commitment to R & D. This varied markedly between firms; in firms with 1–99 employees the probability of having R & D on site in a plant in the South-East was very much higher than the probability of having R & D on site in a Development Area (Thwaites 1982). Clearly the South-East of England must have some advantages for the development of new products in market-system firms in these industries. It is only possible to speculate on the nature of these advantages (Oakey, Thwaites and Nash 1982:1083–4). The most obvious might be links with R & D establishments in the area, while the availability of sources of capital funds might be of significance too. Executives in South-Eastern firms might have a higher level of technical competence while the firms and their executives might be pulled along by the larger high-technology firms which are known to be concentrated in this area. Finally, local shortages of skilled development and production workers may inhibit developments elsewhere in Britain.

Recent data on product innovation by regions and plants are less readily available from the United States but a particularly striking form of the regional concentration of new products and innovations is provided by Silicon Valley which forms part of Santa Clara county south of San Francisco. Although parallels have been drawn with the earlier development of new products and industries along Route 128 out of Boston, the growth of employment in electronic com-

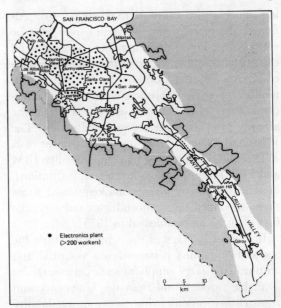

Fig. 6.3 Silicon Valley, California, 1979 (*Source*: Saxenian 1983:15)

ponents in Santa Clara county from 1968 to 1978 of around 27,000 jobs has not been paralleled elsewhere in the United States. The main concentration of these jobs is between Palo Alto and San Jose (Fig. 6.3).

At Palo Alto is Stanford University and 'from this small enclave...the impetus for the transformation of Santa Clara county emerged' (Saxenian 1983:8). The University's role was guided by Frederick Terman who built up a strong technological bias in the University by attracting gifts from large firms, by ensuring a major share of government research contracts came to the area, and by building up one of the two best electrical engineering programmes in the United States. These policies were paralleled by the establishment of the Stanford Industrial Park in the early 1950s. This covered 660 acres and leases were granted only to high-technology firms. Production facilities and research laboratories were made to resemble campus buildings and thus the industrial landscape was one of low-lying modern buildings set in a green landscape. It is from this development that the 'science parks' which form part of many local

industrial policies are derived (Ch. 10). Although Stanford's and Terman's role can be
emphasised, initial developments were aided by
the existence in the region of the research oriented aircraft industry, followed by the arrival of a
number of well-established electrical and electronic firms to take advantage of markets in the
aircraft (and later aerospace) industries. The
1940s and 1950s too saw the establishment of R
& D facilities in the area by companies like IBM
and ITT. From this base of research institutions,
qualified scientists and technology-based firms
there developed the semiconductor industry, the
first plant being established in 1955.

In this early stage of the semiconductor's life
access to qualified personnel was essential and
an unusually large supply of such personnel was
available through and from the University and
research institutions in the area, an availability
probably enhanced by the residential attractiveness of the Californian environment described in
the last chapter. Saxenian (page 11) claims 'no
other area in the United States provided such a
rich concentration of technologically skilled
labour'. Equally important were the economies
associated with access to information and subcontracting systems. As the complex developed
and new small firms sprang up, so personnel and
information were switched (both formally and
informally) between firms and the personnel of
the different firms formed part of intricate friendship networks by which information on new
products could be spread. Once a few firms had
succeeded there was ready access to venture
capital to aid the founding and expansion of new
firms. Interaction between contractors and subcontractors was intense as the complexity of the
integrated systems that were developed often
involved the provision of specific designs for
specific customers, and there developed within
the region numerous small firms to provide
equipment, services and materials essential for
the production of semiconductors. By 1979

the rapid expansion and agglomeration of semiconductor production in Santa Clara county thus
created a single industry boomtown. Today, at least
one-third of Silicon Valley's workers are employed in

the approximately 700 electronics-related companies
in the region, while many of the remainder are in
occupations which support or service this 'high technology' complex (Saxenian 1983:17).

Although there is now increasing evidence of
dispersal of activities from Silicon Valley its
example seems to provide a dramatic illustration
of the significance of access to specialised labour
skills, external economies and venture capital in
the early stages of the product-cycle. However, it
is probably unique in the United States and
there is nothing on a comparable scale in Britain.
The popular press makes much of the Silicon
Glen in central Scotland but this is not a clear
parallel as many of the firms in Scotland manufacture products developed overseas rather than
products developed locally. Some academic
studies (Breheny, Cheshire and Langridge, 1983)
have tried to unravel the changes taking place in
Britain's 'M4 corridor' from London to Bristol
yet as Oakey (1984b:159) observes 'the claims
for the existence of a British Silicon Valley west
of London on the M4 and for a Silicon Glen in
Scotland, have been grossly exaggerated'. The
evidence for a Cambridge effect around the
university city in East Anglia is more convincing
and this is described in Chapter 11.

The mature stage

While there seems to be some support for the
clustering of new products in particular regions,
the finding that the plants of multi-plant firms
are equally innovative throughout Britain suggests care should be exercised before accepting
the existence of a filter-down process. Examination of the mature stage of the filter-down process also counsels caution.

It can be argued if plants in peripheral/rural/
smaller urban places are associated with products in the mature stage of the product-cycle
then this will provide some further support for
the existence of a filter-down process. Clearly,
the spread of branch plants from metropolitan to
non-metropolitan areas cannot be interpreted as
a filtering-down process unless it can be shown
that the branch plants are manufacturing mature
stage products. Traditionally, investigations

have focused upon the areas within which it is expected that mature stage products will predominate. There are studies encompassing North Carolina (Moriarty 1983), Georgia (Park and Wheeler 1983), Kentucky (Cromley and Leinbach 1981), Wisconsin (Erickson 1976) and Vermont (Leinbach 1978). Some of the results of the latter three studies, together with those relating to New Mexico are summarised in Erickson and Leinbach (1979). Most support for the filter-down process comes from plants with five or more employees locating in non-metropolitan Wisconsin between 1969 and 1974. Three features of the plants appeared to support the filter-down process. First the industries in which the plants operated had standardised production processes. Second, when asked reasons for their location in particular communities, the firms stressed the pool of unskilled workers, and third, in response to other questions little reference was made to any advantages which might arise from external economies. Interesting as these results may be they do not focus sufficiently upon the product and the links between these findings and the product-cycle concept are rather tenuous.

A clear focus on products is evident in a study of the pharmaceuticals industry in the United Kingdom. Howells (1983) showed that there were no significant differences in the proportion of a plant's products over ten years old between rural and urban plants, between plants in towns of different sizes and between plants in different regions. Similarly, no significant differences could be discerned within the plants of individual multi-site firms. Admittedly, the use of ten years as the critical divide might have influenced the results but the consistency of the results provides little to support the view that mature-stage products will be manufactured in particular locations.

The evidence for a filter-down process is not very strong. It may be that filter-down interpretations of shifts in production activities have passed their time and, certainly, Vernon (1979) questions the present relevance of the product-cycle concept to the location of international production activities. The concept may have been relevant when firms were spreading their production activities from one region to another but now regional systems are the norm in planning-system firms and a concern with the spatial growth of a firm's production system (Ch. 12) has been replaced by an interest in the spatial reorganisation of production (Chs. 13 and 14).

The implications of the product-cycle concept for patterns of employment change are difficult to establish. There are hints of the way in which the cycle may contribute towards the spatial division of labour discussed in the next chapter and, in the long term, it might be expected that plants producing mature-stage products will face closure as the product reaches the end of its life. The effects of new or improved products on a plant's employment performance are less conjectural.

Thwaites's (1983) study of establishments introducing a new or improved product in Britain indicated that firms believed that the general tendency was for a new product to secure existing employment levels rather than bring about an increase in employment. Analysis of the employment records indicated that, in fact, there was a net gain of five employees per innovating plant; there was no evidence of any regional differentiation in the number of jobs created in innovating plants. The generally positive employment benefits of product innovation must be seen against the general fall in manufacturing employment at this time. Yet one major plant in the study modernised its product, reducing both the number of components used in the product and the time taken to assemble it resulting in the dismissal of 500 employees. It is difficult to separate this kind of product change from the changes associated with the introduction of new technologies into the production process.

PROCESSES

Manufacturing industries use a variety of technologies varying from sewing machines in the clothing industry to catalytic crackers in the oil refining industry, and from biological processes in the drink and pharmaceutical industries to quite straightforward tasks of assembling varying components to make a finished product. Emphasis is placed usually on the variation between industries but technologies can also vary between plants in the same industry. New plants may be capital intensive with few labour inputs whereas the older plants may be labour intensive. Regardless of industry-type industrial technologies fall into three groups (Woodward 1965):

1. Unit and small batch production, for example, subcontract work;
2. Large batch and mass production, for example, automobiles and TV manufacture;
3. Process production (continuous flow production), for example, oil refineries, and modern breweries.

Different technologies can impose different land, labour and capital requirements upon the plants of individual industries and may necessitate different material inputs. The product manufactured by a plant and the technology selected to produce it are the primary determinants of a plant's cost structure which is discussed below. The *cost structure* constrains the way a plant reacts to changes in its environment and ultimately, therefore, the way in which the firm changes the location of its employment opportunities. It is for this reason that this section begins with a brief consideration of inter-industry variations in cost structures. Technology too has a major influence upon the *size of plant* found in different industries. Some industries reap considerable savings when the capacity and output of a plant is high, whereas others gain little advantage from large-scale production. The extent of these inter-industry variations in plant size and their influence on locational change make up the theme of the second part of this section. In the final part of the section it is recognised that technologies, cost structures and plant sizes can be influenced by technological innovations and these innovations are shown to be potential influences on the geography of employment change.

Cost structures

Five main elements contribute towards the distinctive form of a plant's cost structure: material costs, marketing costs, capital costs, land costs and labour costs (Rawstron 1958). The latter three costs are, of course, the factors of production defined in Chapter 4. However, this is a very simple classification and detailed studies of specific plants can subdivide each of these categories to distinguish between the costs associated with different materials, different markets and different types of labour.

The relative importance of these different elements varies quite markedly from plant to plant and is reflected in the aggregate data for individual industries shown in Table 6.1. This picks out the role of labour costs in different industries. Labour costs are shown as a percentage of value added. They are particularly high in industries which still require semi-skilled operatives notably the leather, textile, and apparel industries; costs also appear high in the primary metal and lumber industries since these industries add little value to the raw materials they process. The wages of production workers

Table 6.1 Wages as a percentage of value added, by industry, United States, 1982

Industry	Wages as a percentage of value added*
Leather and leather products	40.0
Primary metal industries	38.9
Lumber and wood products	37.5
Textile mill products	36.8
Apparel and related products	34.6
Rubber and miscellaneous plastics	33.3
Furniture and fixtures	30.7
Fabricated metal products	30.5
Stone, clay and glass products	30.4
Transport equipment	30.1
Paper and allied products	27.3
Machinery, except electrical	24.0
Electric and electronic equipment	22.4
Miscellaneous manufacturing	21.4
Printing and publishing	20.0
Food and kindred products	18.0
Instruments and related products	17.6
Chemicals and allied products	12.8
Petroleum and coal products	12.0
Tobacco products	11.1

(*Source*: US Bureau of Census (1985) estimated from Table 1342)

* Value added estimated from value of shipments less cost of materials.

are particularly unimportant in the chemicals and instrument industries.

Where the costs of the different elements of the cost structure vary systematically from place to place then these variations in cost surfaces can affect patterns of locational change, the effect being influenced by the nature of a plant's cost structure. A firm operating a plant with particular labour requirements may be particularly responsive to spatial variations in the availability of that labour, while one operating a plant with high marketing costs may respond to spatial variations in marketing costs. Such relationships are reflected in aggregate cross-sectional data for specific industries. Instrument manufacture with a dependence on skilled scientists and engineers is responsive to inter-state variations in these elements of the labour force and overall they explain 61 per cent of the variation in state employment in instrument manufacture (Gibson, 1970). Similarly, Stafford (1960) showed that the paperboard container industry which was expected to locate near its markets to minimise transportation costs did just that. The market in the food, textiles, apparel and electrical machinery industry explained 88 per cent of the variation in employment in the paperboard container industry in 'large' counties in the United States.

It is not always the case that cost structures influence location. Where alternative technologies exist location can influence cost structure. This is seen most clearly in the steel industry. Whereas a coastal steel plant would operate oxygen convertors fed by molten iron produced from imported coal and ore, an inland steel firm in an engineering area may well adopt electric arc furnace technology because of the difficulties of access to coal and ore and a ready availability of scrap in the local area. Not only can cost structures be adjusted by using different technologies, the relative importance of the different elements can be altered in some industries by increasing the size of plant. Large capital intensive plants with few labour inputs can replace smaller labour intensive plants with limited capital equipment.

Plant size

Estimates of the relationship between costs and outputs (plant size) in four industries are shown by the long-run average cost curve in Fig. 6.4. The general shape refects *internal economies of scale*. Similar curves may be plotted for firms but the emphasis here is on plants. These internal economies are those which arise from *within* a plant and are to be distinguished from external economies of scale discussed in Chapter 9 which arise from outside the plant. The curves shown in Fig. 6.4 are for illustrative purposes only as it is not possible to consider fully the complexities of establishing the shape of such curves from empirical data. The particular character of the cost curve, downward sloping to the right, arises from the various factors which create internal economies of scale. The more important of these are as follows.

First, there is the existence of indivisibilities. For example, the greater the number of units produced the less will be research and development costs associated with each unit. Also, if a plant has a series of machines with different capacities they will only be used to capacity with

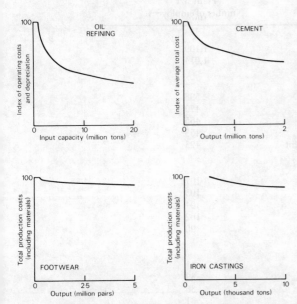

Fig. 6.4 Long-run average costs in selected industries, Britain, late 1960s (*Sources*: Based on Pratten and Dean 1965:53; Pratten 1971:35, 92 and 129)

a common multiple of all the machines. Second, economies of increased dimensions can be important. Costs often increase less than the capacity of a machine, doubling the size of a water tank does not double the amount of material used in the construction of the tank. Third, economies of specialisation are important too. Increased size means that specialist machines and specialist manpower can be employed. Economies arising from massed resources make up the fourth and final category. Discounts may be negotiated for buying in bulk and inventory (stores) costs will be reduced. In the latter case, the number of spare parts needed do not increase in proportion to the number of machines used in the plant.

These different factors will operate with differing force in different industries and, not surprisingly, different industries have different long-run average cost curves. In footwear and iron castings there are few savings in increasing the scale of operations, while in oil refining and the manufacture of cement the savings from building large plants are quite considerable (Fig. 6.4).

Examination of these diagrams suggests that there is a point on the curve where costs of production are minimised and this point marks the *minimum efficient scale (m.e.s.) of production*, that is the minimum efficient size of plant. The m.e.s. is defined normally in terms of output but it can be described in terms of employment. The variations in m.e.s. between industries mean that different industries are characterised by plants of different sizes. This is illustrated in Table 6.2 which shows clearly the variation in minimum efficient scale of plant in United Kingdom industry from 1,109 employees in ordnance and small arms to 31 employees in both spirit distilling and compounding/animal and poultry foods. Many smaller plants do, of course, exist – some operating at less than minimum efficient scale.

Variations in the m.e.s. between industries can affect the relative importance of the different components of change. Births will be rare where *barriers to entry* are high; that is where the m.e.s., measured in output, is very large or where a

Table 6.2   Minimum efficient scale of plant, selected industries, United Kingdom, 1968

Industry	Plant size Number of employees
Very large plants	
Ordnance and small arms	1,109
Wheeled-tractor manufacturing	1,014
Large plants	
Motor cycle and pedal cycle manufacturers	598
Office machinery	470
Asbestos	465
Toilet preparations	453
Broadcast-receiving and reproducing equipment	425
Medium-sized plants	
Plastics products	107
Abrasives	105
Narrow fabrics	104
Scientific and industrial instruments	102
Leather goods	98
Small plant industries	
Brewing and malting	41
Surgical bandages	39
Lace	36
Animal and poultry foods	31
Spirit distilling and compounding	31

(*Source*: Lyons 1980:28–9)

plant of m.e.s. needs to capture a large share of the market to survive. Conversely, where the barriers to entry are low births may be a prominent element among the components of change. In contrast, where the m.e.s. is large there may be a tendency for investments to be added to existing plants if they are below the m.e.s., while employment change in large-plant industries may be characterised by *in situ* shrinkage rather than closure.

The m.e.s. can also constrain the choice of site for entirely new plant. Other things being equal, very small plants can survive in most locations while larger plants are severely constrained by either or both of their initial labour and space requirements. It might also be argued that with larger plants locations will be more carefully evaluated by firms because of the size of the investment at risk. What is more, state and regional development organisations will take an active interest in a change involving a large plant because of the number of jobs and/or the amount of investment involved.

A fascinating insight into the interaction between plant size and locational change is provided by some work in South-West England (Norcliffe 1975). It is particularly at the lower end of the town size spectrum that the size of an urban place appears to impose important limitations on the size to which an industrial plant can grow. This is depicted clearly in Fig. 6.5 which shows the relationship between the population of the largest town and the employment in the largest plant in 69 functional urban areas in South-West England. This work also provided some empirical evidence as to the constraint of town size on an incoming branch plant. Towns with less than 25,000 population were limited to branch plants with less than 200 workers, while only towns with over 50,000 population were able to receive plants with over 500 employees. If this pattern is typical, industries with plants of a m.e.s. of 500 employees are, *ipso facto*, excluded from all centres with less than 50,000 population unless the smaller centres have unemployed labour reserves sufficient to support the large plant.

Of course, the m.e.s. in an industry is rarely

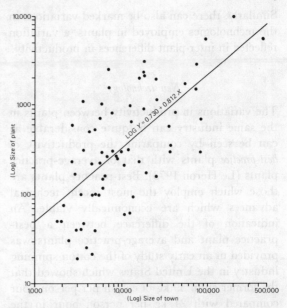

Fig. 6.5 Plant size and town size relationships, 1964 (*Source*: Norcliffe 1975:49)

stable and has tended to increase over time. Although industry output may rise, the number of sites at which employment is provided may fall, and there is evidence that industries with different plant sizes produce different spatial patterns. The relationship between plant size and spatial patterns was explored using cross-sectional data by Florence (1962:1–8). He examined the problem using 13 United Kingdom regions and concluded that industries characterised by small plants were widely dispersed (many plants in each region) as were industries characterised by large plants (a single plant in each region) but medium-sized plant industries tended towards concentration in specific regions. It has already been shown in Chapter 2 how increasing economies of scale in production have encouraged multinational firms to concentrate production of specific products in a limited number of plants as part of their reorganisation plans while the effects of changes in the m.e.s. in industries with high transport costs are explored in Chapter 9.

This discussion may have given the impression that all the plants of an industry are of a given size but this is not so as there is usually a wide range of variation around the most typical size.

Similarly, there can also be marked variations in the technologies employed in plants, a variation reflected in inter-plant differences in productivity.

New technology

The variations in productivity between plants in the same industry can be quite considerable as can be seen by comparing the productivity of *best-practice* plants with that of average-practice plants (Le Heron 1973). Best-practice plants are those which employ the most recent technical advances which are economically viable. An indication of the difference between a best-practice plant and average-practice plants was provided in an early study of the cotton spinning industry in the United States which showed that the former spun 39 kg of cotton per person hour compared with 24 kg per person hour in the latter. Similar contrasts can be seen between a 1945 spinning mill which had a labour cost of $64 per 100 kg while a 1973 mill had a labour cost of $12 per 100 kg (Rothwell 1978:36). Differences such as this may not be due only to process technology (managerial skills, for example, may influence output) but technology plays a major role in explaining these differences. In part, the differences will arise from variations in productivity with size of plant but they will also reflect diffusion of new technologies through an industry's plants. New technologies will be introduced in certain plants and then spread to other ones. There is now some evidence to suggest that the spread of process innovations has a geographical dimension; virtually all of these process innovations take the form of purchased machinery (Oakey, Thwaites and Nash 1982: 1078).

Within Canada Martin *et al.* (1979) discovered distinct delays in the adoption of innovations in five Canadian regions. They considered eight process innovations in five Canadian regions and discovered that the average lag between development in the leading (innovating) region and the Ontario region was 1.4 years but in the peripherally located Atlantic region it was 6.9 years. Similar contrasts have been reported in West Germany (Ewers and Wettmann 1980).

Tufting technology for carpet manufacture was first introduced in that country in 1954–55 and by 1961 60 per cent of potential users in non-assisted regions had adopted this technology but, in the assisted regions, the proportion was only 11 per cent. Overall, there was a delay of 4–5 years in the adoption of tufting technology in the assisted regions.

Further supporting evidence for spatial differences in the adoption of new technologies comes from both Britain and the United States. In Britain studies of the introduction of three process innovations (computerised numerical controls, computers in design and manufacture and the utilisation of microprocessors in products and processes) in nine metal-working industries between 1973 and 1977 showed a difference between the Development Areas (Wales, Scotland and the Northern region) and other areas. When the ten British regions were ranked by the proportion of plants adopting the new technologies, for two of the innovations none of the Development Areas was ranked higher than seventh. These differences between Development Areas and other regions could not be accounted for by either industrial sector or establishment size (Thwaites 1982:377–8).

In the United States, Rees, Briggs and Oakey (1984) examined spatial differences in the adoption of innovations relating to computerised automation within manufacturing with particular reference to machinery manufacturers within two-digit industries 35 and 36. Among seven technological innovations examined one advanced technology (the use of computerised numerical controls – CNC) showed significant differences in the rate of adoption between regions. Whereas 47 per cent of the surveyed plants in the North Central region had adopted CNC the proportion adopting CNC in the South was only 28 per cent. Considering all seven innovations the dominance of the manufacturing belt as a user of new technology stands out. Closer examination of the data shows that it is among the market-system (single-plant) firms that these differences were most marked; it is perhaps because of the ability of multi-plant firms to spread new production technologies that they show much smaller variations in the adoption rates for new technologies. It will be recalled that there was little variation between such plants in the levels of product innovation.

Although considerable interest has been aroused in the recent past in the regional variations in the adoption of new process technologies explanation of the differences is difficult. It is possible that plants in regions that are slow to adopt the new technologies are not receiving the relevant information to enable the new technologies to be introduced; the better performance of the plants of multi-plant firms with access to corporate information sources supports this view. Other possibilities should not, however, be ignored. In the lagging regions, for example, funds may not be able to finance the installation of the new technologies and the relevant back-up facilities to ensure the reliability of the new technology may not be readily available.

The effects of variations in the use and adoption of process technologies on a region's employment performance are varied. New technologies may alter markedly the locational requirements of an industry and encourage the construction of entirely new plants in new locations and the abandonment of older sites which are unsuitable for the new process. This kind of phenomenon was seen, for example, in the development of coalfield areas in Britain with the introduction of steam-based technologies (Ch. 3) but in the kind of time period considered here most interest is focused upon technological changes which adapt and modify existing processes and which through these changes and modifications influence both the number employed in particular plants and the kind of jobs available within them.

New technologies often reduce the number of workers required to manufacture a given level of output. In the British brick industry an interest in improving labour productivity led to increased mechanisation and to standardisation of the types of brick made which 'almost certainly ...involved cuts in labour' (Massey and Meegan 1982:176). Clear evidence of the link between process innovation and employment loss is provided by the employment record of the plants in the nine metal-working industries listed above.

The mean effect of process innovation in these British industries was for the plants to experience employment loss (Thwaites 1983:47–50) but these losses have to be seen in context. The employment losses tended to be less than those experienced by non-innovating plants and, most strikingly, those plants adopting all three of the technologies listed earlier were more likely than average to have experienced *employment growth*. These trends illustrate that while new technologies may reduce jobs, they can enhance the competitiveness of a plant and allow it to avoid job losses associated with the contraction of demand for the products of the non-innovating plant. It is also evident that in successful and innovating plants new processes may create demands for more labour to produce increasing output; it is where plant output is stationary or falling that new technologies are most likely to lead to employment loss.

Not only do new technologies offer the possibility of higher labour productivity with increased output per person they can reduce the labour costs by changing the nature of the jobs within the plant, especially by *de-skilling* the workforce. The latter change is associated primarily with the new technologies associated with the later stages of the product-cycle, and 'in many instances process innovations have encouraged the employment of less skilled labour and shifts in the type of worker employed (female, rather than male, for example)' (Clark 1981:421). Such de-skilling is not new and can be traced back to the development of the auto-assembly line and standardised production techniques (Ch. 3). 'In the years following World War II ... the principle of the assembly line was applied to everything from food processing to the assembly of television sets and the packaging of cosmetics' (Bluestone and Harrison 1982:117). Although the continuing trend towards higher levels of automation is clear, accurate data on changes in the geography of different types of jobs as a result of changes in technology are difficult to obtain. This topic is examined further in the discussion of the characteristics of labour markets in the next chapter.

Exploration of the consequences of the introduction of new technology for the geography of employment change is still in its infancy, although increasingly technological influences are being cited as possible causes of regional differences. For example, a study of employment change in the EEC showed that the central areas experienced a differential loss of *total* (not only manufacturing) employment, whereas peripheral areas showed a differential gain. However, the central regions experienced above average growth of output and the employment decline in the central regions 'strongly suggests a powerful process of capital labour substitution and rising labour productivity' (Keeble, Owens and Thompson 1982a:103). This assertion is based in part on the fact that central regions are showing a tendency towards greater emphasis upon technologically advanced and research-intensive manufacturing industries.

CONCLUSION

Choice of product and choice of production technology to manufacture the selected product are vital decisions for a firm and this chapter has illustrated how both the choice of product and production technology may be influenced by a firm and/or plant's geographical position within a national space economy. This is particularly evident among market-system firms; plants of planning-system firms appear to show fewer regional variations both in the age of the products they manufacture and the processes they use.

There is an important contrast in the employment consequences of the introduction of new products and new processes. Whereas new products help to create jobs in the plants in which they are manufactured the results of process innovations are more equivocal and can produce job loss, but it is a job loss which perhaps helps to ensure the longer run survival of the plant. Explanations of the variations which have been shown to occur, and the full implications of those variations for the geography of employment opportunities are not yet available. Technology, too, determines the minimum efficient scale for an industry's plants which further influences the nature and spatial pattern of industrial change. In the final analysis, it is the products and technology of a firm which have a major influence on the cost structures of its plant or plants and it is this cost structure which creates specific needs for the labour, capital and land resources to which attention is turned next.

7

LABOUR COSTS

Labour costs play a dominant role in the cost structure of many firms and their plants. Indeed, Storper and Walker argue that the labour factor should be in 'the forefront in the analysis of the modern geography of industrial capitalism'. As locational differences in the cost of non-labour commodities have diminished so 'it [is]...more important than ever that corporate executives focus in on the labour factor as the key to locational competitive advantage' (1984:19,22). The increased interest in labour costs has stimulated research in recent years into the various elements which make up labour costs and into the way in which firms respond to or exploit spatial variations in the characteristics of the labour force. Clearly, shortages of labour can act as important constraints on the employment growth of plants; while, in periods of employment decline, regions with high-cost labour may be characterised by both a high failure rate of market-system firms, unable to compete with rivals using lower cost labour, and by the closure of plants of planning-system firms, to permit the concentration of production in plants in areas with low labour costs. Of course, not all workers in manufacturing are employees and, as will be seen in Chapter 11, the characteristics of a region's labour force can influence the supply of potential founders of new firms.

In the short to medium term the main features of a region's labour force are relatively stable, that is workers are both geographically and occupationally immobile. Admittedly some groups of workers do move to homes in different areas, and highly paid white-collar workers are more likely to move between regions than unskilled manual workers. From 1965 to 1970 just over one-quarter of salaried professional and technical workers aged 35 to 44 in the United States migrated between counties in comparison to one in ten of non-farm labourers (Moriarty 1980: 187). Occupationally too, there are few changes in the short to medium term. Despite various retraining schemes an individual's skills, once learnt, tend to be maintained. Overall, the mix of blue-collar and white-collar jobs in a region as well as the mix of particular industrial skills remains stable. Stability too is often a feature of other regional characteristics which affect the labour market such as the education levels, the proportion of males and females, and the proportion of minority groups. Thus, at the present time, in the short to medium term, industrial change rarely acts as a lead to population movements; instead, industrial change responds to the characteristics of different labour markets.

The labour employed in a particular plant will be drawn, for the most part, from the *local labour market* in which the plant is set. The local labour market is the area within commuting distance of the town in which the plant operates. More specifically, Lever (1979:91) argues that from a firm's viewpoint the labour market is 'the geographical area containing those members of the labour force, or potential members of the labour force, that a firm can induce to enter its employ under certain conditions'. Such a definition produces overlapping local labour markets but discrete units can be defined by including in a town's local labour market only those areas which send more commuters to the specified town rather than to any other. The key criterion in most labour market definitions is journey to work which forms the basis of Standard Metropolitan Statistical Areas (SMSAs) in the United States and Travel to Work Areas (TTWAs) in Britain. The areal units can, of course, change from year to year or, at least between censuses as populations rise or fall and journey to work patterns change.

The distinct lines around individual local labour markets tend to mask some of the complex movements between and, more importantly, within the markets they define. They hide the nesting of more localised labour markets within the broader areas, yet for many individuals it is these localised labour markets which are of major significance. Perhaps the major criticism of the typical local labour market is the

implicit ... belief that the collective daily journey-to-work interaction patterns of a metropolitan population represent the spatial boundaries of the exchange relationships for *all* participants in the urban labour market. In reality, however, such broad boundary definitions are more likely to reflect the commuting patterns of the upper income ... suburban residents whose incomes and predisposition to individual daily mobility are most likely to enable them to stretch the limits of such boundaries to their farthest spatial extent (Clark and Gertler 1983:275).

Although criticisms of local labour market data have been made the identification of such markets reflects an attempt to move away from administrative areas in recording the geography of labour supply. Yet descriptions of spatial variations in labour force characteristics often have to rely upon much wider spatial frameworks such as states and regions. This may not be a major disadvantage, particularly for analyses of the changing geography of employment in manufacturing, since differences between adjacent labour markets may be small and it is only over wider areas that geographical differences in those characteristics appear.

This chapter indicates the extent of geographical variations in labour market characteristics. Many of these patterns arise from earlier periods of industrial activity but the emphasis here is upon describing contemporary spatial variations in labour costs and in examining the spatial division of labour.

LABOUR RESERVES AND WAGE RATES

For any firm contemplating expansion or setting up a new plant the size of the labour pool in a labour market may be of some significance. The influence of the size of the labour pool on industrial change will be most critical on growth and particularly on growth at periods of full employment. In recessionary times, only projects requiring a very large labour force in a relatively small local labour market would find local labour reserves inadequate, but at other times when unemployment is below 5 per cent shortages of labour may militate against industrial growth in many areas.

One indicator of the size of the pool is provided by *unemployment* data. Table 7.1 shows clearly that the pattern of unemployment does vary systematically around the United States average of 7.6 per cent with lower levels in the South and West and higher levels in the North. The highest rate of 12.3 per cent in Michigan is to be contrasted with 3.6 per cent in Oklahoma. Rates can be much higher in smaller geographical areas. A United Kingdom average in 1984 of

Table 7.1 Unemployment and female participation rates, United States, 1981

Unemployment rate		Female participation rate	
Lowest rates			*Highest rates*
Oklahoma	3.6	Nevada	61.8
Wyoming	4.1	Minnesota	60.8
Nebraska	4.1	Wyoming	59.7
Kansas	4.2	Colorado	58.0
Highest rates			*Lowest rates*
Indiana	10.1	Pennsylvania	47.5
Alabama	10.7	Louisiana	47.4
West Virginia	10.7	Florida	47.3
Michigan	12.3	Alabama	47.0

(*Source*: US Bureau of Census 1985: Table 628)

13 per cent covered unemployment rates ranging from 6.5 per cent (Basingstoke TTWA) to 23.4 per cent (South Tyneside TTWA). Too much emphasis should not be placed on percentage figures as indicators of labour reserves, the absolute number unemployed is far more critical. An unemployment rate of 5.1 per cent in Dakota arises from 17,000 unemployed whereas a 5.3 per cent unemployment rate in Texas arises from over one-third of a million unemployed. The distinction between percentage and absolute unemployment levels is particularly crucial when considering very small local labour markets, where a high percentage unemployment rate may represent only a small number of workers. The constraints imposed by a place's population size were illustrated in Fig. 6.5.

Unemployment data, of course, only include those recorded by the authorities assembling the information on unemployment and a more general indicator of the size of a potential workforce is the *participation* or *activity* rate. This is defined as the proportion of the population of a given age group in work. The male participation rates tend to be high, rarely dropping below 70 per cent at state level when measured as the percentage of the civilian non-institutionalised population age 16 and over in the civilian labour force. Female participation rates are lower. Variations between states in female participation rates are shown in Table 7.1; the values range from 47.0 per cent in Alabama to 61.8 per cent in Nevada. Regional data for Britain pick up small variations in the activity rate for females. The rate is consistently lower than the British average in Wales and the South-West and persistently higher in the larger English regions of North-West, West Midlands and the South-East. But only 7 percentage points separate the regions with the highest activity rates from those with the lowest. Where female activity rates are low the provision of employment opportunities can draw additional workers into the economically active population.

At the present time, with high unemployment rates in many advanced economies it may be more critical to consider wage rates rather than availability of labour. It is dangerous to compare

Table 7.2 Average weekly earnings* of full-time manual workers on adult rates in the engineering and allied trades, United Kingdom, 1982

Region	Male	Female
	£	£
South-East	128	87
East Anglia	120	82
South-West	127	81
West Midlands	124	86
East Midlands	125	87
Yorkshire and Humberside	129	83
North-West	130	88
North	132	86
Wales	129	89
Scotland	139	95
Northern Ireland	121	94

(*Source*: *Central Statistical Office* 1984:100)
* Data have been standardised on a 41-hour week for males and a 38-hour week for females.

regional variations in wage rates without making allowance for industrial and occupational structures. Regional comparisons can be illustrated with reference to a single occupational group within one industry. This is done in Table 7.2 which examines manual workers in the engineering and allied industries in the United Kingdom. The male workers were predominantly skilled workers and the females predominantly unskilled. Among skilled workers the highest earnings appear in Scotland which has earnings 16 per cent above the low earnings region of East Anglia. Such differences appear among the unskilled workers too. Scotland and Northern Ireland are regions with high earnings, whereas the lowest earnings are found in East Anglia and the South-West. Despite the difficulties of using an average for all manufacturing industries an indication of wage rate variations within the United States is provided by the fact that although during the period 1959 to 1978 there was a significant narrowing on South/non-South wage differences (Newman 1984:5) 'the south's average hourly manufacturing wage rate...remained nearly 20 per cent below the national average' (Moriarty 1980:184). Wage rate differentials tend to be smaller for white-collar workers particularly the higher paid ones with a greater propensity for inter-area migration and regional variations are damped down by national level wage negotiations. Wage rates themselves hide costs of additional payments to labour which supplement their basic wages. As Estall and Buchanan (1980:92) observe, in relation to the United States, 'there is a clear distinction between the north-east (liberal) and the southern (less liberal) regions in every class of fringe benefit – paid holidays and vacations, private health insurance and pension plans and so forth'.

The patterns in wage rates can be modified by government intervention *either* in the form of a pay-roll tax which if restricted to a specific area or areas raises labour costs in those areas *or* in the form of a labour subsidy which effectively reduces a firm's labour costs. Interventions of this form are discussed in Chapter 15. There can also be sudden changes in the relative rankings of different areas. In the West Midlands in Britain the collapse of the manufacturing sector in the region saw a change from 1974, when it had the second highest gross weekly earnings for all men among the seven metropolitan counties, to 1982, when it had the lowest (Healey and Clark 1984:310).

While the availability of labour and prevailing wage rates may be important in explaining some aspects of manufacturing employment change, more critical for the firm is the amount of work undertaken for a particular payment. 'It is', as Czamanski (1981) has observed, 'neither the cost, nor the availability of labour, treated as a homogeneous factor of production, but the distribution of skills, productivity and absence of labour disputes that are of importance.'

PRODUCTIVITY

It is in the area of productivity that certain preconceived facts about certain regions exist and it is particularly here, as was shown in Chapter 5, that firms react to their perceptions of an area's labour productivity rather than to the measurable facts. Thus region A is 'known' for having a high turnover rate, region B 'obviously' suffers from high levels of absenteeism, region C has a 'well-organised and unionised' labour force and region D is 'clearly' the most strike prone in the country. It may be that among planning-

system firms in particular that these preconceived notions exert a greater influence on employment change than the actual patterns of productivity that can be measured. Certainly, the characteristics of a region's labour force are often important inputs to a firm's perception of an area's business climate (Ch. 10).

Turnover rates can affect productivity. High labour turnover means that at any one time a number of employees may be learning the job (thus reducing output) and training costs will be high. On average, turnover rates are low; the number of engagements per 100 employees per month in the United Kingdom is 1.6 (in 1984) while in the United States (in 1980) new hires were 2.1 per 100 employees per month. It is likely that in periods of low unemployment they will be higher than the figures quoted above. In the United Kingdom, for example, the leaving rate in 1973 was twice that of 1984. A comparison of quit rates between Philadelphia and Houston over the period 1970–79 indicates that as local unemployment increases so the rate of quits decreases (Clark 1980:222). Unemployment levels may provide a rough surrogate for regional differences in turnover rates but the extent of regional variations in labour turnover remains unexplored as are their implications for regional employment change (Clark 1982:53).

Productivity will be influenced also by the proportion of the workforce which fails to show up for work, that is the level of *absenteeism*. An early study which compared four branch factories in a peripheral area of Britain with plants elsewhere discovered that in three out of four cases absenteeism was higher in the peripheral area (Hague and Newman 1952:33–56). This does seem to be a general pattern as Fig. 7.1A shows. It appears to relate to all workers and a loss of around 5 days per worker in the South-East increases to about 15 days per worker in the North. These figures must be interpreted cautiously since if they include all employees they cover those employed in less attractive jobs where a higher level of absenteeism is not unexpected and these jobs may be more prevalent in the areas with the high absenteeism rates. Yaseen (1960:65) suggests an absentee rate of 3

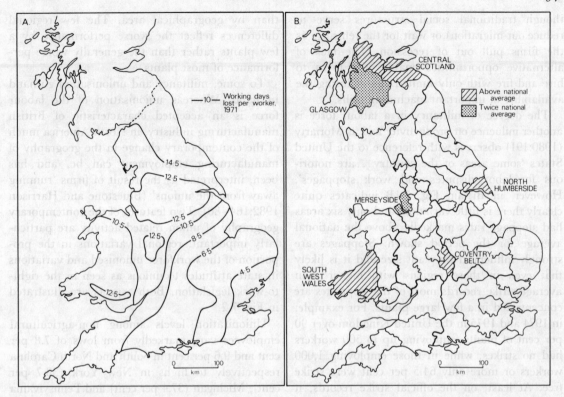

Fig. 7.1 (A) Absenteeism, England and Wales, 1971 (B) Strikes (working days lost), Britain 1968 to 1973 (*Source*: (A) Toyne 1974:125 (B) Based on data from Smith *et al*. 1978)

per cent is typical and where rates are double or triple this level a potentially volatile labour situation may exist. Of course, there are other more subjective elements which affect the productivity of the labour force in a particular area. A willingness to work overtime and the degree to which individuals are prepared to accept different forms of shift working may vary from area to area but whether those differences result in any systematic spatial variation is difficult to establish.

Productivity may also be influenced by the competition for labour within a local labour market and the role a plant plays in that labour market. Lever, McPhail and Norris (1978) drew attention to some 95 company dominated labour markets in Britain where one plant accounted for 12.5 per cent or more of the local workforce. Examples include Rugby (General Electric Company), Luton (General Motors), and St

Helens (Pilkingtons). In at least 13 cases the plants accounted for over one-third of the workforce. In these markets, the dominant plant may exert an influence on wage rates, conditions of service and indeed, 'poach' labour from other firms. The nature of the influence is not, however, clear. For example, a dominant plant may hold labour in a recession conscious of the serious impact its lay-offs will have on the local economy, yet it could equally make large numbers unemployed recognising that because there are insufficient other employers to take up the workers they will still be there if, and when, demand recovers. An example of the latter behaviour is provided by Storper and Walker (1984, 37–8). Jet engines are manufactured in southern New England where the industry so dominates the area that there are not enough job opportunities to absorb the workers laid-off in recession. Workers either have to move (al-

though traditional social structures serve to
reduce out-migration) or wait for the rehirings as
the firms pull out of recession. The lack of
alternative opportunities enables the firms to
hire and fire with only limited risk of losing the
availability of important machining skills.

The degree of militancy in a labour force is
another influence on productivity and as Moriarty
(1980:191) observes with reference to the United
States 'some areas of the country...are notori-
ous for labor disputes and work stoppages'.
However, in Britain Fig. 7.1B indicates quite
clearly there is little variation, and only six areas
had stoppage rates markedly above the national
average for the period shown. Stoppages are
strongly influenced by plant size and it is likely
that even in those regions with higher than
average strike records most of the stoppages are
concentrated in a few large plants. For example,
in 1974 and 1975 in the United Kingdom over 90
per cent of plants employing up to 500 workers
had no strikes, while in those employing 1,000
workers or more only 64.5 per cent were strike
free. At least, on the official strike records, it
seems reasonable to argue that there is little
regional variation in worker militancy, and that
which does exist is influenced more by plant size

than by geographical area. The few regional
differences reflect the worse performance by a
few plants rather than the generally worse performance of most plants.

To some, militancy and unionisation go hand
in hand. Whereas unionisation of the labour
force is an accepted characteristic of British
manufacturing industry, in North America much
of the contemporary change in the geography of
manufacturing employment can be, and has
been, interpreted as the result of firms 'running
away from the unions' (Bluestone and Harrison
1982:164–80). Two features of the contemporary
geography of union related activity are particularly important: regional variations in the proportion of the workforce unionised and variations
in state attitudes to unions as seen in the right-
to-work legislation. Both aspects are illustrated
in Fig. 7.2.

Unionisation levels among non-agricultural
employees vary markedly from lows of 7.8 per
cent and 9.6 per cent in South and North Carolina
respectively to highs in New York (38.7 per
cent), Michigan (37.4 per cent) and Pennsylvania
(34.6 per cent). In general high levels of union
activity are concentrated in the older manufacturing areas. In part these variations reflect the

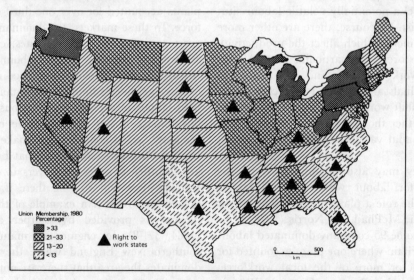

Fig. 7.2 Union membership and right-to-work states, United States, 1980 (*Source*: US Bureau of Census 1983:
Table 582)

presence in these areas of industries which are typified by high levels of union activity. The right-to-work laws show an even more distinct pattern and are indicative not only of attitudes to unions but also provide a guide to a state's 'business climate' (Ch. 10). The anti-union right-to-work laws not only outlaw compulsory union membership in a plant they also outlaw it in plants where the majority of workers vote for it. The implementation of right-to-work laws depends upon the initiatives of state legislatures and as Fig. 7.2 makes clear the right-to-work states are concentrated in the Southern regions, the West North Central region and the Mountain region. As of 1980 not one state in the older manufacturing areas of East North Central, Middle Atlantic and New England had passed a right-to-work law.

A final influence on productivity is the particular mix of labour skills available within a local area. If the particular skills a plant needs can be readily obtained within the local labour market costs can be reduced thereby increasing a plant's competitive advantage. Similarly, regional concentrations of unskilled workers can prove attractive to plants with routine production processes. Regional variations in skill levels as well as variations in militancy, unionisation and productivity create the spatial division of labour.

THE SPATIAL DIVISION OF LABOUR

A feature of advanced societies is the division of labour whereby individuals specialise in particular tasks, and a *spatial division of labour* arises when specialists in particular tasks are concentrated in certain regions. At least two different spatial divisions of labour can be recognised (Massey 1979, 1984).

1. *The sectoral division of labour*. Different industries and their associated skills are concentrated in particular regions. So that, for example, the East Midlands of England is associated with footwear manufacture and the state of Georgia is associated with carpet manufacture.

2. *The intra-sectoral division of labour*. Within each industry different tasks occupy different locations. Plants manufacturing new products (for example) using skilled labour may be located in one area, while those manufacturing well-established products using unskilled labour may be located elsewhere. Equally, as was seen in Chapter 4 head office and research and development functions of planning-system firms predominate in some regions while production activities dominate in other regions.

The sectoral spatial division of labour is well established and many specialist industrial areas developed in the nineteenth century (Ch. 3). More recently newer industries have concentrated in regions like Silicon Valley (Ch. 6) and the Cambridge area in Britain (Ch. 11). While there may be cost advantages to plants in these areas through the ready availability of specialist skills these must be offset against the fact that the concentration may encourage a higher degree of unionisation and union activity.

The intra-sectoral division of labour is a rather more recent phenomenon and is associated closely with the growth and development of planning-system firms and the emergence of locational hierarchies within these firms. If all large firms show broadly similar locational hierarchies then an intra-sectoral spatial division of labour will emerge. There is clear evidence in most countries of a concentration of head office and research activities in particular regions, and white-collar and blue-collar workers in many industries have different geographical patterns (Ch. 4). Although Massey and Meegan (1979:209) claim there is some evidence of a spatial division between skilled and unskilled production workers in specific firms, this does not show up clearly in aggregate data on planning-system firms. Nevertheless, the descriptive material describing regional variations in labour productivity do suggest spatial contrasts in the characteristics of the labour force.

Manufacturing employment changes thus take place in relation to two spatial divisions of labour – one reflecting sectoral specialisation and the other intra-sectoral variations in types of job.

It is now a major area of debate as to the extent to which firms exploit the intra-sectoral spatial division of labour. It seems likely that market-system firms are unable to make use of the spatial division of labour as they operate in a situation where 'the...labour market of classical economists is reproduced, with general skills, usually labour power itself being more or less freely bought and sold' (Danson 1982:259) although regional variations in labour costs may affect the performance of individual plants. However, over the last decade considerable interest has arisen in the spatial employment policies of planning-system firms. These firms may use locational strategies to overcome rigidities in certain local labour markets. An alternative to technological change to cut costs might be to shift older technologies into low wage areas. Similarly, local opposition to the introduction of process innovation may be met by introducing new technologies in new areas. Such shifts do, however, depend upon the existence of the kind of geographical differences in the characteristics of the labour force described in the last section.

To understand a firm's response to and/or exploitation of the intra-sectoral division of labour it is useful to take a closer look at the characteristics of the industrial labour market. This is, in fact, a *dual labour market* (Doeringer and Piore 1971) consisting of primary and secondary sectors. The *primary labour market* is characterised by high incomes, job security, and good prospects of upward mobility, whereas the *secondary labour market* is characterised by limited prospects for upward mobility, little job security, and negligible training. In this secondary market the only reward is cash payment and even this is small. Such a division within the labour market is emphasised where the secondary market is associated with minority groups and, despite equal opportunities legislation, female workers. The primary workers can be further sub-divided into upper primary and lower primary workers. The *upper primary workers* (usually white-collar employees) will be tied to the firm by long-term contracts, promotion will take place internally, wages will relate to professional standards and additional opportunities and rewards will be made available on the basis of the length of time in the job. The *lower primary workers* (usually blue-collar employees) enjoy a similar degree of stability; they may be highly unionised, and possess a range of skills often process specific and learnt through on-the-job training.

As a response to these different segments of the labour market the larger planning-system firms create their own *internal labour markets*, often in collusion with the unions active in their plants. Access to these markets is restricted both by firm and union and entry to the market takes place at a limited number of access points such as on leaving school, on graduation, or on receiving a union ticket. Once into the internal labour market promotion and advancement lie within the firm. These internal labour markets consist principally of primary workers; secondary workers are hired, primarily, from the *external labour market*. Their numbers can be adjusted and adapted rapidly to changing circumstances and they offer the firm flexibility in its personnel planning without affecting the security of those in the internal labour market.

Clark (1981) argues that the different relations which exist between a firm and its employees in the different segments of the labour market will encourage it to separate spatially the different segments of the workforce. Where workers from different segments are located in the same plant or town comparisons between employment contracts will be made. Where R & D staff (which can be equated with the upper primary sector) and production workers (which can be equated with the lower primary sector) occupy the same location, the blue-collar labour force will.be all too aware of the preferential terms offered by the firm to white-collar workers and they may well be able to negotiate some of these benefits for themselves. This reduces the flexibility a firm desires in its relations with its blue-collar workers. Spatial separation offers the opportunity to retain control over the blue-collar workforce. Although empirical evidence often suggests a spatial separation of R & D and production facilities, it is difficult to establish empirically that this arises from a desire to separate spatially two groups of employees which have different contractual relations with a firm. It could arise from the different locational needs of the production site (say, access to materials) and the R & D site (say, access to other R & D institutions).

Shifts between different segments of the blue-collar labour market have been linked to moves from areas with strong union power (often associated with the lower primary market) to those where union power is limited (in the secondary labour market). Such shifts can be related to maturing industrial products making fewer demands for skilled labour, the introduction of new highly automated production systems and to filter-down concepts (Ch. 6). Most of the literature on the exploitation of non-union power tends to adopt the view that conflict between a firm and its union (or unions) is inevitable. It is often forgotten that a good contract (or agreement) with a union can be a considerable help to a firm in organising its relations with its workforce. Similarly fringe benefits are not always obtained from a reluctant firm by a powerful union. Retaining good workers is an important goal of most firms and thus fringe benefits may be granted as a result of enlightened self-interest.

Growth in the southern United States in the 1950s and 1960s is interpreted by Bluestone and Harrison (1982) as a reflection of firms running away from the unions. The 'runaway shop' (complete transfer of operations from one area to another) was unusual but the running was done by both differential expansion of existing plants and through the establishment of branch plants. That they were able to run in this way was aided by, for example, the right-to-work legislation, southern anti-union attitudes (especially in rural areas), insufficient union funds to organise recruitment of new members and, in some cases, the lethargy of the unions concerned who did not recognise the need to gain new members. Not only did the build-up of non-union plant directly avoid union power but in multi-site firms threats to shift production to a firm's non-union plants could be used as a bargaining strategy with its union shops. Even more subtle differences within work contracts can influence shifts of emphasis. Thus Brown and Williamson Tobacco switched activities between southern plants to concentrate on Macon, Georgia, as at that plant there were no maximum allowable machine speeds, manning ratios and restrictive seniority positions and production could be organised to operate the machinery 24 hours a day avoiding even shutdowns for lunch breaks. Similar shifts can be seen in firms which have developed basic assembly work in the semiconductor industry in towns on the Mexican border. They employ mainly women who have little or no industrial experience, who have family obligations before and after work and because of little alternative work and their roles as principal wage-earners they make an ideal, low wage, unmilitant labour force (Storper and Walker 1984:37–8).

Avoidance of unionised labour is difficult to demonstrate in Britain although Massey and Meegan (1982:169) recognised that 'a change in location...[can]...be a device on management's part for avoiding trouble with existing unions' and, as will be shown later, 'union activities' have been blamed for the closure of some plants (Ch. 14). It can be argued that output associated with the late stage of the product cycle will be located 'where semi-skilled workers are...available...where wages are low and where there is little tradition amongst ...workers of organisation and militancy' (Massey 1979:237). This labour will be, for example, in seaside resorts and in specialised industrial regions. However, in the specialised industrial regions the labour will be drawn not from those previously employed in the specialisations but from those outside them and especially women (Cooke 1983:543). Some anecdotal evidence supporting these arguments is provided by a statement from a director of a clothing factory which moved from a traditional clothing centre to Wales.

The labour...(shortage) was not...the main obstacle ...(in the previous location). It was rather the impossibility of adapting a labour force accustomed to traditional methods to mass production line operation ...We had attempted to introduce it and had been forced to abandon it, partly because of our inadequate premises, but chiefly because of worker resistance ...In Wales we employ girls straight from school...It would have been impossible to use mass production methods with our former employees, many of whom were skilled... The element of suspicion and distrust of management which was present to some extent in the traditional clothing centre is very largely absent amongst our present workforce... reactions to management amongst the girls... tend to follow the pattern of school and family, rather than trade union and clothing industry' (Hague and Newman 1952:53–4).

The role of the labour factor in influencing the movement of plants is explored further in Chapter 12 but the general validity of filter-down argument was questioned in the last chapter.

CONCLUSION

While the influence of the labour factor has received considerable attention over the last decade, it is difficult to accept that firms deliberately exploit the spatial division of labour from studies which focus solely upon the characteristics of labour markets (Peet 1983). While the labour factor is clearly important, as indeed is recognised in traditional location theory (Weber 1929:95–103), it must be seen in the context of other influences on industrial change. This is taken up in the afterword to this part of the book (page 136) and the influence of labour in the context of other influences is also illustrated with reference to the different components of change in Part IV. Further, it is difficult to marry studies which claim unskilled labour is exploited by planning-system firms with those studies of mature stage products in the filter-down process which showed no product differentiation between planning-system plants in different areas.

This chapter has, however, shown the differing geographies of labour supply, wage rates, labour turnover, absenteeism, competition for labour, labour militancy, unionisation and labour skills. There is a clear spatial division of labour and planning-system firms can exploit this spatial division to, for example, avoid union power. While areas with certain labour characteristics may experience rapid employment growth, that growth may reflect some other non-labour attributes of the areas, this is most obvious in the case of rural areas which often offer attractive environments (Ch. 5) and unconstrained locations (Ch. 8).

8

CAPITAL AND LAND
COSTS

In turning from the characteristics of labour markets to spatial variations in the availability and cost of capital and land, attention is concentrated on the two other factors of production which may affect regional variations in manufacturing employment change. As was pointed out earlier, the availability and cost of capital, like labour market characteristics, is likely to vary regionally whereas land costs and availability are more likely to vary markedly between urban areas and rural areas. Land costs do, of course, also vary within urban areas but consideration of intra-urban change is outside the scope of this discussion.

CAPITAL FUNDS

For the majority of private sector firms the principal sources of funds for investment come from equities (shares sold to the public), loans (from banks and finance houses) and retained profits. In a new firm personal savings form an important source of initial capital. As Estall (1972:193) points out, a number of writers on industrial location tend to assume that 'new capital funds will be equally available (... within a nation ...) at all places on the same terms for all projects which involve the same degree of risk' and thus dismiss the possibility that the availability and cost of capital will influence locational change. It might also be argued that in periods of de-industrialisation and manufacturing decline the availability of new funds is irrelevant. However, there

is some evidence that capital may not be as widely available as has been supposed and that even at times of *net* employment decline some individuals and firms are seeking funds for new plants or expansion of existing operations. For these firms the availability and cost of capital may be critical, although the emphasis may be placed on availability rather than cost.

The influence of capital funds and the constraints imposed in raising capital differ markedly between the market-system and planning-system firms. The former tend to rely on personal and local sources whereas the latter can raise funds in the national money markets. In the market system the problems of plant and firm are identical, but in the planning-system firm the individual plant may depend upon the allocation of funds by the corporate head office. It is this critical plant–head office relationship which governs the availability of funds for new investment at regional level in planning-system firms.

Market-system firms

There have been few studies of spatial variations in the cost and availability of capital to market-system firms because it has been assumed that such variations do not exist but there are barriers to the free flow of capital within advanced nations. They may be more apparent in nations of considerable spatial extent (like the United States) than in nations of smaller size. Among market-system firms activities will be financed by personal savings and borrowing from financial institutions, especially banks and finance companies based in the local area.

Personal sources of finance (savings, for example, and family help) will be particularly important at the start-up of the firm as will be shown in Chapter 11 but small firms will depend also upon local sources of funds. The attitudes and capabilities of financial institutions in different areas to the supply of funds to small firms may be critical. This is less important in the highly centralised banking system of the United Kingdom, but in the United States, where in the early 1970s 13,000 banks existed to serve local communities, regional contrasts may be large. Not only can individual banks have different lending policies and interest rates, they can lack the resources to support the more successful firm. Particular difficulties may be faced by medium-sized firms whose needs are too large for local institutions but are too small to be attractive to national level investors such as pension funds and insurance companies. Even in Britain some locally based organisations such as the West Midland Enterprise Board have argued that for the medium-sized firm access to capital is more difficult outside the South-East of England (Healey and Clark 1984:315).

Venture capital

While variations in bank policies might be important in North America because of its decentralised banking system, there is increasing interest in both Britain and North America in spatial variations in the presence of specialised financial institutions prepared to supply venture capital. Venture capital (sometimes called risk capital) is capital loaned at considerable risk; indeed substantial losses might be expected on up to 40 per cent of the investments made and even for successful investments it may need between 5 and 10 years for an investment to mature and to offer a profit on selling (Cross 1981:194). Such risks are borne on the assumption that major success and capital gains on a limited number of highly successful 'ventures' will more than offset the losses elsewhere.

Analyses of variations in the availability of venture capital are difficult to make without analyses of the supplying institutions. A focus upon the behaviour of financial institutions is seen in a study of Boston and Philadelphia reported by Estall (1972). In Boston, financial institutions responded to the needs of new science-based industry arising from R & D work and recognised its potential for new business from which the institutions themselves would eventually benefit. The Philadelphia financial institutions behaved rather differently and their attitude may have inhibited the growth of new firms of this type. There are hints of regional contrasts in the availability of venture capital in Britain today. Fewer market-system firms in the South-East believed finance to have been a major constraint on their development than firms located in other parts of England. This suggests that 'it may be more difficult to raise venture finance in peripheral regions due to constraints in the present financial system' (Thwaites 1982:378). This provides some support for the view that lack of venture capital may help to explain the inability of some market-system firms in peripheral regions to generate and manufacture product innovations (Ch. 6). However, the discovery that market-system firms in particular areas make little use of venture capital may reflect neither the attitudes of financial institutions nor the lack of venture capital firms. It could equally well reflect the unwillingness of firms to seek help from firms supplying venture capital or the lack of creditworthiness among the firms themselves.

Planning-system firms

The financial inter-relationships between plants and head offices in planning-system firms have been seen as peripheral to geographical enquiries and have not been explored in depth in the geographical literature. There is an increasing concern with the extent to which plants in particular regions as externally owned (Watts 1981) but 'how control is actually exercised from corporate head offices has received only limited attention' (Hayter and Watts 1983:163). Evidence from studies of financial control within organisations suggests that the essential distinction is between a plant or group of plants which are treated as 'cost' centres (i.e. corporate profits are not associated with particular plants) and those which are regarded as 'profit/loss' centres and are judged by their contribution to corporate profits.

Among plants operated by planning-system firms an important distinction can be made between subsidiaries (which have a separate legal identity although the parent corporation will own more than 50 per cent of the shares) and branches (which have no separate legal identity). Subsidiaries tend to be treated as 'profit centres' whereas branches may be either 'profit centres' or 'cost centres'. Although individual plants may be categorised in this way the 'cost' or 'profit' levels can be controlled by head office both through the allocation of items such as central administrative costs to each plant and through corporate transfer pricing systems by which the firm controls the price at which materials and products are transferred between corporate sites. A plant's costs and profits can also be influenced by restrictions on the sources of materials and services, the products that can be made and the markets that can be served from the plant. Some of the implications of this ability to move costs and profits round the corporate system were touched upon earlier in the discussion of multinational firms (Ch. 2).

Where a plant is a cost centre it will depend entirely on head office for funds for all but minor capital investments but where it is a profit (or loss) centre it may have some funds it can use at its own discretion although the areas in which it has discretion may be constrained by centralised policies such as those imposing limitations upon the proportion of profits to be retained at plant level. Indeed, one of the criticisms of externally-owned plants at regional scale has been that profits 'leak' out to corporate head offices and are not necessarily available for new investment in the local area.

Not only will the investment patterns of planning-system firms affect employment growth at particular plants they may contribute to employment decline where capital equipment replaces

labour and where non-investment over a period of years results in plants becoming less efficient and thus, in times of recession, candidates for closure. There appear to be two important questions which affect the spatial availability of capital within the planning-system firm. The first is how much control over capital spending is exercised by head office? The second is, if funds are controlled by head office, is there any spatial bias in the way in which funds are made available to particular plants?

Few subsidiaries and branches are able to provide for their own capital investment needs from sources external to the firm to which they belong but they can have some influence over capital expenditure decisions. In a study in Wales just under half the branches and over three-quarters of the subsidiaries believed they could make their own capital expenditure decisions but virtually all needed to seek final approval from head office. So although the establishments thought they had discretion in capital expenditure 'those who visited the companies gained the impression that there were not so many autonomous investment centres' as appeared in the initial study (Tomkins and Lovering 1973:13).

Spending limits do vary between plants and can be very low indeed, although the limits tend to be higher in subsidiaries than branches. Examination of 75 plants that had moved over 25 miles to a location in either East Anglia or the Northern region of Britain showed that in 55 per cent of the cases all spending of over £1,000 had to be referred to the parent. To put £1,000 in perspective it represented at this time about one-seventh of the price of an average house in these areas. Of the remaining 19 plants, another 12 had limits of £7,500 or less, 2 had a limit of £20,000 and 5 had undisclosed limits above this latter figure (Townroe 1975:51). A similar control is seen in the Peugeot-Talbot motor vehicle assembly plant which operated in Scotland in the early 1970s. Here the plant in 1974 had an annual turnover of £75 million but the plant level expenditure limit was £15,000 (Hood and Young 1982:74–6).

Clearly, in the interests of a firm as a whole,

individual plants have to have their capital investment plans scrutinised at head office level. Each project will be assessed on its anticipated contribution to corporate profits but the key question is not whether it will generate profit (which might be acceptable at plant level) but its profitability in relation to other projects competing for what may be a limited capital budget. To this assessment must be added risks inherent in the project and projects some distance from head office may be perceived as involving greater risk, especially as those involved in the project may not be very well known to head office staff. As Townroe (1975:51) observed 'a number of interviewees commented on the importance of personal relationships in the acceptance of a proposal from a branch plant or subsidiary company'. The sensitivity of head offices to distance constraints, particularly in new plant investment, is well illustrated by the distance decay function which is evident in the establishment of branch plants (Ch. 12) and Schmenner (1982:232) shows in a sample of United States firms that 'more on-site expansions...occur in the vicinity of headquarters locations than would be expected merely from the distribution of stay-put plants and employment'.

The distance constraint should not, however, be overemphasised. In large multi-regional systems each plant will have a particular role in the corporate production system and the availability or non-availability of investment funds will reflect overall corporate strategies and the way in which the plant fits into those strategies. If the current strategy is to expand output of product X the plant producing X will be expanded regardless of location in relation to head office, but where X is produced in a variety of plants the more peripheral plants may be at a disadvantage with regard to capital investment funds. The role of the existing distribution of products helps to emphasise the strong influence of existing sites on new capital investment and the reasons for this locational conservatism are explored in Chapter 13.

The highly speculative nature of the evidence of spatial variation in the cost and availability of capital is emphasised by the fact that there are no contemporary maps or graphs to illustrate such variations. Such diagrams have been drawn in the past, notably by Lösch (1954:461–8) for North America in the inter-war period, but it would be unwise to regard them as typical of the situation at the present time.

One area where speculation can be replaced by fact is that distinct spatial variations in the availability of capital funds do exist where local, state and national governments have intervened in the capital market. This is discussed in Chapters 10 and 15 but two examples indicate how this might work. First, some states in the United States offer loans to new plants in labour surplus areas while some local administrations in the United Kingdom are prepared to invest their funds in medium-sized firms and thus medium-sized firms based in these areas have access to a source of funds not available elsewhere. Second, in the early 1970s government policies in Britain meant that an investment of £100 cost a firm between £30 and £40 in areas eligible for regional policy aid and £60 elsewhere. The difference between these sums and the £100 being made up by government grants.

LAND AND BUILDINGS

In the process of employment decline and plant closure capital may be released by the sale of buildings and land while the establishment of new plants or the extension of existing ones can meet considerable expense in acquiring the appropriate land and buildings. Land and buildings are required not only for the manufacturing process but also for, as examples, administration, warehousing, car parking, access roads and, in more modern well-designed sites, landscaping. The land and building costs rarely form a key element in the cost structure of a plant but they can play a major role at critical points in a plant's history. New plants can be established only where there are (or are likely to be) adequate land and buildings of the right shape, size and position; existing plants can only expand *in situ* if adjacent land or buildings are available, while strong pressure from competing land users (for example, on the edge of the Central Business

District) might encourage closure of plant to take advantage of its site value. At this point it is assumed that the state does not intervene in the land market but such intervention does occur and is described in Chapters 10 and 15.

At the present time there is considerable debate over whether land costs do have a major influence on employment change. On the one hand there is the argument that with a net decline in manufacturing employment few new plants are being constructed, few plants are being extended, and that 'second-hand' industrial premises are widely available. Yet there is evidence of increasing capital intensity in manufacturing industry which necessitates an increasing amount of floor space per worker. This is reflected in England and Wales floor space data which show an increase of 2.5 per cent in floor space per employee between 1966 and 1971, and a further 4.0 per cent increase between 1971 and 1975 (Fothergill and Gudgin 1982:106). Thus even where employment is stable or is declining slowly there can still be a strong demand for industrial floor space and this demand might accentuate a need for modern well-serviced plants rather than older plants abandoned by earlier manufacturing operations.

Land and building costs

Building costs (that is factory construction costs) appear to vary regionally, at least within the United States, a factor which may be of significance for firms considering new sites or extensions. These differences are shown in Fig. 8.1 which is based on data for 181 metropolitan areas. This indicates lower construction costs in urban areas lying in a belt from North Carolina to southern Alabama with the highest values in the New York area and along the southern shores of the Great Lakes (Smith 1981:263–6). While the figure illustrates differences in costs between urban areas it probably exaggerates the costs of factory construction in the non-metropolitan areas for which data were not available.

In contrast to building costs, land costs are unlikely to be of importance in discriminating between the employment change in different major regions. Good sites can usually be found somewhere in any general area and so the principal spatial contrast is between urban centre and urban periphery locations and between urban and rural areas. The former is illustrated by data for Sydney (Fig. 8.2) which show the percentage decline in the cost of industrial land

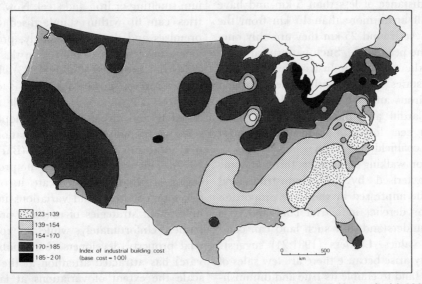

Index of industrial building cost (base cost = 100)
123–139
139–154
154–170
170–185
185–201

Fig. 8.1 Industrial building costs for 181 metropolitan areas, United States, 1980 (*Source*: Smith 1981:266)

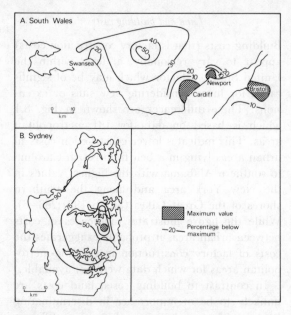

Fig. 8.2 (A) Factory rents on industrial estates in South Wales and Severnside (B) Land costs, Sydney (*Sources*: (A) Bale 1981:30 (B) Logan 1966:456)

with increased distance from its peak value. Although based on 1964 data there is little reason to expect that the general shape of the land cost curve as represented by the percentage values will have changed. In some areas land values halve in a distance of less than 5 km and have halved in all areas more than 15 km from the peak value. At around 25 km they are only one-quarter of the peak value. Such patterns are also evident in the rent for industrial buildings on industrial estates in the South Wales coalfield and its environs and show clearly the peaks in Newport, Cardiff and Bristol and rents more than 50 per cent lower in some of the central parts of the coalfield (Fig. 8.2A).

Any visitor walking or driving through some areas characterised by high industrial land values will be impressed by the large proportion of unused or derelict industrial land and it is difficult to understand how such land can command high values. Lawless (1981:24) suggests that this may arise because there are few sales of inner urban land to enable its true and diminishing value to emerge. The lack of sales tends to

reflect the special nature of land as an investment (essentially a long-term investment) and also the lack of interest in purchasing the land. Developers of industrial land (whether those providing sites for firms or firms developing their own sites) reject re-use of existing sites because of the high costs involved in assembling sufficiently large parcels of land and undertaking the site preparation costs. Greenfield peripheral sites are more attractive in cost and, generally, environmental setting. In Britain too, central land use patterns are stabilised as large areas of land are held by public authorities as part of redevelopment schemes. Yet industrialists are prepared to pay premiums for central rather than peripheral locations and in Sheffield, for example, new industrial plants can be rented (in 1984) for £1.50 per square foot per annum on the periphery but this rises to £2.00 in central areas.

Description of variations in rental patterns emphasises a change which is taking place in the way in which industrial premises are provided. At one time, because of the need for specialised features associated with specific industries, firms acquired sites and built for their own occupation. This is still the prevalent pattern for a firm extending any premises it already owns and indeed for industries with major investments in large and bulky capital equipment, as in aluminium smelting or iron and steel. Now many industries can fit within standardised single-storey premises and thus, increasingly, property developers have become involved in the provision of industrial property (Boddy 1983). Public authorities can be involved too as is discussed in Chapters 10 and 15. It is possible that at both regional and urban scale developers may be selective spatially in choosing locations for industrial estates or industrial parks (Barr 1983; Bale 1977). This may reflect both the propensity of a region or urban area to 'create' its own property development firms and variations in the spatial investment strategies of national property companies. Unfortunately, while the role of industrial property developers (both public and private) has attracted attention at the intra-urban scale the extent of variations at larger spatial scales still awaits exploration. Although little is known of the geography of industrial property development there do appear to be striking variations in building costs, land costs and rents within national economies which might be expected to influence spatial patterns of employment change in manufacturing industry.

Competition for land from competing uses can also be important, notably on the CBD periphery in urban areas. There are numerous examples of central area sites being vacated by manufacturing firms, particularly for office developments. Some of the best examples occur in the British brewing industry where the majority of firms with production facilities in inner London in the 1950s abandoned these facilities and sold or leased sites for property development. These closures have resulted in considerable losses of employment in the brewing industry in central London (Watts 1980b).

The constrained location hypothesis

More critical perhaps than rentals, price of land or building construction costs for the firm which wishes to extend its floor space is simply availability of convenient land. For many plants availability of land in the general area is irrelevant, what is required is land adjacent to the existing plant. Lack of such land can act as a restraint not only on extending production floor space but also on access, parking and introducing new technologies which it might be difficult to fit within existing site boundaries. The constraining role of urban sites is seen as playing a key role in explaining urban–rural shifts in employment in Britain. These shifts were discribed in Chapter 1.

Fothergill and Gudgin (1982:99) argue that 'the single overriding cause of the urban–rural shift in industrial location is the lack of space for physical expansion faced by a large proportion of factories in urban areas'. This is termed the *constrained location* hypothesis. Other explanations such as differences in labour market characteristics and in residential attractiveness are assigned minor or negligible roles. The shift in employment reflects two processes. First, firms in urban areas which desire to increase employment must,

because of their constrained sites, either forego growth or divert production elsewhere. Such diversion might be additional employment at more suitable plants in the corporate system or the establishment of a new branch plant. This does not result in job loss from urban areas but a slower growth in urban areas than elsewhere. Second, where there is no room for expansion and new equipment is introduced the new machinery displaces labour on the shop floor.

It is this major and rapid displacement of labour by capital which is the driving force behind the loss of manufacturing jobs in cities. The same displacement of labour by capital occurs on existing floor space in small towns...but their losses are offset by jobs created in new factories and factory extensions (Fothergill and Gudgin 1982:104–5).

This intuitively appealing argument does need empirical support, particularly evidence that urban locations are more constrained than rural ones. Such evidence is not widely available as it is difficult to obtain from published sources. Fothergill and Gudgin (1982:106–8) cite two pieces of evidence. First, examination of plants in the central area of Birmingham (United Kingdom) showed that in the mid-1970s around 70 per cent of those examined were on sites with no room for expansion and only 17 per cent had the possibility of expansion on site. No less than half the buildings in this study area completely covered the site they occupied. Second, as Table 8.1 shows the larger the city the higher the probability of a factory occupying a constrained location. It is based on the observation that a town 3.2 km across will have an area of about 775 hectares and circumference of approximately 10 km, but a city 16 km across will have an area of about 21,000 hectares (over 25 times larger than the smaller town) but its circumference will only be five times larger than the smaller town. Examination of the trends shown in Table 8.1 illustrates that the proportion of constrained locations decreases markedly as population size falls below 400,000 and falls dramatically as population falls below 35,000. These data support the arguments for the preponderance of constrained locations in larger cities but it is

Table 8.1 Hypothetical estimates of the proportion of
factories in constrained locations

Size of settlement		% of factories in constrained locations
Diameter (km)	Population* (000s)	
3.2	15	4
4.8	35	36
6.4	65	50
11.3	190	71
16.1	400	80
32.2	1,600	90
64.4	6,300	95

(*Source*: Fothergill and Gudgin 1982:107)
* Assuming 5,000 residents per 259 hectares.

perhaps important to remember that the Birmingham data relate to the period before the onset of the present recession and such a recession might offer more opportunities to purchase adjacent buildings previously occupied by failed firms.

The general evidence of the existence of restricted sites in larger centres supports the constrained location explanation of urban–rural shifts. More significantly, it is also supported by many of the other characteristics associated with those shifts. Employment loss has been greatest in the largest cities, that is those cities with the highest proportion of constrained sites. The urban–rural shift is an international phenomenon as is the increasing capital intensity and rising floor space per worker which is associated with it. The acceleration of the urban–rural shift after 1960 can be associated with the faster rise in capital intensity after 1960. Analysis of the components of the shift indicates that it is location of new jobs rather than the loss of old ones which accounts for the better employment record of the rural areas. The urban–rural contrast appears regardless of corporate status, urban areas constraining the growth of both independent plants and branch plants. However, very small plants perform as well in cities as in smaller towns but this can be explained by the fact that since small firms can readily move they are less constrained by their urban locations. Finally, there is some evidence that urban firms have

lower profitability than rural firms and this may reflect an inability to make full use of modern cost-reducing techniques in constrained sites and that industries with high levels of investment show urban–rural contrasts more clearly than industries with low levels of investment (Fothergill and Gudgin 1982:108–11).

Here then there is a very convincing explanation of the role of land, particularly land availability, in influencing the regional pattern of employment change. Keeble (1984:166) indeed argues that 'the current front runner in the debate amongst industrial geographers over ...causes... (of the urban–rural shift in the UK) ...is therefore undoubtedly constrained location theory'.

Yet in reading the evidence it all appears to fit together too neatly. Evaluation of the arguments and evidence indicates that the results are not as might seem on first reading. Much of the analysis is based very much upon interpolations of the experience of one region (the East Midlands) and sometimes on only one county (Leicestershire). Similarly, the causes often have to be inferred and much of the discussion is written in terms of 'possible factors' and 'plausible explanations'. There is also evidence to suggest that as the recession has deepened there is often unused space within existing factories. Healey and Clark (1984:309) note, for example, in Coventry that most job losses arose from massive *in situ* contraction and that some of the major losses have been recorded at larger plants in the outer city which have land available for extension of the premises. Finally, proximity to other plants and to producer services may be enhanced in urban areas thus reducing the attractiveness of a small town or rural location.

CONCLUSION

Capital and land as factors of production are, like labour, receiving increasing attention from industrial geographers in order to assess their influence on the geography of employment change. It is not at all clear whether the geography of financial institutions, especially those supplying venture capital, influences the employment patterns of market-system firms, nor indeed is very much known about the ways in which capital is raised in the branch plants of planning-system firms. Rather more is known about the role of land, particularly land availability, and strong arguments have been put for the important role of the constrained location hypothesis. While land can play a part in an explanation of regional shifts its role, particularly in explaining urban–rural shifts, needs further investigation. After all, rural areas contain the attractive residential environments (Ch. 5) as well as unorganised inexperienced labour (Ch. 7). What is more it might be that at least some of the rural areas offer uncongested access to highway networks, and it is questions of accessibility to markets and supplies that are taken up in the next chapter.

9

THE SUPPLY AND
MARKET CONTEXT

This penultimate chapter in the section on the context of change turns to what used to be seen as the major element in industrial geography and one which used to play an important part in explaining industrial location and, by implication, changes in the regional geography of employment in manufacturing industry. In studies of the contemporary geography of industrial change within a national economic system labour and land costs now occupy the centre of the stage. The main concern of this chapter is with an examination of spatial variations in accessibility to supplies and markets.

Introductory studies of economic geography (Bale 1981:46–67) at regional scale emphasise that transport costs play a key role in industrial location models which pre-date the development of inter-regional freeway/motorway networks. In these models location is determined by the relative location of suppliers, producers and buyers. With reference to these three groups the initial 'problem to be solved is how *transportation costs* influence the distribution of industries' (Weber 1929:41). Similarly, the examination of the locations of producers serving a dispersed set of buyers notes that 'the further away ... (from the producer) ... the price will naturally be higher by the amount of *the freight* and demand consequently will be smaller' (Lösch 1954:106). Each of these two cases and, indeed, some modern introductions to industrial location (Webber 1984:42–66) stress the critical role of transport or freight costs. Implicit too, in these models, is

the assumption that suppliers and producers adopt a pricing policy such that their products are sold at a factory price plus a transport charge reflecting the distance from supplier to factory or from factory to buyer. As Chisholm (1970:163) observes 'formal location theory seems ... to assume that this form of non-discriminatory pricing is usual, if not universal'.

Modern research tends to suggest that transport costs and non-discriminatory pricing play an important role in explaining locational change only in specific industries and at particular geographical scales of analysis. The beginning of this chapter examines the relationship between manufacturing plants and their supplies and markets, and illustrates the current role of transport costs and the nature of present-day pricing policies. The second part considers the roles of access to resources, intermediate goods and producer services through a consideration of linkages. The chapter concludes with an examination of those limited number of cases where patterns of locational change are influenced by competition for the markets or supplies of particular areas.

SUPPLY AND MARKET RELATIONSHIPS

Industrial activity, in its simplest form, takes one or more raw materials, transforms them by some kind of production process and then sells the finished product (Fig. 4.1). At the present time this kind of industry is relatively unimportant as

Table 9.1 Raw material and final market relationships

Category	Examples
First stage resource users producing for the non-final market	Bricks Oil refining
First stage resource users producing for the final market	Milk products Food canning
Second stage resource users producing for the non-final market	Steel tubes Artificial fibres
Second stage resource users producing for the final market	Bread Clothing
Industries for which resources are of indirect significance producing for the non-final market	Metal boxes Wires and cables
Industries for which resources are of indirect significance producing for the final market	Domestic electrical goods Motor vehicles

(*Source*: Duncan *et al.* 1960)

many plants depend upon purchases from other plants as their material inputs and sell semi-finished products to other plants for further processing. The varying degrees of dependence upon raw materials and final markets are shown in Table 9.1. The first stage resource users process raw materials from either mineral, agricultural or forest resources; the second stage resource users tend to utilise the outputs of the first stage, thus milling produces flour which is the input to the second stage resource-using industry, the baking of bread. The industries for which resources are of indirect significance tend to use the outputs of the second stage resource users. Thus steel ingots (first stage) are manufactured into steel sheets (second stage) which are then converted into metal boxes. The final market represents not only domestic consumers but any purchaser who uses the finished product in the form in which it is sold. One of the most important facets of this classification is that it picks out the first stage resource users and it is these industries which are among those having major transport inputs as is shown below.

Transport costs

Transport costs are the costs involved in moving goods to and from a plant and include payments to transport operators for services provided as

well as any costs incurred by the plant in operating its own fleet of vehicles. Apart from an occasional 'hiccup' caused by rises in oil prices the general tendency has been for transport costs to fall as a result of improvements in transport infrastructure and transport technology. Table 9.2 shows transport costs as a percentage of net output for 17 industries in the United Kingdom. Six of these industries incur costs above average (metal manufacture, chemicals, timber and coal/petroleum products) and in two cases (food and

Table 9.2 Transport costs as a percentage of net output, United Kingdom, 1968

Industry	Percentage
Bricks, pottery, glass cement	14.6
Food, drink and tobacco	13.7
Coal and petroleum products	8.8
Timber, furniture, etc.	7.5
Chemicals and allied industries	6.5
Metal manufacture	5.9
Paper, printing and publishing	5.5
Other manufacturing industries	4.4
Leather, leather goods and fur	4.2
Metal goods n.e.s.	4.1
Textiles	3.2
Clothing and footwear	3.1
Mechanical engineering	2.6
Vehicles	2.6
Electrical engineering	2.5
Instrument engineering	1.7
Shipbuilding and marine engineering	1.5

(*Source*: Business Statistics Office: 1972)

drink and bricks and pottery) the costs are more than twice the average. In the case of the bricks, pottery, glass and cement industry transport costs represent 14.6 per cent of net output. Care is needed in interpreting these results since the figures probably underestimate the role of transport costs in industries where transport costs are of major significance because existing locations may be those which allow the plants to minimise transport expenditures. These industries employed just under a third of manufacturing employees in Britain in 1981, thus just over two-thirds of British manufacturing employment is in industries where transport costs are of limited importance. In North America with its larger spatial extent transport costs may be more significant. Whereas the United States saw the dispersal of motor vehicle assembly operations to market locations to reduce delivery charges no such trend can be seen in the more restricted areas covered by the United Kingdom. However, Gough (1984) claims that even in this industry in North America regional markets are becoming less important for plant location.

Pricing policy

Two types of pricing policy predominate in the industrial system of the capitalist world.

1. *Free-on-board (f.o.b.) pricing.* This is where the buyer pays a price which includes the cost of the product plus the cost of loading on to freight vehicles at the point of sale but excludes the cost of transporting the goods from the point of sale to the buyer. It is because of this transport charge that the cost to the buyer increases as distance from the shipment point increases and thus demand will fall as distance increases.

2. *Uniform delivered pricing.* This is where the buyer pays the same price for the product regardless of location and thus demand will not be affected by distance from point of sale. It is sometimes referred to as *c.i.f.* (cost, insurance, freight) *pricing* but this term is most appropriate to an import/export context where prices are quoted c.i.f. a port or seaport. The great advantage of uniform deliver-

ed pricing is its simplicity for both seller and buyer. Instead of a multitude of delivered prices only one price has to be used, though this may, of course, be reduced for bulk orders.

These are not, of course, the only pricing systems and a firm can adopt a mix of pricing policies. Two other policies deserve special mention, both involving combination of the two basic forms. *Zonal pricing* is where prices are uniform within specific zones but vary between zones usually with reference to distance from the factory. *Basing-point prices* are where f.o.b. prices are charged from a series of 'base points' which may (or may not) include the plants manufacturing the product. Although this latter system was declared illegal in the United States in 1948, Moyes (1980:38) claims variants of basing-point pricing 'remain common, especially in capital intensive industries like cement...[and] iron and steel manufacture'. A full discussion of different pricing policies in their geographical context is provided by Chisholm (1970:163–94).

Where *suppliers* sell at a uniform delivered price the cost of supplies will not vary from place to place and there will be no transport cost advantages in expanding or retaining plants close to their suppliers. Proximity may offer some advantages in speed of delivery but the cost savings may be small. It is worth noting that where an input is purchased at a uniform delivered price it is, in Weber's terms, ubiquitous. Similarly, where *producers* sell at a uniform delivered price the most favoured plants will be those at the geographic centre of the market since proximity to large concentrations of demand may not increase sales to those concentrations. Just as reduced transport costs have removed some of the disadvantages of distance from suppliers or markets so the use of uniform delivered prices has reduced the advantages occurring to a plant which result from proximity to either suppliers or markets. There is, however, some debate as to how extensive uniform delivered prices are among manufacturing firms and their suppliers.

Chisholm (1970:177) concluded that 'in Britain, a country of small extent, uniform delivered prices are more usual than f.o.b....prices, except for a very limited range of basic commodities like...coking coal and stone'. More recently Norman (1981:87) noted that 'the use of uniform delivered prices for certain final products is neither new nor exceptional...[and] it would also appear from recent...reports that uniform delivered price systems are applied to a number of intermediate products'. In their conclusions on intermediate products both Chisholm and Norman relied to a large extent upon evidence presented in cases relating to industries with highly oligopolistic market structures and thus their results may not be generalisable across a wider range of industries. Drawing upon survey evidence from firms with significant freight costs (and thus most likely to use f.o.b. pricing) Greenhut (1981:79) confirmed that 'f.o.b. pricing is the exception rather than the rule' with its being applied by only 18 per cent of the surveyed firms in Japan, 21 per cent in West Germany and 33 per cent in the United States. The higher proportion in the United States may reflect the wide spatial extent of the United States market and the influence of the Robinson–Patman Act which attempted to control price discrimination. In all cases less than one-third of the firms used f.o.b. pricing suggesting that models based on such pricing may be unimportant. Uniform delivered prices were characteristic of 21 per cent of United States' firms, 27 per cent of Japanese and 32 per cent of West German – the other 50 per cent of firms tending to use mixed pricing systems. Since these figures relate to high freight cost industries only (which are less likely to use uniform delivered prices) the proportion of firms using uniform delivered prices is likely to be well over half.

These conclusions relate to firms and may, in the market system, apply to plants but the evidence appears to be drawn primarily from planning-system firms. The planning-system firm may sell its products at a uniform delivered price but very little is known of the pricing systems which apply within multi-plant firms operating within national economies. Their transfer pricing policies (Ch. 2) await detailed enquiry. How, for example, would the movement of parts from a plant in Ohio to another plant in Texas be costed? Is it a charge on the Ohio plant, the Texas plant or shared between them? Decisions like this in a planning-system firm with high transport inputs can clearly affect the viability of individual plants.

LINKAGES

Each manufacturing plant is supplied with material inputs and manufactures a product which is distributed to a plant's markets. These flows of inputs and outputs are called *material linkages*. In addition each plant receives inputs from *producer services* (financial and legal advice and plant maintenance contracts are examples) called *service linkages*. In this way each individual plant is tied into the economic system by material and service linkages. Only a brief indication of the scope of linkage studies is possible here as they have developed into a specialised sub-field of industrial geography (McDermott and Taylor 1982). However, it seems reasonable to argue that a plant's employment record can be influenced by the extent to which it can readily draw upon suppliers of materials and services in the local area and can serve markets in the local area.

In industries which are first stage resource users, and these are industries which tend to have high transport inputs compared with the all industry average (Table 9.2), the distribution and availability of resources may have a critical influence on industrial change. Raw material inputs to manufacturing activity are drawn from two broad sectors of economic activity, 'agriculture, forestry and fishing' and 'mining and quarrying'. Here too, it is possible in include fuel and power resources some of which influence locational change in a similar way to raw materials. At any one time the distribution of raw materials and fuel and power resources adopts a particular spatial configuration which imposes important constraints upon the rate of employment change in industries which rely upon them. Growth can be limited by the acreage or yield of a particular crop while in the medium term the output of mines and quarries is limited by the

available technology. Similarly, industrial decline might be precipitated by changes in the
distribution of particular crops, while fishing,
forest and mineral resources can be depleted.

In most advanced countries raw materials are
not only drawn from within the country but are
also imported. Thus from the viewpoint of the
manufacturing sector the system of seaports represents an important potential source of *raw
materials*. The nature of the materials imported
through particular ports will be influenced by
the maximum size of vessel the port can handle,
the prevailing size of ship used for particular
commodities and whether or not specialist
handling facilities are required and are available.
In a few cases (notably oil refining and ore
importing) firms develop their own port facilities
but, in the short to medium term the location of
ports, and thus resource inputs, can be regarded
as fixed.

Firms which are second stage resource users or
firms for which resources are only of indirect
significance are unlikely to be influenced by the
geographical distribution of resources; for these
industries, if access to material supplies is important, it is access to the distribution of industries which serve non-final demand. Emphasis
has already been placed (Ch. 3) on the inherited
spatial pattern of industrial activity and this has
a major influence on the distribution of industries supplying intermediate goods.

All industries, whatever their material sources,
also depend upon service linkages. The distribution of *producer services* is still an under-explored
area (the lack of knowledge concerning financial
institutions and property development companies was seen in the last chapter) but they
appear to be tied closely to the characteristics of
the urban system, occurring more frequently in
larger urban centres and in centrally located
regions. Just like the distribution of industrial
activities the location and size of different centres
within the urban system show a fair degree of
stability in the short to medium term. Whereas
in the past industrial activities, particularly in
the nineteenth century in Europe and in the late
nineteenth and early twentieth centuries in
North America, played an important role in

determining the location of urban growth, at the
present time industrial activity tends to make
adjustments within the existing urban framework.

External economies of scale

The advantages which a plant derives from a
location within an existing urban or industrial
centre are termed *external economies of scale*, that is
they arise outside the plant itself. Internal economies of scale were discussed in Chapter 6.
External and internal economies of scale are in
some cases treated together as *agglomeration
economies*. Geographical analysis divides external
economies into *urbanisation economies* (cost-savings
resulting from an urban location) and *localisation
economies*. The existence of these economies contributes particularly to the significance of *in situ*
growth discussed in Chapter 13.

Localisation economies result from the spatial
proximity of other plants supplying materials or
buying products and can be extended to include
proximity to research centres, labour training
establishments and pools of skilled labour associated with a particular sectoral or, more recently, occupational specialisation. An examination
of localisation economies in the American carpet
industry (Walters and Wheeler 1984) while
stressing the importance of material linkages also
drew attention to the importance of the proximity of machinery suppliers (to reduce delays
caused by servicing requirements) and access to
skilled labour. The influence of labour factors
has usually been treated separately (Ch. 7) and
it is material linkages that have proved to be the
most readily measurable part of localisation
economies.

There is some evidence that material flows
between industries are characteristic of some
industries found in close proximity to one another. Lever (1972) shows that the linkages between the engineering and metal industries are
accompanied by spatial association. Thus the
distribution of motor vehicles is similar to the
distribution of machine tools with which it is
joined by a material linkage. However, not all
spatially associated industries are accompanied

by linkages. Although science-based industries occur together in similar areas only the scientific instruments and radio industry have any material links. Although it can be argued that the existence of linkages gives rise to the spatial association of industries it is also possible to argue that the flows have arisen because of the spatial association. While the direction of causation is not clear there is other evidence to suggest that industries found in the same region are often linked together by flows of materials.

For manufacturing, as a whole, local linkages may be of little significance. A study of Philadelphia concluded that 65.5 per cent of the industries purchased their largest input from non-local sources (Karaska 1969:358). Yet, for small market-system firms dependence on local sources may be high. Among the small firms in the West Midlands metal-manufacturing industry in Britain only 10 per cent of the drop forgers' purchases of materials came from outside the area and only 8 per cent of the lock and latch manufacturers' purchases of materials (Taylor and Wood 1973:133). More significantly, Peck (1985) shows that metal-working plants in urban areas subcontract more work than plants in isolated rural areas, while in high-technology firms in the San Francisco bay area over 60 per cent of the firms purchased more than 50 per cent of their inputs from within a 48 km radius. It is perhaps worth noting that this dependence on local linkages in this successful area is much higher than among similar firms in Scotland and South-East England (Oakey 1984a:78).

Clearly, some plants in some industries do rely on local inputs but the influence of the availability and cost of such inputs upon employment growth and decline is not well established although the existence of beneficial effects is often asserted. It is not difficult to establish whether employment growth is faster (or loss slower) in regional concentrations of particular industries in comparison with isolated pockets of industrial activity. Reference back to the discussion of Fig. 1.6 shows that in the hosiery industry in Britain net gains were most marked in the major regional concentration but in the electronics industry the concentrations were associated with net losses.

The focus of most studies of localisation economies upon material linkages does perhaps underplay the role of other elements, such as access to specialised educational and research centres. Yet by including these elements within the concept of localisation economies it becomes almost impossible to separate localisation economies from the more general urbanisation economies.

Urbanisation economies are associated with urban places and the larger the urban place the greater will be the urbanisation economies. It is also possible to envisage the development of *urbanisation diseconomies* and that the larger the urban place the more marked the diseconomies. Although at any one time urbanisation economies or urbanisation diseconomies may appear to predominate the actual costs of operating in urban areas will reflect both the economies and diseconomies.

At the present time most interest is centred upon the diseconomies associated with an urban location for a manufacturing plant. In the recent past, as Chapter 1 demonstrated, there has been a net loss of employment from more urbanised areas indicative perhaps of the powerful influence of these diseconomies. A convincing case, discussed in Chapter 8, has been presented to support the view that constricted urban sites had some responsibility for employment losses in major urban areas in the 1970s. Despite the apparent strength of urbanisation diseconomies in urban areas evidence of the continued existence of some urbanisation economies is not difficult to find.

Urbanisation economies are those savings available to a manufacturing plant in an urban area which arise in part from the availability and close proximity of services drawn from the *non-manufacturing sector*. These producer services include high-order activities (such as auditing, stockbroking, advertising agencies and provision of venture capital) and low-order activities (such as pay-roll banking, industrial cleaning and electrical maintenance). Only larger urban centres will be able to offer the high-order producer services and the lack of firms providing venture capital has been seen as a possible influence upon the poor innovation performance of market system firms in certain areas (Ch. 6). Further advantages may accrue to a plant as a result of the availability of a large labour supply and the whole developed urban infrastructure of roads, industrial estates, and older buildings which can be adapted for industrial use.

Although the geographical literature has not displayed convincingly the *cost* advantages of an urban location it has shown how plants in urban areas are able to draw upon local services whereas those elsewhere are forced to seek service inputs from more distant locations. An example of such work is provided by the study of the service links of industrial plants in south-east Ontario. Of interest in this context are auditing, major banking services (e.g. loans for capital expenditure), financial services (e.g. stockbrokers) and legal services. Among the Toronto plants local links predominated, but in the non-Toronto plants only in one case did the percentage of plants having links with the local area reach 50 per cent. The tendency for Toronto links to replace local ones was evident across all four services in non-Toronto plants (Britton 1974).

Although there is evidence to suggest that plants can depend upon the area in which they are set for inputs of both materials and services, there are differences between planning-system and market-system firms. Very often the plants of planning-system firms substitute intra-firm links for local ones. For example, Hoare (1978) shows that in Northern Ireland's engineering and metal industries plants owned by firms based outside Northern Ireland received only 13.5 per cent of their material inputs from the local region in contrast to 47 per cent for independent plants; while in the Northern region of Britain, Marshall (1979:546) shows that the major supplier of business services to 73 per cent of the independent plants was in the Northern region but this was true of only 20–25 per cent of the externally owned plants. These constrasts owe much to intra-firm linkages. Britton's (1976: 314) study of plants in the Toronto region showed that many United States owned plants depended upon intra-company links with the United States and similar results showing a dependence on corporate sources for both services and materials is seen in Northern Ireland (Hoare 1978). For planning-system firms it may be the case that 'the achievement of economies within the firm can be more important [than] economies deriving from the proximity of suppliers in the same agglomeration' (Gilmour 1974:356).

ACCESSIBILITY TO SUPPLIES AND MARKETS

The evidence of the effects of localisation economies and urbanisation economies has tended to place emphasis (at least in linkage terms) on access to materials and producer services. In contrast, studies of accessibility have stressed access to markets, although there is no reason why similar approaches could not be adopted to examine access to a spatially dispersed system of suppliers as is found, for example, in many food processing industries.

In industries oriented to local markets or supplies a key question is whether local markets/supplies are sufficient to support a plant of minimum efficient scale. Similar arguments apply at regional scale. For these industries, as for many retail outlets, there are critical *thresholds* which have to be exceeded before a plant of minimum efficient scale can be established. Conversely where local markets or supplies fall it may no longer be possible for a region to support a plant. There is some evidence that particular industries need particular population levels to survive. This is demonstrated clearly at urban level by Hoover (1971:157–8). The manufacture of fur goods and bookbinding, for example, is markedly over-represented in SMSAs with populations in excess of over one-half a million persons. However, it is difficult to separate out the market orientation effect from the effects of the availability of labour (Fig. 6.5 and Ch. 7).

Where a sufficient market (or supply of materials) exists questions of accessibility to that market become important since markets are usually spread over geographical areas. Studies of market accessibility focus on either the potential transport cost or market potential surfaces. The former is a cost surface (supplementing, for example, labour and land-cost surfaces) while the latter is a revenue surface and indicates spatial variations in potential revenues (Ch. 5).

When a plant sells at a uniform delivered price it is possible to estimate the cost of serving a market from a given point (Appendix II). Two examples of a *potential transport cost (PTC) surface* are shown in Fig. 9.1A. The figures show the

minimum transport point for serving either a British or United States market and also the variations in cost around that point. Similar maps can be constructed to show the cost of serving specified regional markets such as the Middle Atlantic region. While there appears to be little relationship between the PTC surface and the distribution of manufacturing activity (Ray 1965:84–8; Rich 1978) there do not appear to have been any attempts to relate it to patterns of change and most emphasis has been placed

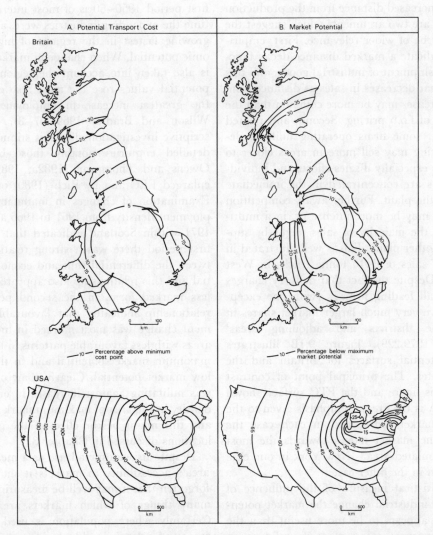

Fig. 9.1 Accessibility to national final market in Britain and to the national manufacturing market in the United States (A) Potential transport costs (B) Market potential (*Sources*: Harris 1954:346; Gudgin 1978:22; Clark 1966: 11)

upon measures of market potential.

The *market potential surface* (sometimes called population potential when markets are measured by population or economic potential when measured by regional income) describes the relative demand at particular locations within a given market area (Appendix II). Critical to an understanding of the model is the assumption that demand decreases as distance from point of sale increases. Although this pattern of demand is most likely in firms operating f.o.b. pricing policies since the total price to the consumer rises with increased distance from the production plant there are two arguments which suggest the model may be of wider relevance. First, empirical data indicate a marked distance decay function in the shipment of industrial goods, and this indicates that decreases in sales as distance from a plant increases may be more common than the occurrence of f.o.b pricing. Second, and related to the first, some firms operating uniform delivered pricing may sell more in areas closer to their plants especially if sales efforts and individual contacts are concentrated in the immediate vicinity of the plant. Further away, competition from rivals may be more intense or, in a multiplant firm, the majority of sales might be supplied by another plant. This is well illustrated in the case of sales of 8–16 tonne trucks in West Germany. Despite the fact that delivery charges are small 'all leading firms...[with one exception]...have very much larger market shares in their home districts and adjoining areas' (Dorward 1979:229). Figure 9.1B illustrates market potential surfaces for Britain and the United States. The principal point of contrast between this figure and the PTC surface shown in Fig. 9.1A is the greater emphasis given to the principal market centre and in each case the centre of the market moves towards the most densely populated area – New York in one case and London in the other case.

As a statistical measure of the influence of markets on industrial change the market potential surface appears to be more useful than the potential transport cost surface if usefulness is assessed in terms of producing a high correlation coefficient. Both Rich (1978) and Beattie and Watts (1983) indicate very high levels of association between industrial activity and market potential in cross-sectional studies and it has become the variable most widely used to measure access to markets.

The association between market potential and employment change was probably first explored in relation to the EEC from 1950 to 1960 and from 1960 to 1965. Since the latter period saw the strengthening of regional policies (Ch. 15) mainly in areas of low market potential and thus making interpretation of the results difficult, the first period 1950–60 is of most interest. At this time the expanding industries were, as expected, growing fastest in the regions of highest economic potential. When change in market potential is also taken into account the regions in which potential values rose the most also experienced the greatest increase in employment (Clark, Wilson and Bradley 1969:207–8). Purely descriptive investigations like this stimulated more detailed enquiries notably those by Keeble, Owens and Thompson (1982a, 1982b) of the enlarged EEC and by Rich (1980) of Scotland. Examination of changes in manufacturing employment density from 1961 to 1966 and 1966 to 1971 within Scotland indicated that within the first period there was a strong relationship between the differential shift and economic potential and this relationship also appeared, but in a less marked form, in the second period. This relationship indicated that favourable employment change was most marked in 'near centre' areas with less favourable patterns in the areas of maximum market potential and in the areas of low market potential. Clearly some other factor was militating against increases in employment density in the area of maximum market potential and this might be the effect of the constrained locations discussed in Chapter 8.

Despite its widespread use as a measure of an area's accessibility to markets it should not be forgotten that it may well be measuring access to many things of which markets are only one. Certainly where population is used as a surrogate of sales it could also be interpreted as measuring access to labour supplies and to the localisation economies and urbanisation economies described earlier in this chapter. It therefore 'makes little sense to interpret measures of [market] potential simply as indices of accessibility to the market' (Rich 1978:223). Unfortunately once this is recognised there is such a mish-mash of factors within the market potential concept that it becomes very difficult to interpret at all! Further, to argue that favourable levels of employment change in association with high scores on a market potential index reflects access to markets is a very dubious exercise, unless the market has been defined carefully in relation to the demand for the products supplied by the industries, firms or plants being considered.

INTER-RELATIONSHIPS BETWEEN PLANTS

The potential transport cost and market potential surfaces assume that the market is given and thus that the location of a firm's markets and the markets of its competitors are fixed. Where competition between firms for market share has no direct spatial element, the proportion of a firm's total markets in each area may remain stable despite fluctuations in the absolute size of its markets, but where firms are competing directly for particular spatial markets (for example, in soft drinks or brewing) or for particular spatial supplies (for example, in timber processing

or agricultural processing industry) locational changes and market (supply) shares may influence one another.

It is very difficult to depict the market and supply areas of different plants as the markets (and supply areas) of different plants overlap (Watts 1975) but it is possible to describe them in general terms using data relating to the distances over which particular industrial commodities are hauled. Table 9.3 shows the percentage of hauls under 50 km in Britain in 1981. Clearly, industries towards the top of the list will have more restricted market or supply areas than those towards the bottom of the list. In planning-system firms operating multi-plant systems much clearer lines are drawn between the market or supply areas of the individual plants of the firm although, of course, these overlap with those of rival firms. The supply areas of British Sugar's sugar-beet processing plant in eastern England typify this kind of system (Fig. 9.2).

The interaction between the market and supply areas of different firms can be examined in one of two ways (Greenhut 1956:25–42) although the distinction between them is not always clearly made.

1. *The locational interdependence framework.* This stresses the attraction or repulsion of a plant caused by the presence (actual or expected) of a rival at a specific location and raises ques-

Table 9.3 Commodities and length of haul by road, Britain, 1981

	Length of haul Percentage (by weight) less than 50 km
Crude minerals	80
Coal and coke	77
Building materials	69
Ores	63
Petrol and petroleum products	56
Machinery and transport equipment	55
Food, drink and tobacco	49
Crude materials	47
Wood, timber, cork	45
Iron and steel products	43
Fertilisers	41
Other metal products	41
Miscellaneous manufactures	33
Chemicals	29

(*Source*: Department of Transport (1982) *Transport Statistics, 1971–81*)

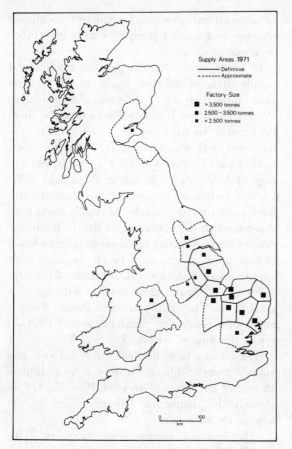

Supply Areas 1971
—— Definitive
----- Approximate

Factory Size
■ > 3.500 tonnes
■ 2.500 – 3.500 tonnes
■ < 2.500 tonnes

0   100
km

Fig. 9.2 Supply areas of sugar-beet processing plant, 1971 (*Source*: Watts 1974:14)

tions as to whether the pattern of plants to serve a specific area will be dispersed or concentrated.

2. *The market area framework.* In contrast to the previous framework, market area analysis does not consider factors influencing the concentration of industrial plants and its framework assumes that plants are never attracted to sites close to their rivals and that in every case a dispersed pattern will be evident.

The locational interdependence framework sees dispersion of plants as a possibility; the market area framework argues dispersion is inevitable. Although in both frameworks plants are assumed to be spatial monopolists, the ideas have been applied to plants that buy all the available sup-

plies in a particular supply area and, thus, are spatial monopsonists.

Locational interdependence

Although proponents of this framework have developed conceptually elegant theories from Hotelling (1929) to Hay (1976) there has been little empirical verification of either the processes or the pattern they produce, at least in the context of the spatial distribution of manufacturing industry. This is not to argue that interdependence effects are unimportant but that these situations, at the present time, are best studied by how firms actually behave in oligopolistic situations.

A concern with the spatial outcomes of interdependence has been particularly evident in the international spread of industrial activities (Ch. 2, page 28) but interdependence can operate at the regional scale too. Unfortunately, it is extremely difficult to study these effects at this scale especially because in contemporary firms they form a very sensitive part of business policy and so in a number of cases industrial geographers have drawn upon historical evidence to illustrate some of the processes at work.

The most obvious examples of interdependence arise where firms actively compete to establish plants or acquire plants in specific areas to capture a specific market. In the first case, new employment opportunities are created but in the second the employment outcomes are more equivocal (Ch. 13). This kind of competition can be illustrated by both the meat-packing and sugar-beet processing industries. In the early twentieth century Chicago meat-packing firms were able to retain employment in the Chicago area, at least in the short run, by restricting access to desirable stockyard sites in the cattle areas so that new processing firms found it difficult to find appropriate sites (Aduddel and Cain 1973). Similarly, in the early 1900s, the principal beet-sugar firm in the United States was controlling new entrants to the industry 'by judiciously supplying capital funds...to turn what might have been an antagonistic interest into a docile appendage of...[its] own industrial empire' (Eichner 1969:229) and at the same time it 'sought to prevent other groups from invading ...[its]...territory with beet-sugar factories of their own...[and through]...strategic moves was able to forestall the building of several other projected factories' (Eichner 1969:239). These two examples relate to supply areas but other empirical evidence has identified similar competitive behaviour for markets in the British brewing industry in the 1960s (Watts 1980b: 184–213) while Mandell's (1975:12) study of Detroit firms found that firms whose competitors had changed location in the last ten years thought a move was more probable than those whose competitors had not moved.

In addition to direct and open competition there is little doubt that in the past (and indeed at present) various forms of collusive behaviour have influenced spatial patterns of change. Many such forms of behaviour are illegal and, therefore, difficult to identify. The best examples of such behaviour are market share agreements where two firms divide a market between them with each having a monopoly in an agreed area. Such agreements allow, for example, the planning of corporate production sytems without fear of competition from a firm's major rivals. A contemporary example is provided by a case in South-East England where regular (but illegal) price fixing meetings were held in public houses and directors' homes. These agreements in the ready-mix concrete industry also included definition of the markets which the firms could supply and, effectively, new firms were prevented from entering the industry. Subsequent enquiries revealed these agreements were characteristic of much of the industry in the late 1970s (Watts 1980c:313). Collusive behaviour, it appears, may be more widespread at the present time than is commonly supposed, despite attempts at government control.

Agreements which divide supply areas have also been traced and can be used to illustrate the way in which collusive agreements have had a direct influence on the location of new plants. In the 1920s two major firms were competing to obtain sugar beet in eastern England. Following considerable disputes when two plants were lo-cated rather close together possibly to 'steal' each other's supplies, the two firms reached agreement that in future they would not come within 30 miles (48 km) of each other's operations (Watts 1980c:301). New plants were built just beyond the agreed 48 km limits. It is interesting that agreements like this which are designed to encourage dispersal of plants produce spatial patterns which are similar to those suggested by the market area framework.

Market areas

The classic analysis of the relationship between market areas and plant location patterns in a single industry is provided by Lösch (1954:105–14) and discussed in a number of introductory texts (Bale 1981:63–5). Although Lösch's analysis was not concerned primarily with change it argues the market will be supplied by a system of regularly spaced plants and that the density of those plants increases as the industry develops until an equilibrium solution is reached. The equilibrium pattern (Fig. 9.3A) reflects the balance between economies of scale in the individual plant (Ch. 6) and either distribution costs (where markets are important) or material assembly costs (where supplies are important).

It is also possible to adapt this framework to show what might happen if demand remained stable but either transport costs decreased to allow plants to serve larger areas or the minimum efficient scale increased, allowing economies of scale to offset any increases in distribution costs which could arise from larger plants serving larger areas (Figs 9.3B and 9.3C). The effects would, of course, be even more marked if both transport costs fell and the m.e.s. increased and would be more complex still if patterns of demand changed. Although the number of plants falls, capacity is not cut and the changes see the concentration of employment in a limited number of large plants. A pattern seen, for example, in Chapter 2 in the reorganisation of multinational production systems from one plant per country to one plant per continent.

Of course, in reality the analysis of change will not show such regular patterns since they will

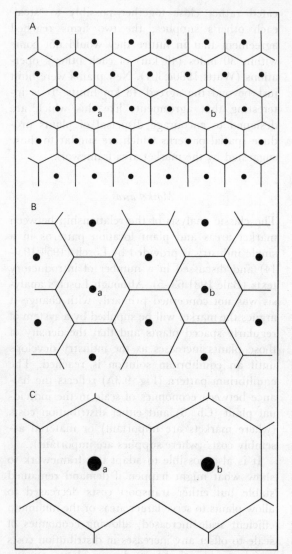

Fig. 9.3 Plant location patterns and market (supply) areas

occur only if all plants are a similar size (or grow to a similar size), if market (or supplies) are evenly distributed and if firms act in an economically rational manner. However, it does not seem unreasonable to expect a tendency towards the pattern shown in Fig. 9.3 which sees a trend from plants oriented to local markets to plants oriented to larger regional markets. A good example of this process can be seen in the British brewing industry. In the mid-nineteenth century

the majority of plants were oriented towards the urban areas in which they were located; in the 1980s market orientation remains but most of the larger plants are oriented towards major regional markets. This emphasises the difficulty of the term 'market orientation' towards which attention was drawn in the preamble to this section.

Market area analysis in its traditional form assumes industries made up of single-plant firms, yet there is within the analysis much of help in understanding the distribution of plants belonging to a single firm operating in a single industry with high transport costs. In these firms the number of their plants and market areas reflect the interaction between economies of scale and transport costs. The larger the plant the lower the average cost of each unit of production but, *ceteris paribus*, the larger the output the greater the radius of the area in which it is sold and hence the higher will be the transport costs. Small plants will have high production costs and low transport costs; large plants will have low production costs and high transport costs. The optimum solution for the firm is where total costs (production and transport) are minimised (Gough 1984). Mathematical solutions to what is known as the 'depot location problem' are widely used in industry and have attracted the attention of industrial geographers.

In their simplest forms these models adapt the PTC model to calculate the optimal solution for 1, 2, 3...*n* sites to serve a national market (Tornqvist *et al.* 1971). For example, Fig. 9.4A compares the plant locations of Anheuser-Busch with a minimum cost transportation solution. As Leamer (1968:236) observes 'the similarity between the actual and the equilibrium locations suggests that Anheuser-Busch responds to locational pressures similar to the ones suggested in...[the] model'. This study does not allow for the fact that as the number of plants increases, average plant size falls and unit costs rise. It is therefore necessary to include internal economies of scale in the calculation.

These were included by Osleeb and Cromley (1978) who calculated an optimal solution to the production–distribution problem faced by Coca-Cola in south-western Ontario. This is shown in

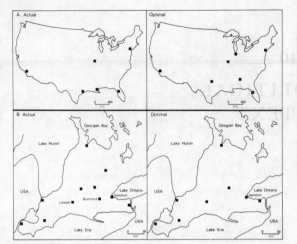

Fig. 9.4 Optimal and actual location patterns (A) Anheuser-Busch c. 1965 (B) Coca-Cola, 1961 (*Sources*: (A) Leamer 1968:238 (B) Osleeb and Cromley 1978: 48)

Fig. 9.4B. No less than seven of the actual 11 locations were replicated in the optimal solution when locations were selected from among 143 potential sites. It would thus appear that in this firm details of its markets, economies of scale and distribution costs are good predictors of its

spatial pattern. More significant to the theme of this discussion is that where optimal and actual patterns do not coincide locational adjustments may take place. For example, the Brantford plant mid-way between Hamilton and London which did not appear in the optimal solution was eventually closed by Coca-Cola. The closure of intervening plants and the widening of a plant's market are characteristics of the behaviour of planning-system firms operating in these industries. Further examples of the widening markets of individual plants in fluid milk processing and auto-assembly are provided by Gough (1984).

CONCLUSION

While there is little doubt that access to supplies and markets and the locational interdependence and market area frameworks provide some insight into the influences which operate upon the changing distribution of employment opportunities it is necessary to be reminded that these ideas are appropriate to only a limited range of firms and industries. This is in marked contrast to the all pervading influence of the political system discussed in the next chapter.

10

THE POLITICAL CONTEXT

It is impossible to ignore the political context within which changes in the geography of employment in manufacturing industry are set. By examining the interaction between politics and industrial geography, industrial geography is drawn into the increasingly important research area which lies at the interface between political and economic geography (Dear and Clark 1978).

Political groups in advanced capitalist economies exert power primarily through the apparatus of the state. Among political groups which exercise power in the capitalist state there are broadly two different views of the role that the state should play in economic activities. One group sees government's (i.e. the state's) role as protective which means that it sets a minimum number of rules to ensure that the market economy functions smoothly and efficiently. The second group sees government as a productive institution which should become involved in key activities and should provide support for 'victims' of the market economy. Such a view necessarily results in a much higher level of government intervention in economic affairs. Since governments change from time to time and since governments rarely countermand in their entirety the decisions of previous administrations western economies are the product of succeeding interventionist and non-interventionist policies.

While past patterns of government behaviour form part of the framework within which change takes place, the immediate context must reflect the view of the group in power at the time that change occurs. Thus Republican governments in the United States and Conservative governments in the United Kingdom reduce the level of state intervention while the Democrats in the United States and the Labour (Socialist) governments in the United Kingdom tend to increase it. It is fluctuations in the popularities of these different parties as reflected in election outcomes which are an important influence on the degree of intervention in the industrial system during a particular time period.

The government of an area represents the actions of not one authority but several authorities. Whereas Britain is characterised mainly by a three-tier structure (national, county and district) the pattern in the United States is much more fragmented and, for example, an average SMSA will be under the control of a state, two or more counties, 13 townships and 21 municipalities (House 1983b:74). Beyond recognising the hierarchical structure of government in any particular area it is difficult to generalise about the kind of intervention at each level because the powers available to different levels of government vary between and within countries and over time. The powers of lower tier authorities are often restricted by the higher tier authorities. In Britain, county and district authority activities are constrained severely by central government and these constraints, at the present time, are a major source of conflict.

Taking all levels of government together intervention can occur in most of the factors discussed in previous chapters in this section. Policies can be aimed at encouraging the adoption of innovations, can be involved in changing the characteristics of labour markets and can be designed to provide capital and land for industrial development. Intervention is perhaps less evident in the supply and market context, although here too it can work indirectly, for example, through improvements in the transport infrastructure. A listing of the policies in operation at one point in time is rapidly outdated but it is important to indicate the type and range of policy measures that may have influenced either directly of indirectly the geography of industrial change.

Three types of policy can be distinguished:
1. *Implicit spatial policies*. These are policies which are not normally thought of as having a spatial outcome and would include such areas as defence policy and merger policy.
2. *Derived spatial policies*. These arise when different lower tier governments pursue different industrial policies such that, for example, one authority may take an active attitude to industrial development whereas another may discourage it.
3. *Explicit spatial policies*. These occur wherever a particular tier of government targets its policies deliberately on one group of areas rather than another, examples being regional policies (usually financial aid to one region rather than another) and urban policies (aid to urban areas rather than non-urban areas).

This three-fold categorisation provides a useful basis upon which to build a discussion of policy but they are interdependent. A cut in navy spending may lead to employment loss in a particular naval shipyard (implicit spatial policy) which leads to the local tier authority to enhance its industrial policy above that of its neighbours (derived spatial policy) while a higher tier authority may designate the area as one to which it will direct regional aid (explicit spatial policy).

Explicit spatial policies are decreasing in importance and the discussion below focuses upon the implicit and derived spatial policies since they have not previously received the attention they deserve. Explicit spatial policies are considered fully in Chapter 15 which illustrates the extent to which the state can, if it so desires, deliberately divert employment opportunities from one area to another.

IMPLICIT SPATIAL POLICY

Virtually all economic policies have some kind of spatial impact. Policies aimed at one sector rather than another influence employment levels in the areas where the aided sector is concentrated; strategies designed to help small firms can have more impact in areas where small firms are dominant; decisions to 'privatise' public sector industries have spin-off effects on employment in towns and regions where the public sector firms are represented. Similarly, national programmes for modernisation of industry and re-training of labour can have a differential spatial impact through regional variations in the extent to which these programmes are taken up at local level. More specifically, there are hints of spatial impacts in environmental protection policy (Stafford 1977; Chapman 1980; Rees and Weinstein 1983:242–8) and in the activities of the Industrial Reorganisation Corporation in Britain (Massey and Meegan 1979) but it is the defence industry which has attracted most attention.

Defence expenditure

Defence expenditure takes several forms. In the United States, almost half goes on pay and pensions to the armed forces, another fifth goes on construction work, provision of services to military installations and research but 30 per cent is spent on 'military prime supply contracts'. Overall, the Department of Defence is 'the world's largest single customer purchasing 15 per cent of all American manufacturing products' (Johnston 1980:17). It is through its purchasing policy for military equipment that the Department of Defence is able to influence the order books, and hence the employment levels, of individual firms.

Isolation of the effects of this defence spending

is not easy. Defence expenditures are not decided in isolation from other spending and an increase or decrease in the Defence budget may cause employment change in defence related industries but such increases/decreases may be paralleled by changes in the spending of other government departments which may themselves have spatial impacts. Ideally these impacts should be set against the defence-related changes in order to calculate the net effects of a change in the Defence budget. Similar difficulties arise in assessing the consequences of a loss or a gain of a defence contract on a particular firm. Obtaining a defence contract may lead a firm to abandon plans to diversify into other activities, while the loss of a defence contract might be accompanied by an active search for new markets to compensate for lost defence sales. In either case the effects of changes in the defence budget would be damped down. Even if these problems can be overcome it is important to recognise that contracts are awarded to firms and the firms rather than the Defence Department influence the allocation of work to both plants within the firm and to subcontractors outside it. This latter point is particularly important because most of the defence-related firms belong to the planning system and hence have the multi-plant multi-regional operations which are characteristic of that system.

The very large firms which produce hardware for defence purposes make up the production side of the *military–industrial complex*. This complex consists predominantly of firms operating in four industries – radio and TV communication equipment, aircraft, guided missiles and space vehicles and aircraft engines and engine parts. Within these industries the ten largest suppliers of manufactured products to the military in 1979 and 1980 accounted for about 30 per cent of all prime contracts awards (including prime contracts for services, construction and research). Some of these firms are highly dependent on sales to the defence sector. For example in 1980, General Dynamics, McDonnell Douglas and Grumman sold over half their output to the Defence Department. Further, these and other similar large firms in the defence industries find that their overseas markets are constrained by the government's policy as to which countries are acceptable or unacceptable as buyers of armaments from the United States.

Clearly, the spatial impacts of changes in defence expenditure will be influenced by the distribution of the industries of the military–industrial complex and the firms operating within them. While the overall pattern may reflect very broadly the industrial distribution, the detail is moulded both by the relative success of different firms in obtaining contracts and the way in which the work received is allocated to plants both within and outside the firm. In the long term the spatial pattern of defence purchases can be influenced by changes in the mix of products being purchased. The shift from automotive products (tanks, armoured vehicles, for example) to missile and aircraft systems in the 1960s resulted in the movement of contracts from auto-firms in the mid-West to newer industries in the West and South-West.

The distribution of prime contracts of over $500,000 in 1979 shows that 70 per cent of them were concentrated in ten states which had only 46 per cent of the United States population. In many cases the pattern reflects the location of single firms such as McDonnell Douglas in Missouri and Boeing in Washington. The other states involved in the South and West were California, Texas and Florida while in the manufacturing belt New York, Massachusetts, Connecticut, Pennsylvania and Michigan made up the ten. Although over 50 per cent of this prime contract work may be subcontracted out there is a tendency for such work to be subcontracted locally (a result in part of spatial concentrations of defence-oriented firms) or for it to go to other prime contract firms on a *quid-pro-quo* basis. Overall, because of these factors there is only a limited dispersion of activity through subcontracting, but it is possible to detect a bias towards the manufacturing belt in subcontracting activities. Texas and Florida subcontract substantial portions of work to Ohio, Vermont and New Jersey which are major subcontract areas although they receive few prime contracts (Malecki 1984).

There is little doubt that defence spending is

concentrated in a limited number of states mainly because of the distribution of defence-related industries and thus increases/decreases in defence budgets will have important impact on the employment levels in these areas. The sensitivity of employment in defence-related firms to changes in the defence budget is well illustrated by Rees (1980) for five major defence firms in Dallas–Fort Worth. Contraction of employment in the five firms reflects the fall in defence spending in the early 1970s. All five firms reached a peak in their employment histories between 1968 and 1970, but by 1971 one had fallen from 30,000 to 23,500 employees, another from 29,000 to 16,000 employees and another from 23,000 to 15,000 employees.

Overall, shifts in the regional patterns of defence spending are small. Table 10.1 examines the shipment of manufactured goods by defence-oriented industries with over 500 employees between 1965 and 1976 and indicates a fall in the relative importance of the manufacturing belt and increases elsewhere. Similar patterns were shown in both prime contract and subcontract data.

Table 10.1 Government contracts by value of shipment per region, United States, 1965 and 1976

Region	1965	1976
Manufacturing belt (New England, Middle Atlantic, East North Central)	41.7	37.3
Periphery (West North Central, South Atlantic, East South Central, West South Central)	26.5	28.7
Pacific	28.9	30.3
Mountain	3.1	3.8

(*Source*: Rees 1980:203)

It is unlikely that such changes reflect conscious policy objectives to shift defence spending from one area to another. They may reflect changes in the distribution of defence-oriented industries, changes in the requirements of the military (the shift from automotive products to missiles has already been referred to), the relative success of different firms in lobbying both the military and Congress and Senate in order to obtain contracts and, it has also been suggested that a pork-barrel effect may be present and elected members of government divert defence spending to their home states. Although prime contract supplies are 'the major areas of pork-barrel politics within the defence budget' (Johnson 1979:158) their influence is not sufficiently large to produce a dominant effect. Nevertheless, in 1972, for example, where a state was represented by a congressman on the Defence Sub-committee of the House of Representatives Appropriation Committee the mean *per capita* receipts from prime supply contracts in the state was $120 whereas states not represented received an average of only $70–73 *per capita*. Interpreted cautiously this might mean that congressmen from states with a major involvement with the military–industrial complex succeed in getting on to committees which influence defence spending, so the pattern may simply reflect the distribution of military–industrial plants!

Although changes in the distribution of employment in manufacturing can result from changes in the allocation of orders for defence equipment, they do not reflect spatial decisions and their effects appear to be small. Rees and Weinstein (1983:248) conclude that 'little evidence has been found to date that ... [Federal purchasing policies] ... contributed in any major way to the decentralisation of ... [United States] ... industry from the Northeast to the Southwest'.

There have been suggestions that defence contracts could be used to stimulate particular industries or particular areas and Britain for some time has given a priority to firms in areas of above average unemployment when tenders for contracts are sought, but only 1 per cent or less of contracts placed in these areas were under the Special Preference Scheme in the mid 1970s (Short 1981; Law 1983). Yet in Britain there are hints that defence policies may have aided areas like Bristol, in the South-West region, which has a high concentration of aerospace industries.

Local communities can have little impact on national government policies and have to adapt to their effects whether they create new jobs through the arrival of large orders from the military or the loss of jobs arising from the cancellation of projects overrunning their expected costs. Yet, under each national government, lower tier authorities do have the ability to develop their own industrial policies.

DERIVED SPATIAL POLICY

As a result of the policies of lower tier authorities different regions and different parts of the urban system vary in their degree of attractiveness to industrial activity. Such variations are not designed deliberately by either central government or by the individual authorities but are derived from place to place variations in the activities of local governments. These variations produce a diverse range of what are termed *business climates*. The term 'business climate' is not unambiguous. To a locational consultant it might relate to legislative actions, to a firm seeking a new site it might be seen in terms of the attitude of public officials while to a local administration it may mirror the availability of finance for industrial development and promotional activities (Weinstein and Firestine 1978:130–44). Two important inputs to spatial variations in business climate arise from local taxation and local industrial policy, the former imposing costs on industrial activities while the latter seeks to promote and develop industrial activities. At times, the two aspects of local government activity may conflict with high local taxes offsetting industrial development initiatives. A third input into an area's business climate – labour characteristics – was discussed in Chapter 7.

Local taxes

Most sub-national governments have power to raise funds to spend upon projects and activities within their own areas. In Britain these funds are raised through a property tax (rates) while in the United States a local level property tax is paralleled by a series of other taxes (for example, corporate income tax) imposed by the state. It does not seem unreasonable to expect industrial change at inter-local or inter-state scale to be influenced by inter-local and/or inter-state variations in tax rates if these rates vary markedly from one area to another. Indeed, firms in high tax areas frequently claim that their actions are influenced by the high tax levels which place them at a competitive disadvantage in comparison with low tax areas.

The tax bill of a particular plant is influenced strongly by the type of industry involved. The variations associated with 5 different industries across 15 states are shown in Table 10.2. This indicates the *total* tax bills (community plus state taxes) for one hypothetical plant per industry. Clearly there are marked spatial variations in tax bills. In England and Wales (outside London) the average rate paid per square metre of industrial floor space varied from £3.50 to £4.70 (Crawford, Fothergill and Monk 1985)

The geography of local property tax revenue *per capita* is shown in Fig. 10.1. This tax is now 'the largest single business tax in most areas' (Stafford 1980:111). The low property taxes characteristic of the South stand out clearly as do the predominantly high property tax levels of the North-East. The two extreme values confirm

Table 10.2 State and local taxes in 5 industries and 15 states

Industry	High	Low	Range	Range as % of:	
	($000)	($000)	($000)	Pre-tax income	Sales
Paper	974	373	601	17.4	1.7
Fabricated metals	265	107	158	9.2	0.9
Machinery	336	137	199	9.0	1.1
Scientific instruments	221	85	136	7.7	1.3
Food	98	40	58	10.4	0.4

(*Source*: Stafford 1980:113)

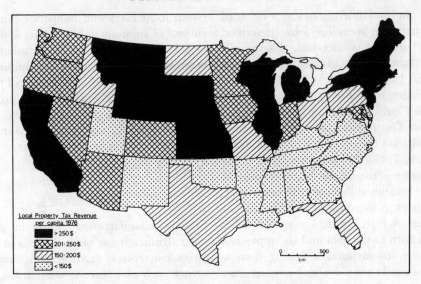

Fig. 10.1   Local property taxes, United States, 1976 (*Source*: Moriarty 1980:249)

this contrast, the local property tax revenue *per capita* in 1976 varying from \$83 in Arkansas to \$384 in Massachusetts. It is also useful to remember that a firm's 'interpretation of high taxes ... [as] ... an expression of a community's hostility could be more significant ... than the dollar magnitudes suggest' (Williams 1967:57).

There is no doubt that tax rates do vary between communites and between states but their locational influence is difficult to measure and an overall assessment of the research results is made difficult by the fact that most studies have been concerned with the impact of local taxes on branch plants or the branch plant location decision (Ch. 12) rather than the impact on the overall pattern of employment change in manufacturing industry. The effects of tax on manufacturing costs was explored by Williams (1967) who found that state and local taxes accounted for only 1 to 2 per cent of the value of shipments across 12 two-digit industries and 38 four-digit industries. These industries (all represented in Minnesota, a high tax state) were then examined to see what effect removal of the Minnesota tax bill would have on Minnesota's relative cost position with reference to other states. The effects were small; in most cases Minnesota's ranking was unchanged and in the

38 four-digit industries Minnesota's rank was improved by 2 or more points in only nine industries. Although the influence of local and state taxes is usually discounted, they are cited as important factors influencing some branch plant location decisions (page 171). What is more Newman (1984:79), by examining changes in relative corporate tax rates between states and by allowing firms time to adjust to those changes, provides some support for the view that low taxes encourage employment growth. However, the exclusion of wage rates from the analysis casts doubt on the validity of the finding.

A recent study of England and Wales (Crawford, Fothergill and Monk 1985) looked directly at the effect of local tax (rates) levels on industrial employment change from 1974 to 1981. Allowance was made for differences between areas in industrial structure, urban–rural mix, plant size, spatial policy measures and peripherality/centrality. The conclusion to their investigation was 'particularly clear cut. It is a consistent finding that, if any effect of rates on the location of manufacturing employment exists, it is too small to detect, despite the large variation in the rate burden between areas' (p. 71).

This limited effect of local and state taxes needs some explanation. There are probably four reasons. First, in the United States as a result of competition between areas for jobs (described below) it is claimed that inter-state differentials on business taxes have all but disappeared (Bluestone and Harrison 1982:185), but for some contrasting evidence see Fig. 10.1. Second, local taxes make up only a small proportion of the value of sales. Third, local taxes may in some cases be set against the other tax bills, an effect which Moriarty (1980:249) suggests reduces the variations in taxes in the United States by around 50 per cent. Finally, differences in taxes may reflect differences in the quality and quantity of public services. A high tax area may well offer more services both to the firm and its employees which offset any disadvantages arising from a high tax location. It should also be noted that local areas may tend to keep their tax structure in line with their neighbours in order to maintain their relative position thus reducing a tendency for industrial activities to be diverted across the borders of local administrations.

Despite the overwhelming weight of the empirical evidence 'the traditional belief...that tax differences between states and localities are an important factor in location decisions...is probably held as strongly as ever' (Moriarity 1980: 246). It is worth asking why this is the case. In part it is due to the fact that general observation relates the pattern of local taxes to the shifts in manufacturing activity in the United States set out in Chapter 1. It seems more likely that the interest in the influence of local taxes arises from the fact that managers can view corporate tax payments in a negative way as an imposed cost rather than payment for services received. A view held by many individuals with regard to their personal tax bills. It is also the principal manufacturing cost over which the firm has little control. Wage bills can be cut, suppliers can be changed and new markets can be sought but it is difficult to adjust local tax liabilities. Local administrations control local tax and therefore it is good business practice to campaign for a reduction in local taxes. Such a campaign is almost inevitably supported and given wider publicity by political parties in opposition. It appears that it is for these reasons that the relationships be-

tween local taxes and industrial change are the subject of vigorous public debate and as Stafford (1980:109) has observed 'the locational influence of taxes...[is]...as much an emotional issue as a financial issue' and it is because of this that the public debate will continue and probably continue to ignore the research evidence. At regional and state level local taxes appear to play a negligible role in influencing the geography of industrial activity.

Local industrial policy

From a manufacturing viewpoint perhaps the most significant use of local tax is in the form of direct assistance to manufacturing firms. Whether or not such assistance is offered, the magnitude of such assistance will mirror local industrial policy. Each local government authority (subject to any constraints imposed by higher level authorities) can develop its own industrial policy and this policy is usually a reflection of its attitude to changes in the level of manufacturing employment within its boundaries. These attitudes may vary markedly from one authority to another and even a cursory inspection of different administrations reveals marked contrasts, for example, between resort areas with little interest in manufacturing and specialised manufacturing towns where local administrations attempt to play an important role in modifying and adjusting the town's industrial structure.

Some of the principal elements which may make up a local industrial policy are listed below, drawing particularly on the British experience (Lawless 1981:59–112). The development policies of municipal areas in Canada are described by Walker (1980a:228–42) and those of the United States by Moriarty (1980). Of course, the powers vary over time and between different levels of authority and the powers are constrained by the policies of central government.

1. *Provision of land*. Local governments can provide single blocks of land, and assemble numerous smaller landholdings into one larger block. Land provided by an authority is usually *serviced land* with sewage, water, power, road network and lighting. This land

is then leased or sold to either firms desiring sites or property (real-estate) firms to develop the industrial buildings.

2. *Provision of buildings*. Factories can be built independently or in association with the private sector and may be built in advance of demand or to meet the needs of a particular firm. Not all factories are new and older premises may be purchased by the authority for further industrial use. Buildings may be sold, leased or rented to firms. These buildings can be grouped on *industrial estates* (Bale 1977) or *industrial parks* (Barr 1983). Most recently the emphasis has been placed on *science parks* (Taylor 1983) for new high-technology industry.

3. *Provision of housing*. Since local authorities manage public sector housing and control access to such housing, housing may be offered to 'key workers' (essential) for plants moving into the area from another local authority.

4. *Financial aid*. Local authorities can offer factories at reduced rents and rent-free periods, can provide mortgages for the development of land and buildings, can provide loans and grants for other purposes, and act as guarantors of loans. It is also possible for a local authority to invest in the shares of local companies as seen, for example, in Britain in the setting up of the West Midland and Greater London Enterprise Boards. In the United States finance for aid to industry may be raised through Industrial Development Bonds.

5. *Industrial promotion*. Industrial development panels may be set up to promote contact between industry and local government and to co-ordinate an authority's approach to industrial activity. Industrial development officers can be appointed whose role is to maintain and expand the area's manufacturing activities. Advertising campaigns are run to draw firms' attention to the attractions of the area (Burgess 1982).

6. *Advice*. Information on markets, suppliers and sources of funds can be provided as can data relating to the availability of local sites and premises. The significance of this information for location decisions was discussed in Chapter 5. In some cases practical training in running a business is available.

Perusal of this list of policies makes it clear that many of them are focused on new plants and few are likely to have an impact on existing plants. Indeed, the provision of loans and grants and the various advice services are the only policies geared to help an existing firm which does not require a new plant or major extension. This balance is likely to change in the future as *industrial retention policies* are developed to help maintain existing manufacturing activities.

There are, of course, less specifically industry-oriented policies which indicate an authority's attitude to industry. The 'right-to-work' legislation (Ch. 7) and training and education policies are two examples as indeed are the individual attitudes of both employees and elected members of local administration with whom the firms come into contact. Firms can have quite different views of local administrations as North and Gough (1983:174–6) show in a study of some local authorities within Greater London. The majority of firms regarded the local authority in a neutral way as having little effect on their activities but among firms that held a view there were marked contrasts. The Southwark and Wandsworth authorities were thought most helpful, while Hackney was regarded as unhelpful. Images like these may be critical in the long run as once a view is established it becomes very difficult to change. They may reflect events outside an authority's control but the image the firm holds may be of critical importance.

Each authority can select from the range of options available a particular mix of policies appropriate to its strategy for employment and industry. For example, in 1978 53 per cent of United Kingdom authorities were developing significant industrial estates and 57 per cent had built or were building new factory units of under 5,000 square feet (Boddy 1983). There were similar variations in the use of promotional material. In a survey of 218 authorities in Britain excluding the Greater London Council 72.5 per cent were producing such material; more significantly, perhaps, slightly over a quarter were not doing so (Burgess 1982).

To gain a quantitative assessment of an authority's policy towards industry, Camina (1974: 133–51) developed an *activity index* to measure the strength of the policy. She measured the presence or absence of 22 policy measures plus the time spent by industrial development officers, the amount of money spent on advertising, the maximum number of houses provided for any one firm and the average number of houses let to key workers at any one time. The data identified five different types of urban area. Out of 89 areas, 19 per cent were inactive and 34.8 per cent either active or very active, the remainder occupying intermediate categories. Most importantly this overall analysis suggested considerable variation among authorities in Britain in their attempts to promote and encourage industrial activity. Counts of the number of policy measures adopted are unable to give adequate assessments of the strength of each policy and ideally one needs to measure the strength of policy by expenditure.

Assembling data on such expenditure is not easy (hence the dependence on counting the number of policies) because of its spread across different departments within an individual authority and the division of functions between different levels of authority. The most complete data for any area appear to be those assembled by Storey (1983b) for the Northern region of England. Here gross expenditure at 1978 prices rose from £3.5 million in 1974–75 to £10.3 million in 1979–80. County variations in expenditure are illustrated in Table 10.3. The amounts can

vary markedly from year to year but Tyne and Wear emerges as the most active authority. Analysis of activity expenditure reveals annual shifts in emphasis. Cumbria shifted its main emphasis from servicing land to loans over the two years considered, while Durham moved from land acquisition to factory construction. These counties are all in areas where at least some central government assistance is available and contrasts between authorities might be greater if similar data were available from elsewhere. The sums quoted must also be placed in context. Over the two-year period 1975–76 to 1977–78 Cleveland received £270 million in Regional Development Grants (see Ch. 15) whereas the total local authority expenditure was under £3 million.

These financial data do not, obviously, include variations in policies with no direct cost, for example land use zoning, yet a very strict zoning policy can serve to inhibit industrial growth. Markusen (1983:26) points out that restrictive policies with effects similar to zoning regulations have been introduced at both county and city level in Silicon Valley (see Ch. 6). Several authorities in the valley have imposed limits on both the number of new plants and the density of employees per acre.

Overall, there is evidence from Britain that there are quite marked policy variations between different local administrations. However, in the United States 'because virtually all states provide similar industrial inducement packages, it can be argued that they have become superfluous in the industrial location calculus' (Rees and Weinstein 1983:252).

Derived spatial policies give rise to spatial variations in business climates. Amalgamating the different influences subsumed within the term 'business climate' is difficult but in 1975 this was attempted by the Fantus Company and the results are shown in Fig. 10.2. This ranking includes not only tax levels but also some of the labour characteristics discussed in Chapter 7. With the exception of Indiana all the manufacturing belt states are seen as having poor business climates, while those of the South and Mid-West tend to be good. In the Far West, and particular-

Table 10.3 Expenditure per head (1980 prices) by local authorities on economic development by county, United Kingdom, 1979–80 and 1980–81

County	1979–80 (£)	1980–81 (£)
Cumbria	1.36	3.58
Cleveland	3.18	3.14
Durham	3.39	5.70
Northumberland	3.99	3.32
Tyne and Wear	5.94	5.94

(*Source*: Storey 1983b:190)

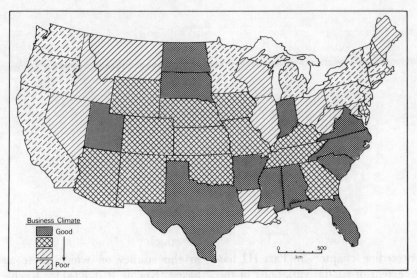

Fig. 10.2   Business climates, United States, mid 1970s (*Source*: Weinstein and Firestine 1978:137)

ly on the Pacific Coast, the business climate is seen as poor.

Business climates are to some extent negotiable and promises of new employment opportunities often cause local administrations to vie with one another to produce the most attractive package. Bluestone and Harrison (1982:183) cite the case of the selection of a site for a Goodyear radial tyre plant in Oklahoma. In the final stages Goodyear solicited bids from six local administrations and indicated that it would locate the plant in the town making the best bid. As part of the winning package interstate highways were moved, access roads built and a school catchment area changed to enable the children of Goodyear managers to attend a selected school. By setting one community against another the large planning-system firms are able to maximise benefits and reduce costs to themselves.

CONCLUSION

The influence of the state on processes of regional employment change clearly encompasses much more than explicit spatial policy which has

usually been the focus of attention. Defence policies, merger policies and, indeed, all industrial policies at national level may have a differential spatial impact as may derived spatial policies. Attempts to unravel the effects of local taxes suggest their effects on employment change are negligible. The effects of local industrial policies have not yet been measured but it is clear that they concentrate upon reducing land and building costs and providing limited financial assistance. Further, by active advertising and public relations activities areas attempt to increase decision-makers' awareness of their more desirable features.

The tasks of isolating the effects of implicit and derived policies are, indeed, exceptionally challenging as is made clear in Chapter 15 where some of the difficulties of isolating the effects of explicit policies are outlined. The major difficulty is that patterns of net employment change may be influenced by all of the variables discussed in Part III and they all need to be considered simultaneously. Some examples of such an approach are illustrated in the afterword to Part III which follows this chapter.

PART III: AFTERWORD

Each of the preceding chapters in Part III has illustrated the extent of spatial variations in the factors which can influence change in the location of industry. They also indicated the ways in which the different factors could affect the spatial pattern of manufacturing employment. In Part II it was shown that the personal preferences of managers and owners might be important particularly where the cost differences between places were small. One of the problems of discussing these different elements in isolation is that change is, in all probability, influenced by more than one of these elements and a full analysis must consider them all simultaneously. Some areas are characterised by pleasant residential environments, by access to new technologies, by productive and cheap labour, by unconstrained locations, by access to markets, and by good business climates while others have poor business climates, limited markets, restricted sites, militant labour, old technologies and coke-town environments. Not only is there a need to know which ones are important and unimportant but also there is need to assess the relative significance of each of the variables identified as important. Examples of this approach can be drawn from Britain although they do not include all the variables that have been discussed. It should also be recalled that different factors operate at different scales and that the conclusions of these examples relate to a Britain divided into about 60 sub-regions. Technical problems of measurement are discussed in detail in the studies on which these summaries are based (Keeble 1976:88–115; Keeble 1980).

Figure III.3 shows the patterns of employment change in manufacturing activity from 1966 to 1971 and from 1971 to 1976. The data for 1966 to 1971 relates to 62 sub-regions and change is expressed in percentage terms. This shows the urban–rural shift with decline or very slow growth along the London to North-West axis and rapid industrialisation of the traditionally rural areas. Around this general pattern there were marked variations seen, for example, in the differences between the sub-regions in East Anglia. The 1971 to 1976 data relate to 64 counties and change is mapped in terms of the differential shift, thus the influence of industrial structure has been excluded. The marked urban–rural dichotomy stands out again. Notable are the performances of the rural counties in West Wales and along the east coast of England; while among urbanised counties a North-West to South-East belt shows small or negative differential shifts. Tabular analysis of these patterns revealed the urban–rural dichotomy even more clearly (Table 1.3).

The variables used to explain these patterns are listed in Table III.1A. Industrial structure is used to explain changes from 1966 to 1971 but is excluded from the 1971–76 study since it has already been allowed for in calculating the differential shift. Residential space preferences are indicative of the potential importance of a firm's image of an area. The consideration of labour

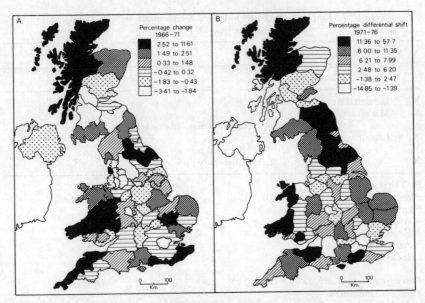

Fig. III.3 United Kingdom (A) Percentage change in manufacturing employment, 1966 to 1971 (B) Percentage differential shift in manufacturing employment, 1971 to 1976 (*Source*: (A) Keeble 1976:96; Keeble 1980:950)

availability and female activity rates indicates a possible role for the influence of labour markets, while measures of agglomeration economies (diseconomies) include aspects of constrained locations in urbanised areas as well as access to suppliers of intermediate industrial products and producer services. The role of markets is included through the measure of market potential while the political context is measured by assisted area status.

The results of the analysis are shown in Table III.1B. For the 1966–71 period, labour availability and market accessibility had no influence upon the changing geography of employment opportunities. Examining the variables having an impact on the changes, three had a positive influence and one a negative influence. Employment growth was greatest in areas which scored highly in terms of residential attractiveness, had some kind of policy assistance and which had a favourable industrial structure. These positive influences on employment growth were damped down where the numbers employed in manufacturing were high, suggesting the operation of agglomeration diseconomies. The 1971–76 period omitted the market accessibility variable which

had not proved important in the earlier period and, in this period, not only are labour influences unimportant again but regional aid and residential preferences have no influence either. Indeed, the only measurable influence was the negative relationship between the differential shift and manufacturing employment density, the latter being a surrogate for agglomeration diseconomies. Both studies emphasise agglomeration diseconomies, of which the most obvious is the nature of restricted sites in urban areas. However, female activity rates vary in the same way as these diseconomies (with high activity rates and diseconomies in urban areas and low activity rates and few diseconomies in rural areas) so the dominance of the diseconomies may hide the attractiveness of unorganised labour as a locational influence! Studies of net changes at this scale suggest that the influence of constrained locations is greater than the influence of labour market characteristics. Yet other variables not considered may be important too since these analyses explain only between 45 and 60 per cent of the changes taking place.

Very few attempts to bring material together in this way have been tried in North America

Table III.1   Employment change in United Kingdom sub-regions (1966 to 1971)
and counties (1971 to 1976)

A. The independent variables

	1966–71 62 sub-regions	1971–76 64 counties
X_1	Industrial structure	—
X_2	Market accessibility	—
X_3	Agglomeration economies/diseconomies	
X_4	Labour availability	Female activity rate
X_5	Regional policy	
X_6	Residential space preference	

B. The results

Percentage change, 1966–71 ($R^2 = 0.60$)   Direction
Significant influences
   Agglomeration diseconomies   –
   Residential space preference   +
   Assisted area status   +
   Industrial structure   +

Percentage differential shift, 1971–76 ($R^2 = 0.45$)   Direction
Significant influences
   Agglomeration diseconomies   –

(*Source*: Keeble 1976; Keeble 1980)

with the exception of the studies undertaken by Burrows, Metcalfe and Kaler (1971) and Wheat (1973). Not surprisingly these placed greater emphasis than the British studies on the role of markets in explaining net manufacturing employment change. A further exception is Peet (1983) who relates net manufacturing employment change to a 'class-struggle' index. This index was constructed by summing a state's ranking on union membership, work stoppages,

average hourly earnings in manufacturing and on the reverse of a business climate index. It thus includes measures of the policy and labour environments in which plants operate. The results of the analysis are shown in Table III.2. This shows that since 1943 the ten highest class struggle states have performed worse than the ten lowest class struggle states. This methodology does not allow separation out of the effects of business climate and the different labour factors

Table III.2   Percentage change in manufacturing employment in industrial cycles 1939 to July 1982

Industrial cycle	United States	Ten highest class-struggle states*	Ten lowest class-struggle states†
1939–43	+71.3	+78.4	+60.0
1943–49	−17.9	−18.5	−12.6
1949–53	+21.5	+14.8	+21.3
1953–61	−6.9	−11.2	+13.1
1961–69	+23.5	+19.6	+46.0
1969–71	−7.6	−10.9	−1.7
1971–73	+8.2	+5.9	+11.8
1973–75	−9.0	−10.0	−6.8
1975–79	+11.7	+12.6	+19.8
1979 to July 1982	−10.7	−13.7	−4.3
1939 to July 1982	+82.1	+56.0	+228.0

(*Source*: Peet 1983:130)
* Michigan, Washington, Pennsylvania, Ohio, Illinois, New York, California, Montana, Minnesota, Oregon.
† Texas, Virginia, North Dakota, Georgia, Arkansas, Mississippi, Florida, South Dakota, South Carolina, North Carolina.

but disaggregation of the data to state level does question the all pervading influence of the 'class struggle' factor. As Peet (1983: 139) observes

the spread of employment to the West Coast is *not* explained by level of class struggle, which in this case loses its immediate, primary determining effect to physical environment (resources, climate) and purely spatial–locational (position) factors and to the regional dimension of ideology and consciousness ('the California image').

An image described so vividly in the quotation in Chapter 5.

Studies of net manufacturing employment demonstrate the need to have a thorough understanding of all the potential influences on the growth and decline of manufacturing employment. Different influences may operate at different scales or at the same scale at different points in time, a point which was emphasised in the preamble. What is more, where the level of explanation is known it is only possible to explain just over half the variations in net employment change. This might reflect the omission of important variables or the fact that net change might not be a particularly useful category for analysis. It will be recalled that net change is the outcome of the operation of the different components of change.

___ PART IV ___

THE COMPONENTS
OF CHANGE

Having considered the general framework within which firms operate, the nature of firms and their decisions and the environmental context in which plants and firms are set, it might be expected that this fourth section would consider how these three sets of influences have moulded industrial change in specific industries and regions. Instead, emphasis is placed upon their effects on the different mechanisms by which change takes place. Industrial geography seeks to interpret the evolving geographies of the different mechanisms of change, just as population geography interprets the geographies of birth, migration and death. Chapters 11 and 12 focus upon the entry of new plants into a regional industrial system, Chapter 11 considering new firms and Chapter 12 the setting up of new plants by existing firms. Chapter 13 examines *in situ* employment growth and Chapter 14 discusses employment decline considering both *in situ* employment decline and plant closure. The four chapters describing and explaining changes in the geographies of the different components of change have very different flavours. That on new firms reports much new empirical evidence, that on movement reports on work that is virtually complete, that on *in situ* growth is essentially speculative while that on employment decline and closure adopts a more conceptual approach.

PART IV: PREAMBLE

The principal reason for disaggregating the geography of employment change is that different components can be influenced by different factors and that the same factor can influence different components in different ways. The founders of new firms may not make locational choices but set up business close to their homes. In contrast, an existing firm setting up a branch plant consciously selects a location. The factors influencing the distribution of potential founders can be different from those influencing branch plant locations. The contrasting influence of the same factor is seen, for example, where high wage rates may discourage the establishment of branch plants but encourage the closure of existing plants. There are also implications for spatial policies. For example, where there is evidence of new plants formed by local people a policy of encouraging the small business might be appropriate. Conversely, in a region where new formations are few there may be little to encourage.

The components of change approach does not have a clearly established and accepted terminology but the four broad categories identified in Chapter 1 (births, deaths, transfers and *in situ* change) can form the basis for a more elaborate classification. In Table IV.1, level one records the basic four-fold categories. A distinction is made between employment change in plants which existed throughout the time period being studied (*in situ* change), employment gains in new plants (births), employment losses in closed plants (deaths) and employment changes in transfers (existing plants which are moved from one location to another). At the second level of classification each plant is classified by its organisational status, that is whether it belongs to a single-plant firm (which operates mainly in the market system) or whether it is a head office or branch plant of a multi-plant firm (which operates mainly in the planning system). It was seen in Chapter 4 that there are important differences in the characteristics of market-system and

Table IV.1 Components of change: a classification

Level 1	Level 2	Level 3
In situ change	Independent plant	
	Head office plant	
	Branch plant	HQ in area
		HQ elsewhere in nation
		HQ overseas
Exits/deaths	Independent plant	
	Head office plant	
	Branch plant	HQ in area
		HQ elsewhere in nation
		HQ overseas
Transfers	Independent plant	
	Head office plant	
	Branch plant	HQ in area
		HQ elsewhere in nation
		HQ overseas
Entries/births	Independent plant	
	Head office plant	
	Branch plant	HQ in area
		HQ elsewhere in nation
		HQ overseas

planning-system firms which make this distinction an important one. At level 3 branches are classified by the location of their head offices. This level is important because there is evidence to suggest that plants with head offices outside a region and, indeed, overseas have different behaviour patterns to more locally based firms (Ch. 2).

Of course, there are inter-relationships between the different components just as there are inter-relationships between individual industries (Appendix I, pages 236–7). Within a firm, changes in all the components are outcomes of investment/disinvestment decisions and, for example, disinvestment in one location may be related to investment in another. Similarly, in a regional environment changes in the individual components may be related to one another such that, for example, a region losing jobs through closures may be one gaining employment in branch plants attracted by the labour released by plant closures. Despite these inter-relationships it is useful to treat each component separately although this can create difficulties as will be seen in the discussion of *in situ* change.

The classification in Table IV.1 gives a general idea of the categories most frequently found in studies using the components of change approach but in practice many of the categories have to be amalgamated because of inadequate data sources and the actual components used in any study are influenced by the nature of the data sources and the purposes of the particular study. Maps of the geographies of each of the components are not readily available. Nevertheless, some employment data for very broad categories are illustrated in the following chapters.

The lack of information reflects the fact that most components of change data have been collected for regions and cities and for individual areas quite detailed *employment accounts* can be built up (Fig. IV.1). The first box represents employment at the beginning of the selected time period (t_1), the final box employment at the end of the period (t_2) while the intermediate boxes record the employment associated with the different components of change. It should be noted

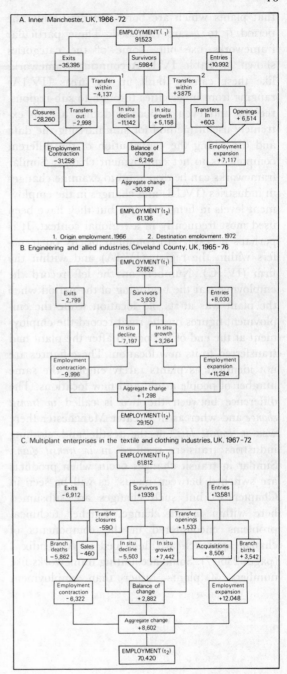

Fig. IV.1 Components of change: accounting frameworks (A) All manufacturing in an area (B) One industry in an area (C) A group of firms (*Sources*: Lloyd and Mason 1978:80 (B) Based on Robinson and Storey 1981:169 (C) Based on Healey 1983:332)

that plants which are born and die within the period t_1 to t_2 are excluded. These particular frameworks use only some of the categories shown in Table IV.1. Accounting frameworks like these can be built up for areas (IV.1A) ranging from inner cities through to sub-regions, regions and even nations and they are an extremely useful method for summarising the data and describing the contribution of the different components to net employment change. Similar frameworks can be drawn up to examine changes in industries (IV.1B) and changes in the employment levels in firms (IV.1C) but they have been used most frequently in a regional context. It is perhaps necessary to comment briefly on transfers within the region (IV.1A) and within the firm (IV.1C). Numbers on the left record the employment at the beginning of the period when the plant was at its old location while the employment figures on the right record the employment at the end of the period after the plant had transferred to its new location. These figures are not identical as plants rarely employ the same number of people at old and new locations. The difference between the two is called *in transit change* and whereas in Greater Manchester there was *in transit loss*, in the textile and clothing industries transfers resulted in *in transit gains*. Similar in transit changes occur when products are switched between plants, as will be seen in Chapter 13 but such changes are subsumed here within *in situ* change. Further technical problems encountered in the components of change approach are described in Appendix I (pages 236–7). Some accounting frameworks use numbers of plants rather than employment

(Bluestone and Harrison 1982:276–7) but these are only worth while if employment data are lacking since they cannot include *in situ* change. The value of these accounting frameworks is that they illustrate the relative importance of the individual components in contributing to net change within a specific region, industry or firm.

Questions as to the relative importance of the different components in contributing to net change are taken up in the afterword of Part IV and the focus of the four chapters is on the different components examined in isolation. In trying to explain the geography of the different components it is necessary to recall briefly some points made in the preamble to Part III. First, regional typology variables (like degree of peripherality) do not provide much of an insight into the reasons for particular geographies. Second, firms may respond to the perceived costs or attributes of areas rather than the measurable costs or attributes. Third, the results of almost any particular enquiry relate only to the spatial scales at which that enquiry was undertaken.

The components of change approach does not offer an explanation for changes in the geography of industrial activity but it is 'a useful way into analysis through descriptive disaggregation' (Massey and Meegan 1982:192). What is more, an important by-product of the approach is that it has turned industrial geography away from an undue interest in the selection of branch plant locations (with its strong business orientation) to a wider concern with all aspects of spatial variations in employment change in manufacturing industry.

11

NEW FIRMS

New firms are added to a population of market-system firms which, to use an analogy, occupy a crowded platform from which the unsuccessful firms fall and on to which new firms climb to take their place, or, indeed, to push them off (Lloyd and Mason 1984:210). The 'market room' on the platform is created by the capture of markets vacated either voluntarily (by retirement, for example) or involuntarily (out competed). At any one time the platform is of limited extent, hence its crowded nature, but there can be a vigorous pattern of arrivals and departures. Through time, the size of a regional platform may expand or contract. Expansion in times of economic prosperity may increase the rate of arrivals and decrease the number of departures whereas in times of economic adversity the platform will contract increasing the rate of departures and reducing the number of arrivals. Some of the features of firms falling from the platform are discussed in Chapter 14; in this chapter emphasis is placed upon the new arrivals.

THE NEW FIRM

The new firm is typified by Cousins Engineering, a small organisation in the English Midlands employing eight people in the early 1970s. The firm was begun by Mr Cousins as a spare-time activity and was initially based on a second-hand lathe installed in his garden shed. An initial order from another local firm was secured via a friend and after six months' experience Mr

Cousins gave up his full-time job. His operations moved from garden shed to an adapted cowshed. From the cowshed the firm moved to a warehouse and finally to a rented unit on an industrial estate. From an initial investment in 1965 of £200 the firm, by 1970, had six lathes worth over £1,000 each. Almost all work was obtained, usually through personal friends, from within a 65 km radius and was all subcontract work. The firm made components for food-handling machinery. The founder had worked as a lathe turner for another firm in a similar industry and had lived for most of his life in the town of Earls Barton where he had established his own firm (Gudgin 1978:122).

This describes just one of a myriad of new firms set up each year but 'the definition of a new firm is not a clear-cut or unambigious issue' (Mason 1983:53). The main problems are those of identifying new manufacturing firms, of establishing the start-up date and of establishing the independence of the new firm. There are also new firms which take over existing manufacturing operations, for example, where a firm is sold to a new owner or where managers buy out the operation of a branch plant from the parent company (Storey 1983a; Wright, Coyne and Lockley 1984). As far as possible new firms of this type are excluded from the analysis since they do not involve a decision to set up a new manufacturing plant.

New firms are difficult to identify mainly because of their small size and they can escape from both official and academic surveys because those concerned with the surveys are unaware of their existence. Traditionally, too, because of the larger number of very small firms, survey work, to reduce time and cost, frequently excludes firms with less than a predetermined number of employees, for example, less than 5 or less than 10. It is also difficult to identify the new *manufacturing* firm since a number of manufacturing firms straddle the service/manufacturing boundary.

Establishing a firm's start-up date is equally problematical. Logically, the firm could be said to be born when it provides the principal source of income of the owner but on pragmatic grounds it is probably useful to define the start-up date in terms of the year in which the first full-time employee is taken on. In the case of firms moving from the service to the manufacturing sector, the start-up date for manufacturing activities will be different from the start-up date for the firm in the service sector. Some studies define start-up dates by the year in which a firm is legally registered but some firms are legally registered only after they have establised themselves successfully while others can be registered before they begin operation.

Drawing a line between a branch plant and an entirely new firm is not easy. Independence is usually expressed in financial terms and independent manufacturing firms can be defined, adopting Johnson and Cathcart (1979), as those whose principal founders are not directors, sole proprietors, partners or major shareholders in any other business. Such a definition hides some of the inter-dependency between new firms and the rest of the industrial system and without detailed survey work it may be difficult to uncover both financial links between small firms and a dependence on other firms arising, for example, from those firms purchasing the majority of the small firms' output. The nature of these inter-dependencies was discussed in Chapter 4.

Most investigators have found it very difficult to identify clearly the new firm and, almost inevitably, the definitions vary from study to study making comparison between them very difficult indeed. It is particularly important to establish whether analyses relate to new plants (Collins 1972) or new firms and whether they relate to *all* new firms (Storey 1982) or to manufacturing firms only. Nevertheless, it is possible to construct a geography of the new manufacturing firm.

THE GEOGRAPHY OF NEW FIRMS

An examination of the geography of new firms focuses attention predominantly on firms operating within the market system. It will be recalled that each firm has only a small share of the market it supplies (although it can have a large share of a small market), it is run by an owner-manager and manufactures a single product or set of related products, usually at a single site. The firms at the time they are founded are very small indeed. In Scotland in the 1960s and 1970s the average employment of new firms was only 2.7 employees (Cross 1981:140). In part this small size reflects the limited capital resources of the founders. In the Scottish data over half the new firms had less than £5,000 invested in them (Cross 1981:239). Initial size does, of course, vary between industries reflecting the different barriers to entry in different sectors, barriers related to the minimum efficient scale of plant (Ch. 6). Data from the East Midlands, which include subsidiaries set up by existing firms as well as new firms, show that the average employment of firms at start-up in the post-war period varied from 2 to 3 employees in printing and engineering to 9 or 10 in clothing or footwear (Gudgin 1978:97).

Where studies are dealing primarily with medium-term change the plants of new independent firms will remain small. If the size of firms established over a ten-year period is measured at the end of the period, plants with over 200 employees are rare. Returning again to Scotland, 95 per cent of the plants at the end of a nine-year period had under 100 employees, 74 per cent had less than 25 employees and 43 per cent had 10 or fewer employees (Cross 1981:143). While in East Anglia the firms founded between 1971 and 1981 and surviving to 1982 provided jobs on average

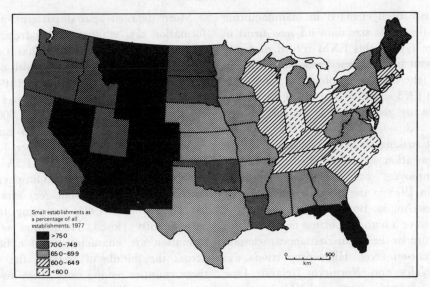

Fig. 11.1 Small plants in the United States, 1977 (*Source*: US Bureau of Census 1985:Table 1382)

for only 12 employees each (estimated from Gould and Keeble 1984:191).

Regional variations in new firm formation rates appear to be quite marked. The pattern in the United State is shown in Fig. 11.1 which illustrates the percentage of all manufacturing establishments with less than 20 employees. It is reasonable to assume that states with high firm birth rates will have a high proportion of small establishments (Gudgin 1978:203). The rates vary from Montana (82.6 per cent) to Pennsylvania (58.8 per cent). Admittedly the high values in some western states may reflect limits on their ability to support larger plants, but the above average birth rates in the West Coast, Florida and parts of New England stand out clearly.

More direct information is available for the United Kingdom. Figure 11.2 depicts employment in enterprises new to manufacturing (ENMs) set up between 1966 and 1975. It includes ENMs with employment levels over 10, except for the Greater London Council area where the cut-off was 20 and some parts of the West Midlands region where the cut-off varied between 20 and 50. It also includes a small proportion of firms (representing about 15 per cent of the total employment in ENMs) set up by firms which were already in existence but had

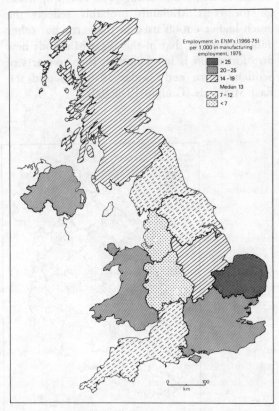

Fig. 11.2 Employment in enterprises new to manufacturing, United Kingdom, 1966 to 1975 (*Source*: Based on Pounce 1981:59)

not previously been engaged in manufacturing activity. If the plant size data for new firms in Scotland are typical this ENM record probably excludes about half the new firms established in this period (the average employment for ENMs surviving to 1975 was 32.6) but it has the advantage of relating to the whole of the United Kingdom.

The most striking feature is that there is considerable variation in employment in ENMs from 6 employees per 1,000 manufacturing employees in 1975 in the North-West to 29 per 1,000 in East Anglia. Both East Anglia and the South-East have a high proportion of ENMs and this high figure for the South-East appears despite its higher cut-off level. High proportions too occur in Wales and Northern Ireland. Low proportions of employment in ENMs are particularly characteristic of the North-West and Yorkshire and Humberside. The low proportion for the West Midlands probably reflects the much higher cut-off used in that area but other data do suggest that in the West Midlands new firm formation is less common than in parts of Scotland (Firn and Swales 1978:210) and the East Midlands (Gudgin 1978:208).

More detailed spatial patterns in new firm formation can be illustrated in Ireland and East Anglia. Although East Anglia has a high rate of new firm formation compared with other British regions (Gould and Keeble 1984:191–3) it is low in relation to Ireland. Ireland has an annual average of 1.1 new firms per 1,000 manufacturing employees in contrast to East Anglia's annual average of 0.37 firms per 1,000 manufacturing employees. Figure 11.3A records all new enterprises with a minimum payroll of three (including the owner-manager) established between 1973 and 1981, including those which subsequently closed. High rates of new firm formation are characteristic of a belt running across the middle of Ireland, the majority of these counties having rates above two firms per annum per 1,000 manufacturing employees. In contrast low rates were recorded in the South-West, mid-West and the South-East. The more successful counties are predominantly rural, a point to which a return is made below. In East Anglia the firm formation rate (surviving firms only) over the ten-year period 1971–81 varies from 0.5 in mid-Suffolk to 21.3 in east Cambridgeshire, the latter county in total accounting

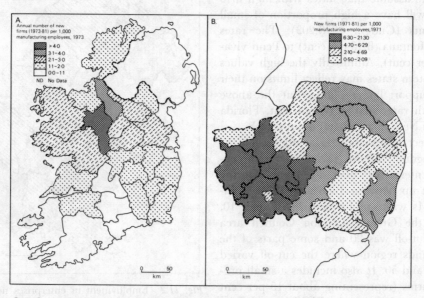

Fig. 11.3 New firm formation rates (A) Eire, 1973 to 1981 (B) East Anglia, 1971 to 1981 (*Sources*: (A) O'Farrell and Crouchley 1984:225 (B) Gould and Keeble 1984:195) *Note*: The shadings on the two maps are *not* comparable

for 45 per cent of the surviving new firms. The pattern shown in Fig. 11.3B displays the clear domination by Cambridge termed by Gould and Keeble (1984:195) the 'Cambridge effect' and the Cambridge area includes a concentration of new high-technology industry to which reference was made in Chapter 6.

The regional contrasts which emerge at these different scales also appear in analyses of new firm formation in relation to an area's urban system. The Eire data show that the new firm formation rate (excluding closures) ranged from 1.91 new firms per 1,000 manufacturing employees per annum in towns with <1,500 population to only 0.54 in Cork and 0.38 in Dublin (O'Farrell and Crouchley 1984:223). Less detailed data for East Anglia showed a range from 0.63 in rural areas to 0.22 in larger towns (Gould and Keeble 1984:195). In the East Midlands from 1968 to 1975 employment in new firms in smaller towns and rural areas was relatively more important than in cities and larger towns (Fothergill and Gudgin 1982:78).

Although it would be premature to make any definitive statements as to the spatial pattern of variations in new firm formation rates because of the inadequacies of the data it is possible to argue quite conclusively that there are sufficiently marked spatial variations in the employment generated in new firms and in the new firm formation rate for them to have an impact on regional employment change. It is then important to try to explain why such variations occur.

ENTREPRENEURS AND LOCATION

The founders of new firms rarely search widely for a location for their new plant and the majority of new firms are set up in the locality in which the entrepreneur lives or works at the time the firm is founded. Although definitions of 'local' vary, North American evidence (cited by Cross 1981:228) suggests 90 per cent or more of founders set up in their local area (perversely, this evidence does not define local). In the Northern Region of Britain no less than 90 per cent of the principal founders in firms established from 1971 to 1973 came from within the

region (Johnson and Cathcart 1979:14), and in the East Midlands 81 per cent of respondents to a survey of new firms said they had strong local associations (Gudgin, 1978:109). A similar proportion (around 80 per cent) were local residents or had worked locally immediately prior to setting up their firms in Greater Manchester, Merseyside and South Hampshire (Lloyd and Mason 1984:214). In Scotland 68 per cent of the founders were employed by a firm based in Scotland before setting up their own business (Cross 1981:229). While in a random sample of new firms in Vancouver all but one of the entrepreneurs had lived in Vancouver for at least 11 years prior to start up (Khan and Hayter 1984:5).

These data all confirm that most new firms do not make an explicit location decision when choosing the region in which to operate. They, simply, set up business in their home region and do not actively consider alternative areas. Returning again to the East Midlands, only 6 per cent of the new firms strongly considered sites more than 50 km from the site at which they were actually operating. Some *local* movement does take place. In Scotland, only one-third of the founders began operation in the same local labour market area (Cross 1981:229) as their previous employer. Similarly, there are some entrepreneurs who move between regions to set up their firms, a proportion of almost one-third in the Scottish case, although this figure is, as yet, atypical. Despite the not insignificant amount of movement by entrepreneurs to set up their own firms it is most useful to work on the assumption that entrepreneurs set up their firms in their local regions.

The reasons why entrepreneurs set up their plants in their home town or town in which they worked were first explored by Hill (1954) some 30 years ago and have been summarised more recently by Gudgin (1978:105–8). The firms are begun with very little capital and thus do not have the resources to undertake elaborate searches for appropriate sites. Their small initial labour and land requirements make a local site feasible as their demands can be met by almost all places within an urban system. By staying in their local region entrepreneurs are able to reduce the uncertainty inherent in the start-up process; not only will they be familiar with many aspects of the local business environment but they will also avoid the stress associated with house sale and purchase. Many firms begin on a part-time basis (in itself a risk-reducing strategy) which ties entrepreneurs to their local areas because of their full-time jobs. Material and service linkages built up during this part-time phase will further tie entrepreneurs to their local areas. Many small firms are aimed at local markets and such market knowledge can be obtained through personal contacts in the local area. The whole start-up process can be eased by using the home as an office, by a knowledge of available premises and by the ability to hire reliable labour through local friendship networks. Finally, capital raised from outside an entrepreneurs' own resources (for example, from local banks or finance houses) may tie the new firm to the local area if the local managers prefer their high risk investments to be close at hand. Stability will be further enhanced where entrepreneurs' loans are secured by second mortgages on their homes. As Cross (1981:228) observes 'this explanation appears convincing and is intuitively appealing in its internal logic'. The locational conservatism reflects the fact that small firms in general have a high degree of locational tolerance (the economic conditions for small firm operation are widespread) while a specific new firm is tied to a founder's local area because of the reduction of uncertainty associated with start-up in a known area.

Although small firms in general can operate anywhere some environments may be more conducive to new firm formation than others. To be a region with a high firm formation rate requires both an adequate supply of local entrepreneurs and an environment which eases the new firm formation process. These two elements are not readily separated and they tend to interact with one another as can be seen from the discussion below.

ENTREPRENEURIAL BEHAVIOUR

Three potential influences on the supply of local entrepreneurs have been investigated. The first is a region's industrial mix, the second is the region's occupational and social characteristics, and the third is its plant size structure. Although it is possible to discuss these influences separately and to argue for the dominant role for any one of them, it is more likely that they all play a part in contributing to regional variations in new firm formation rates.

Industrial structure

At first sight it might appear that the particular mix of economic activities in a region should have little influence on the supply of entrepreneurs and on new firm formation rates since theoretically there is no reason why new firms should be related to previously existing activities. It takes on a potential as a major influence since, in addition to their locational stability, entrepreneurs tend to show at least some links with the industries they have left. This can be illustrated at a broad level of manufacturing versus other activities and at a much finer level of industrial disaggregation.

The majority of founders are drawn from the manufacturing sector. In the East Midlands almost 90 per cent of the founders came from the manufacturing sector (Gudgin 1978:113) while in Scotland the figure was 72 per cent (Cross 1981:233). Since manufacturing employees accounted for less than 40 per cent of employees in these regions, employees from manufacturing activities are over-represented in the new firm formation process. It does not seem unreasonable to argue that regions with a small proportion of manufacturing employees will have their new firm formation rates reduced, although Gudgin and Fothergill (1984:204) argue that manufacturing firms established by people from other sectors can form a high proportion of all new manufacturing firms in districts with little manufacturing industry.

The link between a region's industrial mix and

new firm formation is less straightforward. Fothergill and Gudgin (1982:125) assert (based on East Midlands data) that '85 per cent of founders set up their firms in trades in which they have previous experience', while in Cleveland 72 per cent of new manufacturing firms were set up in the two-digit industry from which the founder originated (estimated from Storey 1982: 114). These figures indicate that the existing industrial mix may be of major significance. Other evidence indicates that founders do not seem to be strongly tied to the industrial group of their previous employer even when industries are classified at the relatively crude order (two-digit) level. In Scotland (estimated from Cross 1981:235) among the founders originating in the manufacturing sector only 64 per cent set up firms in the same two-digit industry, while analysis at three-digit level in the Northern region (Johnson and Cathcart 1979:275) indicated that founders were as likely to establish a firm in the same three-digit industry as they were to establish a firm in another industry. Where changes do take place these may be influenced by the features of the founder's previous industry founders remaining with an industry when its output is growing and/or small units are feasible and moving outside it when output is falling or the minimum efficient scale makes too great demands on the financial resources of an individual.

The extent of inter-sectoral variation in new firm formation is illustrated for Eire and the East Midlands in Table 11.1 (O'Farrell and Crouchley 1984:227). The four industries with the highest entry rates (wood, cork, brushes; furniture; printing and publishing; plastics) are identical in the two countries and are industries characterised by small plants, while one of the lowest entry rates is found in drink and tobacco characterised by large plants. It is perhaps of significance that typical small plant industries with low entry rates (footwear and hosiery) are those suffering from import penetration (Ch. 2) while those with high entry rates have a degree of natural protection with a high bulk or weight to value ratio.

Although studies of net employment change have played down the role of industrial structure in influencing regional variations (Ch. 3) there is sufficient evidence of entrepreneurs establishing a firm in the same sector in which they were previously employed and of varying rates of new firm formation in different sectors to justify exploring the possibility that regional variations in industrial structure explain variations in the geography of new firms. This task was undertaken by Gould and Keeble (1984) who were able to show that industrial structure by no means explains all the variations in the new firm formation rate in East Anglia. Even when the adjustments for structure were made a Cambridge effect still stood out and, perhaps more

Table 11.1 Standardised new firm formation rates, selected industries, East Midlands and Ireland

Industry	East Midlands 1968–75	Ireland 1973–81
Food	0.39	0.36
Drink and tobacco	0.07	0.15
Hosiery	0.36	0.19
Footwear	0.14	0.10
Clothing	0.75	0.74
Wood, cork, brushes	2.52	2.95
Furniture	1.95	4.24
Paper products	0.43	1.11
Printing and publishing	0.79	1.28
Chemicals, fertilisers, pharmaceuticals, etc.	0.27	0.89
Cement, structural clay, glass and pottery	0.27	1.01
Plastics	1.85	2.09

(*Source*: O'Farrell and Crouchley 1984:227)

significantly, the over-representation of new firms in the environmentally attractive Norfolk and Suffolk coasts was very evident.

Clearly, industrial structure must be taken into account when investigating spatial variability in new firm formation but it is not a simple task (Gudgin, 1978:140). The main difficulty is that with small samples of new firms breaking the data down by sector and region leaves many industries unrepresented in many regions, a dilemma noted by O'Farrell and Crouchley (1984:233) and one which makes generalisation across a set of regions extremely difficult. It is because of this dilemma that the role of industrial structure in explaining regional variations in new firm formation has not been fully explored.

Population and occupational characteristics

Not only may regional variations in industrial structure affect new firm formation but also it is possible for the population and occupational characteristics of a region to have an influence. The potential influence of population characteristics has received only limited attention.

Populations may differ in their attitudes to risk with new firm formation held back where there is an aversion to risk taking. Such attitudes are difficult to measure but they may be related to the migration characteristics of a region's population. A marked out-migration may remove those willing to take risks, while a marked in-migration might bring in potential entrepreneurs. Such ideas are essentially speculative.

There is more evidence available to examine the age and educational background of the individuals founding new firms and if new firm formation is related to particular age groups or to individuals with particular educational qualifications then regions in which these elements are well represented may well have higher new firm formation rates. Evidence from a number of British regions suggests the majority of founders lie within the 30–45 age range (Scotland, south Hampshire, Greater Manchester and Merseyside) but there are differences in the proportion of firms founded by older individuals. In three of the regions the proportion of founders over 45

was less than 20 per cent but in south Hampshire the proportion of older founders was 32 per cent (Cross 1981:209; Lloyd and Mason 1984:215).

It is difficult to establish whether higher levels of education increase the propensity to form firms. In Scotland, the majority of founders (57 per cent) had ceased full-time education by the age of 19 (Cross, 1981:215), but 16 per cent did not start full-time employment until they were 22–25. It is not unreasonable to assume that most of these would have been in higher or further education until their early twenties. At present time only about 7 per cent of each age cohort in Britain proceeds to full-time higher education in universities and polytechnics suggesting that this group is over-represented in the new firm formation process.

As is evident from this description of some very limited evidence as to the relationship between population characteristics and new firm formation this type of explanation has not, as yet, been explored in any detail. Most emphasis has been placed on areal variations in occupational mix, the population characteristic for which data are readily available. Of course, occupation and educational levels are related to one another.

One of the striking features of change in local labour markets has been the emergence of a new spatial division of labour which results in a tendency for white-collar and administrative jobs to be spatially separate from the jobs of operatives (Ch. 7). The implication of this for new firm formation is that if people from certain types of occupation have a greater propensity to set up new firms then the distribution of occupations will influence the distribution of new firms. The evidence suggests that this propensity does exist. In Scotland, the majority (63 per cent) of founders had previously occupied managerial positions prior to setting up a new manufacturing enterprise (Cross 1981:214). It would appear that managerial experience is an important prerequisite for new firm formation and regions with low proportions of managerial employees may experience low birth rates.

Figure 11.4 shows that there are some empirical data to support this view. This relates the

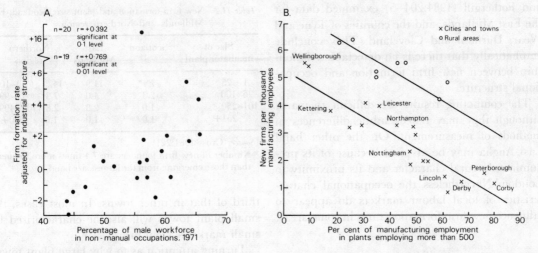

Fig. 11.4 Influences upon new firm formation rates (A) Occupational structure, East Anglia, 1971 to 1981 (B) Employment in large plants, East Midlands, 1968 to 1975 (*Sources*: (A) Gould and Keeble 1984:197 (B) Fothergill and Gudgin 1982:120)

proportion of the male workforce in non-manual occupations in 1971 to the firm formation rate in each of 20 sub-regions of East Anglia. The firm formation rate has been adjusted to allow for differences in industrial structure between sub-regions. Among 19 districts there is a strong relationship between the two variables and as Gould and Keeble (1984:197) conclude, 'local residential occupational structure . . . [is] . . . the chief – and powerful – determinant of recent rates of new manufacturing firm formation in East Anglia'.

Although the occupational data in this case relate to all occupations (not only those in manufacturing) there is a possibility that in-migration to the region of manufacturing plants (discussed in the next chapter) has brought with it some potential entrepreneurs. This may be particularly marked in East Anglia since in-migration was characterised by complete transfers (rather than branches) which brought with them managers and skilled workers with sufficient experience to establish new firms. A weak relationship between the in-migration rate of an area and its new firm formation rate was evident in the East Anglian data (Gould and Keeble 1984:197). Conversely, in-migration of branch plants with their low proportion of managerial staff may damp down

firm formation rates but the evidence here is even more speculative. McDermott's (1979:304) study of the Scottish electronics industry concluded 'few Scottish firms could be traced which owed their existence to spin off from (externally owned) electronics firms'. Similarly, re-working data from Cross (1981) indicates that while only 36 per cent of the Scotland's manufacturing employees were in Scottish-owned plants, 55 per cent of the founders had been employed in a Scottish plant immediately prior to setting up their own firm. This evidence does at least suggest that externally owned plants are less successful than indigenous firms as a source of potential entrepreneurs and it is tempting to argue that this may arise as externally owned plants are characterised by few managerial staff and what managerial staff are present are able to seek advancement within the firm's internal labour market (Ch. 7).

Outside East Anglia, the relationships between occupational structure and new firm formations are less obvious, although these studies confine themselves to relating firm formation to the proportion of non-manual employees in manufacturing. This is justified by the fact that, as we have seen, most firms are founded by those working within manufacturing. Gudgin and Fothergill (1984:204–5) examined data for the East Midlands, and the counties of Tyne and Wear, Durham and Cleveland. They conclude emphatically that there is no detectable relationship between new firm formation and occupational structure.

The conflicting results are difficult to marry although they may reflect subtle differences in methods of measurement. On the other hand East Anglia may be atypical because of its predominantly rural character and its proximity to London. Nevertheless the occupational characteristics of local labour markets do appear to influence new firm formation rates in some areas.

Plant size

Although the industrial, population and occupational characteristics of a region may influence the rate of new firm formation another influence appears to be a region's plant size structure. The greater the dominance of an area by large plants the lower is the birth rate, and conversely, where the proportion of small plants is high so too the birth rate is high (Chinitz 1961:284). It seems reasonable to accept this as a general statement of an observed empirical reality but in explaining why the presence of large plants reduces the new firm formation rate the ideas are still speculative and remain to be confirmed or refuted by detailed empirical analysis.

Cross (1981) has usefully brought together the data on plant size and this is shown in Table 11.2. The data show that employee for employee small plants produce more new firm founders than large ones. The trend in the number of new firm founders is consistent between all three areas and in each area the trend is consistently downwards from high rates associated with small plants and low rates associated with large plants. The general pattern is confirmed if attention is turned to regions with different plant size structures. This is illustrated dramatically in Fig. 11.4B which relates the percentage of manufacturing employment in plants employing more than 500 to the number of new firms per 1,000 manufacturing employees. The rate of new firm formation in large plant towns is almost one-

Table 11.2 New firm formation and plant size: Scotland, East Midlands and Northern region

Size of incubator plant	Scotland	East Midlands	Northern region	
1– 25	7.4*	11.9	14.3	(1–10)
26–100	2.3	4.0	7.3	(11–99)
101–250	1.0	2.8	2.8	(100–499)
251+	1.0	1.0	1.0	(500+)

(*Source*: Cross 1981:221)
* Number of new firm founders are 7.4 times more frequent than those emerging from the largest size band.

third of that in other towns. In most cases, the small plant towns will also be characterised by small market-system firms.

Turning attention as to why large plant towns are less conducive than small plant towns to new firm formation the realm of speculation begins, although it is not difficult to list a number of factors which might explain the observed relationship (Fothergill and Gudgin 1982:124–8). If founders stay with the same industry the fact they are working in a large plant industry may make it impossible for them to raise sufficient capital to start a plant of minimum efficient scale. It was shown in the earlier discussion of industrial structure that new firms were most characteristic of industries where the minimum efficient scale was small. A considerable number of firms begin by undertaking subcontract work for other firms, but many large plants internalise much of their work and what work is put out, is put out to large well-established plants which are perceived as having better quality control and reliability than small firms.

Small firms (and their small plants) provide ideal training grounds for the founders of firms. The head of the small firm is readily accessible and provides a clear example to follow and the small firm may offer a greater variety of work experience than the large firm as individuals undertake a wider range of tasks than the functional specialists found in the larger firm and its larger plants. Arising from this argument is the concept of *splintering* whereby employees leave an existing firm to set up their own operation. Although the splintering process is not confined to small firms, it has been seen as contributing to the survival of concentrations of small firms in cities such as those characteristic of the garment industry of New York and London (Hall 1962) and of other concentrations such as the jewellery industry in Birmingham described in an early study by Wise (1949). It is also possible that it is characteristic of new high-technology industries and, indeed, the Silicon Valley developments (Ch. 6) can be explained in part in this way but there was little evidence of such a process in the United Kingdom instruments industry (Oakey 1981:96–100).

Other factors may have an influence too. The limited availability of premises in large plant towns will restrict new firm formation, while in small plant towns there can be numerous suitable premises through the departure of firms from the crowded platform. Abandoned steel works, sugar mills and car assembly plants can offer little to the small firm unless public or private investors undertake modification of the redundant premises. Ready availability of premises may well ease the barriers to entry in small plant towns although in most centres some premises can be found if a sufficiently careful search is undertaken.

It has also been suggested (Thwaites 1978) that where the large plants are externally owned and associated with the later stages of the product-cycle new firm formation will be damped down. This partly reflects the lack of white-collar jobs noted earlier but also a possible emphasis on unskilled jobs. In the later stages of the product-cycle the stable production technology is unlikely to provide a stimulus to new firm development as spin-offs are more likely when employees are engaged in problem-solving tasks. Further, unskilled jobs tend to be for female workers who have not been noted for entrepreneurial activity in the past.

Finally, the presence of a very active small firm sector will provide plenty of examples for the founder to follow. Contacts with other small firms may be made as part of an employee's job while informal contacts with potential and actual founders are more likely. In such an area the entrepreneur will find access to social clubs and business organisations much easier and will feel less of a 'second-class' citizen if such social groups are not dominated by big business (Chinitz 1961:285).

Although a large number of reasons have been put forward to explain why small firms provide a source of future potential entrepreneurs they are not supported by any strong empirical evidence other than the association between small firms and new firm formation and are, therefore, little more than speculations. It should also be noted that as the number of regional case studies of new firm formation has increased so doubt has been cast on the generality of the relationship between plant size and new firm formation. Gould and Keeble (1984:196) were able to find only a weak relationship between the two variables in their East Anglian data set.

REGIONAL ENVIRONMENTS

While its particular industrial, occupational and plant-size characteristics give a region its own distinctive features which can influence new firm formation rates, important too are other aspects of the regional environment which affect the context within which new firms will operate. Access to capital, to markets and to industrial premises may, to some extent, constrain the opportunities for entrepreneurs to establish new businesses, while some policy environments may be particularly conducive to new firm formation.

New firms place a considerable reliance on personal savings, with loans and overdrafts from banks being of secondary importance. For example 67 per cent of Cleveland firms cited savings as the most important source of start-up capital and 21 per cent cited loans and overdrafts (Storey 1982:149). While in Scotland personal savings were mentioned as a source of capital in 44 per cent of the cases and local banks in 18 per cent of the cases (Cross 1981: 238). In Oakey's (1984a:130) study of high-technology firms personal savings were the main source of capital of 67 per cent of the firms in Scotland, 69 per cent of the firms in South-East England and 52 per cent of the firms in the San Francisco Bay area.

There are variations in savings per head and

income per head by region which may influence the availability of personal savings for new firm formation in different regions. Similarly, for many individuals starting a firm the only security for a loan is an owner-occupied house. For non-owner occupiers there may be difficulties in raising finance and regions with low levels of owner occupation may find new firm formation rates damped down because of the difficulties of raising loans, while variations in house prices will work to restrict the amount a financial institution is likely to lend to a particular individual. Whether or not regional variations in savings, owner occupation and average house prices do affect new firm formation is yet to be established for manufacturing firms. However, examination of these relationships for *all* new VAT registrations in the United Kingdom shows that new firm formation is higher where owner-occupation levels are high (Whittington 1984:255).

Chapter 8 described the nature of spatial variations in venture capital which can be of particular importance to the new firm. Indeed, the significance of venture capital in the North American context is seen with reference to high-technology firms in the San Francisco Bay area where for 30 per cent of the firms venture capital was an important source of funding.

Local markets are of particular significance since most small firms start by serving them. The potential of these markets will be influenced by the purchasing power of the region's occupants (for firms serving final demand) and the existing industrial structure which will influence the availability of industrial markets. New firms in Merseyside, Greater Manchester and south Hampshire mainly served local markets (Lloyd and Mason 1984:217). In Greater Manchester 41 per cent of the firms conducted over half their business within the local area, in south Hampshire the proportion was 50 per cent and in Merseyside almost three-quarters of the firms showed a marked dependence on the local area. In Vancouver over half a sample of new firms sold at least 75 per cent of their output within the Vancouver metropolitan area (Khan and Hayter 1984:7). It seems likely the consumer (and industrial) demand within a region may influ-

ence firm formation rates. Yet local ties may not always be as important as these figures indicate. For example, in the study of new firms in the East Midlands only between 16 and 23 per cent of the firms were able to say that most sales were within 50 km (Gudgin 1978:118). Other things being equal a high local demand may allow more firms to come into operation but whether variations in local demand affect new firm formation rates still has to be established.

The third element, availability of buildings, has already been touched upon as one of the factors which might encourage higher rates of new firm formation in small plant towns. Although it is impossible to measure the number of new firms that have not been set up because they could not find adequate premises, surveys in 1980–81 in Manchester and Merseyside indicated that only 7 per cent of the firms experienced difficulties in finding adequate premises. Most were searching for small premises (around 4,000 sq. ft.) on short leases and cheap rents and they were easy to find in either old adapted nineteenth-century units or in purpose-built small units constructed by private developers or government agencies. This evidence from North-West England need not necessarily reflect the situation in Britain as a whole as in a more prosperous part of Britain (south Hampshire) finding suitable premises was a problem for no less than 70 per cent of the new firms. This may reflect the absence of a major nineteenth-century industrial inheritance, the relatively little interest in building small units (particularly by government agencies) and, until quite recently, the anti-industry planning regulations in the more scenic parts of south Hampshire. This has stopped new firms occupying old industrial premises or former farm buildings and has restricted the development of new industrial sites (Lloyd and Mason 1984:217). It is possible that the limited availability of premises may have restricted new firm formation in south Hampshire and, more generally, may be an influence on new firm formation rates in some areas.

Policy effects on the geography of new firm formation have not, as yet, been measured. National policies to encourage new firm formation may raise the formation rates in regions where there is a tradition of new firm formation, while areal variations resulting from derived spatial policies might arise if some local administrations are more successful than others in encouraging new firm formation.

Although each of these elements: capital, markets, land and industrial policy may independently enhance the new firm formation rate in a region it is possible that certain combinations of the elements provide environments which are *incubators* or *seedbeds* in which new firms can grow. This idea was developed by Vernon and Hoover (1959) to help in understanding the location of economic activity within the New York metropolitan area but the arguments are also applicable at the regional scale. The incubator hypothesis states that new firms 'will be attracted to areas offering services essential to their operation that they, because of their small size and limited resources, would be unable to provide internally' (Struyk and James 1975:109). Such services would include production space to rent, legal and financial services, rapid access to stocks of supplies and components, contacts with other firms offering lucrative subcontract work and access to employee-related services such as public transport and catering facilities. Indeed, this would include the whole range of localisation and urbanisation economies discussed in Chapter 9 as well as the postulated splintering effect described earlier. However, as the description of the spatial pattern of new firm formation made clear the evidence indicates that, at the present time, new firm formation rates are higher in rural areas than urban areas suggesting that, taken as a whole, urban areas do not act as incubators or seedbeds of new firms. Indeed, Oakey (1981:100) argues that in new modern industries the old analogy of industrial concentrations providing a seedbed for new firms is incorrect and they provide only a source of seeds cast into the wind.

The source of 'heat' for the incubator need not necessarily be confined to the traditional urbanisation and localisation economies and, for firms operating in new industries advantages might lie in access to research and development informa-

tion. The significance of access to Stanford University for firms in Silicon Valley has already been mentioned but equally Gould and Keeble observe that although high-technology firms accounted for only 13 per cent of new firm employment in East Anglia, no less than 75 per cent of them were formed within 50 km of Cambridge. Although partly explained by the occupational and industrial structure of the area a more complete explanation will have to

lie in a complex of actual and perceived environmental advantages for high-technology industry, which are rooted in the labour, entrepreneurial and information advantages of the Cambridge region, the historic presence of Cambridge University as a world famous centre of scientific research, and the residential attractiveness of this particular part of East Anglia, coupled perhaps with the prestige of a Cambridge post-code (Gould and Keeble 1984:199).

NEW FIRM FORMATION IN RETROSPECT

The discussion of the variables influencing new firm formation rates indicates the problem of identifying those which are of importance and, within that group, attempting to get some idea of their relative importance. It is also vital to examine the way in which these variables operate in a regional context. The characteristics of entrepreneurs and their new firms are reasonably well established but less is known about their geography and the evidence so far is very conflicting. An attempt to consider some 68 different influences on regional variations in formation rates within Scotland was deemed by its author a failure although it did reach the conclusion that

there are combinations of factors that...exert an influence (on new firm formation)...At a number of spatial scales, the number employed in small plants (employing 100 or less employees), the overall level of administrative employment and the industrial diversity of local industry all appear important influences (Cross 1981:275).

With a more careful selection of variables a study of the spatial variations in new firm formation in Ireland (Fig. 11.3A) produced more use-

Table 11.3 Factors influencing spatial variations in new firm formation rates

Variable	Measure
Increasing markets (+)	Rate of manufacturing employment change
Young plants (+)	Median age of plant stock
Independent single plants (+)	Proportion employment in independent single-plant firms
Small plants (+)	Proportion employment in plants with <20 employees
Rurality (+)	Proportion of population outside towns with over 5,000 population
Agricultural employment (+)	Proportion employed in agriculture
Commercial, retail and wholesale employment (+)	Proportion employed in commercial, retail and wholesale activities
Large plants (−)	Proportion employed in large plants
Industry/sector	Not measured
Occupational mix	Not measured

(*Source*: Based on O'Farrell and Crouchley 1984)

ful results. The variables included in this study are listed in Table 11.3 and include many of the factors discussed earlier in the chapter although they do not include the effects of industrial structure or occupational mix, the former being excluded because of inadequate data. Some 50 per cent of the regional variation was explained by the proportion of employees in plants with less than 20 employees and the degree of rurality. None of the other variables made a significant contribution to the regression equation. A one-percentage point increase in the proportion of plants in a county employing fewer than 20 increased new firm formation by 0.04 per 1,000 manufacturing employees per annum, while a one-percentage increase in a county's population resident outside towns with over 5,000 residents increases new firm formation by 0.03 per 1,000 employees, having controlled for the effects of plant size. Unfortunately the influence of rurality needs to be disaggregated to see why it behaves in this way as it may be a surrogate measure or indeed a composite measure of some of the other influences discussed in the last section. The difficulty of interpreting these regional typology variables was stressed in the preamble to Parts III and IV.

The multi-variate approaches have not, as yet, proved very successful. There are few data sets relating to new firm formation in different areas and complementary data sets running across the whole range of possible explanatory variables are difficult to assemble. An alternative approach is to calculate an index of regional entrepreneurship which then might be correlated with regional variations in new firm formation. Such an index has been developed by Storey (1981:183–202).

This index averages a region's ranking upon six principal indicators which may be associated with high levels of entrepreneurship. These are the percentage of small firms, the percentage of population that are managers, the percentage of the population with degrees, savings per head of population, the percentage of houses owner occupied and their price, the percentage of the workforce in low entry barrier industries and the regional income distribution. The distribution of the index values is shown in Fig. 11.5; they are much as would be expected. The Northern regions and Wales score badly on the index, while the South-East and South-West score particularly highly with East Anglia ranking third. Admittedly, this is a simple index built solely on rankings and ignoring relationships between variables but it does provide a vivid illustration of the way in which entrepreneurship might vary between regions. It has yet to be related to

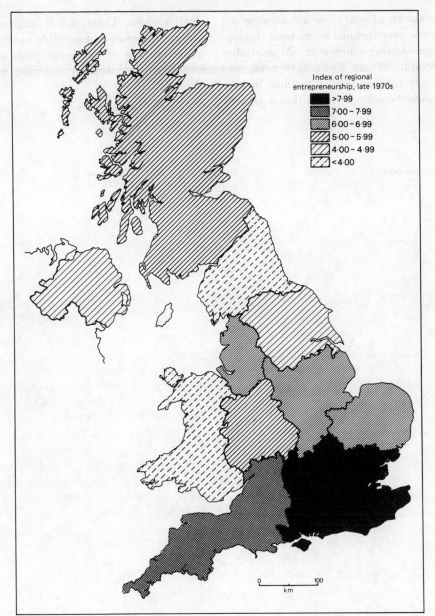

Fig. 11.5 Regional entrepreneurship in the United Kingdom, late 1970s (*Source*: Based on Storey 1982:196)

spatial variations in the formation rates of new manufacturing firms and as comparison with Fig. 11.2 makes clear any relationship is not a simple one. Wales scores highly on employment in enterprises new to manufacturing but has one of the lowest scores on the index of regional entrepreneurship.

CONCLUSION

Despite the current enthusiasm for studies of new firm formation their relatively small contribution to gross job creation will be shown in the afterword of Part IV. Even where marked variations in the geography of new firm formation can be shown to exist their influence on net change may be overwhelmed by massive employment changes in other components. Most studies of the geography of new firms have been confined to single regions or to variations in new firm formation between areas within relatively small regions. There is still some considerable way to go before it is possible to arrive at a full understanding of the geographies of new firm formation described in the first part of this chapter.

12

MOVEMENT AND ACQUISITION

The last chapter illustrated some of the factors influencing the location of new firms and their associated new plants. New plants are the focus of this chapter too but here the interest lies in industrial movement which arises from new plants set up by existing firms. The chapter also considers plants acquired by firms which are new to a firm but which previously had an independent existence. To many people industrial movement is associated with the *runaway shop* described by Bluestone and Harrison (1982: 25) in these terms:

Just after the Second World War, in one fell swoop the Chance-Vought Division of United Aircraft moved an entire industrial complex from Bridgeport, Connecticut, to Dallas, Texas. This particular relocation, which had financial assistance from the federal government, has been described as one of the most spectacular migrations in industrial history – fifteen hundred people, two thousand machines, and fifty million pounds of equipment were involved.

These physical relocations, or 'transfers', are a part of industrial movement but often more significant in long distance movement, is the establishment of a new production unit (a branch plant) to supplement a firm's existing production capacity. By establishing a branch plant new capacity needed by the firm is set up not on the firm's existing site but is 'moved' to a new location. Typical examples of major new branch plants are the motor vehicle assembly plant established recently by a Japanese firm, Nissan, in northern England (Dicken 1983) and that established by the West German firm (Volkswagen) in Pennsylvania (Krumme 1981a). Of course branch plants are also established within a firm's home country. Branches and transfers are normally grouped together as the main elements of industrial movement (Sant 1975b; Townroe 1979) or more unusually, industrial migration (Keeble, 1976; Hoare, 1983). While transfers move a firm from one area to another, branches extend the influence of a firm to another area although control functions may remain at head office. The distinction between branches and transfers is not always clear in empirical investigation (Appendix I). Despite the interest in different types of branches (Ch. 4) this is rarely taken into account in considering the geography of branch plants and the lack of information on the age of products manufactured in branch plants make it difficult to relate much of the branch plant literature to filter-down ideas (Ch. 6). An alternative to establishing a branch plant for many firms is to acquire another firm and its plant or plants. This only involves a change of ownership for the acquired plants rather than new employment but the change of ownership may have important consequences for the subsequent employment history of the plants (see Ch. 13) and thus the geography of acquisitions has increasingly attracted the attention of industrial geographers.

Not all movement is of relevance to the changing geography of employment opportunities since very short distance moves make little difference to the total number of jobs in local labour markets. Admittedly different moves will affect different individuals in different ways and employees on low wages may find that even a very short distance move may take a job outside the area defined by their own time and cost constraints. Short distance moves may be of significance to these individuals but more generally interest is focused upon jobs which are moved between different labour markets. If moves of up to 19 km are defined as moves *within* local labour markets then just over 29,000 jobs were moved *between* local labour markets in the United Kingdom from 1976 to 1980. Of the employment in these longer distance moves 71 per cent was in branches rather than transfers. In contrast, just over 60 per cent of employment in moves within local labour markets was in transfers and only around 40 per cent of the employment was in branches (Killick 1983:468). Movers thus consist of a *dual population* (Keeble 1976) made up of short distance movement dominated by transfers and long distance movement dominated by branches. At the present time in the United Kingdom branches and transfers are of a similar size with between 50 and 60 employees each.

The movement of industry has been studied exhaustively for a number of reasons. First, the search for a new production site relates clearly to industrial location theory with its emphasis upon the best location for a plant. In this context, theory and practice are related closely. Second, the problem is very much a practical one thus allowing geographers to develop an expertise which can be of clear value to business interests. Third, movement is amenable to policy initiatives, particularly policies which attempt to divert moves from one destination to another. The practical value of the research to regional and district authorities is self-evident. Fourth, in the more prosperous 1960s and 1970s industrial movement was a very obvious feature in the changing geography of employment opportunities. The four factors apply widely but the final factor, availability of data, relates only to Britain where central government has collected data on industrial movement for almost 40 years. The geography of acquisition has received limited

attention and only very general outlines have been built up from studies of specific firms or from samples of a small number of acquiring firms.

The first section of the chapter illustrates the contemporary geography of industrial movement and acquisition. The second section considers why some regions attract more migrant plants than others, while the third probes into the ways in which managers decide about the location of a new plant. The findings reported in the second and third sections go some way towards explaining the patterns described in the first section. The illustrations in the first section are drawn predominantly from Britain as 'there is no source which can give... [an]... overall picture of the geographical distribution of industrial moves in the United States' (Townroe 1979:90). To compensate for this emphasis the discussion in sections two and three draws examples primarily from research in the United States on location factors and the location decision. The majority of the discussion is concerned with the establishment of branch plants and acquisition patterns; only limited attention is given to short distance transfers.

THE GEOGRAPHY OF MOVEMENT AND ACQUISITION

Movements and acquisitions are undertaken by firms. Establishing the *spatial growth* patterns of individual firms requires a detailed probing of corporate histories. Figure 12.1A illustrates the spread of the operations of a soap and detergent manufacturer, Proctor and Gamble, through the United States from 1886 to 1963. The case illustrated in Fig. 12.1B is particularly interesting as Clarks' policy was to expand footwear production away from its main location to gain access to labour resources but to constrain that movement to within the range of a daily journey from the main plant. Each axis, as can be seen in the diagram, maintained a particular specialisation to ease supervision and the movement of technical staff, supplies and products. Whereas Clarks spread by the establishment of branch plants, Fig. 12.1C illustrates the spatial growth

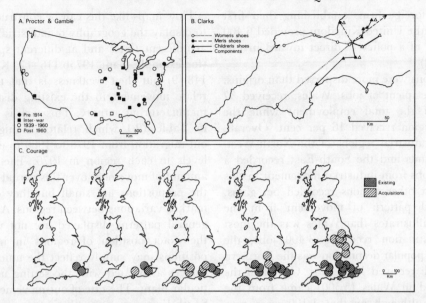

Fig. 12.1 The spatial growth of corporate systems (A) Proctor and Gamble, 1886 to 1963 (B) Clarks, 1939 to 1967: branch plant growth (C) Courage, 1951 to 1972: growth by acquisition (*Sources*: (A) Rees 1974:201 (B) Spooner 1972:210 (C) Watts 1980b:198)

of Courage (a British brewing firm) whose acquisitions (seen earlier in Fig. 4.2) were undertaken primarily to capture regional markets. Each of these corporate maps suggest interesting problems in themselves as well as contributing to aggregate patterns of movement and acquisition.

An examination of aggregate industrial movement patterns raises three questions. Which regions are contributing most (least) employment to industrial movement? Which regions are receiving most (least) jobs from industrial movement? In what ways are the origins and destinations of moves related to one another? Figure 12.2 relates to employment in 1980 in the 299 inter-regional moves in the United Kingdom between 1976 and 1980. The major origin for the moves was the South-East which accounted for over half the employment in inter-regional moves (59 per cent) while the second most important region (the North-West) created only 11 per cent of the jobs. Regions like Wales, Northern region and Scotland recorded negligible outward movement and Northern Ireland generated no outward movement at all. While the South-East generated 8,700 jobs and the North-West only

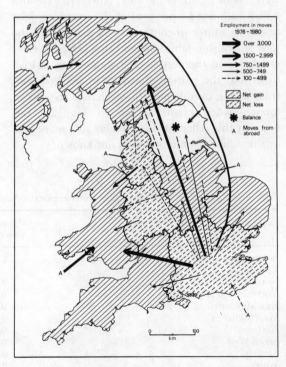

Fig. 12.2 Inter-regional movement of employment, United Kingdom, 1976 to 1980 (*Source*: Based on Killick 1983:468)

1,600 jobs, foreign firms establishing their first branches in the United Kingdom provided 6,400 jobs as part of a policy of direct inward investment (Ch. 2).

Destinations were more dispersed than origins. The chief recipient of jobs, Wales, received 37 per cent of the total employment while the Northern region received 16 per cent. Overall, the major industrial regions of the North-West, West Midlands and the South-East recorded a net loss of jobs from industrial movement in this period; most other regions recorded net gains. The general pattern of movement from the South-East illustrates that Wales was the most popular destination receiving 3,400 jobs, the second most popular destination was the Northern region which received 1,900 jobs. Over half the jobs received in Wales (5,500) came from the South-East, although another 1,100 were contributed by the North-West. Examination of the firms setting up their first manufacturing plant in Britain shows that the preferred destinations were Wales, Scotland and Northern Ireland which received 65 per cent of the incoming jobs from this source in contrast to 44 per cent of the jobs of British origin. Foreign firms placed greater emphasis on the peripheral regions than British firms and the pattern shown is in marked contrast to the overall pattern of change in jobs in foreign-owned plants shown in Fig. 2.5 but whether this reflects the particular sub-set of jobs or the different time period is not known.

Flow maps like this can be constructed readily to display the geography of industrial movement at different times and at different spatial scales (for example, Sant 1975b:116–17; Keeble 1976: 148–9) but their weakness is that they do not relate movement to the existing distribution of manufacturing activity. This task is undertaken in Table 12.1 which relates in-migration and out-migration from 1976 to 1980 to employment levels in each region in 1976. The very small amount of movement over this period means that the proportions are small but they do indicate marked variations between regions. Although the general patterns displayed are not unexpected, the exact position of regions in intermediate positions may simply reflect the unique circumstances associated with the setting up of a particular plant. The rate of out-movement from the South-East was twice that of any other region but the other regions were arranged along a continuum with no clear break in between. In recipient regions employment in in-moving British plants is three times more important in Wales than it is in the Northern region while in the Northern region it is twice as important as in East Anglia.

It is less easy to establish even the basic spatial pattern of acquisition but an example of the spread of corporate activities by acquisition is illustrated in Fig. 12.3. This describes acquisitions by firms based in New York City, Los Angeles and Chicago. Although it relates to

Table 12.1 Inter-regional industrial movement, Britain, 1976–80

Out-migration	% of 1976 employment	In-migration*	% of 1976 employment
South-East	0.47	Wales	2.37
East Anglia	0.20	Northern	0.73
North-West	0.16	East Anglia	0.31
Yorkshire and Humberside	0.15	Scotland	0.31
East Midlands	0.12	East Midlands	0.28
West Midlands	0.11	South-West	0.21
Northern	0.09	North-West	0.15
South-West	0.07	Yorkshire and Humberside	0.13
Scotland	0.07	South-East	0.07
Wales	0.03	West Midlands	0.03

(*Source*: Based on Killick 1983:468)
* Excludes first United Kingdom operations of overseas firms.

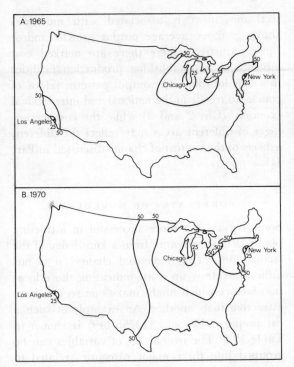

Fig. 12.3 Acquisition fields of firms in Los Angeles, Chicago and New York (A) 1965 (B) 1970 (*Source*: Green and Cromley 1984: 299)

firms in all sectors (not only manufacturing) it indicates well the kind of spatial patterns generated by acquisition activity. Between 1965 and 1970 the acquisition fields of the three cities witnessed major expansion and their influence spread over longer distances. The most notable differences occur in the case of Los Angeles, in that whereas 50 per cent of all acquisitions were within California in 1965 by 1970 the 50 per cent contour was well to the east of Denver and Santa Fe (Green and Cromley 1984).

In contrast to the previous study which examined all economic sectors Leigh and North (1978) examined only four sectors within United Kingdom manufacturing industry. The food, chemicals, textiles and clothing sectors upon which attention was concentrated all showed consistent levels of acquisition activity from year to year and attention was focused on the data for 1973–74, the latest available at the time of study. A striking feature was the concentration of acquiring firms in South-East England and although the South-East was the leading employment region for chemicals, clothing and food (28 per cent, 24 per cent, 21 per cent of employment shares respectively) its share of acquiring firms in these sectors was much higher (56 per cent, 62 per cent, and 65 per cent respectively). Even in textiles, the South-East had 17.8 per cent of acquiring firms although it had only a 3.5 per cent share of employment.

Acquisitions and movement (especially the setting up of branch plants) tend to be associated with the spatial growth of planning-system firms, but the part they play must not be over-stressed. Many market-system firms acquire rival organisations and can transfer operations to a larger site or establish a branch plant. A survey of new plants established by existing firms between 1964 and 1967 indicated that only 25 per cent had been established by the largest 500 firms in the United Kingdom (Inquiry Into Location Attitudes and Experience 1973:529). Yet multi-plant firms established 62 per cent of the plants compared with an estimate that only 21 per cent of UK-firms in 1963 were multi-plant (Keeble 1976: 132), which perhaps is indicative of the fact that planning-system firms are over-represented among the firms establishing branch plants.

A move to a new site is stimulated by output growth and/or pressures to cut costs. It is not confined to a few industrial sectors but is characteristic of almost all of them. Every two-digit industry in the United Kingdom experienced over 15 moves of over 35 km from 1966 to 1975 – the mechanical engineering sector recording no less than 491 moves. More detailed data relating to all moves at three-digit level indicate that out of 122 three-digit industries only five had no recorded openings between 1972 and 1975 (Pounce 1981:75). There is a strong relationship between above average sectoral output growth and above average employment in migrant plants (Keeble 1971:26–7). The two-digit industries with above average employment in movement in the United Kingdom from 1945 to 1965 were instrument engineering, electrical engineering, coal and petroleum products, chemicals,

clothing and other manufacturing. These industries still had above average movement rates
from 1966 to 1975 (Pounce 1981). The vehicles
sector was also important in the 1960s but this
was mainly a reflection of government initiatives.

Although industrial movement is typically
associated with growing industries it can also
arise where new plants are used to introduce new
technologies and to cut costs. More generally
Massey and Meegan (1982:128) stress that 'quite
significant levels of mobile employment can be
generated even...[where]...overall job opportunities are declining'.

While the stimulus to move may come from
plans to change output or cut costs it will be
further influenced by spatial variations in cost
and revenue surfaces (page 65). These surfaces
occur in one of three combinations (Keeble 1976:
131–2).

1. Spatial variations in the surfaces are small. In
other words costs and revenues do not vary
markedly. Movement to a new location is
unlikely either to increase revenue or to reduce
production costs and therefore movement will
tend to occur only if there is very rapid output
growth to stimulate it. Engineering industries
with stable technologies and mature products
would probably fall within this category.

2. Spatial variations in both surfaces are marked
and costs fall and/or revenues increase away
from the existing location. This may be characteristic of industries which have high labour
inputs and which are eager to exploit cheaper
labour or less organised labour or to obtain
more space for production (Chs 7 and 8). In
these circumstances movement may occur
without growth and may be accentuated
when profit margins fall.

3. Spatial variations in both surfaces are marked
and costs rise and/or revenues fall away from
the existing location. This might apply to
those industries which derive cost savings
from localisation and urbanisation economies
(Ch. 9). Many small subcontracting firms
may fall within this category. Such a pattern
of cost surfaces will tend to inhibit industrial
movement.

The evidence appears to suggest that industrial movement is associated with industries
showing above average output growth and/or
those industries where there are marked cost
advantages in establishing production facilities
in a new location. The output patterns relate, of
course, to trends in the national and international
economy (Chs 2 and 3) while the cost advantages of different areas may reflect the different
aspects of the context of change discussed in Part
III.

CORRELATES OF MOVEMENT

Some regions are more successful in attracting
plants than others and, from a knowledge of the
factors influencing industrial change 'it is not
difficult to draw up a list indicating those location factors which might make one region more
attractive than another. An example of such a
list prepared by Sant (1975b:149) is shown in
Table 12.2. The overall list of variables can be
grouped into three major categories related to
the constrained location influences, labour influ-

Table 12.2   Independent variables expected to influence
number of surviving moves in United Kingdom
regions

Constrained locations
1. Employees per urban acre
2. Per cent sub-region with urban status
3. Size of region (estimated radius)

Labour factors
4. Total number unemployed
5. Female activity rate
6. Average male manual earnings
7. Average female manual earnings
8. Male unemployed (per cent)
9. Female unemployed (per cent)
10. Total unemployed (per cent)

Explicit policy factors
11. Per cent employment in Assisted Areas
12. Target population of new towns as a percentage
of base year population
13. Total employment in Assisted Areas
14. Total target population in new towns

Frictional factor
15. Modified gravity weight related to size of
originating areas and their distance from
sub-region

(*Source*: Sant 1975b:138 and 149)

ences (discussed in Part III) and explicit policy influences (discussed in Ch. 15). The first group are surrogate measures for the availability of land, the second group measure different aspects of labour supply and the third are rather crude measures of policy initiatives. Excluded from the list are more subjective influences related to the perception of areas by industrialists. Most of the measures are straightforward and only variable 15 (the modified gravity weight) needs further explanation. This is derived from the market potential concept (Ch. 9 and Appendix II). The attractive power of a given region is derived from a summation of the number of moves generated by the major source regions divided by the distance between the sources and the area under consideration (Sant 1975b:140).

By using the number of surviving moves in each of 61 regions Sant obtained results which showed that during the period 1966 to 1971 the amount of labour available, short distance from the source regions and the availability of regional assistance were of approximately equal significance in influencing the number of moves to a region. Of secondary, but nonetheless significant, importance in attracting industry was new town development policy. The only significant and negative regression coefficient indicated that in regions where urban employment densities were high the number of incoming plants was reduced. The regression equation explained about 60 per cent of the variation between regions and on examination of the residuals provided hints that regions with high environmental values might be attracting more plants than predicted by the regression equation. This does appear to be the case, as Keeble (1976:142–50) in a study of the same period included a measure of residential attractiveness in his regression analysis and it emerged as one of the few significant regression coefficients and showing an expected positive association with inward movement.

In addition to trying to explain the overall patterns of movement it is sometimes useful to examine a sub-set of moves to investigate a particular problem. A useful example of this is a study by (Keeble 1971) which tried to explain the amount of movement into different Assisted

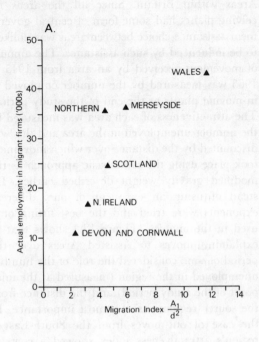

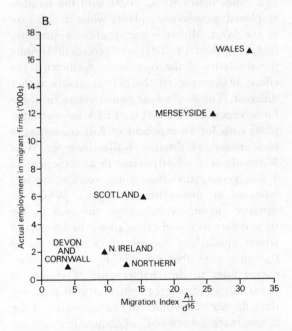

Fig. 12.4 Predicted and actual employment in plants moving to peripheral areas, United Kingdom, 1945 to 1965 (A) Movement from South-East England (B) Movement from the West Midlands conurbation (*Source*: Keeble 1971:57–8)

Areas within Britain. Since all the areas receiving plants had some form of central government assistance choice between areas was unlikely
to be influenced by such assistance. The amount
of movement received by an area from 1945 to
1965 was measured by the number employed in
in-moving plants at the end of the study period.
The attractiveness of each area was measured by
the number unemployed in the area and this was
discounted by the distance over which movement
took place using the same basic approach as the
modified gravity weight described earlier. Instead of using an exponent of one, different
exponents were tried and the best fitting ones
used in the analysis. Figure 12.4 shows that in
explaining moves to Assisted Areas over the
period of time considered the role of the number
unemployed in the region (measured at the mid-
point of the study period) and the distance from
the source region was of utmost importance. In
the case of out-moves from the South-East a
region's attractiveness index showed a correlation (Spearman's R) of +0.94 with the number
employed in in-moving plants while in the case
of the West Midlands conurbation a similarly
high coefficient (+ 0.93) was recorded. Despite
the similarity of the correlation coefficients the
effects of distance on the two areas are rather
different. The South-East moves relate to a distance exponent of 2.5 (Fig. 12.4A however displays data for an exponent of 2.0) suggesting a
high friction of distance while those for West
Midlands (Fig. 12.4B) relate to an exponent of
1.5 suggesting that increasing distance has less
influence on moves from that area. While the
distance exponents vary (and the reasons for
these differences need exploration) the key role of
labour availability stands out clearly. Some of
the difficulties this variable presents are discussed later in the chapter and, of course, it
needs further disaggregation to try to pick out
the influence of the different characteristics of the
labour market discussed in Chapter 7.

Similar distance decay functions have been
used to explain the acquisition fields of the North
American cities shown in Fig. 12.3. For both
New York and Chicago a distance decay function explained around 50 to 60 per cent of the

variations in acquisition patterns, although this
dropped to just under 40 per cent in the case of
Los Angeles (Green and Cromley 1984:297).

These examples give a broad indication of the
flavour of correlation studies of industrial movement and acquisition and the techniques used
can be applied to movement data for different
time periods and different places. The methodology provides a useful insight into the factors
influencing the destination of industrial movement although the 'factors' themselves may, in
fact, be summary measures of a yet wider range
of characteristics. This is most obvious where
'policy' is summarised by a single variable.
Similarly, the role of residential attractiveness
has been challenged because of its association
with non- or less-unionised labour. Equally
fuzzy is the influence of distance from the source
region which avoids questions as to the mechanisms which create the friction of distance.
More fundamentally, these studies tend to hide
the fact that firms are involved in the processes
of change. It is then necessary to explore the
factors which influence firms in making decisions
to select a particular location for a branch plant.

LOCATION FACTORS AND THE LOCATION DECISION

Conventionally, studies of the factors influencing
new plant locations select a sample of plants and
attempt to generalise from that sample, but a
case can be made for detailed in-depth studies of
particular location decisions. This is particularly
so where a single new investment is expected to
generate a large number of new jobs. Cases such
as these inevitably generate considerable public
interest and may be subject to particular political pressures as areas and communities compete
for the new jobs. Although there was a time
when the majority of industrial geographers were
dismissive of studies of this sort it is now recognised that a single decision involving one large
plant may have far more impact on a region's
employment opportunities (or its lack of them)
than a myriad of decisions taken by much smaller
firms.

The majority of studies collect data on location factors and location decisions from a number of firms. These studies vary considerably in their methodologies making comparisons between them very difficult. Some studies question firms that have moved, others ask about possible moves; some ask only about recent moves, others about all moves; some studies have very low response rates, others successfully interview most sampled firms; the status of the person approached varies between firms and many studies fail to recognise that decisions, especially in planning-system firms, are made by groups rather than individuals. The common method of putting questions to plant managers is often inappropriate as they may have had little to do with the location decision. Finally there are the quite critical difficulties in asking 'why was this location selected?' to a varied group of branch plants.

The chief difficulty with the question is that, as has been argued earlier (pages 76–8), different influences will operate at different scales. Suppose the firm argues that a particular location was selected primarily because of 'labour supply'. Does this relate to labour supply in the town or the region? Suppose again the answer had been 'access to markets', does this relate to the local market, the regional market or indeed better accessibility to the national market than other locations operated by the firm? It is only fair to say it is very difficult to resolve this problem without making questionnaires too long and unwieldy or focusing upon the reasons for location selection at a particular geographic scale.

The heterogeneous nature of branch plants raises further difficulties. Part-process plants and cloned plants (Ch. 4) as well as plants in different industries might be expected to be influenced by different location factors. There is evidence in the aggregate data (Fig. 12.2) which suggests foreign firms select different locations from domestic firms while analysis of the development of multinational firms drew attention to the distinction between cost-led and market-led expansion. Some of the distinctions between the different types of branch plants are taken up by

Moriarty (1983) but here branch plants are treated mainly as an undifferentiated group.

Location factors

There is a long tradition of identifying 'location factors' in studies in industrial geography both in North America (Logan 1970; Nishioka and Krumme 1973) and Britain (Inquiry into Location Attitudes and Experience 1973; Herron 1981). The most useful recent studies of location factors appear to be those of Schmenner (1982) and Moriarty (1983).

Moriarty examined a sample of the 530 manufacturing plants established in North Carolina between 1969 and 1974 and which were still in operation in 1975; attention here is concentrated upon the responses of the 60 plants established by US firms based outside North Carolina. North Carolina is reasonably distant from the manufacturing belt and at the time of the survey had the lowest average manufacturing wage in the United States as well as lowest level of unionisation. In this study firms were asked to assess whether 58 location factors were essential, very important, important, unimportant or not considered in site evaluation. Table 12.3 lists 49 of these factors and excludes nine factors (mainly amenity and local or state inducement factors) because they were not sufficiently important to any group of respondents.

The location factors, which apply to a variety of scales, are indicative of the wide range of factors which have some influence on branch plant locations. All the factors are clearly drawn from the literature discussed in the last two sections of the book. The categories were devised by the investigator and a surprising omission is that there are no questions about accessibility to other plants of the firm or indeed to its head office.

The major significance of labour factors stands out distinctly in Table 12.3 thus confirming the patterns identified in correlation studies. These branch plants are searching for locations with non-unionised and semi- or unskilled labour with high levels of productivity. The most important

Table 12.3 Location factors for branch plants in North Carolina

Location factors	Essential or very important (%)	Unimportant or not considered (%)
Labour factors		
Labour costs*	70	8
Availability of semi and unskilled labour	75	10
Availability of skilled labour	52	17
Labour productivity	70	8
Extent of labour unionisation	72	11
Labour climate	80	5
Right-to-work-law	63	22
Accessibility factors		
Suitability of rail service	43	43
Suitability of motor freight service	78	3
Suitability of air service	35	32
Suitability of access roads and highways	72	10
Proximity to production material sources	43	28
Proximity to national markets	45	38
Proximity to regional markets	52	35
Proximity to large city (> 50,000)	18	57
Community factors		
Physical attractiveness	22	37
Community attitude towards industry	80	7
Social make-up of inhabitants	22	35
Suitability of housing	22	25
Community race relations	43	27
Fire protection and insurance	47	13
Police protection	32	20
Adequacy of local schools	37	32
Suitability of medical facilities	30	28
Suitability of shopping facilities	22	48
Business climate factors†		
Suitability of repair and maintenance services	20	43
Suitability of business, financial and legal services	22	43
Compatability of other industry	37	40
Suitability of building codes	52	22
Suitability of zoning restrictions	55	22
Suitability of environmental regulations	58	22
Availability of public technical training	35	30
State or local planning assistance	23	52
Utility factors		
Suitability of electrical service	78	7
Suitability of telephone service	57	15
Availability of natural gas	42	42
Adequacy and cost of water supply	57	22
Suitability of waste disposal service	35	35

Table 12.3 (Cont'd)

Location factors	Essential or very important (%)	Unimportant or not considered (%)
Plant site factors		
Suitability of site parking facilities	27	38
Site development and construction costs	47	17
Room for expansion	77	5
Plant site topographic features	45	18
Plant site flood risk	50	27
Plant site adequacy and costs	62	10
Plant buildings for sale or lease	10	77
Financial and special factors		
Hometown of company official	2	90
State taxes	50	13
Local taxes	52	10
Availability of direct loans	12	73

(*Source*: Adapted from Moriarty 1983:70–71)
* Italicised factors cited as essential or very important by 50 per cent or more of all respondents.
† This definition of business climate differs from that used in this text.

labour factor of those listed is a favourable labour climate, which can be interpreted as an indicator of a malleable and co-operative workforce. While these factors illustrate the influence of the labour market characteristics discussed in Chapter 7 high scores are also recorded by room for expansion (77 per cent) and community attitudes (80 per cent). The stress on room for expansion provides support for those who argue that less industrialised areas offer unconstrained locations (Ch. 8). The importance of community attitudes supports the role of business climate described in Chapter 10 as indeed does the fact that over 50 per cent of plants considered local zoning restrictions, environmental regulations and the levels of state and local taxes as essential or very important. There are hints here that taxes may be more important to branch plants than to the net changes examined in Chapter 10 but no tax-related effects have been identified in studies of the correlates movement nor, indeed, in the other studies of location factors described below. Accessibility to markets or material sources was less important than any of these factors.

This North Carolina study picks up some variables which relate to regional characteristics (such as access to national markets) and others which relate clearly to a specific site (suitability of access roads). Further, studies based upon branch plants arriving in particular areas run the risk of identifying factors relevant to a specific region, rather than factors which influence branch plants in general.

Schmenner's (1982) study tried to overcome both these deficiencies. It examined a number of firms which had set up branch plants throughout the United States and considered choice of region or state as well as choice of site. Managers were asked to identify those factors which were perceived as 'musts' for any region/state or site. The results of this work are shown in Table 12.4.

At regional/state level considerable emphasis is placed upon labour climate as a location factor with access to markets as the second most important. This indicates that branch plant location may be cost-led or market-led as indeed was seen, at a different scale, in the location of foreign branches. Community attitudes at state/region scale were not important. Attractiveness for the upper primary workers (Ch. 7) was regarded as important as was nearness to company facilities which was cited by a quarter of the plants, an indication of how branches have to fit within an existing corporate system. In contrast, at site level emphasis is placed upon access to

Table 12.4   Location factors for branch plants for 410 major US manufacturers 1970s

A Region/state level

Location factor	Plant openings citing at least one factor (%)
Favourable labour climate	76
Near market	55
Attractive place for engineers, managers to live	35
Near supplies and resources	31
Low labour rates	30
Near existing company facilities	25
Environmental permits	17
Others	6
Community attitude	0

B Site level

Location factor	Plant openings citing at least one factor (%)
Rail service	47
On expressway	42
Special provision of utilities	34
Rural area	27
Environmental permits	23
Within metropolitan area	21
On water	16
Available land/building	8
Others	7

(*Source*: Adapted from Schmenner 1982:150)

transportation facilities and utilities, although some firms seem to have marked preferences for rural sites while others opt for metropolitan sites. This latter finding suggests the sample may include different types of branches. Returning to the North Carolina data it was evident that one group of firms manufacturing the state's traditional products sought locations in small towns and rural areas where low production costs would allow them to remain competitive while another group of high technology plants located near the high wage large cities to be accessible to skilled labour and specialised services (Moriarty 1983:78–9).

In looking through Tables 12.3 and 12.4 there is little emphasis upon personal influences. The influence of the home town of an official appeared in one case in North Carolina but more subjective influences do not appear. This may, in fact, reflect the structured listing of location factors. The listing of potential location factors in these studies does force respondents to relate to factors thought to be important by the investigators. A less structured response can probably be achieved by content analysis of a relatively unstructured interview session.

Stafford (1974) examined decisions by large firms to locate, relocate or significantly expand eight plants (with between 50 and 200 employees) in south-eastern Ohio. The plants were primarily metal fabricators of machinery or components and interviews were conducted among six personnel in the six firms which had been involved in the eight decisions. In tape-recorded interviews, interviewees were asked to describe briefly the corporate situation at the time the decision was made, to indicate how they were involved and to describe the actual location decision-making process. The content of the transcriptions of the interview was then analysed separately by

Table 12.5 Location factors identified by content analysis (all scales)

Factor	Number of evaluated responses	
Labour		197
Productivity	108	
Availability	50	
Rates	39	
Personal contacts		117
Local amenities		49
Transport facilities		42
Dispersion tendencies		28
Executive convenience		27
Facilities and utilities		25
Corporate communications		20
Access to supplies		17
Induced amenities		13
Markets		12
Taxes		1

(*Source*: Based on Stafford 1974:174)

three individuals and the results combined to indicate the factors mentioned, the scale at which they applied and whether a factor was 'evaluated' as good or bad or whether it was treated in a 'neutral' manner. The results for the evaluated responses are shown in Table 12.5 which indicates that there are some 12 key factors or 14 if the labour category is broken down into its constituent parts. The main interest of such a list is that it reiterates the significance of labour considerations but at the same time stresses more clearly than traditional studies the role of personal contacts and local amenities. The former included the personal co-operation of the town's leading citizens, the information supplied by the town and information and co-operation from state officials or power companies. The latter related to the firm's impression of a town's shopping, housing, schools and recreation facilities. The breakdown of 'labour' into different aspects stresses the firm's emphasis on productivity, with amount of labour and wage rates being of secondary but equal importance. In this study labour 'rates' also included whether it was a union or non-union area and the degree of competition in the local labour market. Analysis of the influences at different scales brought out very clearly the fact that some factors operate at different scales. For example, market and supply accessibility became less and less important in

moving from sub-national, regional to local level in terms of evaluated responses, and whereas labour productivity and personal contacts were of almost equal importance at sub-national and regional scale; at local level personal contacts were about twice as important as labour productivity.

Content analysis allows respondents to introduce their own location factors, permits identification of the scale or scales at which a factor works and through the count of the number of responses (mentions) provides an indication of the relative importance of each factor. It does appear to pull-out the amenity and personal factors rather more readily than traditional approaches although as Stafford (1974:180) observes 'the high number of response counts in this category…[personal contacts]…may… reflect a natural tendency for interviewees to talk overmuch about the people with whom they dealt'. Despite the advantages of this approach the time required for analysis makes it impractical in many situations.

These interview studies confirm the significant variables identified in aggregate analyses and perhaps throw greater light on personal and amenity influences. It is perhaps not surprising that in the search for new locations by existing firms the factors discussed in Part III do appear to play an important role (with the exception of capital). Yet a fundamental dilemma emerges from these studies. If most managers claim they were attracted to particular locations by availability of labour or labour climate then availability of labour or labour climate does not discriminate between locations. They may be necessary conditions for a plant to locate in a specific area but it does not explain why one site with labour available is preferred to another site where labour is available. In recession this criticism has even greater force as labour is available in almost all locations, although there may be local shortages of specific skills. Clearly, there is still some way to go before the key location factors are fully understood.

Whereas the characteristics of areas can have an important influence on where branch plants are located, and the firm has an almost infinite number of potential locations, the situation with relation to acquisitions is rather different. The characteristics of the firms may be more important than the features of the areas in which their plants are located and the 'location' of acquired firms is very much circumscribed by the location of potential acquisition candidates. Nevertheless, some evidence suggests that firms are more aware of potential candidates in their home areas. Healey (1983:336) describes a significant neighbourhood effect with twice as many plants being acquired in the same region as firm's head office than would be expected from the distribution of the industries concerned. In a market-oriented or supply-oriented industries there are hints of acquisitions to capture regional markets and supplies, often influenced by competition between firms (Ch. 9). Such expansion to capture markets by acquisition is confirmed in the acquisition behaviour of British brewing companies in the 1960s (Watts 1980b:191–207). Thus proximity to head office and access to markets and/or supplies appear to be 'location factors' which can influence the acquisition decision.

Location decisions

From the preceding discussion, it is evident that plant location decisions must reflect rather more than sticking a pin in the map or selecting a site next to a golf course. Exponents of the golf course location argument tend to forget that there are a large number of golf courses from which to choose! Analyses of location factors indicate that there are influences which work upon the location of new plants in a systematic manner. There remains the question of how the various factors and influences are considered within the location decision-making process and as Stafford (1969:143) observes 'a key element in the understanding of industrial location patterns is an enquiry into the decision-making process'. Attention has already been drawn to the influence of 'information available' and 'ability' in Chapter 5.

A business-oriented approach to industrial geography might ask, legitimately, what is the best way of selecting a new location. This kind of task has been undertaken in guides for managers such as those prepared by Townroe (1976) and Stafford (1980). In contrast, the central concern in this chapter is with how branch plant location decisions are taken not with how they ought to be taken. Such a concern gives a clearer insight into contemporary patterns of change than an interest in what ought to be done. Two approaches have been adopted: the first, and most frequently used, investigates procedures in actual firms; the second simulates the decision in a gaming situation.

An important precursor to the decision to select a new site is the decision to move. Industrial geographers, because of their particular expertise, have tended to focus most attention on the former rather than the latter. Although investment decisions may be taken quite frequently, decisions to invest in a branch plant or to transfer locations are relatively rare, although in larger planning-system firms branch plants might be established more frequently. Rees (1974:199), for example, cites the case of the Monsanto Chemical Company in the United States which located an average of two branch plants per year between 1958 and 1969, but even in medium-sized companies the rate may be much lower than this. Laulajainen (1982:403) suggests from a study of three Scandinavian firms over almost 100 years new locations were selected on average only every 5.3 years. While Healey's (1983) study of 64 multi-plant firms shows that they only established 51 branches during a six-year period. Acquisitions were made rather more frequently in the latter study with 80 acquisitions in the six-year period.

Only a limited number of managers are directly involved in the location decision and the decision itself is handled within the firm. The use of location consultants is rare in Britain and found only among larger firms in the United States (Townroe 1979:166). Within different firms the responsibilities may rest in different departments. Rees's study (1974:199) showed that in a shoe plant with high labour requirements the location was selected by personnel and manufacturing departments but the location of a canning plant which depended upon sales to specific customers was selected by the sales department. In many smaller and privately owned firms the decision may rest in the hands of one person either the owner or managing director. It is unlikely that selecting a location will be an individual's full-time task. Cooper's (1975:81) examination of 64 firms setting up branches or transfers in the North-West and West Midlands of Britain in 1971–72 indicates that 'a majority of decision-makers spent either a negligible proportion or between 1 and 10 per cent of their total time on ... [the] ... decision during the period of its formulation and implementation'. The search for a new site and implementation takes on average around two years (Rees 1974:197), this broadly compares with Townroe's (1971:59–60) evidence that just under half a sample of moves into the West Midlands and Northern regions of Britain took between 6 and 18 months to search for a site and a similar proportion took as long from choice of site to commencement of production. Of course, some moves took longer and others took less time. The time span would be significantly longer if it also included the time taken to decide to move to a new site. The number of personnel involved and the time taken to provide the immediate context within which the location decision is taken.

A number of writers have tried to present the decision sequence in diagrammatic form (for example, Townroe 1969:22; Rees 1974:191; North 1974:236; Cooper 1975:58) but such is the variety of experience uncovered in investigations of individual firms that it is very difficult to generalise. Figure 12.5 provides an indication of the kind of processes and factors involved in the location decision based upon the earlier work. It assumes a decision to move has been made and that the main problem is to find a location for either the transferred plant or a branch plant.

The study of location factors identified the critical fact that different factors can operate at different scales and it is partly as a consequence of this that the search for a site can operate through a hierarchical sequence selecting first a region, then a sub-region and finally a site.

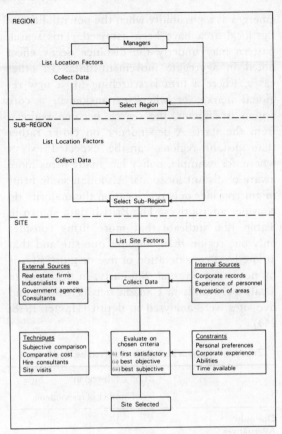

Fig. 12.5 A three-stage industrial location decision sequence

There are however interactions between the different levels and in practice it is difficult to consider them independently. At regional/sub-regional scales firms appear to operate in one of two ways; they either subjectively draw up a list of areas which appear acceptable or draw up a list of desirable attributes for a new location, collect data on locations and then search for locations which provide the desired attributes. It is assumed in the figure that one region or one sub-region is selected at each stage; in practice, for example, two regions might be retained for further examination at sub-regional level.

In many cases the initial search will be confined to regions in which the firm already operates, the search positively moving outwards from the parent plant and choice between regions only emerges as a possibility when the potentialities of the local area have been assessed. This search pattern may underly the distance decay effect noted in aggregate movement data. In other cases, where a firm is searching for a new regional market or where expansion in a core region is difficult, the search become regional from the start. A dependence on closer rather than distant regions can be expected except where, for example, policy has made firms more aware of distant locations. Although some firms might consider only one location the majority do consider alternatives. The British data shown in Table 12.6 indicate that more firms consider only one region than consider one site and that at site level consideration of five or more sites is by no means unusual. Similarly, in decisions to locate pulp mills in Canada between three and five sites were analysed in depth (Hayter 1978: 244).

Table 12.6   Regions and sites considered by British firms

	Region/sub-region	Sites
	Number of respondents	
One only	17	5
Alternatives		
2 to 4	13	13
5 to 7	13	10
>7	16	31
	42	54

(*Source*: Townroe 1971:56–7)

Data are collected from a variety of sources some of which were listed in Table 5.1. Although most data may be provided free it was shown in Chapter 5 that even free data involve a cost in the time involved in their collection. A glance at the table indicates the role of both government and private organisations with state and local development agencies providing data to help to promote employment opportunities in their areas and real-estate agents eager to sell or lease land. The extensive nature of promotional activities has been summarised by Burgess (1982) and a typical 'promotion pack' sent to firms in 1984 by the Welsh Development Agency in Britain included the following items: list of factories available, details of investment services provided by the agency, information on the small business unit, plans of standard 4,500 and 3,000 square feet factories, statement of the agency's policies and programmes, its strategy for the provision of finance and advice to industry, a news-sheet recording recent successes and an annual report on the agency operation showing the range of its investments and activities and full. details of financial assistance which could be made available by central government.

The evaluation and assessment of the data collected varies from subjective assessment through to detailed quantitative evaluations. Stafford (1974:185) suggests that as the area of search gets smaller so more detailed evaluations are made. Thus, whereas regions may be selected on arbitrary or impressionistic grounds (perhaps influenced by the kind of mental maps shown earlier in Fig. 5.3) the final sites may be assessed in very detailed terms. This is particularly true of very large firms and Rees (1974:196) cites the case of a large diversified firm with a New Jersey plant which was searching for a new plant on the eastern seaboard of the United States. In this case the regional location was determined by the site of the parent plant but at site level 'for each of 15 ... [sites] ... sufficient information was obtained to draw up a pro forma profit and loss statement'. Townroe (1979:166) suggests that in the early stages many places are ruled out as impractical; at the second stage more data are collected and visits to areas are undertaken and then at the third stage detailed evaluations are made.

Such detailed evaluations are not always expressed in cost terms. Schmenner found that in firms establishing new plants with over 100 employees over 40 per cent of the plants were not formally costed out. A British survey put the proportion even higher with 66 per cent failing to compare costs between sites, although about half of this 66 per cent did cost out the final site (Townroe 1971:69). Many decisions then depend upon the 'judgement' of the firms' managers since many of the 'quantifiable' factors give little guidance as to future patterns and as North (1974:235) observes 'companies had little confidence in their calculations because so many vital factors, such as labour quality, defied quantification'. Even where cost or profit data are accepted they may well provide similar assessments for different sites so that the decision itself must depend upon a firm's 'hunch' as to the best site. Cooper (1975:87) discovered that no less than 55 per cent of the sampled firms selected the first satisfactory site they found – a clear example of the satisficing behaviour described in Chapter 4. This still means that 45 per cent of firms did have to select between sites and since a mechanistic response to projected costings is unlikely a closer evaluation of the actual decision-making is required. An approach is to simulate the decision-making process.

The one reported use of a game situation is by Stafford (1972:208–9) who utilised the Metfab game devised for the High School Geography Project in the United States. The game has five players (President, Sales Manager, Production Manager, Personnel Manager and a Finance Manager) who have to select the best location for a new plant out of a pre-selected set of 25 cities. It thus relates to the choice of location at one scale only. Each participant was provided with some general data about the firm (Metfab) and some more detailed data relating specifically to their managerial roles within the hypothetical firm. Extensive observation of the game in progress indicated a number of important generalisations.

Decision-makers, it appears, may wish to find quantitative answers but they rapidly move towards an acceptance of judgemental solutions. Such solutions are aided by rapid simplification of the data. Short lists quickly emerge and then effort is spent on ranking the short list. The final decision, although it cannot be shown to be economically optimal, is judged by the players to be the best solution and one which emerges from a rational decision process. When the game is played within a limited time span more reliance is placed on 'data' whereas with longer time spans judgemental influences take on a more critical role. Restriction of the time span of the game also showed that in the short run most emphasis was placed upon minimising cost whereas in longer runs of the game the emphasis

switched to solutions which emphasised future areal variations in demand.

These findings are broadly in line with those which emerge from studies of respondents' memories of what actually happened in firms. Particularly interesting are the confirmation of the speed with which the final list of sites emerges and the emphasis upon judgemental solutions when selecting between them. It is because choice of location is a key element in the branch plant or transfer location decision that industrial geographers have contributed to studies of the branch plant location decision. Since in the case of the acquisition decision space may only be of limited relevance, the geographical contribution has been to emphasise that it is a variable that needs to be included in studies of the decision to acquire.

CONCLUSION

Firms, either by branch plants or transfers, move their production activities between regions. In this process some regions gain jobs and other regions lose jobs. Correlates of movement studies indicate that the geographical patterns of movement owe much to labour availability and distance from the source region and studies of location factors also place emphasis upon the labour factor. These findings do provide support for those who contend that various aspects of geographical variations in labour markets play an important part in explaining locational change. It should not be forgotten that despite the dominant role of labour-related factors, other factors such as community attitudes can be as important. Industrial movement studies are the only group of analyses of the components of industrial change which permit insights into how decisions are taken, and as will be shown, there are no similar studies, for example, looking at how a decision to select an existing plant for closure or expansion is taken. It is only in movement studies that there is a feeling that investigators have got inside the firm to examine the way it operates and to see how those operations express themselves in the changing geography of employment opportunities.

13

IN SITU CHANGE:
EMPLOYMENT GROWTH

It will be recalled that *in situ* employment change is concerned with the growth and decline of employment in plants which neither open nor close during the time period being examined. In other words it encompasses changes taking place in an area's permanent stock of plants. The role of *in situ* change, whether contributing to job gain or job loss, has been underemphasised in the past. This is not because it is unimportant. Reference back to Tables 1.6 and 1.7 and examination of Fig. IV.1 shows that it can make a very important contribution to employment change. The lack of interest arises because it is a middle stage between the distinct events of birth and death and it is difficult to separate out its contribution to the changing geography of employment opportunities.

While a number of studies provide data on net *in situ* change within a region (employment growth in permanent plants less employment loss in permanent plants), a distinction can be made between plants experiencing employment growth and those experiencing employment decline. It is the former category – plants experiencing *in situ* growth of output and employment – which is the main interest of this chapter. Output growth and employment decline is considered in the next chapter.

The inherent stability of employment sites in manufacturing activity is most vividly displayed by the continued use of industrial buildings located to take advantage of rail or water transport by firms which make no use of those facilities.

Some industries and firms originating in the nineteenth century still occupy their nineteenth-century sites, and in parts of Europe some eighteenth-century sites (admittedly much altered) are still utilised. Kuklinski (1967:17) claims that probably 60 to 80 per cent of investment in manufacturing industry in developed countries is allocated to the expansion of existing plants and only somewhere under 40 per cent to the construction of new ones.

The geography of *in situ* employment growth in Scotland from 1968 to 1977 is shown in Fig. 13.1 as an illustration of the range of regional variations that can occur in this component of change. *In situ* employment growth as a percentage of 1968 employment varied from 0.8 per cent in the Grampian region to 48 per cent in the Highlands and Islands region. No consistent spatial pattern emerges as even within the central manufacturing belt of Scotland the growth rates varied from 4.7 to 38.0 per cent.

In looking at variations in *in situ* growth in this way it is important to remember that the data may include only part of the employment growth generated by each plant because growth can be diverted into a new branch plant or, in the case of a multi-plant firm, to another site within the corporate system. Table 13.1 illustrates how a proportion of growth can be diverted from permanent plants to new branches. This, of course, excludes growth diverted to other plants in a corporate system and acquisition of rival firms to obtain more capacity. The loss of *in situ* growth

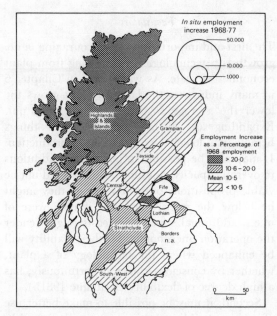

Fig. 13.1 In situ employment growth, Scotland, 1968 to 1977 (*Source*: Based on Cross 1981:58)

Despite the difficulties of establishing the geography of *in situ* employment growth it is important to try to understand why such variations occur. The first section of the chapter considers the factors that encourage and discourage employment growth at a particular plant, while the second describes in more detail those relationships which have been established through empirical enquiry. In the third and final section attention is concentrated upon plants which are part of planning-system firms to illustrate how the growth experience of a particular plant is often inextricably tied into changes taking place elsewhere in the corporate system. It has already been shown how branch plant location is sometimes influenced by accessibility within the corporate spatial structure and in the next chapter it will be seen that *in situ* decline and closures too have to be studied in their corporate context.

IN SITU EMPLOYMENT GROWTH

Commonly offered explanations for the significance of *in situ* growth are the concepts of geographical inertia and geographical momentum, sometimes referred to simply as inertia and momentum. There are parallels here with the concepts of adoption and adaption described in Chapter 5. Inertia is taken to be indicative of a lack of flexibility in the plant's management and the plant survives and grows because it is 'adopted' by its local environment; in contrast, momentum suggests that positive actions are taken by management to 'adapt' the plant to the environment in which it is set (Hoare 1983:68–70). However, inertia and momentum are terms that are best forgotten.

The terms are so imprecise and ill-defined that their use contributes very little to understanding the reasons for the importance of *in situ* growth or, indeed, for variations in its importance between regions. The terms also carry with them an implication that a plant is in a poor location. Certainly, in some cases, if a new plant were being built a different location might be selected, but where an old plant exists its costs may be cheaper. For example, in Britain in the 1950s the well-located iron and steel plant at Port Talbot,

from Northamptonshire and Leicestershire appears to be at twice the rate for Nottinghamshire/Derbyshire and Lincolnshire. Similarly, re-examination of Table 12.1 suggests that in England the South-East region loses the highest proportion of locally generated employment growth through the out-migration of industrial establishments whereas in Wales very little employment growth is lost through this particular mechanism.

Table 13.1 Employment in permanent plants and branches established from 1948 to 1967, East Midland firms, United Kingdom

Sub-region	Total employment ('000s)	Employment in new branches (%)
Leicestershire	161	14.9
Northamptonshire*	61	13.4
Nottinghamshire, Derbyshire†	238	8.0
Lincolnshire‡	48	7.5

(*Source*: Gudgin 1978:253)
* Excluding steelworks employment.
† Excluding Newark, Retford and Chesterfield.
‡ Including Newark and Retford.

adjacent to a dock for importing iron ore, produced steel strip at a higher cost than a plant at Shotton located inland. Much of this difference reflected the fact that Shotton had low capital charges as it had been built before the inflation in costs associated with the war and post-war years (Warren 1970:245). Old sites, if all costs are considered, may offer lower costs than production in entirely new plants and firms are therefore making a positive and sensible decision to remain at a particular site. Further, inertia and momentum cover a variety of processes and to use them as the explanation for continued growth at a particular site is rather like saying the location of a branch plant in a region reflects the operation of location factors. To reach a full understanding of the major significance of *in situ* growth and its regional variations it is of utmost importance to dissect the terms inertia and momentum to identify the various processes subsumed within them.

In discussing the causes of *in situ* growth, there are parallels with the causes of industrial movement. The factors encouraging industrial movement are those that discourage *in situ* growth while the factors that discourage industrial movement are those that encourage *in situ* growth. The degree of locational stability in the industrial system reflects the extent to which the forces encouraging *in situ* growth are balanced against those discouraging it. A discussion of the factors encouraging and discouraging *in situ* growth provides a useful first step towards understanding regional variations in *in situ* growth as it seems reasonable to argue that if these factors can be identified clearly then regional variations in their occurrence may be major influences on the geography of *in situ* growth. Emphasis is placed in this discussion on the stability of individual plants. Localisation and urbanisation economies (Ch. 9) clearly contribute to this stability as will be seen below but there are also plant-related factors which have not yet been discussed. It is necessary to make the assumption here that output growth leads to employment growth and to recall that growth or lack of growth is influenced by an industry or firm's international competitiveness (Ch. 2).

Facilitators

The first and important factor encouraging *in situ* growth is a technological one arising from plant economies of scale. As was shown in Chapter 6 in many industries the larger a plant grows the lower the average cost of each unit of output. Expanding an existing site will, other things being equal, lower the overall cost of production. It may also be possible to make small additions to overall capacity, additions which would not be viable propositions on a new site as they might be below the m.e.s. and even if they were of m.e.s. additional supervisory costs might render the operation uneconomic. Further, stability will be enhanced where the technology of a plant, whether by conscious choice or fortuitously, has a high degree of flexibility (Krumme 1981b).

Second, it may be possible to make better use of existing buildings and increase capacity without new construction work; even if new work is required extension and redevelopment of an existing site may be cheaper than placing new developments on entirely new sites. A 1960s plan for an integrated steel works in Britain estimated a *greenfield* (i.e. new) site would cost 50 per cent more than a *brownfield* (i.e. redevelopment of existing works) site (Warren 1969). Obviously, the difference in cost between extensions and greenfield sites will vary from case to case but this example illustrates the cost advantages of expanding on site.

Such cost advantages may be further enhanced where the amount of capital invested in a site is high. Technically, machinery can be moved but the life or depreciation period of the machinery and buildings might govern the life of the plant. Equipment and buildings remain in use until the repair and maintenance costs begin to exceed the interest on and repayment of the capital necessary to replace them. Where there is a large amount of capital investment in a plant this situation is unlikely to be reached especially if the plant consists of several large units with varying lives. Selective renewal of different facilities at different points in time ties subsequent developments to the same site. In a steel plant, new coke-ovens at t_1 may be used to justify a new blast furnace at t_2, the new blast furnace will justify a new steel furnace at t_3 and the new steel furnace a new strip mill at t_4. The latter in turn will justify renewal of the original coke ovens at t_5.

Risk and uncertainty play a part too. An existing plant has a well-established system of suppliers and a set of marketing channels. Expansion at an alternative site may require re-evaluation of supplies and markets with all the uncertainty that this involves; on site expansion may involve only increasing orders to existing suppliers. An increased labour force might be achieved via a local grapevine and only limited time need be devoted to recruitment.

This rather descriptive analysis of the factors facilitating *in situ* growth is indicative of how little attention has been focused upon differential rates of expansion among a set of industrial plants. Yet, a pioneering piece of work by Dziewonski (1966) perhaps deserves attention. This study argued that it was useful to divide the forces encouraging *in situ* change into two more general categories. First *inertial forces* which bind a given activity to a specific site but, once overcome, do not create any obstacles to movement. A new owner-occupied factory might bind a firm to a particular site but once the factory building needs replacing it ceases to act as a binding force. Second, *frictional forces* which can never be overcome but are always present to a greater or lesser extent. In this category would come, for example, a plant's links with its local environment which were discussed in the context of urbanisation and localisation economies in Chapter 9. A change of location between local labour markets instead of *in situ* growth would require those links to be either stretched or broken.

Constraints

Opposing and counteracting the forces facilitating and encouraging *in situ* growth are those which constrain it. Again, it is possible only to provide a descriptive listing of potential influences.

Technologically, large plants may present quite severe diseconomies of scale. In major continuous process plants (e.g. oil refineries) a breakdown in part of the system can result in the loss of total production through the need to shut down the whole system. Thus production in two 5 million tonne plants will offer greater stability than concentrating all production in one 10 million tonne plant. Many of the diseconomies of scale arise from the workforce in that larger plants appear to be more strike prone (Ch. 7) and where a firm's operations are concentrated in one key plant labour power is, almost inevitably, stronger.

The labour and land markets within which a plant operates may be of significance too. Labour shortages, high wage rates or low productivity in particular areas may discourage a plant from expanding on site and this will be aggravated where adjacent land is either not available or available only at high cost. Keeble (1968) shows that over a ten-year period of relatively stable prices generally, land prices trebled in one of the more important industrial areas in London during a period of rapid industrial growth. More recently it has been suggested that the lack of convenient land adjacent to the factory premises may be more critical than price. This constrained location hypothesis was discussed in Chapter 8.

The political framework is not without its influence and this has, in the past, operated restrictions forbidding additions to existing industrial plants in certain areas. The effect of labour, land and capital subsidies on discouraging *in situ* growth is less easy to evaluate as so much depends on whether management of particular plants is aware of the nature of these subsidies and the geographical areas to which they apply.

Finally, plants dependent upon localised materials may be discouraged if local supplies of materials are exhausted (in the case of minerals) or cease to be available (in the case of intermediate products). Similarly local markets may disappear (with the closure of major local industries) or, in local market-oriented industries, local demand may be insufficient to support new capacity.

These ideas are very much speculative ones but a useful attempt to identify the forces discouraging *in situ* growth is found in the work of Sant (1975b:147). This study was concerned primarily with explaining the number of outward moves generated by a number of British regions; it can be assumed that a high level outward movement indicates the existence of constraints on *in situ* growth. High levels of outward movement between 1966 and 1971 were positively associated with a large number of employees in manufacturing, a high density of manufacturing employees per urban area, a large proportion of an area with urban status, a region of large spatial extent, and high earnings. However, where regions had access to government regional policy grants the outward movement was damped down. These variables accounted for around 60 per cent of the variations in a region's outward movement.

Following this listing of the factors which constrain the quantity of *in situ* employment growth found in particular regions, it is essential to stress again that whether or not a plant will expand its employment *in situ* will depend upon the balance between the facilitating and constraining influences. These influences will operate through the industrial and size structure of the plants, the age of the plants, and the kind of organisations to which they belong.

DETERMINANTS OF EMPLOYMENT GROWTH

There are few studies of variations in employment growth rates among a set of plants displaying employment growth and very little is known about medium-term employment change in individual plants. As a result it is difficult to ascertain the likely employment record of a group of plants which neither open nor close during a given time period. Yet, the limited evidence suggests that the industry group to which a plant belongs is of little significance. Data from Leicestershire which relate to all permanent plants, including those whose employment was declining *in situ* as well as those in which employment was growing (Gudgin 1978: 165–9), indicated that industry differences accounted for only a small part of the variation in

employment change between plants. Examining the data at the three-digit level the most obvious feature was the wide dispersion of growth rates within any one industry. It is thus apparent that there is considerable scope for other variables to influence the *in situ* employment growth of individual plants.

One of the most obvious of these is the effect of plant size. Empirical data suggest there is an inverse relationship between plant size and employment growth. An illustration of this relationship is provided in Table 13.2 which expresses *in situ* growth as a percentage of employment in each plant size category at the beginning of the period. Whereas *in situ* growth to 1975 represented 19 per cent of the 1972 employment in plants of 11 to 20 employees it represented only 6 per cent of that employment in plants with over 500 employees. As size of plant increases *in situ* growth rates display a downward trend. Similar results are reported for the East Midlands (Gudgin 1978:160–5) and Ontario (Collins 1972).

Table 13.2   In situ employment growth by size of plant, 1972–75, Britain

Employment size group	*In situ* employment growth as per cent of 1972 employment in size band
11– 20	19
21– 50	14
51–200	12
201–500	9
>500	6

(*Source*: Estimated from Macey 1982:Tables 2.4 and 2.5, p. 19)

The observed relationship could be interpreted partly as a reflection of the fact that, as an example, doubling the workforce from 5 to 10 may be easier than doubling it from 200 to 400, partly because the larger plant may be reaching the limits of existing site, and partly because larger plants might have a greater tendency to divert growth to branches or (in multi-plant firms) to other parts of the corporate system. Nevertheless, given the generality of this relationship it might be reasonable to expect that in regions where many of the permanent stock of plants are small *in situ* growth rates might be higher than in other regions, yet because of their small size the employment generated by *in situ* growth might make only a small contribution to overall patterns of employment change.

The better performance of small plants may reflect a greater proportion of young plants within the small plant population and rather more is known about recently established (i.e. youthful) plants. Little is known about plants which have only a short life but the more successful plants experience a period of self-sustaining growth in the years immediately after opening, although the length of time this self-sustaining growth lasts and the extent to which it is influenced by the economic cycle is open to debate. It might be expected that regions with a high proportion of youthful plant might gain employment from the growth experiences of these young plants.

An illustration of this early growth in employment among new openings in the United Kingdom is shown in Table 13.3. It will be recalled that these data exclude small new plants (pages 147–8). Among plants established between 1960 and 1970 employment had doubled after five years' operation and had increased by a further 50 per cent at the end of nine years. For a later period (1966 to 1975) there was only a 50 per cent increase in the first five years of operation and most of this occurred within the first two years. The rate of build-up was even slower

in plants established between 1974 and 1978. Plants established during a period of economic growth appear to grow more rapidly and sustain that growth over a longer period than those plants established during a recession.

These plants in aggregate are, of course, made up of new firms and new branches and it is not unreasonable to expect the influences of age and ownership to interact. A more rapid growth might be expected in branches since they have access to the established marketing and distribution systems of the parent company, to the whole range of managerial services and expertise of the parent, and they may find that the financial constraints which can limit the growth of new firms may be absent because of access to the financial resources of the parent firm. More detailed analysis of the data shown in Table 13.3 showed that branch plants opened in the period 1966 to 1975 had almost doubled in size in two years and had increased almost 2.5 times in 5 years. Thus a region with a high proportion of recently established branches might expect to find its employment growth rates enhanced.

Independent births (new firms) had much lower growth rates and had not even doubled in size over five years. To understand the post-foundation growth of these new firms it is useful to look at the influence of the life-cycle of a firm and the characteristics of the firm's founders.

The life-cycle of the firm has not been fully articulated in the geographical literature and discussions do not clearly indicate the relationships between the life-cycle and employment trends. Broadly, one might envisage a formative period, one of rapid employment growth, then slower growth in maturity ending with a phase of employment decline. It seems likely that the life-cycle of the firm will be interwoven with the product cycle (Ch. 6). Firms introducing new products may mirror the product cycle in their own cycle, whereas others which enter an industry and begin manufacturing a product at a late stage of the product-cycle will show less correspondence. Thus among a set of market-system firms there can be up to nine combinations of characteristics based on the mix of young, mature and old firms and young, mature and old

Table 13.3 Employment growth in new plants, United Kingdom, 1960–78

Years after opening	Index of employment		
	1960–70	1966–75	1974–78
0	100	100	100
1	140	133	123
2	163	151	142
3	181	162	156
4	194	167	
5	206	167	
6	218	166	
7	220	166	
8	229	164	
9	244	154	

(*Source*: Pounce 1981:25)

products. Regional variations in the mix of product and firm life-cycle stages may influence a region's employment change, and certainly particular regions are characterised by distinctive types of firm. In the Canadian Prairies, for example, Ajao and Ironside (1982:179) found that the two most common categories of firm were mature firm/mature product and young firm/mature product.

An important influence on a region's performance may be the relationship between the number of young firms associated with young products in contrast to those young firms dealing with mature old products. These two classes can be related to two different types of entrepreneur the 'opportunist' and the 'craftsperson'. Opportunists aim to run and develop their own firms and take up opportunities as they arise. Day-to-day activities are characterised by a search for new markets and new products. In contrast, the craftspersons have no long-term objectives to found their own firms and are often forced into establishing a firm by some kind of crisis (e.g. unemployment). After establishment the firm's growth can be constrained by the limited ambitions of the founder.

The potential importance of this distinction between craftsperson and opportunist is found in a study of 52 firms in Michigan founded since 1945 (cited in Gudgin 1978:97–100). Admittedly it was a small sample, but firms run by the opportunists grew *twelve* times as fast as those run by craftspersons. Similarly, Fothergill and Gudgin (1982:129) show that of 44 new firms established in the East Midlands between 1965 and 1975 and surviving to 1979, those founded by graduates (a surrogate for opportunists) employed (on average) 26 employees in 1979 while those founded by manual workers (a surrogate for craftspersons) employed only 18 workers in 1979.

THE CORPORATE CONTEXT

While the life-cycle of a firm and the characteristics of the firm's founder can have a direct influence on a plant's employment performance in a single-plant market-system firm, in a planning-system firm the overall growth experience of a firm is not necessarily reflected in the employment record of every plant. For example, among multi-plant firms in the United Kingdom textile and clothing industries from 1967 to 1972 employment increases in plants in the Assisted Areas were twice as frequent as those elsewhere (Healey 1983:338). Although the Assisted Areas had only 9 per cent of the plants in the sample they had 17 per cent of the plants experiencing employment increases. This kind of shift in emphasis may reflect both the early growth experience of branch plants referred to above and the fact that the branch plants tended to be newer and in more modern and efficient premises. Regional aid may also have had an influence but the difficulties of assessing this are discussed in Chapter 15.

Underlying these shifts are two aspects of the behaviour of planning-system firms. The first is the spatial allocation of investment within the planning-system firm and some evidence was presented earlier to suggest that some spatial biases were evident in the allocation procedures (Ch. 8). The second, relates to the allocation of orders which is of major significance to plants which have no control over their marketing and sales (Ch. 4). Their whole performance will depend upon the way in which the head office allocates the orders it receives.

It is difficult to probe into the mechanisms for the allocation of investments and allocation of the corporate order book but there has been some interest in the way in which planning-system firms change the products manufactured at particular plants. Admittedly product change at plant level can lead to *in situ* employment decline as well as *in situ* employment growth and may be related to the opening and closing of plants elsewhere in the corporate system. Within a planning-system firm it is difficult to examine a plant in isolation for as Hayter (1978:212) observes plant level adjustments often form part of 'a sequential and frequently highly integrated chain of on-site and inter-site...adjustments within corporate activity patterns'. Such inter-relationships have already been demonstrated in the reorganisation of international production systems described in Chapter 2 and in the previous chapter it was argued that some new branch plants were established to replace out-dated facilities. In order to comprehend the corporate context of *in situ* expansion and *in situ* decline and closure geographers have examined corporate spatial reorganisation strategies within national economic systems.

Locational adjustment

Locational adjustment defines the process by which multi-plant firms reorganise their production facilities. The essential features are that it involves more than one plant and no increase in the number of plants operated. Spatial growth (associated with an increase in the number of plants a firm operates) was discussed in the last chapter.

A common adjustment is to introduce new products to a plant. This may include new products arising from the innovations discussed in Chapter 6, but it also includes growing or mature products which are only new to the plant. Berry (1967) in a study of the plants operated by the 494 largest American corporations over the five-year period 1960 to 1965, suggested that they survived by shifting their product emphasis frequently from one industrial category to another. In Britain, one-third of a sample of 1,500 firms (*not* plants) examined by Hamilton (1978) claimed that they had substantially altered their production profiles between 1960 and 1972. In the United Kingdom textile and clothing industry from 1967 to 1972 product change decisions were taken as frequently as decisions to establish branch plants or to acquire other firms. Product changes at plant level were usually to products closely related to those already manufactured by the plant. For example, one firm faced with a decline in the demand for gloves started to produce slippers, while a blanket manufacturer started to make continental quilts. A few new products were entirely unrelated to existing products and markets. For instance, two firms started to manufacture plastic products. Plants gaining products were those whose main products were in declining industries (Healey 1981a).

This would appear to suggest that planning system firms are allowing these particular plants to survive by introducing new products to replace those in decline. As Steed (1971:324) has observed 'the continued existence of [a] plant, if it is not to be solely a function of pure chance, must...depend upon management's ability to interpret their changing environment and chart a suitable path of adaptation'.

In addition to introducing new products to a plant, firms can also reorganise the distribution of products within the firm's spatial structure. The possibilities inherent in this form of locational adjustment are illustrated in Fig. 13.2 where the firm is seen to have a set of activities spread over a number of sites giving rise to *activity locations*. The first locational adjustment policy – specialisation – concentrates activities on specific sites with the advantage of longer production runs and the reduction of costs through economies of scale. This is the logic underlying the global integration and plant-per-

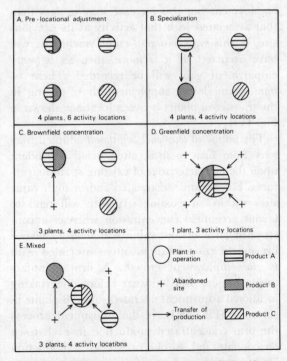

Fig. 13.2 Some locational adjustment policies (*Source*: Healey 1984:137)

product strategy of multinational firms (Ch. 2). The second policy 'brownfield concentration' offers not only economies of scale but savings in administration costs and inter-plant linkages together with income from the sale or lease of abandoned sites. The third policy of 'greenfield concentration' releases all the other sites for alternative uses and allows construction to proceed without disturbing the production capacity of existing units. Mixes of these strategies may also occur (an example is shown in Fig. 13.2E) and, in some cases, products may be exchanged between plants.

Clearly these policies have implications not only for *in situ* employment change but also for branch plant decisions (in the case of greenfield concentration) and plant closure (in the case of both brownfield and greenfield concentration). Branch plant decisions were discussed in the last chapter and plant closures are considered fully in the next one. *Locational adjustment* can also involve the transfer of activities between sites and contributes to *in-transit* changes in employment. Adding a product to a plant may increase its employment but this increase may be less than that associated with that activity at its previous site, in this way, *in-transit* employment loss will have occurred. If it is more, then an *in-transit* employment gain will be recorded. These *in-transit* gains/losses supplement those arising in the transfer of plants between locations shown in Fig. IV.1.

The policy of *locational adjustment* adopted may vary from firm to firm, often being dependent upon the characteristics of existing spatial structures. For example, congested and/or high value sites within an existing structure will tend to favour greenfield concentration whereas unconstrained sites of low value will tend to favour brownfield concentration, often associated with *in situ* employment growth. A firm manufacturing hosiery and knitwear before undertaking locational adjustment operated some 18 plants in six areas (Fig. 13.3). In the adjustment process the firm concentrated production in each town on one site and, in one case, ceased production in one region and transferred activities to the main plant of the firm. Few technical changes

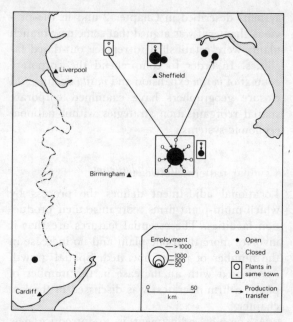

Fig. 13.3 Locational adjustment in a hosiery and knitwear firm (*Source*: Healey 1984:140)

were involved in this industry and machinery and equipment could, if necessary, be readily utilised on existing sites (Healey 1984:139). In contrast, the advent of new large-scale technologies in the British brewing industry meant that where existing sites were too small the 'greenfield concentration' option was chosen (Watts 1980b).

Reorganisation of a firm's production system is not necessarily confined to existing or new sites of the firm and in many cases reorganisation may follow the restructuring of an industrial sector (Ch. 4) through the merger between larger firms (Massey and Meegan 1979) or the acquisition of small firms by large ones. As was seen in Chapter 4, a frequent target for the acquisition policy of planning-system firms is the rapidly growing small firm. In the Northern region of Britain over 75 per cent of the acquired firms were in two-digit industries where employment growth was above the regional average (Smith 1979:423). Not all the evidence supports this view in that out of state acquisitions of Nebraska firms suggested that the acquired firms were typical of all Nebraskan firms (Brue 1972: 45).

Acquisition seems to damp down employment growth, possibly as a result of post-acquisition locational adjustments. In Nebraska, manufacturing firms showed a pre-merger employment growth rate of +1.6 per cent in contrast to a post-merger decline of −11.1 per cent (Brue 1972:48). Returning again to the Northern region, data relating to 52 single-plant firms show a similar pattern. Between 1963 and the year of acquisition the firms expanded employment by 18 per cent, whereas between the year of acquisition and 1973 employment declined by 14 per cent. Overall, 35 companies recorded an employment fall after takeover compared with only 15 which recorded an increase (Smith 1979:435). However, some contrasting evidence comes from Massey and Meegan's (1979:225, 227, 229) examination of post-acquisition adjustments by large firms in the British electrical engineering industry. While 21 per cent of the employment losses were in assisted areas these areas included well over one-quarter of the pre-acquisition employment of the surveyed firms. Examination of the post-acquisition employment record of ac-

quired plants moves the discussion from *in situ* growth towards *in situ* decline.

CONCLUSION

It is clearly difficult to separate analytically *in situ* employment growth from *in situ* employment decline and it is equally difficult to separate them from the distinct events of birth and death. While it appears correct to move attention away from the movement of industry to the birth of new firms and to the closure of plants such an emphasis still leaves untouched the employment record of a permanent stock of plants. If the number of jobs generated by plants expanding their employment was small this would not be a matter of concern but, as will by shown later, they often provide a major contribution to job creation. Industrial geographers have not as yet developed appropriate concepts for analysing variations in employment growth rates within a set of permanent plants. In contrast to this, employment decline has received more attention and progress is being made towards understanding its essential features. It is the critical geography of employment decline and plant closure that is the concern of the next chapter.

In contrast to the last three chapters which were concerned predominantly with employment creation this chapter turns to a discussion of employment decline. Although *in situ* employment decline and plant closures are always present in components of change analysis of regional employment patterns they tend to play a more dominant role in times of recession and it was a shift in public attention towards job losses that pushed industrial geographers towards research into the geography of employment decline. Nevertheless, the geography of employment decline is a relatively unexplored area. Although research into this aspect of change began at about the same time as research into the birth of new firms (Ch. 11) the latter has proceeded more rapidly because of the major policy interest in job creation.

Employment decline is not necessarily associated with output decline, as has been noted for some time (Sant, 1975a; Leigh and North, 1978) and Massey and Meegan (1982:18) draw attention to the operation of three different processes.

1. *Intensification.* Employment decline associated usually with increased output resulting from a rise in labour productivity without major new investment. It is a decline in employment associated primarily with the reorganisation of production and labour within existing plants.
2. *Rationalisation.* Employment decline associated with cuts in output. Plants may be closed as part of the rationalisation process. Rationalisation arises primarily from lack of profitability in the sectors with excess capacity. It is, of course, not necessarily excess in terms of social need, but excess in terms of production for profit. Some excess capacity results from the process of competition between firms where capacity is built up in an unco-ordinated manner. The lack of co-ordination eventually leads to cuts to bring production into line with demand at the prices set by the competing firms. Excess capacity also arises, for example, where new products replace old ones (Ch. 6) and where domestic products are unable to meet competition from imports (Ch. 2). Closures arising from the rationalisation process are termed excess capacity closures.
3. *Technical change.* This produces employment decline by producing the same or increased output with less labour. It is often associated with the introduction of new technologies (Ch. 6) which reduce production costs. Technical change is associated with investment in specific sites and the abandonment of others; the sites abandoned are seen as investment-related closures.

Although allocation of particular job losses to these three categories is not straightforward, analyses based on these concepts provide some interesting insights into 'why' employment decline takes place but they give us only a limited understanding as to why decline is concentrated in specific areas, a problem of vital significance in trying to understand why one community or area is affected by employment decline whereas another is not so affected.

The variations in employment decline between areas are demonstrated in the empirical evidence in the first section of the chapter. The second and third sections of the chapter focus specifically on plant closures, the second section discussing some major variables which are thought to influence spatial variations in plant closure rates. In the third and final section emphasis is placed upon closures by planning-system firms because it is suspected that they have the ability to choose where closures take place.

REGIONAL VARIATIONS IN EMPLOYMENT DECLINE

Whereas Chapter 1 presented several examples of regional variations in *net* employment decline interest here is focused upon *absolute* employment

decline for which data are less readily available. Indeed, in many cases the data force attention on employment loss through closure which plays down the role of lay-offs in plants which continue in operation. Although Birch (1979:4) claimed 'the rate of job loss due to ... [deaths plus contractions] ... is about the same everywhere ... [in the United States]' the empirical evidence now available does not support this view.

Figure 14.1 illustrates the geography of job loss in closings and contractions of private business establishments in the United States. This includes stores and shops as well as manufacturing plants. On average about 60 per cent of the jobs existing is 1969 had been lost by 1976, and these losses were lowest in the manufacturing belt and highest in parts of the south and west. Overall, job losses ranged from 53 per cent of the 1969 employment in the East North Central region to 75 per cent in the Mountain region.

This broad overview of the geography of job

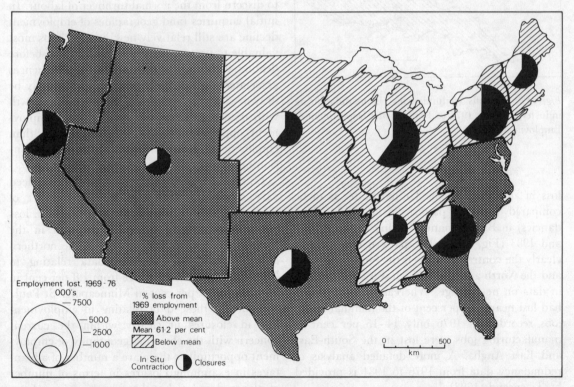

Fig. 14.1 Employment decline in *all* private business establishments, United States, 1969 to 1976 (*Source*: Bluestone and Harrison 1982:30)

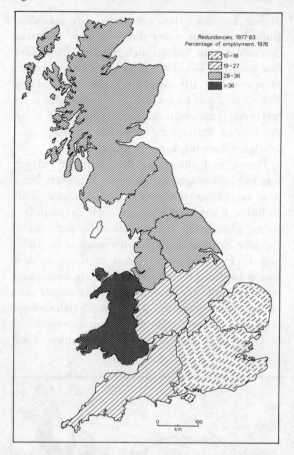

Fig. 14.2 Lay-offs (redundancies) in manufacturing industry, Britain, 1977 to 1983 (*Source*: Department of Employment)

loss in all sectors in the United States is to be compared with the pattern of lay-offs (redundancies) in British manufacturing between 1977 and 1983 (Fig. 14.2). The pattern here depicts clearly the contrasts between the South and East and the North and West which were also evident in data on net change. Whereas by 1983 Wales had lost nearly 40 per cent of the manufacturing jobs recorded in 1976 only 14–15 per cent of manufacturing jobs were lost in the South-East and East Anglia. A more detailed analysis of redundancy data from 1976 to 1981 is provided by Townsend (1983).

Regrettably, it is not possible to explore re-

gional patterns of absolute job loss any further because of the lack of data, although an indication of the importance of *in situ* decline in relation to plant closure is provided in Table IV.3. It is variations in employment losses arising through closure and variations in plant closure rates which form the focus of the remainder of this chapter. They do, however, influence the patterns of employment loss described above.

Although several investigators have suggested it is unwise to separate closure from *in situ* shrinkage (Massey and Meegan 1982:192), mainly because *in situ* decline often precedes closure, two important considerations point to the value of concentrating attention upon plant closures. First, closure is more final, more dramatic and more painful than merely reducing employment levels. A plant, once closed, is unlikely to re-open; a plant with contracting employment may subsequently increase its labour demands. Second, closure is a clearly distinguished event, whereas lay-offs may be difficult to discern from the normal turnover of labour. In initial enquiries (and geographies of employment decline are still relatively new) it is perhaps most valuable to try to understand the extremes before dealing with the nuances and subtle influences associated with *in situ* change. A parallel may be drawn with early studies of employment growth with tended to stress the generation of employment opportunities in new plants rather than employment created through the *in situ* expansion of existing plants.

Employment loss through closure does indeed vary regionally. Estimates from a number of studies (Table 14.1) indicate a percentage loss per annum ranging from 1.2 per cent in the Northern region to 3.1 per cent in the northern city of Manchester. Similar data relating to North American cities range from 1.8 per cent in Phoenix to 3.7 per cent in Minneapolis–St Paul.

Although these data relating to employment loss in closures fit clearly within the current concern with the changing geography of employment opportunities there are a number of advantages in examining closures in terms of number of plants closed rather than employees in plants closed. Calculation of employment loss due to

Table 14.1 Employment loss through closure, 1960s and 1970s

	Percentage loss per annum from base year*
Inter-regional: Britain	
East Midlands, 1968–75	1.7
Scotland, 1968–77	1.3
Northern, 1963–73	1.2
Inter-urban: Britain	
Manchester, 1966–75	3.1
Clydeside, 1968–77	1.3
East Midland cities, 1968–75	1.7
Inter-urban: United States	
Minneapolis–St Paul, 1965–68	3.7
Boston, 1965–68	2.7
Cleveland, 1965–68	2.6
Phoenix, 1965–68	1.8

(*Sources*: Struyk and James 1975:41, 58, 75, 90; Smith 1979: 429; Mason 1980:180; Fothergill and Gudgin 1982: 78; Cross 1981:52, 54, 58)

* These data use a variety of definitions of closure and thus provide only a very broad indication of spatial variations in plant closures rates.

closures demands knowledge of both the number of plant closures over a time period and their employment. It also raises the question as to whether employment should be measured as at the beginning of the time period, at peak employment, at closure or, indeed, some average of employment levels over a certain number of years. An emphasis upon plant closure rates avoids the difficulties associated with employment data and at the same time allows analogies to be draw with those studies which focus upon the establishment of new plants. A further advantage is that plant closure data are more

readily available than data on employment in closures.

Plant closure rates do vary between regions. In the United States in a sample of plants with over 100 employees in 1969 one-third of the plants in operation in the South had closed seven years later at the end of 1976. In contrast the North Central division recorded a 25 per cent closure rate. In even the most favoured region a plant had a one in four chance of a shut-down in a seven-year period (Bluestone and Harrison 1982:32). Equally dramatic levels of plant closings are recorded in United Kingdom data for manufacturing plants with over 10 employees. Approximately 20 per cent of the Scottish manufacturing plants of 1971 had closed by 1975 compared with a closure rate of 10 to 11 per cent in East Anglia and Wales (estimated from Nunn 1980:9).

The above data relate all closings to initial plant stock. British evidence examines closures among recent start-ups. (Table 14.2). These data show quite distinct regional variations in closure rates. Among new firms, closure rates are very high in Scotland, and there is a distinct difference between peripheral areas and the rest of the United Kingdom. There is a more marked range of regional variations in the closure rates of inter-regional moves which, it will be recalled, tend to be branch plants. Only in the case of intra-regional moves (which in all probability were transfers) was the range of regional variation small.

Data at this very broad scale can hide quite important variations within the regional bound-

Table 14.2 Plant closure ratios, United Kingdom, 1966–75

Area	Moves inter-regional	Moves intra-regional	Enterprises new to manufacturing
	Closure ratio*		
Scotland	135	108	144
Peripheral areas	114	95	114
Rest of UK	79	102	93
UK	100	100	100

(*Source*: Henderson 1980:159)

* Closure rate is the percentage of recorded openings between 1966 and 1975 that had closed by the end of 1975; the closure ratio is derived from an area's closure rate expressed as a percentage of the UK figure.

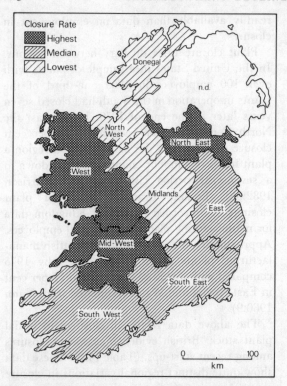

Closure Rate
■ Highest
▨ Median
▧ Lowest

Donegal

n.d.

North
West

North East

West

Midlands

East

Mid-West

South East

South West

0   100
km

Fig. 14.3 Plant closure rates in grant-aided plants, Eire, 1960 to 1973 (*Source*: O'Farrell 1976: 443)

aries. Examination of variations in closures among plants with 11 or more employees in Scotland showed that the annual closure rate in Glasgow (the largest city in Scotland) of 4.2 per cent was significantly higher than the rate of 3.0 per cent for the rest of Scotland (Henderson 1980:169). Within New England the high closure rate in Massachusetts could be contrasted with boom conditions in the southern towns of New Hampshire (Bluestone and Harrison 1982:33). Similarly, in Eire the closure rate of grant-aided plants set up from 1960 to 1973 varied from over 20 per cent in the North-East, West and mid-West to rates of only 8 or 9 per cent in Donegal and the North-West (Fig. 14.3).

While regional patterns of closure, revealed by variations in employment lost in closures and by variations in closure rates, differ between places and between different time periods the critical feature is that variations do exist. These variations, like those of the other components of

change, contribute towards the geography of net employment change and therefore raise important questions as to why such regional variations occur.

CLOSURE FACTORS

Plant closures present an intriguing problem for research workers since it is extremely difficult to collect data about closed plants unless they were part of planning-system firms. Johnson and Cathcart (1979:271–2) made 'considerable effort ... to trace the former management and shareholders of... [closed plants but]... nearly all seemed to have disappeared without trace'. Barkley (1978) tried to overcome the problem by asking knowledgeable individuals in the communities in which the plants were set but this would work only in small communities. The collection of data relating to closed market-system firms and their plants is likely to remain a particularly intractable problem except where 'historical' data sets allow comparisons to be made with present patterns.

A critical point in a plant's history occurs when it moves from the profit-making to loss-making category. In planning-system firms this point is still of significance, although some profits may themselves be seen as too low for the operation to continue (see page 200). However, the level of profitability may be affected by a variety of area, plant and corporate characteristics so that practical efforts towards understanding plant closure rates must involve the use of measures which are thought to be associated with plant profitability. A review of the empirical analysis of closure patterns indicates that most emphasis has been placed on plant-related variables (notably sector, size, age and ownership) and little attention has been paid to the plants environment (for example, labour market characteristics, land availability and accessibility to supplies and markets).

Industrial structure

Underlying the association between industrial structure and the probability of plant closure is the implicit assumption that industries with relatively low levels of profitability are more likely to be characterised by unprofitable plants and hence high closure rates. It might also be expected that industries likely to suffer greater variations in demand are likely to experience high closure rates. As plausible as these arguments appear it is possible to reason in a completely opposite direction that plants in growing sectors are at least as liable, and perhaps even more liable to closure than are plants in slow growth or declining (low profit) industries. If growth industries are experiencing rapid technological change then existing facilities may find themselves rapidly outmoded. The microcomputer and software industry would provide a good example at the present time. As more and more firms enter a new industry a shaking out process might be expected with some of the pioneers closing because of insufficient managerial experience, lack of financial resources to grow or even because of a poor location. Locational deficiencies can be masked by the high profit levels and only become obvious if profit levels fall. As is to be expected from these arguments the empirical evidence of the effects of industrial structure on closures are rather mixed.

There is no doubt that closure rates do vary by sector whether this is examined in non-metropolitan Wisconsin (Erickson 1980:498), Scotland (Henderson 1980:167) or Eire (O'Farrell and Crouchley 1983:418). Across these studies clothing/apparel and wood and furniture appear among the industries with high closure rates. In non-metropolitan Wisconsin there is fairly clear evidence that closure rates are related to output change. Whereas industries with above average rates of output growth recorded a closure rate of 16 per cent those with below average growth rates recorded closure rates of 29 per cent (Erickson 1980:498). These data related only to branch plants and Henderson's (1980:166) study of all types of plant across 13 sectors in Scotland provided a contrasting result in that there was no statistically significant relationship between either an industry's output or employment growth rate and its closure rate. Although predicting a region's closure rate from its industrial structure

is a risky business it is a variable which has to be considered.

Size of plant

If there is a relationship between plant size and closure regional patterns of closure may reflect, in part, the underlying distribution of plant sizes. There are a number of reasons for expecting small plants to be more liable to closure than larger ones. Plant size is, of course, related to industrial sector (Ch. 6).

In the case of a market-system (single-plant) firm, which is the most characteristic of organisational form found among small plants, there are a number of features which place it at risk. It usually depends upon a single product or process, it has limited financial and managerial resources and thus its flexibility, if faced with a financial crisis, is very restricted. Further, there may be problems of succession when an owner retires, especially in countries where there are high tax liabilities on death. Finally, because of the small size any loss of demand might have to be met by closure rather than reduction of size since a reduction in size might reduce the viability of the operation taking it below the minimum efficient scale. For these reasons small plants would appear to be more liable to close than large ones.

Even in planning-system multi-plant firms where several of the above reasons do not apply (for example, a small plant within a planning-system firm would have access to financial and managerial resources) there are still grounds for expecting the smaller plant to close. The loss of a small plant would have little effect on the total organisation, few workers would lose their jobs or have to be transferred to other sites, any economies of scale available are less likely to have been achieved in small plants than large ones, and little capital will be invested in the site.

The empirical evidence confirms these expectations with a high degree of consistency although a number of writers also include data on closure and *firm* size. Among the studies confirming that a relationship between *plant* size and closure

Table 14.3   Plant closure and plant size, United States, 1969–76

Plant size, 1969 (employees)	Percentage closed by 1976			
	North-East	North-Central	South	West
1– 20	53	48	53	53
21– 50	40	30	36	39
51–100	37	27	36	36
101–500	33	27	34	31
>500	21	15	28	16

(*Source*: Bluestone and Harrison 1982:272)

exists are those of New Jersey (James and Hughes 1973), Eire (O'Farrell 1976; O'Farrell and Crouchley 1983) and Scotland (Henderson 1980). The principal feature these studies reveal is that closure is a negative function of plant size. The relationship is illustrated in Table 14.3 which shows the remarkable degree of consistency typical of the results of this type of research. Take the North-East region as an example. Whereas 53 per cent of the plants with 1 to 20 employees at the end of 1969 had closed by the end of 1976 this was true of only 21 per cent of the plants with over 500 employees. The same pattern appears in the other three regions; in each region as plant size increases so the proportion of plants closed decreases.

Age of plant

Small plant size can be associated with youthfulness (Ch. 11). In the medium term plants are most at risk during their early years of operation, although in the very long term as products and building fabric age so the risk of closure increases again. Most research has concentrated upon what O'Farrell and Crouchley (1983:418) term *infant mortality*. In the early years of a market-system firm's operation profits may be low and costs high as the firm has to establish its markets and suppliers, set its prices and wage rates and develop its own management structure. Founders may find they lack the competence and skills to run a business and they may have underestimated their need for financial reserves to meet their initial set-up costs. As Gudgin (1978:182) observed 'the disadvantages of youthfulness are mainly associated with inexperience'.

These problems are less likely to affect branch plants of planning-system firms and transfers but there are still learning costs to be incurred and Townroe (1979:191) argues that 'many initial post-move problems are more functions of inadequate managerial skills than anything else'.

It is simplest to examine the effects of age on closure where data are available on the number of plants established each year. Two such data sets exist, for Scotland (Henderson, 1980) and for Eire (O'Farrell and Crouchley, 1983). The Scottish data relate to all new plants established between 1960 and 1974 and closures were defined to include not only shut-downs but also transfers and a fall in employment below 11 employees. The catholic definition of closure inflates the closure rates but does not invalidate the contrasts which emerged. Whereas the average closure rate in the first five years of operation was just over 6 per cent, in the succeeding ten years the closure rate fell to slightly over 3.5 per cent. The age specific closure rates for Irish plant from 1973 to 1981 indicate the highest probability of closure occurs in the early years and the lowest in the seventh year of operation. Closure rates during the first four years of a plant's life are approximately double those between years five and seven.

Whereas these two studies examined all plants, an analysis of branch plants indicates closure comes rather later than in single-plant new firms presumably because branch plants have fewer problems in their early years. In plants moving between 49 British regions from 1945 to 1966 the highest closure rates occurred after five to eight years of operation and then after the eighth year the closure rate returned to its previous level

(Sant 1975b). In contrast, a study of grant-aided plants established in Eire from 1960 to 1973 (O'Farrell 1976) was unable to find any relationship between age of plant and closure but this might reflect the high level of subsidies given to those Irish plants enabling them to overcome any financial difficulties in their first few years of operation.

While youthfulness brings an increased risk of closure it does not seem unreasonable to suggest that among a well-established stock of plants it is the very old plant that will close. Among these plants the factory structures will be old. They may cause major maintenance costs and fail to meet modern safety and work environment requirements. In Chapter 8 the difficulties of adapting older buildings to modern space requirements were stressed. In human terms many market-system firms, still run by their founders or their families, may hit problems associated with finding a successor to the founder after 30 or 40 years of operation. Curiously, the relationship between old age and plant closure has not been explored in recent studies except by Healey (1981b:403) who found no empirical support for the view that old plants within multi-plant firms were more likely to be closed or to have their workforce reduced.

Ownership

This final variable has attracted considerable attention in the recent past with the suggestion that plants with different ownership characteristics have differing propensities to close. Branch plants are thought to be most at risk and from this basic notion have arisen a number of enquiries which have moved from studies of differences between branch and independent plants to investigations into the closure rates associated with different types of branches. Branches, for examples, can be classified by nationality of ownership (Ch. 2) and by the ways in which they are linked into the organisation of the parent firm (Ch. 4).

Branch plants

It is possible to argue that branch plants of planning-system firms are *either* more likely *or* less likely to close than a single-plant market-system firm (Erickson 1981:146–9). The argument for the higher closure rate goes something like this. Since a branch plant is only one of a number of plants its closure does not necessarily result in the liquidation of the firm. In the case of a single-plant firm such a liquidation would be almost inevitable. Thus, the decision to close a branch plant is rather less fundamental from the point of view of the firm than the decision to close a single-plant firm. Similarly, the single-plant firm is forced to adjust on site or face the cost of moving elsewhere, while the multi-plant firm can switch capacity and products between sites and closure of one site can be offset by expansion elsewhere (Ch. 13). Further, if overall demand is falling or major new investment is required production can be concentrated on a particular site and other plants closed. Closure of a branch plant may also be more likely because the decision to close will be made some distance from the locality of the plant, making it an easier decision since the employees will not be known to the decision makers and the decision-makers will feel little sense of loyalty to the town in which the plant is located.

It can be argued, in opposition to these views, that with access to the financial resources of the owning firm, a branch plant might be able to survive a downturn in the business cycle better than a single-plant firm, and large conglomerate firms may be prepared to subsidise, at least in the short run, any of their plants experiencing difficulties. Despite this counter argument it seems likely that closure rates will be higher among branch plants than among independent plants.

There is some evidence that branch plants do *not* have a greater propensity to close than independent plants. From a study of branch plants in non-metropolitan Wisconsin, Erickson (1980: 500) concluded that 'non-metropolitan branch plants do not have a particularly high closure rate...[and]...compared to business enterprises, in general,...[the]...closure rates appear to be relatively low' while Keeble (1976: 238) and Townroe (1975:57) concurred from

British evidence available to them that there was little evidence to support the view that branch plants had a greater propensity to close than independent ones. If these findings are widely supported it would suggest that ownership is not an important variable influencing closure rates: other evidence suggests that ownership does influence closing rates.

The higher closure rate of branch plants is confirmed by Barkley's (1978) study of plants in rural Iowa between 1965 and 1975. Plants were classified into local plants and plants which were part of multi-plant corporations. When closures were expressed as a proportion of total plant stock in the area in 1973–74 the proportion of local plants closed (12.50) was significantly different from the proportion closed (21.43) in the multi-plant group. The closure rate in the latter group was almost twice that of the local group and these differences appeared in all plant size groups and for all industries except non-durable goods (i.e. food, textiles, chemicals). Data from Sweden (relating to the county of Skaraborg between Stockholm and Gothenburg) for the period between 1963 and 1971 show a similar pattern of a closure rate of 27 per cent in externally owned branch plants in contrast to a rate of 11 per cent among independent plants and this did not reflect variations in plant size structure (Clark 1976).

It is then possible to identify differences in closure rates between branch plants and independent plants, and these differences appear even when a control for plant size is introduced. While the direction of the difference may be a matter for debate (both theoretical and empirical evidence can support arguments for opposing directions) there is sufficient evidence to suggest that ownership is an important variable that ought to be included within studies of regional variations in plant closure rates.

Nationality

A foreign firm is expected to have little commitment to either the host country or to any of the areas within it and therefore might be expected to close plants more readily than indigenous firms. The typical pattern of closures expected of

foreign-owned firms is seen in Eire where almost one-third of the foreign-owned plants of 1973 had closed by 1981 in contrast to only one-quarter of the Irish single-plant firms (O'Farrell and Crouchley 1983:423). Yet from 1963 to 1973 overseas-owned plants in the Northern region were *less* prone to closure than plants controlled from elsewhere in Britain (Smith 1982:243), while in Scotland from 1968 to 1977 the closure rate of UK-owned firms (31 per cent) was much higher than that of overseas-owned firms (12 per cent) (Cross 1981:22, 199). However, since 1973 closures of foreign-owned plants in the Northern region have begun to accelerate, a phenomenon also seen in Scotland where an average of 8 to 9 closures per annum in foreign-owned plants from 1976 to 1978 rose to an average of 11–12 from 1979 to 1981 (Hood and Young 1982:30). This evidence, like that on ownership in general, can only indicate that overseas ownership may be an important variable influencing closure rates but it would be wrong to assume that foreign-owned plants are always more vulnerable then their indigenous counterparts.

Organisational structure

A highly autonomous branch may have more in common with a market-system firm than with a branch plant belonging to a highly centralised organisation and thus there may be variations in closure rates between different types of branches. The effects of organisational structure on closure rates were explored by Erickson (1980) in the study of non-metropolitan Wisconsin referred to earlier. He argued that in diversified firms branch plants will be very much affected by their own decisions while in a vertically integrated firm (with part-process branches) or large single-product firms (with cloned branches) individual plants may be closed not only because of their own problems but because of the way they fit (or do not fit) within the entire set of plants in the corporate system (Ch. 4). The evidence provides support for this view as the closure rate for plants belonging to diversified firms was only 10 per cent whereas in the other two groups the rate was between 27 and 30 per cent. However, in view of the contrasting patterns which have emerged in other studies of the ownership variable too much should not be read into this one piece of evidence.

Acquisition

Whereas a plant's sector, size and age change slowly, ownership can change rapidly by acquisition and the 'popular media portrayal of... [acquisitions]... is that they tend to lead to mass plant closures' (Leigh and North 1978:240). Some evidence, mainly from Britain, supports this view. In the Northern region, over a ten-year period plants which had been acquired in earlier years showed a closure rate four times the regional average (Smith 1979) and in the iron foundry industry in the United Kingdom from 1967 to 1981 plants which changed ownership had a closure rate between 64 and 66 per cent while independent single-plant firms had a closure rate of 55 per cent (Smith and Taylor 1983:655). Not surprisingly, contrasting evidence is also available, notably from the Wisconsin study (Erickson 1980), which showed that the closure rate for acquired plants was not as high as that for all branch plants.

The variables discussed above may all influence regional variations in plant closure rates but in many cases they have been analysed in an aspatial framework. It is possible to suggest why certain plants in area A are closed but there are few studies which try to explain variations in closure rates between areas. An exception is Gudgin (1978:266–81) who claims for example from a study of closures in Leicestershire from 1947 to 1967 that most of the spatial variations in closure rates can be explained by plant size and industrial structure with perhaps some influence from high entry rates which indicate areas with relatively youthful plant. Perhaps more typical are Henderson's (1980:169–71) results from Scotland. It will be recalled that Glasgow showed a higher closure rate than other areas of Scotland. Yet, there was no evidence to suggest that Glasgow had an over-representation of those plant size groups or industries which were especially liable to closure, nor did it have a high number of young firms which might also

tend to push up the closure rate. It would then appear that Glasgow's higher closure rate must reflect other variables excluded from the analysis.

Despite the increasing interest in closures it is clear that very little is known about why some areas experience more closures than others. Business failure may explain many of the closures in small, single-plant market-system firms which are forced either voluntarily or involuntarily from the crowded platform (Ch. 11). Yet in many cases closures arise not because a business has failed but because planning-system firms, with multi-plant multi-regional and often multinational operations decide to close a plant. Increasingly, interest has been drawn towards these corporate closures partly because of the large size of many of the plants involved and partly because individuals feel so helpless when affected by a corporate decision often made many miles from the plant concerned. What is more there is a suspicion that at least some of these firms deliberately exploit spatial differences in the characteristics of the labour force and quite happily abandon profitable plants in a search for yet higher profits elsewhere. In essence, attention has become concentrated upon plant closures in their corporate context.

CLOSURES AND PLANNING SYSTEM FIRMS

Evidence of the dramatic changes created by closures undertaken by planning-system firms is not difficult to find. Between January 1979 and December 1980 domestic automobile manufacturers in the United States closed or announced the closure of 20 facilities, while on one day in 1979 United States Steel announced the closure of 14 plants and mills in eight states. The latter included a steel mill in Youngstown, Ohio which by itself led to a loss of 3,500 jobs (Bluestone and Harrison 1982:36–7). Similarly in Britain, British Leyland announced the loss of some 10,000 jobs in the West Midlands in September 1979, while British Steel announced, for example, closures and job losses at Corby (6,700 jobs in 1977 and 1979) and Consett (4,600 jobs in 1979) (Townsend 1981:34–5). Figures like these indicate only the *direct* job losses and do not include losses arising in plants supplying the closed plant with either services or material inputs.

Closures in planning-system firms differ from those in single-plant firms. The most vital distinctions are that in the single-plant market-system firm closure results in the demise of the firm whereas in the case of the multi-plant operation the firm survives and while the single-plant firm has no choice over which plant to close the planning-system firm can select a plant for closure from the 2+ plants it operates. It is this potential for selection which makes the study of closures within planning-system firms of such importance. Bluestone and Harrison (1982:34) summarise the distinction between closures in the two types of firm in this way: a corporate and especially a conglomerate closing is... 'likely to be the result of a planned strategy to increase company wide profits... [while] ... the closing of an independently owned business is more likely to be the result of a truly involuntary failure'. The interest in closures in planning-system firms arises because of their ability to select between plants, and because of the suspicion raised by some observers that planning-system firms are more likely than market-system firms to close profitable plants.

Examination of closures in planning-system firms suggests that there are two important but closely related questions to which answers must be sought.

1. Why is it necessary to close a plant (or plants)? The *motivation* question.
2. Why has a particular plant (or plants) been selected as a candidate for closure? The *selection* question.

The distinction between these two questions has not been made clearly in the past (see, for example, Cross 1981:102) and it is a distinction which is of particular significance to the planning-system firm. Obviously selection between plants is not possible for the market-system firm operating only one plant. The distinction between motivation and selection is seen most vividly in new plant location studies where the factors influencing the need for expansion (motivation) are separated from those influ-

encing the search for a new location (selection) but it is less well drawn in the disinvestment literature. In some cases the motivation for a closure has a direct link to where closure occurs but in other cases it is necessary to look at the way in which plants are chosen for closure.

Plant closures within planning-system firms can be classified into one of the three categories (Watts and Stafford 1986). These categories relate specifically to the geographies of plant closure within these firms.

1. *Cessation closures*. The decision by a firm to abandon the production of a product (or product-mix) may lead to the closure of plants no longer needed although there are alternatives such as the sale of the plant to another company or a management buyout. The simplest situation is a firm which closes the one plant responsible for the entire output of the product lines to be discontinued. This is illustrated in Fig. 14.4A where plant 2 is closed following a decision to cease production of product B. More complex situations may involve the closure of several plants within a conglomerate. Location has very little to do with this closure decision or its consequences. In such situations the motivation and selection questions are conflated (although the poor performance of a product might reflect poor production locations).
2. *Default closure*. The most obvious type of default closure is shown in Fig. 14.4B. As a result of locational adjustment policies (Ch. 13) a decision has been made to increase production at plant 2 and other plants, by default, are closed. Questions about 'what is the best location for product B lead to the closure of sites 1 and 3 when 2 is selected for expansion. Default closures can follow from the expansion of an existing brownfield site which is selected from sites already operated by the firm (the situation shown in Fig. 14.4B) or from the opening of a greenfield plant which replaces capacity in older plants which are then all closed. Default closures arising from greenfield expansion were shown in Fig. 13.2. Investment in one plant may create a need to close only some of the re-

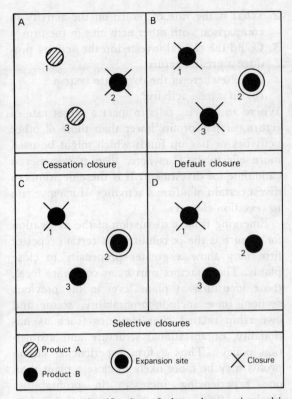

Fig. 14.4 A classification of plant closures in multi-plant firms (*Source*: Watts and Stafford, 1986)

maining plants and, thus, the need to select between them. This leads to a consideration of the third category.

3. *Selective closure.* Two circumstances under which selective closures are made are shown in Fig. 14.4C and Fig. 14.4D. In the case of Fig. 14.4C some expansion has occurred at site 2 but the firm has to select between plants 1 and 3 for closure. This is a selective closure arising from a brownfield concentration policy shown in Fig. 13.2. In Fig. 14.4D no expansion has occurred and it is necessary to select between sites 1, 2 and 3. These are the most explicitly spatial types of closure decision, as a firm decides to close one (or more) plants from a set of several similar facilities. If, for example, a firm has several plants producing (or capable of producing) identical products, it must then carefully assess the merits of each to determine which should be closed. The decision to close a plant is prior to, and

separate from, the decision of which plant to close.

Some indication of the relative importance of the different types of closures are provided in Table 14.4. Only one-quarter of the closures in this sample were associated with what are here called cessation closures; and only 12 per cent were associated with investment in a new plant. The latter group would form part of default closures in the categorisation used in this analysis. The remaining major category accounting for some 61 per cent of the closures would include default closures associated with brownfield investment and selective closures associated with cuts in overall firm capacity.

Table 14.4 Disposal of plants in a sample of multi-plant firms in the United States, 1970s

	Per cent of closures
Cessation closures	
'The company got out of the business'	24
'The operations were subcontracted'	2
'Government contract was completed'	1
Default closures (part)	
'The operations were relocated to a *new* plant	12
Unclassified closures	
'The operations were absorbed by one or more existing company plants'	61

(*Source*: Schmenner 1982:237)

The different types of closure are explained in different ways. Default closures need little attention as these arise from investment decisions which are clearly related to the branch plant location decisions discussed in Chapter 12. Most interest has been focused on cessation and selective closures. Understanding cessation closures needs a careful consideration of the motivations which lead a firm to abandon a product; understanding selective closures requires a consideration of factors influencing the choice of plant for closure.

Motivation

Firms need profits to survive and, as part of the process of long-run survival, resources are switched between activities. Some activities are abandoned, others are introduced, and yet others change in their relative importance within the corporate system. One of the outcomes of this financial reorganisation and re-appraisal may be the closure of plants. The motives for such re-appraisals are varied and range from adjustments stimulated by changes in the business cycle, through reorganisation of activities consequent upon acquisition of another firm's activities, to adjustments arising from longer term trends. Regardless of the solution the eventual aims of the re-appraisal will be to improve profits or reduce costs. Many of these adjustments are part of the process of 'creative destruction' as the capitalist economy grows and develops, but 'destruction' has now become such a major feature of manufacturing activity that reference is made increasingly to de-industrialisation (Ch. 1). The forces leading to closures are perhaps more obvious during de-industrialisation, but they do, of course, help to explain why closures also occur in other time periods.

The search for profits and corporate survival places pressures upon a planning-system firm to grow and to expand its market share. Such growth depends on the availability of funds to finance growth and a particularly valuable source of funds is the organisation's retained profits. Where the retained profits are not sufficient to fund a firm's plan, one course of action is to redeploy corporate assets. Redeployment actions may be classified into two groups: *forced redeployment* where reorganisation is necessary to avoid bankruptcy of either the firm or part of its activities; and *opportunistic redeployment* where the shifting of assets from one activity to another results not from the threat of bankruptcy, but from the attraction of higher returns elsewhere. These opportunistic redeployments may lead to abandonment by the firm of marginally, but not sufficiently, profitable activities.

Each planning-system firm will have its own acceptable rate of return on individual products or divisions. What is, or is not, acceptable, may be assessed in one or more ways.

1. Does the activity meet the target rate of return set by the firm?

2. What is the rate of return on the activity in comparison with other activities in the firm?
3. Could the capital invested in the activity produce a greater return
   (a) elsewhere in the corporate system
   (b) in a new activity?

Where an activity fails to meet a target rate of return, or has profits lower than those of other activities or ties up funds which might be used more effectively elsewhere, then it becomes a candidate for divestment. It is these decisions to divest certain of a firm's activities which give rise to cessation closures.

Emerging from a discussion of the motivation for closure is the possibility that certain types of firm may show a greater propensity to close plants. These factors mirror, at corporate level, those identified at plant level in the previous section, these include profitability, sector and ownership related characteristics (such as nationality, organisational structure and acquisition policy). Thus a firm experiencing falling profits may be more likely to close a plant than one experiencing increases in profitability. Healey's (1982) study which examined a variety of firm-related characteristics to establish their effect on closure found only one relationship of significance. Closures were least frequent in enterprises following a growth oriented strategy. Overall company profitability can be important, especially among planning-system firms operating in an oligopolistic environment. In Britain, for example, six newsprint plants were operated by three firms and two were subsequently closed. The differential spatial closure pattern had little to do with the regions which lost the plants, it was related more closely to the relative financial strength of the firms operating the plants (Massey and Meegan 1982:158–9). However, data relating to larger groups of firms do not support the view that the firms with the lowest profits show the highest closure rates (Healey 1982:44). Relationships between corporate level characteristics and propensity to close plants may be of value to analyses of regional closure patterns if certain types of firm are concentrated in certain regions; a more direct route would focus upon selective closure.

Selection

A survey of the disinvestment and closure literature by Watts and Stafford (1986) produced a plethora of variables which researchers have suggested or utilised in their efforts at explanation of individual closures and/or spatial patterns

of closure and this section is based on their work. Table 14.5 presents a list of the variables that may influence a planning-system firm's selection of a plant for closure. Table 14.5 is not necessarily exhaustive but it includes all the most frequently cited variables. Sectoral influences are excluded since a decision to abandon a product

Table 14.5 Selective closure: the variables

The probability of a plant being selected for closure increases as the predictive variable increases (+) or decreases (−)

Category	Plant level	Area level
Access to markets	Links with region (−) Links with firm (−)	Accessibility to markets (−)
Access to supplies	Links with regions (−) Links with firm (−)	Accessibility to material inputs (−) Accessibility to business services (−) Accessibility to head office (−)
Land		Site value/rent (+) Space for expansion (−)
Capital	Capital intensity (−) Machinery valuation (−) Age of machinery (+) Age of buildings (+) Size of plant (−)	
Labour	Per cent female labour (+) Labour productivity (−) Labour intensity (+)	Wage rates (+) Labour relations (−) Unionisation of labour force (+)
Organisation	Managerial autonomy (−) Length of ownership (−) Management expertise (−)	Corporate interaction (+)
Technology	Flexibility of operations (−) Appropriateness of technology (−)	
Policy Environment		Regional policy environment (−) Local policy environment (−) Local taxes (+) Environmental regulations (+)
Personal	Personal attachments (−)	Residential amenities (−) Community dependence upon plant (−)

(*Source*: Watts and Stafford (1986))

would be treated as a cessation closure. The list in Table 14.5 has been simplified by *excluding* relative measures and measures of change.

Perhaps the most obvious omission from the list is a consideration of profits and costs, especially as in their public statements large firms tend to emphasise the high costs of the plants they plan to close. For example, in the London Brick Company in Britain 'the selection of works for closure was made, above all, on the basis of internal production costs and productivity' (Massey and Meegan 1982:174). While the profits and costs of individual plants may provide a route to understanding selective closures, access to a firm's projections for even one plant is usually impossible. Even if cost/profit data are available they raise questions as to why costs are high/profits low in particular plants. Attention has already been drawn (page 115) to the problems raised by transfer pricing and the procedures for allocating central overheads to individual plants can be the subject of acrimonious debate. Thus, practical efforts towards understanding selective closure must involve the use of other measures which are thought to be associated with closure probabilities; these are the variables listed in Table 14.5. These variables may be surrogates for cost and profit but, equally, they may be more fundamental explanations of a plant's financial record.

The variables are classified in two ways. The first column allocates them to the categories found in traditional location studies and the other two columns take up Massey and Meegan's (1982:147–8) dichotomisation of closure factors on the basis of those relating to plants and those relating to areas. Several variables could have been placed in more than one category but they have been listed in the category that seems most appropriate to the analysis of selective closures in planning-system firms. An indication of the directions in which the variables might operate is also provided. The allocations to categories and the direction of the relationship is, of course, open to debate, but it is the categorisation which is of most relevance here.

Despite the range of characteristics included in the table a striking feature is that the vast majority of them can be classified to categories recognised in the traditional work in industrial location such as land, labour, capital and access to supplies and markets which were discussed in Part III of this book. Investigators have been drawing implicitly, if not explicitly, upon the existing body of location theory. Although O'Farrell (1976:434) claimed that 'there is no existing body of theory which outlines the causal variables of plant closure' the links with traditional location theory are evident.

Equally important in Table 14.5 is the distinction between area and plant variables. It will be noted that the plant variables include measures of the plant's 'position' in the firm to which it belongs (Erickson 1980). The crucial distinction emerges from the recognition that most plant level variables can be manipulated by the firm (for example, by changing a plant's purchasing pattern, or by increasing a plant's autonomy) while the area related variables are often outside the control of the firm. This distinction is least easy to make in relation to access to supplies and markets and in relation to labour characteristics. A firm cannot decide to sell more or buy more from a local region if the potential buyers or sellers do not exist. Similarly, while a firm can try to manipulate its own labour policies it may well be constrained by regional labour force attitudes to such things as unionisation. Inevitably, a dichotomisation of the variables in this way tends to hide the way in which the plant and the area variables can be interrelated but it does help to stress the difference between the two.

There are few detailed analyses of selective closures in planning-system firms although both Bluestone and Harrison (1982) and Massey and Meegan (1982) draw together a wide range of evidence. Particularly interesting are Peck and Townsend's (1984) case studies and Healey's (1982) study of closures in multi-plant firms in the textile and clothing industry.

The former study examined three large firms – British Shipbuilders, Plessey (an electronics company) and Metal Box – and an important part of the work was trying to establish why certain plants were selected for closure. The evidence from the three firms indicated a number of factors which made the closure of a specific plant more likely.

1. *A recent history of labour difficulties*. This was evident in the Haverton Hill shipyard which had closed with a loss of 1,420 jobs in 1979. Despite the fact it was a modern yard it had failed to win orders possibly because of fears of late delivery arising from labour troubles. There appears to be support here for the role of labour influences in the closure decision.

2. *Restricted site*. This was cited as the major reason for the closure of a plant at Speke. The site was just too small to accommodate new production lines. There are hints here of the influence of the constrained location hypothesis.

3. *Age of equipment*. This may have been the reason for the closure of a Sunderland plant. The equipment was older than that in another potential closure candidate.

4. *Unsuitable buildings*. In Metal Box its Rochester plant proved incapable of conversion to new technologies primarily because of height restrictions.

5. *Loss of markets*. At Winsford the Metal Box plant lost its contract to supply major local brewing firms with metal cans, the market being captured by a rival firm.

The listing hides some of the complexities of the closure decision but it indicates some of the different variables involved.

Healey (1982) adopted a wider ranging approach and examined 64 multi-plant firms in the United Kingdom clothing and textile industry. This confirms some of the relationships noted in the earlier part of the chapter, notably that small plants are more likely to close, and that acquired plants have a greater propensity to be closed (especially five or more years after acquisition). Closure rates were lower in plants with space for expansion, in plants with high degrees of managerial autonomy and in plants at which the site of the company head office was located. Plants acquired by firms as part of a horizontal acquisition were more likely to close than those taken over by firms operating in different industries. In contrast to hints as to the significance of age of buildings in the case studies there was, as was seen in the discussion of age and closure, no evidence that plants in older buildings were closed. Similarly, there was no evidence that distance from head office increased the probability of closure. This study did not include any measures of labour force characteristics (other than number of employees) nor did it include any aspects of policy.

It ought to be possible to move beyond these case studies and external assessments to examine selective closure decisions in planning-system firms. Despite widespread use of survey techniques to establish the factors influencing new firm formation and the location of branch plants the published evidence suggests that they have not been used in the context of closure.

Examination of the plant closure decision will allow identification of the closure factors as perceived by firms and will assist in assessing the relative importance of the different factors. It may also be effective in picking up the influence of personal and subjective factors and will help in distinguishing the way in which firms respond to an area's characteristics as distinct from a plant's characteristics. The extent to which the selection of a plant for closure follows carefully established decision-making procedures or reflects simply a 'business hunch' is still open to debate. A hunch decision may supplement or override a cost/profit decision. It will supplement it where cost/profit data do not themselves indicate a specific course of action at a specific site, and may override them where there is a 'gut-feeling' that a certain plant is the 'obvious' one to close.

It might be argued that, even where it appears a selective closure has taken place, management rarely makes a conscious choice between alternatives when deciding to close a plant; the choice of which plant to close usually is 'obvious'. If this is true – and research is needed to substantiate the idea – then the implication is that there is little new knowledge of the geography of plant closures to be obtained through examination of selective closure decisions. However, even 'obvious' decisions have their rationale and where such 'obvious' decisions are recorded it will be necessary to probe into why a particular plant was the obvious candidate for closure. Such a probing should help to reveal the factors influencing a selective closure decision.

CONCLUSION

Despite assertions about the uniformity of the regional experience of employment loss through closure and *in situ* shrinkage there is evidence that regional variations in these components of change are as marked as those considered in previous chapters. Data sources have meant that analyses have focused on closures and on closure rates rather than employment loss through closures. In aggregate it seems that a region's industrial structure, its plant size structure, the age

of its plants and various aspects of plant ownership may all influence plant closure rates.

Most interest in recent times has been on closures implemented by planning-system firms and analysis of closures by these firms can be allocated to one of three classes: cessation, default or selective. Analysis of cessation closures demands that attention concentrate on the motives that lead firms to abandon products (and, as a result, close the plants producing them); default closures can be understood by examining the processes affecting the location of investment decisions and analysis of selective closures demands clear identification of closure factors and, perhaps in the future, investigation of the selective closure decision.

PART IV: AFTERWORD

Examining each component in turn reveals little of their overall impacts upon net employment change. Comparison of the impacts in different regions is made difficult by the lack of comparability in different studies. The studies described below have been selected as they identify the five main components discussed in the last four chapters. Only studies which separated *in situ* growth from *in situ* decline were considered. No such data meeting these requirements are readily available from the United States or Canada and components of change analysis appears to be a distinctly British activity.

The data in Tables IV.2 to IV.4 give an indication of the differences between different areas but they do not report precise measures of the relative importance of each of the five components. They differ, particularly, in their treatment of branches and transfers. The key features illustrated in these tables are the relative roles of job creation and job loss and the relative importance of the different mechanisms contributing to job creation and job loss.

Table IV.2 examines the balance between job creation and job loss for three major regions, four cities and three areas with different levels of

Table IV.2 Job creation and job loss‡

	Gains	Losses	Net change
Area			
Ireland, 1973–81	+ 92,181	− 72,789	+19,392
Scotland, 1968–77	+128,991	−195,922	−66,931
East Midlands, 1968–75	+140,196	−146,279	− 6,083
Cities/Industrial Areas			
Coventry, 1974–81	+ 5,578	− 59,284	−53,706
East Midland cities, 1968–75*	+ 56,715	− 79,800	−23,085
Cleveland, 1965–76	+ 23,310	− 34,467	−11,157
Urban–Rural (East Midlands, 1968–75)			
Large towns†	+ 17,492	− 18,576	− 1,084
Smaller towns	+ 49,672	− 41,582	+ 8,090
Rural areas	+ 17,096	− 9,788	+ 7,308

(*Source*: Estimated from Cross 1981:49–50; Robinson and Storey 1981:169; Fothergill and Gudgin 1982:77–8; Healey and Clark 1984:307; O'Farrell 1984:158)

† Lincoln, Northampton, Peterborough, Mansfield.

‡ All figures are estimated from tables in original studies and may differ slightly from figures derived by the authors of those studies from raw data.

* Nottingham, Derby, Leicester.

Table IV.3 Job loss

	Closures (% of all job losses)	Contractions	Total
Areas			
Ireland, 1973–81	−36,477* (50)	− 36,312 (50)	− 72,789
Scotland, 1968–77	−82,719 (42)	−113,203 (58)	−195,922
East Midlands, 1968–75	−68,112 (46)	− 81,167 (54)	−149,279
Cities/Industrial Areas			
Coventry, 1974–81	−13,506† (23)	− 45,778 (77)	− 59,284
East Midlands cities, 1968–75	−35,340‡ (44)	− 44,460 (56)	− 79,800
Cleveland, 1965–76	− 9,955 (29)	− 24,512 (71)	− 34,467
Urban–Rural (East Midlands, 1968–75)			
Large towns	− 7,972 (43)	− 10,604 (57)	− 18,576
Smaller towns	−21,519 (52)	− 20,063 (48)	− 41,582
Rural areas	− 4,263 (44)	− 5,525 (56)	9,788

(*Source:* see Table IV.2)
* Excludes plants <50 in Dublin.
† Includes transfer to locations within and outside Coventry.
‡ Includes transfers out of area.

rurality. Among the major regions, only Ireland records a positive net change in jobs. Job gains outweigh job losses in Ireland but despite the apparent strength of the area's employment record massive job losses have occurred. In Scotland, despite a large negative net change around 130,000 new jobs were created. In the East Midlands net change figures appear to indicate a relatively stable employment record yet just less than 150,000 jobs were lost and 140,000 jobs gained. Although in the East Midland cities there was a significant net loss of jobs much of gross job losses were offset by job creation. It is only in Coventry that net changes reflect gross job loss as there has been so little job creation in the city. Finally, in the large towns job creation almost offsets job loss; in smaller towns the job gain more than offsets job losses giving a net gain; while in the rural areas job gains are almost twice the job losses. These figures indicate clearly how net changes emerge

from very different patterns of job gain and job loss.

Theoretically, the categories of job loss and job creation can be disaggregated further but it is only possible to break empirical data on job loss into *in situ* contractions and closures. Table IV.3 shows that the broad pattern is for the two processes to be of almost equal importance in terms of employment with a slight bias towards a dominance by *in situ* contractions. The two exceptions (Cleveland and Coventry) are areas dominated by large plants. Although the major plants have not all been closed they have shed large numbers of jobs.

Table IV.4 identifies the contribution of new firms, branches and *in situ* expansion to job creation. The single most important source of new jobs in virtually every area was the *in situ* expansion of existing plants, the poor performance of this sector in Ireland probably reflects the fact that *in situ* expansion of the headquarters

Table IV.4 Job creation

	New firms	Branches (% of all jobs created)	*In situ* expansion	Other	Total
Areas					
Ireland, 1973–81	18,032	32,365	23,676	18,108*	92,181
	(20)	(34)	(26)	(20)	
Scotland, 1968–77	12,194	37,636	74,853	4,308†	128,991
	(9)	(29)	(59)	(3)	
East Midlands, 1968–75	23,271	12,487	84,572	19,866‡	140,196
	(17)	(9)	(60)	(14)	
Cities					
Coventry, 1974–81	1,040	818§	3,720	3,689¶	9,267
	(11)	(9)	(40)	(40)	
East Midland cities, 1968–75	10,260	2,565	33,915	9,975‡	56,715
	(18)	(5)	(59)	(18)	
Urban–Rural (East Midlands, 1968–75)					
Large towns	2,245	3,173	8,901	3,173‡	17,492
	(13)	(18)	(51)	(18)	
Smaller towns	7,766	6,472	29,933	5,501‡	49,672
	(16)	(13)	(60)	(11)	
Rural areas	2,697	2,306	10,831	1,262‡	17,096
	(16)	(13)	(64)	(7)	

(*Sources*: see Table IV.2)
* Irish multi-plant enterprises.
† Scottish multi-plant branches.
‡ Branches of East Midland firms.
§ Branches from within and outside Coventry.
¶ Transfer opening from within and outside Coventry.

plants of Irish firms is not separately identified. Just as *in situ* decline accounts for around 50 per cent of job losses, so *in situ* growth in the areas and time periods for which data are available accounts for well over half of all jobs created.

The relative importance of job creation through branches varies from high inputs in areas peripheral to the European economy (Scotland and Ireland) to much lower levels elsewhere (for example, a contribution as low as 5 per cent in the East Midland cities). In the areas described in Table IV.4 the new firm's role in job creation varies between 9 and 20 per cent, being high in the East Midlands and Ireland and low in Scotland. It is through an understanding of the geographies of these different forms of job creation that it is possible to understand regional variations in the job creation processes.

The most striking results to emerge from this disaggregation of employment change is the emergence of *in situ* change as an important mechanism influencing job creation and job loss. This should not be surprising since an area's permanent stock of plants is often much greater than the number that open and close, but such a finding does suggest that industrial geography with its emphasis on new firms, branches and closures is scarcely touching an important mechanism influencing the creation and loss of employment opportunities in different regions. It is not alone, for policy makers too when trying to create jobs have until recently concentrated upon diverting jobs between regions. Where attention has been focused upon a region's indigenous potential emphasis has been placed upon the creation of new firms rather than the expansion of existing plants. It is the impact of explicit spatial policies upon employment opportunities in different regions which is considered next.

PART V

POLICIES AND
RESEARCH
PRIORITIES

In the discussion so far it has been an implicit assumption that changes in employment patterns in specific regions reflect the decisions taken by firms although those decisions are constrained by the framework within which the firms operate. In this final part of the book it is shown how the geography of industrial change can be modified by direct government intervention. Such intervention is usually expensive but some governments have succeeded in diverting employment opportunities between areas. Intervention is the theme of Chapter 15 and then Chapter 16 tries to assess the nature of the gaps in our current knowledge of industrial geography and to indicate the new directions which industrial geography may follow in the 1990s.

15

INTERVENTION

In the preceding chapters various factors influencing net change, births, movement, *in situ* change and deaths have been considered and in different chapters there are hints of 'policy effects'. In this chapter the role of central government in diverting industrial activity from one area to another is discussed. It begins by discussing explicit spatial policy measures (Ch. 9) and then considers their effects on the geography of employment change in manufacturing industry. Most of the evidence is drawn from the United Kingdom which has a long history of explicit spatial policies.

EXPLICIT SPATIAL POLICIES

The most extreme form of policy occurs where government issues a directive as to where a particular form of locational change is (or is not) to take place. The direction of industry is relatively unusual but, in exceptional circumstances, it is undertaken. This is made possible where there are major government shareholdings in particular firms, or where the fortunes of the firm are dependent particularly on other government controls. For example, a threat to remove import tariffs on a firm's or industry's products would encourage the firm to accept government advice on location. Two contemporary examples illustrate direction of industry. One relates to closure, the other relates to an opening.

In the late 1970s the British government established INMOS a state-backed company to help to develop the British semiconductor (microchip) industry. The initial (pre-production phase) facilities were established in Bristol and the firm put forward plans to set up production facilities in the same area. Public outcry at this decision led, after numerous behind-the-scene manœuvres, to the setting up of the production plant in the nearby declining coalfield area of South Wales. In essence, the firm had been directed to set up its production plant in that area (Sweet 1981:37–8).

The second example concerns the British steel industry and plans to cut capacity in 1982. The public-sector firm proposed reducing the number of its steel making plants from five to four, the most likely candidate for closure being the Ravenscraig plant in Scotland. Strong pressure on the Conservative Prime Minister by the Conservative Secretary of State in Scotland led to discussion of the proposed closure at Cabinet level. In December 1982 the government told British Steel to prepare its corporate plan on the basis that steel making will continue at all five sites. In effect, the firm was being directed not to close the Ravenscraig plant at this point in time.

More common than direction and, indeed, dominating explicit spatial policy measures are policies to maintain or increase employment levels in industry in specific areas. Policies of this type were for many years called 'regional policies' but the areas to which policies now apply are so diverse in size and scope that the term 'regional' is no longer appropriate. These policies in Britain saw their greatest development from the mid-1960s to the mid-1970s but in the United States Rees and Weinstein (1983:248) observe 'economic development assistance for the more distressed parts of the country has been given a low funding priority, resulting in very little impact on the industrial geography of the United States'. The detailed history of spatial policies varies markedly from country to country as does the range of policies and the speed with which such policies change. It is therefore inappropriate in a work such as this to describe either the evolution of policy or the nature of current policies. The historical context of such policies in the United States is described by House (1983a:34–79); a similar historical perspective for Britain is provided by McCallum (1979:3–41).

Perhaps the most distinctive feature of these explicit spatial policies is that some areas are eligible for aid and others are not, and in some cases, the level of aid varies between *Assisted Areas*. The criteria for delimiting Assisted Area varies from country to country but the guidelines of the Canadian Area Development Agency provide a good example (Walker 1980a:60).

This agency offered assistance to areas which met at least one of three conditions.
1. The area's average family income was below the national average ($5,449) and during the previous five years there had been
   (a) unemployment at least twice the national average;
   (b) unemployment at least one and a half times the national average plus an employment growth rate half the national average.
2. Employment decline in the area was over 10 per cent per annum over the previous five years.
3. Average family income was below $4,250; 40 per cent or more families in the area with an average annual income below $3,000.

Utilising measures like these and, it must be admitted, occasionally reflecting the interests of the party in power, countries are divided into policy zones.

Figure 15.1 illustrates the Assisted Areas in the United Kingdom in 1978 and 1984. In 1978 aid was highest in the Special Development Areas (SDAs), lower in the Development Areas

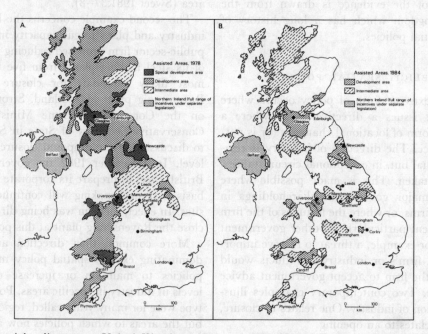

Fig. 15.1 Spatial policy zones, United Kingdom, 1978 and 1984 (*Source*: *Trade and Industry*, 3 March 1978, Special Report: 27 and *British Business*, 30 November 1984:533)

(DAs) and lowest of all in the Intermediate Areas. The Assisted Areas covered much of the West and North of the United Kingdom and excluded most of the Midlands, East Anglia and the South-East. The wide coverage of these areas reflects the essentially interventionist nature of a Labour administration. By 1984 the Assisted Areas had been cut back dramatically under the Conservative administration but the government did recognise the changed role of the Midlands and in 1984 both Corby and the Birmingham area were eligible for aid. Selected local administrations (not shown on Fig. 15.1) were also able to offer an Enterprise Zone free of local taxes (see page 214).

Within the Assisted Areas the levels of the inducements (like the boundaries) have varied over time. Such variability makes decision making a difficult task and from a firm's viewpoint both the nature and spatial pattern of policy instruments should be stable, at least in the medium term. The explicit spatial policy instruments are either inducements or restrictions and they were the precursors of the policies followed by local administrators to create the derived spatial policies described in Chapter 10. Usually, from the financial viewpoint, the sums involved are much greater (Table 10.3).

Inducements

The amount of money spent on inducements in Britain is shown in Table 15.1 which relates to the period from 1962/3 to 1983/4. At 1970–71 prices spending rose from £22 million at the beginning of the period to a peak of £332 million in 1975–76. By the end of the period the spending had fallen back to the level of the mid-1960s. These figures exaggerate the spending as they include funds which have a large recoverable element (mainly loans) and in the long term these will reduce the cost of the spatial policies.

Where aid is offered to firms in particular areas governments have to make two choices as to the eligibility of firms for aid. In some cases (particularly in times of growth) aid may be offered only to new plants moving into an area from elsewhere. In other cases (often in times of em-

Table 15.1 Regional policy funds, Britain, 1962–63 to 1983–84

	Amount* (£m)		Amount (£m)
1962–63	22	1973–74	227
1963–64	41	1974–75	327
1964–65	53	1975–76	332
1965–66	117	1976–77	311
1966–67	108	1977–78	247
1967–68	173	1978–79	277
1968–69	288	1979–80	247
1969–70	324	1980–81	233
1970–71	291	1981–82	256
1971–72	246	1982–83	225
1972–73	232	1983–84	184

(*Source*: Pounce 1981:107 and estimated from data in Martin 1985:383)
* At constant 1970–71 prices.

ployment decline) aid will be offered to all existing plants plus any newcomers. A similar kind of choice has to be made as to whether aid will be automatic or discretionary. In the former case all plants of a particular type will be eligible for aid. This policy is expensive and it may make very marginal projects viable. Further, it may aid plants which have no need for assistance, and which provide little employment. Unattractive though this kind of policy may be to government it is most attractive to firms as it is easy to establish the amount of aid that will be available. Discretionary aid may be focused more carefully and given only to those projects which clearly help to meet the government's policy objectives. It should be more cost-effective than automatic aid but experience has shown discretionary aid is difficult to administer (staff, for example, are needed to evaluate all potential projects) and to a firm it is not clear how much aid will be available for a given project.

Inducements can be grouped into a number of categories of which grants, loans, tax allowances, equity investment, infrastructure improvements and labour subsidies are probably most important.

1. *Grants*. Grants can be given to cover part of the cost of new buildings and machinery. They may be either a fixed proportion (for example, 30 per cent) or a proportion based upon the employment generated. The best

examples of such grants are the Regional Development Grants set up in Britain by the Industry Act of 1972 and which accounted for 80 per cent of British government regional spending in 1977–78 (Pounce 1981:107).

2. *Loans.* Loans can be offered at either commercial or subsidised rates of interest and may be limited to projects which cannot raise funds from usual sources. It is usual to limit government loans to a certain proportion of the total investment. Examples of this policy are provided by loans made in the United States by the Business Development Assistance Program of the Economic Development Administration (EDA) set up by the Public Works and Economic Development Act of 1965. In these cases, firms must have been turned down by at least two commercial banks and assistance is limited to not more than $10,000 for each job saved or created (Moriarty 1980:280). Where loans are not made it is possible to provide loan guarantees where the government undertakes to repay a commercial loan if the borrower defaults, such loan guarantees were established in Canada in the Regional Development Incentives Act of 1960 (Brewis 1974:317).

3. *Tax allowances.* These allowances permit firms to set certain items of expenditure against their pre-tax profits and thus reduce their tax bills. The Area Development Agency set up in Canada in 1963 offered such allowances and, a more generous measure, offered a three-year Federal tax exemption on new plants (Walker 1980a:60). Closely related to these tax exemptions and allowances are 'free port' schemes where goods may be landed at a limited number of specified sites and perhaps processed and re-exported without payment of import or excise duties. These were introduced in Britain in 1984. The various tax-related schemes are similar to those incentives offered by local government which reduce local tax levels and, indeed, in the British case it was central government which selected, from a large number of applicants, the urban administrations which could create areas free of local tax (Enterprise Zones).

4. *Equity investment.* In this case the government purchases shares in a firm. This allows a firm to raise extra funds while at the same time the government, as a shareholder, may have the right to influence a firm's behaviour. At regional scale the best examples are the work of the Welsh Development Agency (WDA) and the Scottish Development Agency (SDA) in Britain (Eirug 1983; Rich 1983). These agencies were set up to co-ordinate and implement regional policies in Wales and Scotland and they have powers to invest in private industry. The extent to which these powers are used is difficult to ascertain since published data on investment activity do not distinguish between equity and loan investments; the proportion in equity is probably small as investments represented only 11 per cent of total expenditure of the SDA and 14 per cent of the WDA in 1978–79 (Cooke 1980).

5. *Industrial infrastructure.* Investment in the industrial infrastructure is intended to make an area more suitable for industrial development or redevelopment. At the lowest level this can involve the provision of serviced land on industrial estates but may be extended to include the provision of factories either for specific customers or in advance of demand. The latter are termed *advance factories* (Slowe 1981). Such policies have played an important role in Britain where, for example, the government-owned English Estates Company is required to conduct its business to further the government's regional and industrial policies. The spatial allocation of resources made available by central government takes account of the severity of unemployment and the amount of vacant factory space already available in each travel-to-work area. Overall the system of resource allocation attempts to strike a balance between social need for new premises and the likely demand for floor space from potential occupiers. In March 1984 English Estates was managing 1.68 million square metres (m^2) of leased properties, had a further 0.49 million square metres not leased and had sold 1.17 million

square metres of properties, approximately half being sold to existing occupiers and half to new tenants. Factories vary in size from 28 square metres to 27,900 square metres and are built either for specific customers or in advance of demand (English Estates 1984).

6. *General infrastructure*. Instead of focusing upon manufacturing activity a general up-grading of an area's infrastructure may be undertaken with the development primarily of public utilities such as water supplies, sewerage and roads. This kind of policy was one of the policies followed in the United States by the Economic Development Administration. From its inception to 1978 it had spent some two-thirds of its funds on public works projects (Hansen 1980:46). Similarly the Appalachian Regional Commission, set up under the Appalachian Regional Development Act of 1965, spent most of its funds during its first few years of operation on highway construction projects (Hansen 1974:291). Perhaps the most dramatic form of policy of this type was the British government's policy of establishing new towns, notably in South-East England (Fothergill, Kitson and Monk 1983). An alternative to infrastructure improvement, or even in addition to it, can be the subsidisation of transport costs a policy followed by Canada for its Atlantic region. The Maritime Freight Rates Act and the Atlantic Region Freight Assistance Act provided for federal subsidies for the movement of goods by rail and motor truck (Brewis 1974:326).

7. *Labour subsidy*. A policy aimed at reducing a firm's labour costs may attract new industries as well as encourage existing firms to retain their employment levels. For about ten years in the 1960s and 1970s the British government offered a Regional Employment Premium in a number of areas and at its inception it was a weekly subsidy of £1.50 per man, £0.75 for women and boys and £0.47½ for girls. This was before 'equal opportunity' arguments gained a firm hold!

This listing of policies is not intended to be exhaustive and there are many other types of policy. For example, rent-free periods may be offered in government factories, grants may be made available to assist in the re-training of workers and, to aid entirely new plants, grants can be offered to help overcome operational costs over the early years of the plant's life. Some government-financed agencies may undertake promotional activities for their areas, thus supplementing similar work by local government.

At present time, the two policy zones in the United Kingdom receive only two direct forms of assistance from the British government although other assistance is provided by, for example, English Estates and the European Regional Development Fund. Regional Development Grants (RDGs) offer a 15 per cent grant towards the capital cost of a project. The RDG is only payable in the Development Areas. Plants in these areas can also receive selective assistance and this is the only form of assistance available to the Intermediate Areas. Selective assistance provides grants for approved projects, the size of the grant being related to capital costs and the number of jobs being created.

There is no doubt that the various government inducements can affect the costs of firms' operations. For example in the late 1960s labour subsidies in Britain were reducing the labour costs of average firms in some areas by around 8 per cent. Similarly, as was seen in Chapter 8, in the early 1970s the net cost of £100 of investment in an area receiving government assistance was (at maximum) £40 compared with a net cost of £60 elsewhere in the nation. This illustrates the repercussions of inducements on a firm's costs at one point in time, but the particular mix of inducements available (and their magnitude) varies in time as well as between countries and between areas within the same country. These variations explain, at least in part, why it is so difficult to isolate the effects of explicit spatial policies on the geography of employment change.

Restrictions

Unlike inducements, which can be used in times of both growth and decline of employment, restrictions can be applied most effectively, as should be self-evident, only where there is growth to restrict. Such restrictions may be used to raise revenue, for example a pay-roll tax levied only in areas where it is intended to limit growth or can be regulatory controls with no financial implications other than the costs involved in implementing them. Restrictions run the risk of causing firms either to abandon expansion plans or to locate them overseas but usually it is hoped that the planned expansions will be diverted to other areas which, in policy terms, are regarded as needing new employment.

The operation of a restrictive policy depends both on a government having the legal authority to restrict industrial growth and the extent to which that authority is exercised. Direct measures to curb growth have not been operated by the federal government in the United States but Britain introduced a system of Industrial Development Certificates (IDCs) in the Town and Country Planning Act of 1947. The IDC system, although subject to various adjustments, remained in operation for just over 30 years. The system required all firms erecting a new plant or an extension of over a given size (initially 5,000 sq. ft.) to apply for an IDC. This policy served to restrict growth at particular sites in a number of ways. Most obviously, outright refusal of an IDC was important but so too was informal advice by government officials that an IDC might not be granted (and so no application was made). What is more, in many areas, firms thought it would be impossible to obtain an IDC and so did not even approach government officers. There were no clear guidelines as to why an IDC might or might not be granted so that firms found it difficult to assess the likely response to a particular proposal.

Although the policy was introduced in 1947 it was implemented with varying force (Table 15.2). Refusals in the Midland and South-East regions from 1956 to 1972 peaked between 1964 and 1966 when the refusal rate was more than twice the rates of 1958 and 1972.

Small market-system firms can escape restrictions of this type since their plants tend to fall under the size limits and it is probable that restrictions will have most influence on larger market-system firms and smaller planning-

Table 15.2   IDC refusal rates in the Midland and South-East regions, 1956–72

	Refusals rates		Refusals rates
	(Refusals as a percentage of applications)		
1956	0.4	1965	10.3
1957	0.4	1966	9.9
1958	3.8	1967	8.8
1959	8.9	1968	5.5
1960	8.5	1969	6.0
1961	7.1	1970	6.4
1962	9.0	1971	6.2
1963	6.8	1972	3.9
1964	10.1		

(*Source*: Pounce 1981:97)

system firms. Large planning-system firms are able to come to 'understandings' with government officials. For example, Ford was allowed to expand in South-East England on the condition that further expansion would take place in Assisted Areas and similarly Courtaulds had a 'running dialogue' such that a particular group of IDCs would be approved side by side with expansion taking place at one of its plants in an Assisted Area (Watts 1980b:270–2). In negotiations of this type a move is being made towards a closer involvement by government in the process of choosing a location for expansion and it is not far removed from the most explicit spatial policy measure – the direction of industry – with which this discussion opened.

POLICY EFFECTS

Following through the general theme of explaining changes in the distribution of employment in manufacturing industry the particular interest in this discussion is the effect of policy on the distribution of industrial activity. It is also possible to ask questions about the effects on, for example, unemployment, social structures and *per capita* incomes but they lie outside the scope of the present discussion. Readers interested in the wider effects of regional policy should consult Diamond and Spence (1983). The policy effects are considered by looking at the aggregate effect of policy, at the effects of different 'regional' policy instruments and at the effect of infrastructure investment.

Explicit spatial policies tend to have the 'broad objective of influencing the distribution of economic activity in favour of... assisted areas' (Ashcroft 1982:287). If they achieve that objective it is necessary to ask what have been the effects of policy on areas with restrictions or lacking inducements and what have been the effects on areas where one or more inducements are available. The first question has received little attention (for an exception, see Tyler 1980) and most effort has to be devoted to measuring the impact of policy on manufacturing employment in assisted areas. This has been undertaken in a number of ways.

One approach is to examine the effect of policy on location decisions. This was discussed in relation to industrial movement in Chapter 12 and these studies show that policy is picked up both in aggregate relationships and as a factor cited by some firms. This conclusion, of course, says nothing of the policy effects on the other components of change. It is probable that decision-makers will not rate the influence of policy very highly as it is variable, uncertain and subject to the winds of political change and therefore cannot be allowed to play a major role in decision-making. As Stafford (1980:117) observes policy may only 'tip the balance when other things are equal or be a marginal bonus'.

A second approach is to identify plants receiving aid as plants affected by policy. This procedure is of dubious value. To assume that a firm receiving aid has retained labour, expanded or even been set up because of that aid is unacceptable as such aid may have been a 'free gift' or 'windfall' and the changes may have taken place for very different reasons. True some firms receiving aid will have been influenced by it but others will not and the problem is estimating the proportion falling in each category.

In view of the difficulty of assessing policy effects by these two approaches most interest has focused upon analysis of aggregate employment data. There is an extensive literature, particularly relating to British and European experience, and methods for measuring policy effects have been developed, adapted and refined over the past decade. Useful reviews which focus particularly on the technical problems involved are provided by Schofield (1979), Ashcroft (1982), Nicol (1982) and Diamond and Spence (1983). These problems are indicative of the difficulties of measuring a policy effect on net employment changes.

To begin, it is useful to caution against the most 'obvious' way of assessing policy effects. It is unwise to correlate employment change in a set of areas with the level of inducements in those areas. For example, when national levels of unemployment are low, high unemployment levels in particular areas encourage governments to provide inducements in those areas, and industrial growth may then occur there. However, does this growth reflect the availability of labour or the inducements? This point is emphasised forcefully by Hansen (1980:54).

The non-metropolitan areas [of the United States] that have experienced economic... growth in the past decade... tend to lie within territories covered by the Appalachian Regional Commission, the Economic Development Administration and the original Title V regional commission... However, few observers would go so far as to credit them with the major responsibility for non-metropolitan revival. The agencies involved have had too little money, too little time, and little in the way of coherent and systematic strategies for development.

In moving on to consider more sophisticated assessments it is necessary to spell out some difficulties which face all assessments, regardless of the technique used.

1. There will be a time-lag between the introduction of a policy and the results arising from it which raises questions as to the length of the time-lag. Such lags will vary between policies; factory construction policies taking longer to effect employment than, say, employment subsidies.

2. It is difficult to isolate short-run from medium-term effects. Any jobs created by policy are not permanent jobs as has been seen in the geography of *in situ* decline and closure and the effects will be modified by the age of the plants at the end of the period being examined.

Numerous young plants will enhance the policy effect especially if they are reaching the end of their rapid growth period, while many old ones will depress it.

3. Isolation of the explicitly spatial policies for examination is often a matter of judgement and drawing a clear line between explicit spatial policies and derived or aspatial policies is not always easy.

4. The policies are rarely stable and the mix of policies is constantly changing. Some 13 Acts directly associated with regional policy measures were introduced in Britain between 1960 and 1975 (Pounce 1981:105–6). In Canada, major changes to policies first introduced in 1963 were made in 1965, 1968 and 1973–74 (Walker 1980a:59–74).

5. Not only do statutory powers vary but the way in which discretionary policies are applied can change as was seen, for example, in the case of IDCs discussed above.

6. The policy zones are unstable too and coverage varies from year to year. Multi-county Economic Development Districts in the United States had risen from six districts to 214 districts by the late 1970s (Hansen 1980: 55) while the Assisted Areas pre-1979 covered about 40 per cent of the employed population in Britain a proportion which dropped to around 25 per cent in mid-1982 (Frost and Spence 1981:327).

Despite these difficulties it is possible to allow in various ways for the problems they raise and to try to measure policy effects. Two approaches have been used – multiple regression and what is termed the residual approach, the latter being the most popular.

In multiple regression studies variations in net employment change across a set of regions is the dependent variable and Assisted Area status is one of the independent variables. This allows policy to be seen in the context of other variables which influence regional employment change. A good example is Keeble's (1976; 1980) study of change in United Kingdom sub-regions described in the afterword to Part III. In the first period from 1966 to 1971 policy did appear as a significant regression coefficient in the best fit

equation explaining percentage change in employment but it did not appear as significant in the second period from 1971 to 1976. Similarly, as was seen in Chapter 12, policy appears as a significant variable in studies of industrial movement. Unfortunately data deficiencies usually mean that policy can be measured only by a dummy variable which fails to measure variations in the intensity of policy between areas and this dummy variable is itself correlated closely with high unemployment levels. While this method does identify whether or not policy played a role in influencing manufacturing employment change it does not reveal the number of jobs affected by policy measures, for this, reliance has been based on the residual approach.

This approach requires that investigators of policy effects try to estimate what would have happened in the absence of explicit spatial policy and from this predict an 'expected', 'hypothetical' or 'counter-factual' position (different terms are used in different studies) against which the actual position may be compared. A difficulty of this method which is discussed rarely is that there is an implicit assumption that with no regional policy there will be no other industrial policy which might have a regional effect, yet if funds were saved from abandonment of regional policies they might well be spent on other forms of assistance to manufacturing industry. Indeed as Schofield (1979:254) points out 'establishment of the counter-factual situation will never be wholly exact (we will never be absolutely sure about what would have happened in the absence of policy)'.

In practical terms it is essential too to have a 'no policy' or 'policy-off' period from which projections of the counter-factual position can be made into the 'policy' or 'policy-on' period. As with all projections, as distance from the base upon which the projection is founded increases so the estimates become more inaccurate. Straight line projections of long-term trends may well produce ludicrous results such as the almost total loss of manufacturing employment. It follows that the 'policy-off' period needs to be close in time to the 'policy-on' period for this method to have any reasonable degree of accuracy.

It is also important to adjust for changes in the pressure of demand, particularly demand for labour. To quote Schofield (1979:252) again 'when...labour shortages appear in prosperous regions, firms expand more readily in depressed areas than they do in less expansionary conditions'. Thus, if national pressure of demand increases as policy incentives increase in Assisted Areas the better employment record of Assisted Areas may reflect the increased demand for labour in prosperous areas forcing firms into areas where labour is more readily available.

The usual method of predicting the counterfactual position is to use shift–share (Ch. 3) as a standardisation technique. It will be recalled that shift–share removes the structural effects and allows examination of a residual (or differential) element which includes non-structural influences such as policy. In the simplest situation, a 'prediction' from t_1 to t_2 for a particular region when no policy applies will provide a reasonably accurate estimate of t_2 employment but, if policy is having an effect on a region the actual employment will be greater than the predicted employment. Since the predictions related to structure rarely explain all regional variations (if they did there would be little scope for industrial geography!) even in policy-off periods the procedure is adopted of

fitting a trend line to the divergence between the actual and predicted in the 'policy-off' period, which is then projected into the 'policy-on' period to provide a hypothetical 'policy-off' position. The size of the policy effect is then measured by the difference between the trend values and the actual values of the actual minus expected series (Nicol 1982:202).

If actual employment begins to exceed predicted employment at the point in time when policy is introduced or strengthened this difference may be attributed to a policy effect. However, it is not possible to draw a direct link between policy and effect and care must be taken to ensure that there are not other valid interpretations of either all or part of the difference. Moore and Rhodes (1973) wrote the seminal paper which introduced this method and their work shows how explicit spatial policies can modify the spatial

patterns of manufacturing employment change.

Their study examined the effects of British regional economic policy on the distribution of manufacturing employment between 1950 and 1971. From an examination of the relevant legislation and government expenditure they suggest that a move to a more active regional policy came between 1960 and 1963 and that 1963 should be seen as the year when the effects of the move to a higher level of regional policy should become apparent. The analysis is based primarily on the study of four Assisted Areas: Scotland, Wales, the Northern region and Northern Ireland which for much of the policy period had at least some form of regional assistance in most of the areas they encompassed. As a further simplification, they excluded metal manufacture (mainly the iron and steel industry) and shipbuilding as these had been targets of separate government initiatives.

The results of their prediction of the hypothetical position (using Order level data) and the actual employment level are shown in Fig. 15.2. For most of the 1950s the actual and expected series coincide but from 1963 the actual employment series exceeds the expected series. Since 1963 was established as the year the effects of a strengthened regional policy should have become apparent it is not unreasonable to associate the change with a regional policy effect. Yet to establish this it is necessary to consider other evidence with provides support.

Examination of the South-East and Midlands shows that from the early 1960s actual employment is *less* than would have been expected and

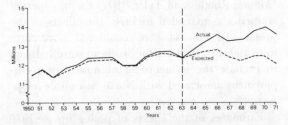

Fig. 15.2 Actual and expected employment in manufacturing industries (excluding shipbuilding and metals), United Kingdom development areas, 1951 to 1971 (*Source*: Moore and Rhodes 1973:94)

this, of course, is what might have been expected to happen if regional policy did divert manufacturing employment growth from the prosperous regions to Assisted Areas. Separate examination of the construction and service sectors (to which, in general, regional policy did not apply) failed to reveal any improvement in performance in the Assisted Areas after 1963, suggesting that the trend in manufacturing must reflect some factor that relates to that sector only, i.e. regional policy. It might also be argued that the post-1963 effects might reflect infrastructure improvements, notably the development of the motorway network but as Moore and Rhodes (1973) argue (p. 100) if motorways were important

It is difficult to explain why Northern Ireland fully shared the benefits and why the relative improvement in the Development Areas started in 1963 when the M1 had only reached Rugby, the M4 had only reached Maidenhead and the Midlands section of the M6 was still under construction.

There remains the difficult problem of the effects of the pressure of demand although it is suggested that since unemployment was higher in the prosperous areas in the 1960s than in the 1950s it is likely that firms had little need to seek out the labour reserves in the Assisted Areas in the 1960s so this too must be discounted. The net result of their research suggests that from 1963 to 1970 the employment generated in manufacturing industry (excluding metal manufacture and shipbuilding) was 150,000 jobs. Using very similar methods McKay and Thompson (1979) identified a policy effect of about 190,000 jobs to 1973. In a subsequent study (Moore, Rhodes and Tyler, 1977) the time period studied was extended to 1976, the effects of the pressure of demand were considered more carefully and the estimates for Scotland were reduced to exclude the influence of manufacturing employment associated with North Sea oil developments.

Estimates of the effects of policy up to 1979 were prepared by Fothergill and Gudgin (1982: 134–52) using a 77 industry disaggregation. They also took into account the urban–rural shift in manufacturing industry which was noted in

Chapters 1 and 8. They show that the increasing urban–rural shift had little to do with regional policy yet some of the improved employment performance of the Assisted Areas may be due to the balance of urban and rural areas within them. They calculate that by 1979 (from 1960) employment in the Assisted Areas was 90,000 jobs higher as a result of the urban–rural shift and this ought, therefore, to be removed from the regional policy effect. Allowing for this shift and making a number of other minor adjustments they were able to conclude 'regional policy has raised manufacturing employment in the four ... [assisted] ... area regions ... (from 1960 to 1979) ... by around 185,000 jobs' (p. 147).

Estimates of policy effects can be criticised. An alternative interpretation of the association of employment growth in Assisted Areas with increased policy incentives in the 1960s has been proposed by Massey (1979). She argues that the mid-1960s also coincided with the marked development of locational hierarchies within large planning-system firms thus providing firms with the opportunities (for the first time) to shift jobs to areas characterised by non-militant labour and it was this change rather than policy which played a major role in the employment gains in the Assisted Areas. Other more technical criticisms are provided, for example, by Chisholm (1976) who in commenting on the 1973 study by Moore and Rhodes was particularly unhappy with the use of an invariant geographical area (when Assisted Areas were constantly changing) with the inclusion of industries such as textiles and motor vehicles which like shipbuilding and metals had had industry specific policies applied to them, and finally, with the identification of 1963 as a key year. He argues policies were not really strengthened until 1966 and then, if allowance is made for lags, a regional policy upturn ought not to have appeared in 1967 to 1968. A more general criticism, which has taken on more force in the 1980s, is that the 1950s are no longer an appropriate base from which to predict a 'no-policy' situation. It is a criticism it is difficult to counter.

While the studies discussed above reveal something of the overall impact of explicit spatial policies there is little to indicate the workings of specific policy instruments. Moore and Rhodes (1976) measured the effects of different policies on moves to the Assisted Areas from 1960 to 1971. Their analysis suggests that almost 90 per cent of the moves were influenced by regional policy and, in employment terms, over half the employment generated in the Assisted Areas through policy was obtained from plants moving into the area. It is then appropriate to assess the relative importance of the different policies in relation to employment in moves.

They tried to assess the relative importance of factory-building policies, investment incentives and labour subsidies by using multiple regression techniques. The analysis indicated that all three policies were important. Out of the jobs created through moves 12 per cent arose through labour subsidies, 26 per cent as a result of investment incentives and 56 per cent through factory-building policies. The remaining 6 per cent arose from slightly higher incentives in some small areas. The emphasis on factory-building policies arises in part from the fact it reflects the combined effect of constraints in factory building (through IDCs) in non-Assisted Areas and policies of factory construction in the Assisted Areas.

Finally, attention is turned to the effect of investment in an area's infrastructure, in this case policies implemented in Britain from 1947 to create new towns and to encourage town expansion schemes. A town's 'no policy' performance was assessed by the rate of employment change in towns of similar size in the same part of the country and during the same time period. The difference between the 'no policy' performance and the actual employment record indicates the policy effect (Fothergill, Kitson and Monk 1983). Between 1960 and 1978 policy diverted between 118,000 and 138,000 jobs into the new and expanded towns. This is a large diversion of jobs and should be compared with the 150,000–200,000 jobs created by policy in the Assisted Areas.

CONCLUSION

It is clear from all these studies that direct government intervention can markedly influence the geographical distribution of employment opportunities. However, it would also appear that this requires strong government interest in explicit spatial policies backed up by spending to reflect that interest. Equally, it seems to require a large amount of potentially mobile industry to respond to the incentives on offer. Certainly, in the United Kingdom in the current recession and with an essentially non-interventionist government, policy effects will be difficult to discern and, indeed may be non-existent. For the 1980s it may be appropriate to echo the words of Rees and Weinstein (1983:248) quoted at the beginning of this chapter and say that at the present time economic development assistance has very little impact on the changing industrial geography of the United States and the United Kingdom.

16

REFLECTIONS AND
DIRECTIONS

The central task of industrial geography is to explain changes in the spatial patterns of industrial activity. The intrinsic fascination with the question as to why some areas experience industrial employment growth while others experience employment decline has attracted work adopting behavioural, neo-classical and structuralist approaches. By bringing this work together in an eclectic approach, the previous chapters have tried to illustrate the extent of our understanding of the geography of industrial change in the late 1970s and early 1980s. This final chapter reflects upon the material selected for inclusion in the discussion and indicates some unexplored avenues. It is argued that future work will build upon and develop the studies already completed as well as introducing new themes.

REFLECTIONS

Changes in the spatial distribution of industrial activity have taken place throughout history and at a variety of spatial scales. Contemporary industrial geography with its concern with changes over 5 to 10 year time span explores only part of a constantly changing geography of industrial activity. Concentration in this discussion upon changes taking place at regional scale has meant that only brief attention has been paid to intra-urban industrial change (micro-scale studies) and to international patterns of change (macro-scale studies). Regional analyses, which fall between these scales, are influenced by the inter-national framework and themselves have impacts upon the patterns of change within urban areas. The focus on the regional scale allows attention to be concentrated on those changes which have a direct influence upon patterns of regional and urban development within national economic systems.

Discussion of the forces influencing changes in the regional pattern of industrial activity within national economic systems has, quite deliberately, excluded two areas of interest to industrial geography. First, it has excluded consideration of the planned economies – notably those of Eastern Europe and the Soviet Union – and second, it has excluded work on the industrial geography of the Third World. These exclusions arise partly from space constraints but they are also a reflection of the fact that apart from a few specialists working on these areas most work in industrial geography is concerned with the societies within which most industrial geographers live. However, it can be argued that many of the influences operating within advanced capitalist societies will operate too within the planned economies. For example, there are parallels between the work of sector planners in the planned economies and corporate planners in large planning-system firms. Similarly, the geography of industrial employment change in the Third World will, like industrial change in the United States or United Kingdom, be influenced by the international environment in which it operates, by the past evolution of industrial activities within its boundaries, by different types of firms and their decisions, by the availability (or non-availability) of products, processes, land, labour, and capital, by accessibility to supplies and markets and by the political system operating within a particular country.

A review of industrial geography in the 1970s and 1980s shows that it is distinctive in four ways: in its emphasis upon change; in its concentration upon the geography of employment opportunities; in its focus on the components of change; and in its concern with the corporate organisation of industry.

An emphasis upon understanding the *changing* geography of industrial activity is the first of the features that distinguishes industrial geography of the mid-1980s from that of earlier time periods. Smith (1981:215–30) devoted less than 20 pages to the time dimension while Estall and Buchanan (1980:28) were of the view that 'the geographer is primarily concerned with what exists on the ground now'. Explaining the distribution of industry x or industry y at one point in time is a rather arid exercise. It is of little interest to anyone except academic geographers. Yet immediately the emphasis is switched to explaining changes in the spatial pattern of industrial activity the important nature of the work is more obvious. These changes have a direct influence upon our lives through their effects upon urban and regional development.

A second distinguishing feature of contemporary industrial geography is its break away from a business-oriented approach which sought to 'inform the decisions on industrial investment currently being made' (Estall and Buchanan 1980:12) and which advised on 'how to make *better* locational decisions' (Smith 1981:viii). Industrial geography can assist business in making location decisions but equally it must contribute to an understanding of the impacts of business on the spatial organisation of society. It is the latter view which led industrial geographers to examine the ways in which business firms modify the *employment opportunities* in different places.

A third distinctive feature of industrial geography in the 1980s is that emphasis is placed upon understanding the mechanisms by which change takes place. Traditionally, geographers considered net changes in employment opportunities. Now, changes in the geography of industrial activity are examined in terms of the geography of the different *components of change*: births, deaths, migrations and the *in situ* expansion or contraction of activities at particular factories.

The fourth, and final, distinguishing feature of contemporary industrial geography is that it recognises the different types of organisation which control the distribution of employment opportunities. These vary from the large multinational corporation with factories in many countries to the small one-person operation in a city back street. Contemporary industrial geography examines explicitly the effects of *planning-system and market-system firms* and the interdependencies between them on changing employment opportunities in different areas in contrast to earlier works which pay little attention to the firm or decision-making precedures within it. To them, 'how decision-makers...behave...[was]...a matter of secondary interest' (Smith 1981:viii).

DEVELOPMENTS

The preceding chapters have shown how over the last two decades industrial geographers have worked towards a greater understanding of the factors influencing geographical patterns of industrial change. In most cases the important factors influencing industrial change have been identified but their relative importance and how much they explain at any one point in time is still a matter for debate. The patterns of change illustrated in Chapter 1 are still not fully understood. Nowhere is the vigour of the debate seen more clearly than in trying to understand the processes involved in non-metropolitan industrialisation. Does it reflect the availability of non-unionised labour? Does it result from the availability of space for development? Does it arise from the residential attractiveness of rural areas? Does it arise because production costs in rural areas are lower than those in towns? Are all four elements involved? If all four are involved, what is their relative importance? There is still considerable scope to build upon and develop the themes of the previous chapters.

It is only in the 1980s that industrial geographers have begun to explore the implications of changes in a firm's international competitiveness on changes in the spatial pattern of economic activity within national economic systems. Not only may some firms in some regions be effective in fighting competition from imports but also the extent to which a region's firms can develop and increase their export markets may have an important influence upon the rate at which employment change takes place. Examination of the export behaviour of a region's firms is likely to be paralleled by increasing interest in the extent to which plants which are part of multinational production systems are influenced by the corporate reorganisation strategies of the firms to which they belong. Emphasis on new inward investment may be replaced by closer examination of multinational disinvestment strategies and particular attention will be paid to the policies of domestic multinationals. It will be useful to probe into the policies of these latter firms to explore the extent to which domestic production is being switched abroad and whether such production changes have spin-off effects on certain types of region within the domestic economy.

Some of the ideas which are being developed at the international scale may be adopted, as they have been in the past, to contribute towards further understanding of the spatial growth and locational adjustment of planning-system firms within a multi-regional framework. Of particular interest here is the influence of a plant's autonomy within the firm on various aspects of its performance. There appears to be a need to get closer to the processes inside the firm. Various aspects of decision-making may be important but apart from the branch plant location decision they have not been investigated fully. Some of the pitfalls arising in examining other location decisions can be avoided by drawing upon the branch plant location literature. Not all emphasis should be placed on these larger firms important though they are, for a large part of industrial activity is controlled by the medium-sized firm which lies mid-way between the archetypal planning-system and market-system firm. Rather more should be known about this group; similarly exploration of inter-firm interdependencies within the segmented economy is important since it is a current area of ignorance. Special attention needs to be given to assessing both the extent to which small firms are dependent upon orders from large ones as well as upon the employment and regional effects of such independence. By switching emphasis to the medium-sized firm and to the interdependencies between large and small firms industrial geography will move away from its current dichotomous (large/ small firm) structure. Despite a need to break from this dichotomous structure it has provided a useful framework in the recent past.

In trying to understand regional variations in the manufacture of new products and the introduction of new processes it is market-system firms which perhaps produce the greatest challenge. Some small firms in some regions are slower to adopt new ideas and investigations of the reasons for this may throw light upon the reasons for spatial variations in the introduction of technological change. There have been suggestions that planning-system firms 'filter-down' new products into particular parts of a national economic system but direct assessment of the relevence of the filter-down idea in terms of the age of products manufactured in particular plants is still relatively rare. More usually, filter-down processes are assumed where plants locate to utilise concentrations of unskilled labour, unskilled labour being associated with the later stages of the product-cycle.

Interest in the role of the labour factor in contributing towards patterns of industrial change is likely to remain paramount in the near future. Careful exploration of the influence of unskilled and unorganised labour is likely to remain difficult. Anecdotal evidence is easy to collect and correlations between such labour and rapid industrial growth are easy to establish. Unfortunately the anecdotal evidence provides no indication of how widespread is the influence while correlation studies are open to alternative interpretations. Probing into decision-making is unlikely to offer a route forward since an objective to exploit an unorganised labour force might not be admitted.

The influences of land and capital form less sensitive topics for investigations than labour market characteristics. There is certainly scope for further investigation of whether constrained locations do have an influence on locational change since most of the evidence available relates to only a limited number of areas, but perhaps a higher priority is examination of the organisations supplying capital, land and buildings to industrial firms. Little is known of the regional pattern (if any) of lending or of the distribution of firms prepared to supply venture capital or indeed of firms selling new technologies. Many smaller firms occupy rented or leased premises provided by local or national property development firms and it is possible that these firms are spatially selective both in the number and type of premises that they provide.

For many years questions of accessibility to markets or supplies have been seen as central to an understanding of changes in the geography of industrial activity. These may still be of importance at the international scale but at the regional scale examined here their influence has been eclipsed, notably by examination of the role of labour supply variables. Thus, examination of the role of accessibility to supplies and markets might be expected to have a low priority in future work. Yet, as profit margins have been squeezed firms are showing greater interest in cutting stocks and moving towards just-in-time delivery systems which may serve to restore questions of accessibility to a more central role in industrial geography. There may also be scope for developing models which optimise plant location and capacity in industries with marked economies of scale and high assembly and distribution costs.

Turning to the political context within which change occurs it is very necessary to demonstrate for a wide range of industrial policies their past and possible future effects on regional patterns; it is a demonstration which is required whether it be to demonstrate there is no spatially selective outcome or that it does have a marked spatial effect. Emerging too is a necessity to evaluate the effects of derived spatial policies; this is especially the case where local administrations claim policy effects but are unable to demonstrate the no policy alternative. Carefully controlled comparisons of administrations with different policies would seem to offer the greatest potential in this area. Considerable progress has been made in evaluating the extent to which explicit spatial policies can divert employment between areas although questions can be raised as to the extent to which the diversions create long-term or short-term jobs. The effects have been most marked in Britain but such effects are measured against any increasingly distant 'no-policy' period; it may well be that assessments of past effects should be related to 'back projections' from the present relatively inactive policy period.

Each of these various influences can be examined in relation to both net change and the different components of change. It will be recalled that industrial movement has been extensively researched but even here there is scope to tighten up the handling of questions of scale in the analysis of location factors. What is more, while the distinction between branches and transfers is well established in the movement literature it might be useful to concentrate upon the location factors associated with the different types of branches. Examination of job creation in new firms has become virtually a growth industry in itself but in a geographical context there seems to be a need to change the emphasis from who founds new firms towards the reasons for regional variations in new firm formation rates. An enthusiasm for new firm studies should not blind investigators to the fact that most new jobs are created in existing plants and the geography of *in situ* employment growth still awaits both concepts and empirical enquiry. In market-system firms, firm life-cycles and different ownership characteristics (craftsperson or opportunist) may offer a way forward while in planning-system firms the degree of plant control over sales and the procedures for allocating a firm's orders to particular plants may offer some useful insights. In both types of firm, examination of the role of intrapreneurial behaviour (entrepreneurship within the firm) may produce some results of interest.

In the current recession it is perhaps not surprising that the early 1980s saw a rise in the interest in the geography of job loss. Some of the critical variations in that geography were hidden through a consideration of only net loss but as data on gross job loss through *in situ* contraction and plant closures have become more widely available greater thought has been given to ways of analysing the job loss data. Two key questions need to be resolved in relation to plant closures in planning-system firms. The first is to establish whether closures are best understood by examining the motives for closure (as would be the case if cessation closures are important), by examining the factors influencing the location of investment within a given set of plants (as would be the case if default closures are important) or by focusing on the factors influencing plant closure where a choice has to be made between plants (in the case of selective closures). The second arises from the first in that if selective closures are important there is considerable scope for both examining the closure decision process and identifying the factors taken into account in the closure decision. Such an enquiry might reveal whether area characteristics are important at all or whether decisions reflect more strongly the characteristics of the plant. This will parallel studies of smaller firms which might usefully try to establish the factors that are associated with high rates of firm failure and bankruptcy and to see whether these are in any way related to the regional environments in which the firm operates.

Most of the development envisaged above involves taking selected parts of industrial geography and examining them in greater depth. While such an approach does produce manageable research problems it tends to hide the inter-relationships between the different parts of the industrial system. Such inter-relationships are most evident in patterns of plant adjustment and change within multi-plant corporate systems and there is still potential for examining adjustment patterns within large corporate systems provided that these changes are related back to the con-

cepts, ideas and empirical evidence already available. Integration too may come from a closer consideration of spatial variations in costs. Most of the features discussed in previous chapters either impose a cost on a firm or can be assessed themselves in terms of cost. Industrial geography in its empirical enquiries has tended to shy away from costs and revenues; it is perhaps time to return to these fundamental financial characteristics.

In the next decade many of the areas for development will be followed up. In some cases research has just begun and in others it is already well advanced and the initial results are beginning to circulate among the research community. The development of established ideas has been paralleled by the emergence of new themes which may become prominent in the 1990s.

THEMES

As the 1980s progressed it has become evident that industrial geography is moving away from a focus upon changes in the location of employment in manufacturing plants to a wider concern with all types of activities controlled by manufacturing firms. To some, for example Massey (1984:10), industrial geography has become synonymous with economic geography and it examines all activities listed within standard industrial classifications of economic activities. This is perhaps an atypical use of the term but increasingly industrial geography has been drawn towards a closer examination of service industries. Examination of retailing has been encouraged by the forward integration of manufacturing firms into retailing and the backward integration of retailing firms into manufacturing. The whole area between retailing and manufacturing – wholesale distribution – is virtually unexplored. However, most emphasis has been placed upon producer services. These services (as was shown in Ch. 9) may themselves influence changes in the distribution of manufacturing activity and with the development of detached head offices and R & D sites (Ch. 4) in planning-system firms explanations of changes in their locational patterns might best be approached through the office location literature.

There is a steadily increasing interest in the nature of changes in the location of head offices and R & D activities and, as was seen in Table 3.3, employment in central administrative offices and auxiliary units was the fastest growing 'manufacturing' sector in the United States in the 1970s. Although Armstrong (1979) evaluates the geography of employment in these offices and auxiliary units most studies of change work in terms of counts of the number of offices or the proportion of turnover controlled. Initial results of the latter studies suggest an increasing centralisation of head offices in the South-East of Britain (Goddard and Smith 1978) and a tendency to dispersion across the nine major regions of the United States (Semple and Phipps 1982). Trends in R & D employment in industrial firms are difficult to discover but analysis of locational trends in R & D activities in large United States' firms show that despite some locational shifts R & D has remained quite concentrated in large metropolitan areas (Malecki 1979). Distinctions between in-house and bought-in office and research services are likely to become increasingly blurred and while some industrial geographers may be drawn into analyses of producer services it is worth recalling the view that 'manufacturing activities will clearly continue to have a key role in our industrial future' (Daniels 1983:308).

Paralleling the interest in office activities in manufacturing firms an interest has been developing not in changes in the quantity of employment in different areas but in changes in the quality and type of employment. Very little is known about changes in the geography of skilled and unskilled work, or about the differential impact of manufacturing employment change upon minority groups, upon part-time employment, upon youth employment and upon women's employment. Increasingly questions are being asked about the nature of changes in the geography of employment opportunities for women (Women and Geography Study Group 1984:67–88). Such questions lead to a wider concern with the impact of manufacturing employment change on society.

The fact that changes in employment in manufacturing industry have a major impact on regional variations in unemployment rates is widely recognised but their impact on social structures is only now coming to light (Massey 1984). In part this impact arises through the creation of areas dependent upon welfare benefits as the result of a net decline in employment opportunities but even where new job opportunities are provided the changes can be profound. Not only may individuals be forced to change from skilled to unskilled jobs but the very role a person plays in society can be changed. Nowhere is this seen more clearly than in areas once dominated by older industries like iron and steel with predominantly male employment opportunities creating an essentially patriarchal social structure. As was seen in Chapter 7 when new jobs arrive to replace the old in this kind of area they frequently bring opportunities not for the old employees but for their wives. Through these changes the women gain increasing power and in many households become the breadwinner. With changes like this the older patriarchal structures are challenged and male-dominated households may increasingly give way to households where all tasks are shared equally.

Change too, and especially marked employment decline, can stimulate increased politicisation of a community or region and encourage the exploration of forms of work organisation which offer alternatives to the capitalist firm. The experience of fighting a 'Save Our Works' campaign shows both the knowledge that can be gained through working together and, perhaps more importantly, the difficulties of trying to modify corporate policies. Among the alternative forms of work organisation that have been examined the worker co-operative has attracted particular attention.

Changes in the economic, social and political characteristics of regions consequent upon changes in the geography of employment opportunities in manufacturing activity have an important influence upon the quality of life in particular areas. A more direct influence on the quality of life is the impact of industrial activity upon the physical environment whether this be a spectacular fire depositing asbestos dust on the surrounding area or a lethal escape of gas or a more long-term effect arising from the regular emission of smoke, effluents and noise. Even the aesthetic attractions of an area can be damaged by an intrusive industrial facility. Although industrial geographers have considered environmental controls as location factors there is likely to be increasing interest in the impact of industrial activity on the environment.

The arrival of a particular plant may give rise to quantifiable environmental effects and the direction of the relationship is usually quite clear. A specific noise arises, of necessity, from a specific industrial facility. Such one-way relationships are less evident in considering the impact of industrial activity upon other regional characteristics. Nowhere is this seen more clearly than in the relationships between the geographies of population change and industrial change. The assumption made usually in short-term studies of industrial change is that firms respond to existing population distributions treating them either as markets or as potential sources of labour. Yet it is not as simple as this

as the population geographers are stressing (White, forthcoming) and an investigation of the effects of population change on industrial change and vice versa within a regional framework needs much closer examination. Has industry followed population to the West and South of the United States? Has population followed industry? Are both processes at work?

Finally, it is appropriate to ask whether industrial geography has any practical value. There is no doubt that it has. Industrial geographers have provided guides to firms on new location decisions (Stafford 1980: Townroe 1976) and have become involved in community industrial development processes (Moriarty 1980; Walker 1980b) but their contributions to public debates on regional and urban development need to be both more frequent and more widely publicised. The real value of industrial geography is measured not by asking whether firms consult geographers about the location of investment or disinvestment but by asking whether industrial geography contributes towards an understanding of the way in which manufacturing firms modify the geography of employment opportunities.

APPENDIX I

DESCRIBING THE
GEOGRAPHY OF
INDUSTRIAL CHANGE

MEASURES

Throughout the discussion, changes in employment levels are used as indicators of changes in the distribution of industrial activity but it has to be stressed that employment trends are *not* necessarily reflections of output trends. For example, in the EEC output and employment both increased from 1950 to 1965; but while output increased from 1965 to 1975 employment was relatively stable and from 1975 onwards as output rose, employment fell (Rothwell 1982: 362). Output growth can be associated with declining, stable or rising employment but output decline (other than in the short term) is always associated with employment decline. Similarly, employment decline can be associated with falling, stable or rising output but employment growth is virtually always associated with output growth. An illustration of these relationships is shown in Table A.1. In these three-digit industries output and employment move in parallel in locomotive manufacture but in synthetic resins a

Table A.1 Output and employment change in selected industries, United Kingdom, 1968–73

	Employment change (%)	Output change (%)
Locomotives	−19	−20
Tailored outerwear	− 6	+ 6
Synthetic resins, etc.	−20	+43

(*Source*: Massey and Meegan 1982:36, 65, 102)

decline of employment by one-fifth is matched by an almost 50 per cent increase in output.

Despite these employment/output relationships, the advantages of employment measures were outlined in Chapter 1. Alternative measures of the amount of industrial activity have a number of disadvantages for geographical analyses.

1. *Physical output*. This indicates the quantity which an industry has produced or is able to produce during a particular time period. Using this measure the steel industry is discussed in terms of ingot tonnes per annum and the oil refining industry in terms of barrels of crude oil per annum. Physical output measures are used primarily in the study of a single industry mainly because it is so difficult to compare industries. How, for example, can ingot tonnes of steel be compared with barrels of crude oil?

2. *Floor space*. This is expressed normally in square feet or square metres. It is a measure used frequently by managers and industrial planners, as can be seen in advertisements of factories for sale or to let in specific sizes such as 10,000, 15,000 or 50,000 square feet, but data on floor space are difficult to obtain.

3. *Financial data*. Sales or turnover data are usually inappropriate since they include the value of purchased materials and instead *value added* (or, a closely related measure, *net output*) per annum is used. A useful working definition of value added is that it is the value added to the material inputs by the processes

operating in a plant, that is it is the value of the products when sold by a plant minus the value of the material inputs. A major difficulty with this measure, or indeed any measure which uses monetary values, is that when considering change it is necessary to remove the effects of inflation on the value of money by expressing all the values as index numbers related to a particular base year.

SPATIAL FRAMEWORKS

In most of the figures and tables employment change associated with individual plants has been aggregated to give figures for particular areas. This is the most common way of illustrating patterns of change partly because published data relate primarily to administrative areas and plant data (usually unpublished) have to be grouped in some way to aid analysis or to disguise the employment figures for individual plants which have to remain confidential. Where reliance is placed on published sources the spatial patterns of change have to be related to the administrative areas used in the sources. Where data are available at plant level the choice of patterns examined lies with the investigators as they can work on the data in their original form or group the plants into areas of their own choosing. The common practice in the latter case is to group the data into a square grid, the size of the grid depending upon the spatial scale of the particular investigation. The implications of using different size grids were considered on pages 77–8.

Alternatives to area based patterns of change are two. First, changes in the point pattern of plants can be considered. This is used primarily where employment data are not available. Second, changes in the employment records of individual plants can be depicted. This is difficult in studies of all manufacturing activity as the density of manufacturing plants in many urban areas is very high but it is a feasible method of displaying the pattern of industrial change in individual firms and industries.

TEMPORAL FRAMEWORKS

Most descriptions of change use the *comparative static approach*. This examines change by comparing two cross-sections (static pictures) in time, one showing the distribution of industry at the beginning of the time period being considered (t_1), the other showing the distribution at the end of the period (t_2).

The advantages of the comparative static approach are that it can be used readily where data are available only at 5- or 10- year intervals (as is common with industrial employment data) and that it can be handled easily by both non-parametric statistics and linear regression models. It does, however, have one major limitation in that it gives no indication of events which occurred between t_1 and t_2; imagine two stills of a soccer game in the first and thirteenth minutes, it would clearly be impossible to re-create the moves of the players in the intervening period. This can become a major problem if the number of years between t_1 and t_2 becomes very long, but in studies of 5 to 10 years' duration the problems are probably not too severe. Even over this short period use of comparative statics tends to exclude many short-lived plants from analyses because they are born and die within the period and therefore do not appear in data sets relating to t_1 or t_2.

There are a number of practical constraints which influence the choice of years to be compared. The time intervals between censuses may offer little choice but an interest in contemporary change dictates that the most recent data available should be used for t_2 but when it is published it can be several years out of date. Conventional practice appears to be that investigations examine trends over 5 or 10 years but direct comparison may not be possible if there have been any changes in the way industry is classified or if the areas to which the data refer have been changed. In many studies which use comparative statics investigators have spent many hours adjusting and modifying data to ensure that as far as possible like is compared with like. It is also necessary to consider carefully the relationship between the period being examined and business cycles. Rather different problems are being examined in comparing peak/peak (or trough/trough) patterns which tend to identify long-term trends whereas comparing changes between peak and trough or trough and peak may identify cyclical changes associated with short-term decline or growth of economic activity.

DESCRIPTIVE TECHNIQUES

The simplest way of describing industrial change where comparable employment data are available is to record the *absolute change* in employment in an area. In this way it can be shown that area A experienced a decrease in employment of 500 jobs while in area B the number of employees increased by 50. More usually interest lies in *relative change* in employment when the absolute change in an area is related to either employment in the area at t_1 (by calculating percentage change) or to changes in employment over the same time period in some larger spatial unit (by undertaking shift analysis).

Percentage change

Percentage change relates the amount of change between t_1 and t_2 to that existing in the area at t_1, so that changes are described by showing that employment decreased by 10 per cent in area A and increased by 5 per cent in area B. Unfortunately percentage change values are subject to the *small base value effect*. It is quite feasible for an area's industrial employment to increase from 50 to 100 employees over a five-year period, but it is very unlikely an area with 25,000 employees will raise its employment to 50,000 over the same time period. In areas with a small number of employees high percentage increases are more likely than in areas with a large number of employees. The effect of small base values can usually be seen clearly in maps showing percentage manufacturing employment change in rural and urban areas; in times of growth the rural areas, with the smaller initial employment levels, stand out as the areas of greatest percentage growth. It is because of this problem that maps showing the spatial pattern

of percentage employment change should be interpreted very cautiously. Despite this difficulty percentage change provides a useful way of summarising contemporary changes in the geography of industrial activity.

Shift analysis

Shift analysis relates the rate of employment change in an area to the rate of employment change in some larger unit of which the area is a part. It is most appropriate for describing changes in industrial sectors or firms. National change can be related to world trends, regional changes to national trends, and sub-regional changes to regional trends. The term 'shift analysis' is used because where, for example, a region is increasing its share of the national employment in an industry the industry is said to be shifting towards the region. If employment in an industry grows (or declines) in all regions at exactly the national rate there will be no shifts but this is unlikely and a shift towards a region occurs when:

1. Industry grows in a region while national employment in the industry is static;
2. Industry grows in a region while national employment is declining;
3. Industry grows in the region at a *faster* rate than the industry is growing nationally;
4. Industry declines in the region as a *slower* rate than industry is declining nationally.

In each of these four cases a region's share of an industry will increase. Conversely, a shift away from a region occurs when:

1. Industry declines in a region while national employment in the industry is static;
2. Industry declines in a region while national employment is growing;
3. Industry declines in a region at a *faster* rate than the industry is declining nationally;
4. Industry grows at a *slower* rate than the industry is growing nationally.

In each of these four cases a region's share of an industry will decrease.

An example of this technique is provided in Table A.2. In this case the net shift represented 24 per cent of the increase in jobs and thus 10,000 jobs were involved in the redistribution of

Table A.2   Shift analysis of the British electronic computer and radio, radar and electronic capital goods industries, 1974 to 1981

	Expected*		Actual	Difference	
	1974 (000s)	1981 (000s)	1981 (000s)	Net gain (+) (000s)	Net loss (−) (000s)
South-East	83	110	106	−	−4
East Anglia	3	4	2	−	−2
South-West	4	5	10	+5	−
West Midlands	6	8	8	−	−
East Midlands	3	4	5	+1	−
Yorkshire and Humberside	1	1	3	+2	−
North-West	11	15	13	−	−2
North	1	1	2	+1	−
Wales	2	3	4	+1	−
Scotland	15	20	18	−	−2
Great Britain	129	−	171	+10	−10
Increase: 42,000		Net shift: 10,000		Net shift as percentage of increase: 24	

* 1974 figure × national rate of growth 1974 to 1981 (171/129)
South-East = 83 × 1.33 = 110.

employment between regions. The gains and losses can each be expressed as a proportion of the net shift to give the net gains and losses shown in Table A.2 and Fig. 1.6B. This industry is shifting its employment from its main centres of activities to areas where it is less well represented.

Shift–share analysis

Shift–share analysis is a development from shift analysis and is most appropriate for analysing net changes in all manufacturing activity. Shift analysis is not particularly useful in examining all manufacturing since net shifts will include major structural influences. The technique of shift–share analysis, which was described briefly in Chapter 3, breaks down the manufacturing employment change in a region into three elements: regional share, structural shift, differential shift. It examines the effect of industrial structure on the rate of manufacturing employment change in a region. The differential shift can also be interpreted as reflecting the strength of the locational advantages/disadvantages of a region. The main features of the techniques are best described mathematically and the results interpreted with reference to a specific example.

Definition of terms

G = national employment in manufacturing industry

E_i = national employment in industry i

E_j = total employment in manufacturing industry in region j

$$\Sigma E_j = G$$

e_{ij} = employment in industry i in region j

t_1 data are represented by

$$G^0 \quad E_i^0 \quad E_j^0 \quad e_{ij}^0$$

t_2 data are represented by

$$G^1 \quad E_i^1 \quad E_j^1 \quad e_{ij}^1$$

Total shift (TS)

$$TS = E_j^1 - \left[E_j^0 \, \frac{G^1}{G^0} \right]$$

The *difference* between the expected employment at t_2 if the region had changed at the national rate and the actual employment at t_2.

Regionae ,share component (RS)

$$RS = \left[E_j^0 \, \frac{G^1}{G^0} \right] - E_j^0$$

The *amount* by which manufacturing employment

in the region would have changed between t_1 and t_2 if it had changed at the national rate.

Structural shift component (SS)

$$SS = \Sigma \left[e_{ij}^0 \left(\frac{E_i^1}{E_i^0} - \frac{G^1}{G^0} \right) \right]$$

This estimates the change expected in the region if each industry in the region (e_{ij}^0) had changed at its own national rate (E_i^1/E_i^0), excluding the effect generated by the national rate of change for all manufacturing (G^1/G^0). Some industries will perform *better* than the national average for *all* industry and some will perform *worse*.

Differential shift component (DS)

$$DS = \Sigma \left[e_{ij}^1 - \left(e_{ij}^0 \frac{E_i^1}{E_i^0} \right) \right]$$

This is based on the difference between the employment at t_2 in an industry in a region (e_{ij}^l) and the employment it would have had if it had grown at the national rate for that industry

$$e_{ij}^0 \left(\frac{E_i^1}{E_i^0} \right)$$

This is, of course, the calculation undertaken for a single industry for purposes of shift analysis as shown in Table A2. Industries in some regions will perform *better* than the national average for *their* industry and some will perform *worse*.

Analysis

The first stage of the analysis involves calculating the national rate of change in each industry (Table A.3, Col. 4) and the rate of change in all industry (Table A.3, Col. 5). Calculating the difference between the two (Table A.3, Col. 6) indicates the relative performance of each industry against the national average.

This difference is used in Table A.4a to calculate the structural effect in the area being investigated, in this case, Wales. Since food, drink and tobacco performed better than the average for all industries nationally its presence in the region might be expected to contribute an additional 2,000 jobs.

Calculation of the differential shift is shown in Table A.4b. If the food, drink and tobacco industry in Wales had changed its employment at the national rate for that industry there would have been a fall of 3,000 jobs, but in fact the fall

Table A.3 Employment change, Great Britain, 1974–81

1 Industry	2 t_1 1974	3 t_2 1981	4 Industry ratio	5 All industry ratio	6 Difference
Food, drink and tobacco	740	629	0.8500	0.7687	+0.0813
Coal and petroleum products	39	28	0.7179	0.7687	−0.0508
Chemical and allied industries	432	403	0.9328	0.7687	+0.1641
Metal manufacture	507	314	0.6193	0.7687	−0.1494
Mechanical engineering	965	767	0.7948	0.7687	+0.0261
Instrument engineering	159	133	0.8365	0.7687	+0.0678
Electrical engineering	830	673	0.8108	0.7687	+0.0421
Shipbuilding	175	144	0.8229	0.7687	+0.0542
Vehicles	783	590	0.7535	0.7687	−0.0152
Metal goods n.e.s.	577	445	0.7712	0.7687	+0.0025
Textiles	546	315	0.5769	0.7687	−0.1918
Leather	42	30	0.7143	0.7687	−0.0544
Clothing and footwear	404	265	0.6559	0.7687	−0.1128
Bricks, pottery, etc.	295	213	0.7220	0.7687	−0.0467
Timber and furniture	278	216	0.7770	0.7687	+0.0083
Paper, printing and publishing	582	508	0.8729	0.7687	+0.1042
Other manufacturing	351	250	0.7123	0.7687	−0.0564
Total	7,705	5,923	0.7687		

(*Source: Employment Gazette*, 1975 and 1983.)

Table A.4a   Calculating the structural shift: Wales 1974–81

Industry orders	t_1 (000s)	Difference (Table A.3)	Structural effect (000s)
Food, drink and tobacco	19	+0.0813	+2
Coal and petroleum products	6	−0.0508	*
Chemical and allied industries	17	+0.1641	+3
Metal manufacture	83	−0.1494	−12
Mechanical engineering	27	+0.0261	+1
Instrument engineering	5	+0.0678	*
Electrical engineering	35	+0.0421	+1
Shipbuilding	2	+0.0542	*
Vehicles	26	−0.0152	*
Metal goods n.e.s.	23	+0.0025	*
Textiles	17	−0.1918	−3
Leather	1	−0.0544	*
Clothing and footwear	16	−0.1128	−2
Bricks, pottery, etc.	12	−0.0467	−1
Timber and furniture	9	+0.0083	*
Paper, printing and publishing	13	+0.1042	+1
Other manufacturing	25	−0.0564	−1
		Structural shift	−11

* Structural effect < 1,000 jobs.

Table A.4b   Calculating the differential shift, Wales 1974–81

Industry orders	t_1 (000s)	National change in industry ratio	Expected t_2 (000s)	Actual t_2 (000s)	Difference (000s)
Food, drink and tobacco	19	0.8500	16	18	+2
Coal and petroleum products	6	0.7179	4	4	−
Chemical and allied industries	17	0.9328	16	15	−1
Metal manufacture	83	0.6193	51	40	−11
Mechanical engineering	27	0.7948	21	20	−1
Instrument engineering	5	0.8365	4	4	−
Electrical engineering	35	0.8108	28	29	+1
Shipbuilding	2	0.8229	2	1	−1
Vehicles	26	0.7535	21	25	+4
Metal goods n.e.s.	23	0.7712	18	15	−3
Textiles	17	0.5769	10	10	−
Leather	1	0.7143	1	1	−
Clothing and footwear	16	0.6559	10	11	+1
Bricks, pottery, etc.	12	0.7220	9	8	−1
Timber and furniture	9	0.7770	7	8	+1
Paper, printing and publishing	13	0.8729	11	12	+1
Other manufacturing	25	0.7123	18	14	−4
				Differential shift	−12

was of only 1,000 jobs producing a differential gain of 2,000 jobs. Summing the final columns in Tables A.4a and A.4b gives the estimate of the structural and differential shifts. The overall results of the analysis are summarised in Table A.5.

Calculation of the total shift shows (Table A.5) that manufacturing lost 23,000 more jobs than would have been expected if its employment had changed at the national rate.

Examination of the regional share (or national trend) shows that national trends de-

Table A.5   Shift–share analysis: Wales, 1974 to 1981 ('000s)

Actual employment 1981	Expected employment* 1981	Total shift†	Regional‡ share	Structural§ shift	Differential shift¶
235	258	−23	−78	−11	−12

* Employment at t_1 (336) multiplied by national rate of change (0.7687).
† Actual less expected employment.
‡ Employment at t_1 (336) multiplied by national rate of change (0.7687) less employment at t_1.
§ See Table A.4a.
¶ See Table A.4b.

stroyed 78,000 jobs in Wales over the period 1974 to 1981 but this trend was modified by the structural and differential shifts. The trend effect plus the total shift equal the net loss of 101,000 jobs or 30 per cent of the 1974 workforce.

The loss of 23,000 jobs additional to those lost through national trends were accounted for almost equally by structural factors (−11,000 jobs) and the differential shift (−12,000 jobs).

Closer examination of the performance of each sector shows that much of the structural shift was due to the major presence of the metal manufacturing sector which suffered major losses nationally, a rate of job loss only exceeded by textiles which also contributed another important element to the structural shift. The only industry in the region to make a major positive contribution to the structural shift was the chemical industry which had the best national performance.

Not only did the poor national performance of metals contribute to employment decline in Wales, the Welsh metals industry had an even worse employment record than the national industry and thus performed even worse, contributing−11,000 jobs to the differential shift. Employment in metals in Wales was falling faster than employment in metals nationally. A more rapid employment loss than the national industry was also recorded by metal goods and other manufacturing industries. Two industries having a markedly better employment performance in Wales and therefore offsetting some of the negative differential shifts were vehicles and food and drink.

Interpreting these results needs care. When all industries have growing employment a more rapid employment growth rate than the national average for all manufacturing or the national average for an industry is usually indicative of output growth. In a period of overall job loss, industries and regions having job losses higher than average may be the most successful in the long term. Job loss with increased output raises productivity and enhances an industry's competitive standing in world markets. Industries losing jobs at a slow rate may be failing to adapt to change circumstances. Shift–share too tends to assume an atomistic economy. Yet the performance in metal in all probability reflects the long-term strategies of a single firm (British Steel) while the performance in vehicles possibly reflects the arrival of a major new production plant of the multinational Ford organisation.

Used with care shift–share analyses permit the isolation of structural influences on employment change but the technique is not without critics and one of the strongest has been H. W. Richardson. He claims that 'the advantages of the technique are illusory... [and that it is]... a harmless pastime for small... [persons]... with pocket calculators' (Richardson 1978:202–3) but a spirited defence is provided by Fothergill and Gudgin (1979). Detailed examination of the case against shift–share analysis suggests that there are three major criticisms if shift–share is used as a descriptive technique to isolate the effects of industrial structure on regional employment change.

First, there is the fact that the finer the industrial classification the greater will be the structural influence. This can be demonstrated in hypothetical examples and may be particularly evident if at one level of disaggregation industrial categories with diverse characteristics are grouped together while at a finer level they are allocated to different categories. Despite this criticism empirical studies have indicated the differences are relatively small (Dennis 1978:66). Nevertheless, the technique should be applied very cautiously in small regions where it is possible that specialist parts of an industry may dominate a sector and overemphasise the differential component.

A second criticism is that the outcome of the analysis will be influenced by the base years used in the calculation. In the example here, the initial year (t_1) was used but estimates can be made from t_2 or from some intermediate year. Yet, evidence from the United Kingdom regions based on estimates calculated first from 1952 and second from 1975 showed that the differential shift had a remarkable degree of stability (Fothergill and Gudgin 1979:313).

The third criticism is that the technique does not allow for multiplier effects between industries, in that decline in one sector may well lead to decline in others. This may be true in a few specialised regions with high local multiplier effects but the more general relationships are built into shift–share analysis through linkages at the national level which result in similar trends of decline or growth in industries which have strong links.

Clearly, there are problems in using shift–share analysis but as long as the technique is used carefully, it is a useful standardisation technique which allows the research worker to identify and remove the effects of industrial structure and to leave those elements of change that may reflect locational advantage or disadvantage as measured by the differential shift.

CLASSIFICATION OF INDUSTRIAL ACTIVITIES

Industries

Industrial classifications are based in part on the materials which are used in the production pro-cess, thus the broad groupings relate to different types of material inputs such as agricultural products, metals, ores and so on. This does, at times, make it difficult to study particular industries if they are defined in terms of products. A particularly pertinent example is the manufacture of gloves which in Britain could be classified to either textiles, leather or rubber industries depending upon the raw material from which they were made. Any classification will, of course, have its anomalies; all the student can hope for is that the data are available in as fine detail as possible to allow them to be reorganised to meet the needs of a particular enquiry and that the classifications remain unchanged over reasonable periods of time.

Classifications of this type are widely accepted but because of their technological bias they ignore many of the more human aspects of industrial activity such as the kind of jobs provided and the different forms of organisation controlling industrial activity.

Within any data source which classifies factories by their industrial category the data always appear with each factory allocated to a particular industrial activity. This hides the complexity of the industrial system in that the single industry factory is the exception rather than the rule. Most factories are allocated in the classification procedures to only one industry, that is the activity which accounts for most of the factory's output or, if that is not available, the activity with the highest number of employees. The degree of simplification this involves does vary from industry to industry. Some 10 per cent of the United Kingdom's biscuits are produced by factories classified to other industries whereas 45 per cent of animal feeding stuffs come from factories classified to other industrial categories. As a result of the classification procedures much of the fuzziness which tends to merge one industrial activity with another is hidden and a set of clearly defined industries emerges.

Components of change analysis

Increasingly, studies of individual industries have been replaced by studies of components of change yet, like industries, they are by no means as clearly defined as the tables, graphs and accounting frameworks which appear in published work suggest. Assigning plants to particular components can be problematical as two examples will illustrate. An independent plant might be acquired by another firm during the period being examined requiring a decision to be made as to whether it should be grouped with plants of similar status at t_1 (independent firms) or with those of similar status at t_2 (branch plants) or indeed, whether the framework should be expanded to allow for plants changing ownership. Other problems are presented by branches and transfers. A firm may establish a branch plant just before t_1 so that at t_1 the plant is clearly a branch but it may later switch all its operations from head office to the branch and cease operations at the head office site. Clearly, by t_2 the plant is a transfer rather than a branch.

Problems of classification are one difficulty arising in components of change analysis, another is that of assembling the data set. In its full form the components of change approach makes huge data demands. The minimum requirement is a list of plants and their employment totals at t_1 and t_2. Considerable effort has to go into collecting, editing and handling data on computer files. Not surprisingly complete tables have been drawn up mainly in an urban context and they exist in comprehensive form for only a few areas. These huge data demands have led some research in this area to focus its efforts on data manipulation and description, that is exploration of the data with little regard to explanation of the patterns that are identified but such descrip-

Table A.6 Measuring components of change: hypothetical data

		Employment (t_1) 10,000
Openings	1,000	
In situ expansion	3,000	
In situ contraction	−1,000	
Closures	−2,000	
Net change		+1,000
		Employment (t_2) 11,000

Openings as a percentage of t_1 employment 10 per cent.
Openings as a percentage of all new jobs 25 per cent.

tive work has been an important precursor of studies of particular components in greater depth.

A final difficulty has arisen in measuring the relative importance of the different components. Most importantly they should *not* be measured with reference to net change as Table A.6 makes clear. Openings appear to account for all the net growth of 1,000 jobs but without *in situ* expansion the net change would be negative. The usual practice is to express the numbers associated with each component as a percentage of base year employment or as a percentage of all jobs created/jobs lost. Regardless of how relative importance is measured the results will be influenced by a number of factors. The time period being examined is particularly important. In periods of recession, closures and *in situ* contraction are likely to be more important than in a time of growth. It has also to be recognised, although this is rarely done by those using the components of change approach, that variations may also be caused by the differences between regions in plant size and industrial structure.

— APPENDIX II —
POTENTIAL TRANSPORT COST AND MARKET POTENTIAL

In calculating a potential transport cost surface or a market potential surface much depends upon how areas, transport costs and markets are measured.

DEFINITIONS

Areas

It is usual to assume that the geographical region to be supplied by a firm is known. This region is then sub-divided into areas, either grid squares or administrative units, and it is assumed that within each area all customers are concentrated either at the mid-point of the grid square or the principal town within the administrative unit. While it would be possible to use data relating to the location of every individual customer, grouping them into areas reduces considerably the calculations. A broad grid or very large administrative areas give only very approximate answers; the smaller the grid or the smaller the administrative areas the more accurate the result. For illustrative purposes calculations are based on Wales and the eight planning regions of England.

Markets

The measure of market size (or possible market size) depends on the industry or industries being examined. A firm serving final demand might use retail sales or population data; a firm serving

Table A.7 Markets (manufacturing employment in planning regions, millions, 1981)

Wales	0.23
Yorkshire and Humberside	0.57
North-West	0.82
Northern	0.34
East Midlands	0.51
West Midlands	0.77
South-West	0.37
East Anglia	0.18
South-East	1.64

(*Source: Employment Gazette* 1983:61–5)

intermediate demand might use employment in manufacturing as an indication of the possible demand in each area. Manufacturing employment is used as a *surrogate* for the manufacturing market in Table A.7.

Transport costs

While it is possible to use actual road or rail rates in many cases such data are not available and the distances between places are used as surrogates for transport costs. Costs are calculated by the straight line (crow-fly) distances between the mid-point of each grid square or between the principal town of each administrative area. These distances are used to build up a *transport cost matrix* (Table A.8). In this example, it is assumed that the centre of each area is also a possible plant location. Estimating point-to-point distances presents little difficulty but the 'cost' of serving the local area (represented by the princi-

Table A.8 Transport cost matrix (km)*

	Cardiff	Leeds	Manchester	Newcastle	Nottingham	Birmingham	Bristol	Norwich	London
Cardiff	5	29	26	45	23	16	5	34	21
Leeds	29	5	6	13	11	16	29	24	29
Manchester	26	6	5	19	10	13	24	27	29
Newcastle	45	13	19	5	26	29	42	35	44
Nottingham	23	11	10	26	5	8	21	18	19
Birmingham	16	16	13	29	8	5	13	23	18
Bristol	5	29	24	42	21	13	5	32	18
Norwich	34	24	27	35	18	23	32	5	18
London	21	29	29	44	19	18	18	18	5

* PTC_i It is assumed for intra-regional sales goods move a mean distance of 50 km.

pal diagonal) is more problematical. It is usual to estimate the average distance from the midpoint to the rest of the grid square or area. In Table A.8 a mean distance of 50 km is assumed.

POTENTIAL TRANSPORT COST

The assumption is made that sales per head will not decline with increased distance from the point of production – a not unreasonable assumption with a policy of uniform delivered pricing. Potential transport cost (PTC) for a given point (excluding exports) is calculated (following Harris 1954) from the following formula

$$PTC_i = \sum M_j . D_{ij}$$

M_j measures the market (M) in a given part (j) of the total market, and D_{ij} indicates the transport cost (D) from a point (i) to the market (j). The index (PTC_i) by itself is meaningless but when calculated for a number of points it permits the identification of the minimum transport cost location to serve the market (minimum PTC_i) and the construction of a potential transport cost surface showing variations around that minimum cost location.

Using the data in Tables A.7 and A.8 the value of Cardiff is calculated as shown in Table A.9. By calculating the values for other cities the *minimum* value of T indicates the lowest cost point for serving the industrial market of England and Wales. By drawing isolines to indicate the extent to which other areas have higher costs, a transport cost surface can be constructed. Ex-

Table A.9 Potential transport cost and market potential indices

Potential transport cost (Cardiff)			Market potential (Leeds)	
M*	d†		M/d	
0.23	5	1.15	0.23/29	0.0079
0.57	29	16.53	0.57/ 5	0.1140
0.82	26	21.32	0.82/ 6	0.1367
0.34	45	15.30	0.34/13	0.0262
0.51	23	11.73	0.51/11	0.0464
0.77	16	12.32	0.77/16	0.0482
0.37	5	1.85	0.37/29	0.0128
0.18	34	6.12	0.18/24	0.0075
1.64	21	34.44	1.64/29	0.0566
Potential transport cost		120.76	Market potential	0.4563

* From Table A.7.
† From Table A.8.

amples of such surfaces were provided in Fig. 9.1.

MARKET POTENTIAL

Market potential calculations assume that demand per head decreases as distance from the point of sales increases. This is likely to occur under f.o.b. pricing but as was pointed out in Chapter 9 this distance decay pattern occurs quite widely.

Market potential (MP_i) for a given market but excluding exports is calculated from the following formula

$$MP_i = \sum \frac{M_j}{D_{ij}^d}$$

The terms to the right of the equation are identical to those in the PTC_i equation but in this case there is also an exponent (d) which describes the friction of distance. A high exponent (2 or 3) increases the friction so that potential demand falls rapidly from the point of sale, while a low exponent (for example, 0.5) reduces the friction. The exponent used varies between studies but it is usually selected with reference to empirical data. A number of studies adopt the convention of using an exponent of one because of 'the absence of clear theoretical justification for other values' (Keeble, Owens and Thompson 1982b: 423). Not only are the outcomes of the model sensitive to the values of the exponent (d) they can also be influenced markedly by the estimates of the value of intra-area movements costs (Dii)

which are central to the calculation of self-potential for a particular site. The higher the value of Dii the lower the demand in the area adjacent to the point of sale. As Houston observes (1969:227) 'the particular combination of d and Dii is...critical to the usefulness of the market potential idea'. Using the data in Tables A.7 and A.8 the value for Leeds can be calculated as shown in Table A.9. By calculating values for other cities the *maximum* value of MP_i indicates the point of maximum demand for a plant designed to serve the market in England and Wales. By drawing isolines to indicate the extent to which other areas have lower demand, a market potential surface can be constructed. Examples of such surfaces were provided in Fig. 9.1.

REFERENCES AND
── BIBLIOGRAPHY ──

Aduddel R, Cain L P 1973 Location and collusion in the meat packing industry. In Cain L P, Uselding P J (eds) *Business enterprise and economic change*. Kent State University Press, pp. 85–117

Ajao A J, Ironside R G 1982 Development in peripheral areas: aspects of the life cycle of manufacturing firms in the Canadian Prairies. In Collins L (ed.) *Industrial decline and regeneration*. Centre of Canadian Studies, University of Edinburgh, pp. 159–85

Allen M (ed.) 1983 *The Times 1000, 1983-4*. Times Books

Armstrong R B 1979 National trends in office construction, employment and headquarter location in US metropolitan areas. In Daniels P W (ed.) *Spatial patterns of office growth and location*. Wiley, pp. 61–93

Ashcroft B 1982 The measurement of the impact of regional policies in Europe: a survey and critique, *Regional Studies* 16: 287–305

Averitt R T 1968 *The dual economy: the dynamics of American industry*. Norton

Bale J R 1977 Industrial estate development and location in post-war Britain, *Geography* 62: 87–92

Bale J R. 1981 *The location of manufacturing industry: an introductory approach*. Oliver and Boyd

Barkley D L 1978 Plant ownership characteristics and the locational stability of rural Iowa manufacturers, *Land Economics* 54: 92–9

Barr B M 1983 Industrial parks as locational environments. In Hamilton F E I, Linge G J R (eds) *Spatial analysis, industry and the industrial environment Vol 3 Regional economies and industrial systems*. Wiley, pp. 423–40

Beattie E, Watts H D 1983 Some relationships between manufacturing and the urban system, *Geoforum* 14: 125–32

Berry C H 1967 Corporate bigness and diversification in manufacturing, *Ohio State Law Journal* 28: 402–26

Birch D L 1979 *The job generation process*. Summary Report: M I T Program on Neighbourhood and Regional Change. Cambridge

Blackaby F (ed.) 1978 *Deindustrialization*. Heinemann

Bloomfield G T 1981 The changing spatial organisation of multinational corporations in the world automotive industry. In Hamilton F E I, Linge G J R (eds) *Spatial analysis, industry and the industrial environment*. Wiley, vol. 2, pp. 357–94

Bluestone B, Harrison B 1982 *The deindustrialisation of America*. Basic Books

Boas C W 1961 Locational patterns of American automobile assembly plants, 1895–1958, *Economic Geography* 37: 218–30

Boddy M 1983 Changing public–private sector relationships in the industrial development process. In Young K, Mason C (eds) *Urban economic development: new roles and relationships*. Macmillan, pp. 34–52

Borchert J R 1978 Major control points in American economic geography, *Annals of the Association of American Geographers* 68: 214–32

Breheny M, Cheshire P, Langridge R 1983 The anatomy of job creation? Industrial change in Britain's M4 corridor, *Built Environment* 9: 61–71

Brewis T N 1974 Regional economic policy in Canada. In Hansen N M *Public policy and regional economic development*. Ballinger, pp. 305–33

Britton J N H 1974 Environmental adaptation of industrial plants, service linkages, locational environment and organisation. In Hamilton F E I (ed.) *Spatial perspectives on industrial organisation and decision-making*. John Wiley, pp. 363–90

Britton J N H 1976 The influence of corporate organisation and ownership on the linkages of industrial plants: a Canadian enquiry, *Economic Geography* **52**: 311–24

Brue S L 1972 *Local economic impacts of corporate mergers: the Nebraska experience.* University of Nebraska Studies, New Series No 43, University of Nebraska

Burgess J 1982 Selling places: environmental images for the executive, *Regional Studies* **16**: 1–17

Burrows J C, Metcalfe C E, Kaler J B 1971 *Industrial location in the United States.* D C Heath

Business Statistics Office 1972 *Report of the census of production 1968: Part 156.* HMSO

Business Statistics Office 1980 *Business monitor 1980: summary tables PA 1002.* HMSO

Camina M M 1974 Local authorities and the attraction of industry, *Progress in Planning* **3**: 83–182

Central Statistical Office 1984 *Regional trends 1984.* HMSO

Central Statistical Office 1985 *Annual abstract of statistics 1985.* HMSO

Chandler A D 1962 *Strategy and structure: chapters in the history of American industrial enterprise.* MIT Press

Channon D F 1973 *The strategy and structure of British enterprise.* Macmillan

Chapman K 1980 Environmental policy and industrial location, *Area* **12**: 209–16

Chapman S D 1972 *The cotton industry in the Industrial Revolution.* Macmillan

Chinitz B 1961 Contrasts in agglomeration: New York and Pittsburg, *American Economic Review: Papers and Proceedings Supplement* **51**: 279–89

Chisholm M 1970 *Geography and economics.* Bell

Chisholm M 1976 Regional policies in an era of new population growth and higher unemployment, *Regional Studies* **10**: 201–13

Chisholm M, Oeppen J 1973 *The changing pattern of employment: regional specialisation and industrial localisation in Britain.* Croom Helm

Clark C 1966 Industrial location and economic potential, *Lloyds Bank Review* **82**: 1–17

Clark C, Wilson F, Bradley J 1969 Industrial location and economic potential in western Europe, *Regional Studies* **3**: 197–212

Clark G L 1980 Local labor market dynamics and the determinants of quits and lay-offs, *Urban Geography* **1**: 215–28

Clark G L 1981 The employment relation and spatial division of labor: a hypothesis, *Annals of the Association of American Geographers* **71**: 412–24

Clark G L 1982 Local labor markets: a brief report and research agenda. In Robson B T, Rees J (eds) *Geographical agenda for a changing world.* Social Science Research Council

Clark G L, Gertler M 1983 Local labor markets: theories and policies in the US during the 1970s, *Professional Geographer* **35**: 274–85

Clark U E G 1976 The cyclical sensitivity of employment in branch and parent plants, *Regional Studies* **10**: 293–8

Collins L 1972 *Industrial Migration in Ontario.* Statistics Canada, Ottawa

Cooke P 1980 Discretionary intervention and the Welsh development agency, *Area* **12**: 269–77

Cooke P 1983 Labour market discontinuity and spatial development, *Progress in Human Geography* **7**: 543–65

Cooper M J M 1975 *The industrial location decision making process.* Occasional Paper No 34 Centre for Urban and Regional Studies, University of Birmingham

Crawford P, Fothergill S, Monk S 1985 *The effect of business rates on the location of employment.* Department of Land Economy, Cambridge

Cromley R G, Leinbach T R 1981 The pattern and impact of the filter-down process in nonmetropolitan Kentucky, *Economic Geography* **57**: 208–24

Cross M 1981 *New firm formation and regional development.* Gower

Czamanski D Z 1981 A contribution to the study of industrial location decisions, *Environment and Planning A* **13**: 29–42

Daniels P 1983 Service industries: supporting role or centre stage, *Area* **15**: 301–9

Danson M W 1982 The industrial structure and labour market segmentation: urban and regional implications, *Regional Studies* **16**: 255–65

Danson M W, Lever W F, Malcolm J F 1980 The inner-city employment problem in Great Britain, 1952–76: a shift–share analysis, *Urban Studies* **17**: 193–210

Darby H C (ed.) 1973 *A new historical geography of England.* Cambridge University Press

Deane P, Cole W A 1964 *British economic growth 1688–1959: trends and structure.* Cambridge University Press

Dear M, Clark G L 1978 The state and geographic process: a critical review, *Environment and Planning A* **10**: 173–83

Dennis R 1978 The decline of manufacturing employment in Greater London: 1966–74, *Urban Studies* **15**: 63–73

Department of Transport 1982 *Transport statistics, 1971–1981.* HMSO

Diamond D R, Spence N A 1983 *Regional policy evaluation.* Gower

Dicken P 1983 Japanese manufacturing investment in the UK, *Area* **15**: 273–84

Dicken P, Lloyd P E 1980 Patterns and processes of change in the spatial distribution of foreign-controlled manufacturing employment in the United Kingdom, 1963–75, *Environment and Planning A* **12**: 1405–26

Dodgshon R A, Butlin R A 1978 *An historical geography of England and Wales*. Academic Press

Doeringer P B, Piore M J 1971 *Internal labour markets and manpower analysis*. D C Heath

Dorward N M M 1979 Market area analysis and product differentiation: a case study of the West German truck industry. In Hamilton F E I, Linge G J R (eds) *Spatial analysis, industry and the industrial environment*. Wiley, vol. 1, pp. 213–60

Duncan O D, Scott W R et al. 1960 *Metropolis and region*. John Hopkins Press

Dunning J H (ed) 1971 *The multinational enterprise*. Allen & Unwin

Dunning J H 1981 *International production and the multinational enterprise*. Allen & Unwin

Dunning J H, Pearce R D 1981 *The world's largest industrial enterprises*. Gower

Dziewonski K 1966 A new approach to theory and empirical analysis of location, *Papers and Proceedings of the Regional Science Association* **16**: 17–25

Eichner A S 1969 *The emergence of oligopoly*. John Hopkins Press

Eirug A 1983 The Welsh development agency, *Geoforum* **14**: 375–88

English Estates 1984 *Industry in England*. English Estates

Erickson R A 1976 The filtering-down process: industrial location in a nonmetropolitan area, *Professional Geographer* **28**: 254–60

Erickson R A 1980 Corporate organisation and manufacturing branch plant closures in non-metropolitan areas, *Regional Studies* **14**: 491–501

Erickson R A 1981 Corporations, branch plants and employment stability in non-metropolitan areas. In Rees J, Hewings G J D, Stafford H A (eds) *Industrial location and regional systems*. Bergin, pp. 135–53

Erickson R A, Leinbach T R 1979 Characteristics of branch plants attracted to nonmetropolitan areas. In Lonsdale R E, Seyler H L (eds) *Nonmetropolitan industrialisation*. Winston and Sons, pp. 57–78

Estall R C 1972 Some observations on the internal mobility of investment capital, *Area* **4**: 193–7

Estall R C 1983 The decentralisation of manufacturing industry: recent American experience in perspective, *Geoforum* **14**: 133–47

Estall R C, Buchanan R O 1980 *Industrial activity and economic geography*. Hutchinson

Ewers H J, Wettmann R W 1980 Innovation-oriented regional policy, *Regional Studies* **14**: 161–79

Firn J R, Swales J K 1978 The formation of new manufacturing establishments in Central Clydeside and the West Midlands, 1963–72: a comparative analysis. *Regional Studies* **12**: 199–213

Florence P S 1962 *Post-war investment, location and size of plant*. National Institute of Economic and Social Research, Occasional Paper XIX. Cambridge University Press

Fothergill S, Gudgin G 1979 In defence of shift–share, *Urban Studies* **16**: 309–19

Fothergill S, Gudgin G 1982 *Unequal growth: urban and regional employment change in the UK*. Heinemann Educational

Fothergill S, Kitson M, Monk S 1983 The impact of new and expanded towns on industrial location in Britain, 1960–78, *Regional Studies* **17**: 251–60

Frank R H, Freeman R T 1978 *The distributional consequences of direct foreign investment*. Academic Press

Fredriksson C G, Lindmark L 1979 From firms to systems of firms: a study of inter-regional dependence in a dynamic society. In Hamilton F E I, Linge G J R (eds) *Spatial analysis, industry and the industrial environment vol I Industrial systems*. John Wiley, Ch. 9, pp. 155–86

Frost M, Spence N 1981 Policy responses to urban and regional economic change in Britain, *Geographical Journal* **147**: 321–49

Fuchs V R 1962 *Changes in the location of manufacturing in the United States since 1929*. Yale University Press

Gaffikin F, Nickson A 1984 *Jobs crisis and the multinationals: deindustrialisation in the West Midlands*. Trade Union Resource Centre

Galbraith J K 1967 *The new industrial state*. Hamish Hamilton

Gibson L J 1970 An analysis of the location of instrument manufacture in the United States, *Annals of the Association of American Geographers* **60**: 352–67

Gilmour J M 1974 External economies of scale, inter-industrial linkages and decision making in manufacturing. In Hamilton F E I (ed.) *Spatial perspectives on industrial organisation and decision-making*. Wiley, pp. 335–62

Goddard J B, Smith I J 1978 Changes in corporate control in the British urban system 1972–77, *Environment and Planning A* **10**: 1073–84

Gough P 1984 Location theory and the multi-plant firm: a framework for empirical studies, *Canadian Geographer* **28**: 127–41

Gould A, Keeble D 1984 New firms and rural industrialisation in East Anglia, *Regional Studies* **18**: 189–201

Gould P R, White R R 1968 The mental maps of British school leavers. *Regional Studies* **2**: 161–82

Gray H et al. 1972 *Foreign direct investment in Canada.* (The Gray Report) Government of Canada, Ottawa

Green M B, Cromley R G 1984 Merger and acquisition fields for large United States cities 1955–1970, *Regional Studies* **18**: 291–301

Greenhut M L 1956 *Plant location in theory and in practice: the economics of space.* University of North Carolina Press

Greenhut M L 1981 Spatial pricing in the United States, West Germany and Japan. *Economica* **48**: 79–86

Gregory D 1982 *Regional transformation and industrial revolution: a geography of the Yorkshire woollen industry.* Macmillan

Gudgin G 1978 *Industrial location processes and regional employment growth.* Saxon House

Gudgin G, Crum R, Bailey S 1979 White collar employment in UK manufacturing industry. In Daniels P W (ed.) *Spatial patterns of office growth and location.* Wiley, pp. 127–57

Gudgin G, Fothergill S 1984 Geographical variation in the rate of formation of new manufacturing firms, *Regional Studies* **18**: 203–6

Gwynne R N 1979 Oligopolistic reaction, *Area* **11**: 315–19

Hague D C, Newman P K 1952 *Costs in alternative locations: the clothing industry.* National Institute of Economic and Social Research, Occasional Paper XV, Cambridge University Press

Hall P G 1962 *The industries of London since 1861.* Hutchinson

Hamilton F E I 1978 Aspects of industrial mobility in the British economy, *Regional Studies* **12**: 153–65

Hamilton F E I 1984 Industrial restructuring: an international problem, *Geoforum* **15**: 349–64

Hamilton F E I, Linge G J R 1983 Regional economies and industrial systems. In Hamilton F E I, Linge G J R *Spatial analysis, industry and the industrial environment, vol 3, Regional economies and industrial systems.* Wiley, pp. 1–39

Hannah L 1976 *The rise of the corporate economy.* Methuen

Hansen N M 1974 Regional policy in the United States. In Hansen N M (ed.) *Public policy and regional economic development: the experience of nine western countries.* Ballinger, pp. 271–303

Hansen N M 1980 Subnational regional policies in the United States. In Hoffmann G W (ed.) *Federalism and regional development.* University of Texas Press, pp. 43–68

Haren C C, Holling R W 1979 Industrial development in nonmetropolitan America: a locational perspective. In Lonsdale R E, Seyler H L (eds) *Nonmetropolitan industrialisation.* Winston, pp. 13–45

Harris C D 1954 The market as a factor in the localization of industry in the United States, *Annals of the Association of American Geographers* **44**: 315–48

Hawkins R G 1972 Job displacement and the multinational firm. *Occasional Paper 3* Centre for Multinational Studies, Washington

Hay A M 1979 Positivism in human geography: response to critics. In Herbert D T, Johnston R J *Geography and the urban environment.* Wiley, vol. 2, pp. 1–26

Hay D A 1976 Sequential entry and entry deterring strategies in spatial competition, *Oxford Economic Papers* **28**: 240–57

Hayter R 1978 Corporate strategies and industrial change in the Canadian forest products industry, *Geographical Review* **66**: 209–28

Hayter R 1978 Locational decision-making in a resource based manufacturing sector: case studies from the pulp and paper industry of British Columbia, *Professional Geographer* **30**: 240–9

Hayter R 1981 Patterns of entry and the role of foreign-controlled investments in the forest-product sector of British Columbia, *Tijdscrift voor Economische en Sociale Geografie* **72**: 99–113

Hayter R, Watts H D 1983 The geography of enterprise: a re-appraisal, *Progress in Human Geography* **7**: 157–81

Healey M J 1981a Product changes in multi-plant enterprises, *Geoforum* **12**: 359–70

Healey M J 1981b Locational adjustment and the characteristics of manufacturing plants, *Transactions of the Institute of British Geographers* **NS6**: 394–412

Healey M J 1982 Plant closures in multi-plant enterprises – the case of a declining industrial sector, *Regional Studies* **16**: 37–51

Healey M J 1983 Components of locational change in multi-plant enterprises, *Urban Studies* **20**: 327–41

Healey M J 1984 Spatial growth and spatial rationalization in multi-plant enterprises, *GeoJournal* **9**: 133–44

Healey M J, Clark D 1984 Industrial decline and government response in the West Midlands: the case of Coventry, *Regional Studies* **18**: 303–18

Healey M J, Watts H D 1987 The multi-plant firm. In Lever W F (ed.) *Industrial change in the United Kingdom.* Longman

Helleiner G K 1981 *Intra-firm trade and the developing countries.* Macmillan

Henderson R A 1980 An analysis of closures amongst

Scottish manufacturing plants between 1966 and 1975, *Scottish Journal of Political Economy* **27**: 152–74

Henderson W O 1969 *The industrialization of Europe 1780–1914*. Thames and Hudson

Herron F 1981 *Post-Industry Act (1972) – industrial movement into and expansion in the assisted areas of Great Britain: some survey findings*. Government Economic Service Working Paper No 46, Department of Trade and Industry

Hill C 1954 Some aspects of industrial location, *Journal of Industrial Economics* **2**: 184–92

Hirsch S 1972 The United States electronics industry in international trade. In Wells L T (ed.) *The product life cycle and international trade*. Harvard Business School.

Hoare A G 1973 The spheres of influence of industrial location factors, *Regional Studies* **7**: 301–14

Hoare A G 1978 Industrial linkages and the dual economy: the case of Northern Ireland, *Regional Studies* **12**: 167–80

Hoare A G 1983 *The location of industry in Britain*. Cambridge University Press

Holland S 1976 *Capital versus the regions*. Macmillan

Hood N, Young S 1982 *Multinationals in retreat: the Scottish experience*. Edinburgh University Press

Hoover E M 1971 *An introduction to regional economics*. Knopf

Hotelling H 1929 Stability in competition, *Economic Journal* **3**: 41–57

House J W (ed.) 1983a *United States public policy: a geographical review*. Clarendon Press

House J W 1983b Regional and area development. In House J W (ed.) *United States public policy: a geographical review*. Clarendon Press, pp. 34–79

Houston C 1969 Market potential and potential transportation costs: an evaluation of the concepts and their surface patterns in the USSR, *Canadian Geographer* **13**: 216–36

Howells J R 1983 Filter-down theory: location and technology in the UK pharmaceutical industry, *Environment and Planning A* **15**: 147–64

Inquiry into Location Attitudes and Experience 1973 *Expenditure Committee: Regional development incentives, session 1973–74, House of Commons, 85–I*. HMSO

International Labour Office 1984 *Yearbook of labour statistics, 1984*. International Labour Office, Geneva

James F J, Hughes J W 1973 The process of employment location change: an empirical analysis, *Land Economics* **49**: 404–13

Johnson P S, Cathcart D G 1979 New manufacturing firms and regional development: some evidence from the Northern region, *Regional Studies* **13**: 269–80

Johnston R J 1979 Congressional committees and the inter-state distribution of military spending, *Geoforum* **10**: 151–62

Johnston R J 1980 *The geography of federal spending in the United States of Amercia*. Research Studies Press, John Wiley

Karaska G J 1969 Manufacturing linkages in the Philadelphia economy. *Geographical Analysis* **1**: 354–69

Keeble D 1968 Industrial decentralization and the metropolis: the north-west London case. *Transactions of the Institute of British Geographers* **44**: 1–54

Keeble D 1971 Employment mobility in Britain. In Chisholm M, Manners G (eds) *Spatial policy problems of the British economy*. Cambridge University Press, pp. 24–68

Keeble D 1976 *Industrial location and planning in the United Kingdom*. Methuen

Keeble D 1980 Industrial decline, regional policy and the urban–rural manufacturing shift. *Environment and Planning A* **12**: 945–61

Keeble D 1984 The urban–rural manufacturing shift. *Geography* **69**: 163–6

Keeble D, Owens P L, Thompson D 1982a *Centrality, peripherality and EEC regional development*. HMSO Books

Keeble D, Owens P L, Thompson D 1982b Regional accessibility and economic potential in the European community, *Regional Studies* **16**: 419–31

Khan A, Hayter R 1984 The linkages of new manufacturing firms: an exploratory enquiry in the Vancouver metropolitan area, *The Albertan Geographer* **20**: 1–13

Killick T 1983 Manufacturing plant openings, 1976–80, *British Business* 17 June: 466–8

Kondratieff N D 1978 The long waves in economic life, *Lloyds Bank Review* **129**: 41–60

Kroos H E 1974 *American economic development: the progress of a business civilization*. Prentice Hall

Krumme G 1981a Making it abroad: the evolution of Volkswagen's North American production plans. In Hamilton F E I, Linge G J R (eds) *Spatial analysis, industry and the industrial environment, vol 2, International industrial sytems*. Wiley, pp. 329–56

Krumme G 1981b Flexibility views in industrial location and location decision theory. In Rees J, Hewings G J D, Stafford H A (eds) *Industrial location and regional systems*. Bergin, pp. 107–21

Kuklinski A 1967 *Criteria for location of industrial plant*. United Nations

Laulajainen R 1981 Three tests on locational matching, *Geografiska Annaler* **63B**: 35–45

Laulajainen R 1982 Temporal hierarchy in corporate

space, *GeoJournal* **6**: 399–408

Law C M 1983 The defence sector in British regional development, *Geoforum* **14**: 169–84

Lawless P 1981 *Britain's inner cities: problems and policies.* Harper and Row

Leamer E E 1968 Locational equilibria, *Journal of Regional Science* **8**: 229–42

Lee C H 1979 *British regional employment statistics 1841–1971.* Cambridge University Press

Le Heron R B 1973 Best practice technology, technical leadership and regional economic development, *Environment and Planning A* **5**: 735–49

Leigh R, North D J 1978 Regional aspects of acquisition activity in British manufacturing industry, *Regional Studies* **12**: 227–45

Leinbach T R 1978 Locational trends in nonmetropolitan growth: some evidence from Vermont. *Professional Geographer* **30**: 30–6

Lever W F 1972 Industrial movement, spatial association and functional linkage. *Regional Studies* **6**: 371–84

Lever W F 1979 Industry and labour markets in Great Britain. In Hamilton F E, Linge G J R (eds) *Spatial analysis, industry and the industrial environment.* Wiley, vol. 1, pp. 89–114

Lever W F, McPhail C I, Norris G M 1978 Company dominated labour markets: the British case. *Tidschrift voor Economische en Sociale Geografie* **69**: 306–12

Linge G J R, Hamilton F E I 1981 International industrial systems. In Hamilton F E I, Linge G J R (eds) *Spatial analysis, industry and the industrial environment.* Wiley, vol. 2, pp. 1–117

Lloyd P E, Mason C M 1978 Manufacturing industry in the inner city, *Transactions of the Institute of British Geographers*, New Series 3: 66–90

Lloyd P E, Mason C M 1984 Spatial variations in new firm formation in the United Kingdom: comparative evidence from Merseyside, Greater Manchester and South Hampshire, *Regional Studies* **18**: 207–20

Logan M I 1966 Locational behaviour of manufacturing firms in urban areas, *Annals of the Association of American Geographers* **56**: 451–66

Logan M I 1970 Locational decisions in industrial plants in Wisconsin, *Land Economics* **46**: 325–8

Lösch A 1954 *The economics of location.* Yale University Press

Luttrell W F 1962 *Factory location and industrial movement.* National Institute of Economic and Social Research vol. 1

Lyons B R 1980 A new measure of minimum efficient plant size in UK manufacturing industry, *Economica* **47**: 19–34

McCallum J D 1979 The development of British regional policy. In Maclennan D, Parr J B (eds) *Regional policy: past experience and new directions.* Martin Robertson, pp. 3–41

McConnell J E 1980 Foreign direct investment in the United States, *Annals of the Association of American Geographers* **70**: 259–70

McConnell J E 1983 The international location of manufacturing investments: recent behaviour of foreign-owned corporations in the United States. In Hamilton F E I, Linge G J R (eds) *Spatial analysis, industry and the industrial environment.* Wiley, vol. 3, pp. 337–58

McDermott P J 1973 Spatial margins and industrial location in New Zealand, *New Zealand Geographer* **29**: 64–74

McDermott P J 1979 Multinational manufacturing firms and regional development, *Scottish Journal of Political Economy* **26**: 287–306

McDermott P J, Taylor M J 1982 *Industrial organisation and location.* Cambridge University Press

Macey R D 1982 *Job generation in British manufacturing industry: employment change by size of establishment and by region.* Government Economic Service Working Paper no 55, Department of Industry

McKay R R, Thomson L 1979 Important trends in regional policy and regional employment – a modified interpretation, *Scottish Journal of Political Economy* **26**: 233–60

Maclennan D, Parr J B 1979 *Regional policy: past experience and new directions.* Martin Robertson

Malecki E J 1979 Locational trends in R & D by large US corporations, 1965–77, *Economic Geography* **55**: 309–23

Malecki E J 1981 Government funded R & D: some regional economic implications, *Professional Geographer* **33**: 72–82

Malecki E J 1984 Military spending and the US defense industry: regional patterns of military contracts and subcontracts, *Environment and Planning C* **2**: 31–44

Mandell L 1975 *Industrial location decisions: Detroit compared with Atlanta and Chicago.* Praeger

Markusen A R 1983 High-tech jobs, markets and economic development prospects: evidence from California, *Built Environment* **9**: 18–28

Marshall J N 1979 Ownership, organisation and industrial linkage: a case study in the northern region of England, *Regional Studies* **13**: 531–57

Martin F *et al.* 1979 *The interregional diffusion of innovations in Canada.* Ministry of Supply and Services, Canada

Martin R L 1985 Monetarism masquerading as region policy? The government's new system of regional aid. *Regional Studies* **19**: 379–88

Mason C M 1980 Industrial decline in Greater Manchester, 1966–1975: a components of change approach. *Urban Studies* **17**: 173–84

Mason C M 1983 Some definitional problems in new firm research, *Area* **15**: 53–60

Massey D 1975 Approaches to industrial location theory: a possible spatial framework. In Cripps E L (ed.) *Regional science – new concepts and old problems.* Pion, pp. 84–108

Massey D 1979 In what sense a regional problem, *Regional Studies* **13**: 233–43

Massey D 1984 *Spatial divisions of labour: social structures and the geography of production.* Macmillan

Massey D, Meegan R 1979 The geography of industrial re-organisation: the spatial effects of the restructuring of the electrical engineering sector under the Industrial Reorganisation Corporation, *Progress in Planning* **10**: 155–237

Massey D, Meegan R 1982 *The anatomy of job loss.* Methuen

Mathias P 1983 *The first industrial nation: an economic history of Britain, 1700–1914.* Methuen

Mitchell B. R, Deane P 1962 *Abstract of British historical statistics.* Cambridge University Press

Moore B, Rhodes J 1973 Evaluating the effects of British regional economic policy, *Economic Journal* **83**: 87–110

Moore B, Rhodes J 1976 Regional economic policy and the movement of manufacturing firms to the development areas, *Economica* **43**: 17–31

Moore B, Rhodes J, Tyler P 1977 The impact of regional policies in the 1970s, *Centre for Environmental Studies Review* **1**: 67–77

Morgan A D 1978 Foreign manufacturing by UK firms. In Blackaby F (ed.) *De-industrialisation.* Heinemann, pp. 78–94

Moriarty B M 1980 *Industrial location and community development.* University of North Carolina

Moriarty B M 1983 Hierarchies of cities and the spatial filtering of industrial development, *Papers of the Regional Science Association* **53**: 59–82

Mounfield P R 1964–67 *The footwear industry of the East Midlands.* Department of Geography, University of Nottingham

Mounfield P R, Unwin D J, Guy K 1982 *Processes of change in the footwear industry of the East Midlands.* Department of Geography, University of Leicester

Moyes A 1980 Can spatially variable prices ever be fair? Some observations on the Price Commission's judgements on British cement prices, *Regional Studies* **14**: 37–53

Mumford L 1961 *The city in history.* Secker and Warburg

Newman R J 1984 *Growth in the American south.* New York University Press

Nicol W R 1982 Estimating the effects of regional policy: a critique of European experience, *Regional Studies* **16**: 199–210

Nishioka H, Krumme G 1973 Location conditions, factors and decisions: an evaluation of selected location surveys. *Land Economics* **49**: 195–205

Norcliffe G 1975 A theory of manufacturing places. In Collins L, Walker D F (eds) *Locational dynamics of manufacturing activities.* Wiley, pp. 19–51

Norman C 1981 Uniform pricing as an optimal spatial pricing policy, *Economica* **48**: 87–92

North D J 1974 The process of locational change in different manufacturing organisations. In Hamilton F E I (ed) *Spatial perspectives on industrial organisation and decision-making.* Wiley, pp. 213–44

North D J, Gough J 1983 The impact of local authorities on manufacturing firms: recent experience in London. In Young, K. Mason C (eds) *Urban economic development: new roles and relationships.* Macmillan, pp. 155–83

Norton R D, Rees J 1979 The product cycle and the spatial decentralization of American manufacturing, *Regional Studies* **13**: 141–51

Nunn D 1980 *The opening and closure of manufacturing units in the United Kingdom 1966–75.* Government Economic Service Working Paper No 36, Department of Industry.

Oakey R P 1981 *High technology industry and industrial location.* Gower

Oakey R P 1984a *High technology small firms.* Pinter

Oakey R P 1984b High technology industry, *Geography* **69**: 157–9

Oakey R P, Thwaites A T, Nash P A 1980 The regional distribution of innovative manufacturing establishments in Britain, *Regional Studies* **14**: 235–53

Oakey R P, Thwaites A T, Nash P A 1982 Technological change and regional development: some evidence on regional variations in product and process innovation, *Environment and Planning A* **14**: 1073–86

O'Farrell P N 1976 An analysis of industrial closures: Irish experience 1960–73, *Regional Studies* **10**: 433–48

O'Farrell P N 1984 Components of manufacturing employment change in Ireland 1973–1981, *Urban Studies* **21**: 155–76

O'Farrell P N, Crouchley R 1983 Industrial closures in Ireland, 1973–81: analysis and implications, *Regional Studies* **17**: 411–28

O'Farrell P N, Crouchley R 1984 An industrial and spatial analysis of new firm formation in Ireland, *Regional Studies* **18**: 221–36

Osleeb J P, Cromley R G 1978 The location of plants of the uniform delivered price manufacturer: a case study of Coca-Cola Ltd, *Economic Geography* **54**: 40–52

Owens P R 1980 Direct foreign investment – some implications for the source economy, *Tijdschrift voor Economische en Social Geografie* **71**: 50–62

Park S O, Wheeler J O 1983 The filtering down process in Georgia: the third stage of the product life cycle, *Professional Geographer* **35**: 18–31

Peet R 1982 International capital, international culture. In Taylor M J, Thrift N (eds) *A geography of multinationals*. Croom Helm, pp. 275–302

Peet R 1983 Relations of production and the relocation of United States manufacturing industry since 1960, *Economic Geography* **59**: 112–43

Peck F W 1985 The use of matched pairs research design in industrial surveys. *Environment and Planning A* **17**: 981–9

Peck F, Townsend A R 1984 Contrasting experience of recession and spatial restructuring: British Shipbuilders, Plessey, Metal Box. *Regional Studies* **18**: 319–38

Penrose E 1980 *The theory of the growth of the firm* 2nd edn. Blackwell

Perloff H S, Dunn E S, Lampard E E, Muth R F 1960 *Regions, resources and economic growth*. John Hopkins Press

Perry P J 1975 *A geography of nineteenth century Britain*. Batsford

Pocock D, Hudson R 1978 *Images of the urban environment* Methuen

Pollard S 1962 *The development of the British economy, 1914–1950*. Edward Arnold

Potter J 1974 *The American economy between the world wars*. Macmillan

Pounce R J 1981 *Industrial movement in the United Kingdom, 1966–75*. HMSO

Prais S J 1976 *The evolution of giant firms in Britain*. Cambridge University Press

Pratten C F 1971 *Economies of scale in manufacturing industry*. Cambridge University Press

Pratten C F, Dean R M 1965 *The economies of scale in large scale production in British industry: an introductory study*. Cambridge University Press

Pred A 1967 Behaviour and location: foundations for a geographic and dynamic location theory, Part I, *Lund Studies in Geography B* No 27. Gleerup, Lund

Pred A 1969 Behaviour and location: foundations for a geographic and dynamic location theory, Part II, *Lund Studies in Geography B* No 28. Gleerup, Lund

Pred A 1977 *City-systems in advanced economics*. Hutchinson

Rawstron E M 1958 Three principles of industrial location, *Transactions of the Institute of British Geographers* **25**: 132–42

Ray D M 1965 *Market potential and economic shadow*. Department of Geography Research Paper No 101, University of Chicago Press

Rees J 1972 The industrial corporation and location decision analysis, *Area* **4**: 199–205

Rees J 1974 Decision-making, the growth of the firm and the business environment. In Hamilton F E I (ed.) *Spatial perspectives on industrial organisation and decision-making*. Wiley, pp. 189–211

Rees J 1978 On the spatial spread and oligopolistic behaviour of large rubber companies, *Geoforum* **9**: 319–30

Rees J 1980 The impact of defense spending on regional industrial change in the United States. In Hoffmann G (ed.) *Federalism and regional development*. University of Texas Press, pp. 193–222

Rees J, Briggs R, Oakey R 1984 The adoption of new technology in the American machinery industry, *Regional Studies* **18**: 489–504

Rees J, Weinstein B L 1983 Government policy and industrial location. In House J W (ed.) *United States public policy: a geographical view*. Clarendon Press, pp. 213–62

Rich D C 1978 Population potential, potential transportation costs and industrial location, *Area* **10**: 222–6

Rich D C 1980 Locational disadvantage and the regional problem: manufacturing industry in Scotland, 1961–71, *Regional Studies* **14**: 399–417

Rich D C 1983 The Scottish Development Agency and the industrial regeneration of Scotland, *Geographical Review* **73**: 271–86

Richardson H W 1978 *Regional and urban economics*. Penguin

Robertson R M, Walton G M 1979 *History of the American economy*. Harcourt, Brace, Jovanovich

Robinson J F F, Storey D J 1981 Employment change in manufacturing industry in Cleveland, 1965–76, *Regional Studies* **15**: 161–72

Rothwell R 1978 The effects of technological change on employment. In Gerstenfeld A, Brainard R (eds) *Technological innovation: government–industry co-operation*. Wiley, pp. 20–40

Rothwell R 1982 The role of technology in industrial change: implications for regional policy, *Regional Studies* **16**: 361–9

Sant M 1975a Interregional industrial movement: the

case of the non-survivors. In Phillips A D M, Turton B J *Environment, man and economic change*. Longman, pp. 355–70

Sant M 1975b *Industrial movement and the regional problem: the British case*. Pergamon

Saxenian A 1983 The genesis of Silicon valley, *Built Environment* **9**: 7–17

Schmenner R W 1982 *Making business location decisions*. Prentice-Hall

Schofield J A 1979 Macro-evaluations of the impact of regional policy in Britain, *Urban Studies* **16**: 251–69

Scott A J 1982 Production system dynamics and metropolitan development, *Annals of the Association of American Geographers* **72**: 185–200

Semple R K, Phipps A G 1982 The spatial evolution of corporate headquarters within an urban system. *Urban Geography* **3**: 258–79

Sheard P 1983 Auto-production systems in Japan: some organisational and locational features, *Australian Geographical Studies* **21**: 49–68

Short J 1981 Defence spending in the UK regions, *Regional Studies* **15**: 101–10

Simon H A 1955 A behavioural model of 'rational choice. *Quarterly Journal of Economics* **69**: 99–118

Slowe P M 1981 *The advance factory in regional development*. Gower

Smith C T B *et al.* 1978 *Strikes in Britain: a research study of industrial stoppages in the United Kingdom*. HMSO

Smith D M 1966 A theoretical framework for geographical studies of industrial location, *Economic Geography* **42**: 95–113

Smith D M 1981 *Industrial location: an economic geographical analysis*. Wiley

Smith I J 1979 The effect of external takeovers on manufacturing employment change in the Northern Region between 1963 and 1973, *Regional Studies* **13**: 421–37

Smith I J 1982 The role of acquisition in the spatial distribution of the foreign manufacturing sector in the United Kingdom. In Taylor M, Thrift N (eds) *The geography of multinationals*. Croom Helm, pp. 221–51

Smith I J, Taylor M J 1983 Takeover, closures and the restructuring of the United Kingdom ironfoundry industry, *Environment and Planning A* **15**: 639–61

Smith W 1949 *An economic geography of Great Britain*. Methuen

Sobel R 1972 *The age of giant corporations*. Greenwood Press

Spooner D J 1972 Industrial movement and the rural periphery: the case of Devon and Cornwall, *Regional Studies* **6**: 197–215

Stafford H A 1960 Factors in the location of the paper-board container industry, *Economic Geography* **36**: 260–6

Stafford H A 1969 An industrial location decision model, *Proceedings of the Association of American Geographers* **1**: 141–5

Stafford H A 1972 The geography of manufacturers, *Progress in Geography* **4**: 181–215

Stafford H A 1974 The anatomy of the location decision: content analysis of case studies. In Hamilton F E I (ed.) *Spatial perspectives on industrial organisation and decision-making*. Wiley, pp. 169–87

Stafford H A 1977 Environmental regulations and the location of US manufacturing: speculations, *Geoforum* **8**: 243–8

Stafford H A 1980 *Principles of industrial facility location*. Conway Publications

Starbuck W H 1971 Organisational growth and development. In Starbuck W H (ed.) *Organisational growth and development*. Penguin, pp. 11–141

Steed G P F 1971 Plant adaptation, firm environment and location analysis, *Professional Geographer* **23**: 324–8

Steed G P F 1978 Global industrial systems – a case study of the clothing industry, *Geoforum* **9**: 35–47

Steed G P F 1981 International location and comparative advantage: the clothing industries in developing countries. In Hamilton F E I, Linge G J R (eds) *Spatial analysis, industry and the industrial environment*. Wiley, vol. 2, pp. 265–303

Sternlieb G, Hughes J W 1975 *Post-industrial America: metropolitan decline and inter-regional job shifts*. Centre for Urban Policy Research, New Brunswick

Storey D J 1981 New firm formation, employment change and the small firm: the case of Cleveland County, *Urban Studies* **18**: 335–45

Storey D J 1982 *Entrepreneurship and the new firm*. Croom Helm

Storey D J 1983a Indigenising a regional economy: the importance of management buyouts, *Regional Studies* **17**: 471–5

Storey D J 1983b Local employment initiatives in north-east England: evaluation and assessment problems. In Young K, Mason C (eds) *Urban economic development: new roles and relationships*. Macmillan, pp. 184–209

Storper M, Walker M 1984 The spatial division of labor: labor and the location of industries. In Sawers L, Tabb W K (eds) *Sunbelt/snowbelt: urban development and regional restructuring*. Oxford University Press, pp. 19–47

Struyk R J, James F J 1975 *Intrametropolitan industrial location: the pattern and process of change*. D C Heath

Swales J K 1979 Entrepreneurship and regional development: implications for regional policy. In Maclennan D, Parr, J B *Regional policy: past experiences and new directions*. Martin Robertson

Sweet M L 1981 *Industrial location policy for economic revitalization: national and international perspectives*. Praeger

Taylor M J 1970 Location decisions of small firms, *Area* **2**, Number 2, 51–4

Taylor M J 1984 *The geography of Australian corporate power*. Croom Helm

Taylor M J, Thrift N 1982a Industrial linkage and the segmented economy: 1. Some theoretical proposals, *Environment and Planning A* **14**: 1601–13

Taylor M J, Thrift N 1982b Industrial linkage and the segmented economy: 2. An empirical re-interpretation, *Environment and Planning A* **14**: 1615–32

Taylor M J, Thrift N 1983 Business organisation, segmentation and location, *Regional Studies* **17**: 445–65

Taylor M J, Wood P A 1973 Industrial linkage and local agglomeration in the West Midlands metals industry, *Transactions of the Institute of British Geographers* **59**: 129–54

Taylor T 1983 High-technology industry and the development of science parks, *Built Environment* **9**: 72–8

Thomas M D 1975 Growth pole theory, technological change and regional economic growth. *Papers of the Regional Science Association* **34**: 3–25

Thomas M D 1981 Growth and change and the innovative firm, *Geoforum* **12**: 1–17

Thompson W 1973 The economic base of urban problems. In Chamberlain N W *Contemporary economic issues*. Irwin, pp. 1–47

Thwaites A T 1978 Technological change, mobile plants and regional development, *Regional Studies* **12**: 445–61

Thwaites A T 1982 Some evidence of regional variations in the introduction and diffusion of industrial products and processes within British manufacturing industry, *Regional Studies* **16**: 371–81

Thwaites A T 1983 The employment implications of technological change in a regional context. In Gillespie A (ed.) *Technological change and regional development*. Pion, pp. 36–53

Tiebout C M 1957 Location theory, empirical evidence and economic evolution, *Papers and Proceedings of the Regional Science Association* **3**: 74–86

Tomkins C, Lovering J 1973 *Location, size, ownership and control tables for Welsh industry*. Welsh Council

Tornqvist G, Nordbeck S, Rystedt B, Gould P 1971 Multiple location analysis, *Lund Studies in Geography, Series C no 12*. Gleerup, Lund

Townroe P M 1969 Locational choice and the individual firm, *Regional Studies* **3**: 15–24

Townroe P M 1971 *Industrial location decisions: a study in management behaviour*. Occasional Paper No 15, Centre for Urban and Regional Studies, University of Birmingham

Townroe P M 1975 Branch plants and regional development, *Town Planning Review* **46**: 47–62

Townroe P M 1976 *Planning industrial location*. Leonard Hill

Townroe P 1979 *Industrial movement: experience in the US and the UK*. Saxon House

Townsend A R 1981 Geographical perspectives on major job losses in the UK, *Area* **13**: 31–8

Townsend A R 1983 *The impact of recession*. Croom Helm

Toyne P 1974 *Organisation, location, behaviour: decision making in economic geography*, Macmillan

Tyler P 1980 The impact of regional policy on a prosperous region: the experience of the West Midlands, *Oxford Economic Papers* **32**: 151–62

US Bureau of Census 1973 *County business patterns, 1972*. US Government Printing Office

US Bureau of Census (various dates) *Statistical abstract of the United States*. US Government Printing Office

US Bureau of Census 1982 *County business patterns, 1981*. US Government Printing Office

US Department of Commerce 1975 *Historical statistics of the United States: colonial times to 1970*. US Government Printing Office

Vernon R 1971 *Sovereignity at bay: the multinational spread of US enterprises*. Basic Books

Vernon R 1979 The product cycle hypothesis in a new international environment, *Oxford Bulletin of Economics and Statistics* **41**: 255–67

Vernon R, Hoover E M 1959 *Anatomy of a metropolis*. Harvard University Press

Walker D F 1980a *Canada's industrial space economy*. Bell and Hyman

Walker D F (ed) 1980b *Planning industrial development*. Wiley

Walters B J, Wheeler J O 1984 Localization economies in the American carpet industry, *Geographical Review* **74**: 183–91

Warren K 1969 Recent changes in the geographical location of the British steel industry, *Geographical Journal* **135**: 343–61

Warren K 1970 *The British iron and steel sheet industry since 1840*. Bell

Warren K 1973 *The American steel industry 1850–1870: a geographical intepretation*. Clarendon Press

Watts H D 1971 The location of the beet sugar industry in England and Wales, 1912–36, *Transactions of the Institute of British Geographers* **53**: 95–116

Watts H D 1974 Locational adjustment in the British beet sugar industry, *Geography* **59**: 10–23

Watts H D 1975 The market area of a firm. In Collins L, Walker D F (eds) *Locational dynamics of manufacturing activity*. Wiley, pp. 357–83

Watts H D 1978 Inter-organisational relations and the location of industry *Regional Studies* **12**: 215–25

Watts H D 1980a The location of European investment in the United Kingdom, *Tijdschrift voor Economische en Sociale Geografie* **71**: 3–14

Watts H D 1980b *The large industrial enterprise: some spatial perspectives*. Croom Helm

Watts H D 1980c Conflict and collusion in the British sugar industry, 1924 to 1928, *Journal of Historical Geography* **6**: 291–314

Watts H D 1981 *The branch plant economy*. Longman

Watts H D 1982 The inter-regional distribution of West German multinationals in the United Kingdom. In Taylor M J, Thrift N. *A geography of multinationals*. Croom Helm, pp. 61–89

Watts H D, Stafford H A (1986) Plant closures and the multi-plant firm: some conceptual issues, *Progress in Human Geography* **10**: 206–27

Webber M J 1984 *Industrial location*. Sage

Weber A 1929 *Alfred Weber's theory of the location of industries*. University of Chicago Press

Weinstein B L, Firestine R E 1978 *Regional growth and decline in the United States: the rise of the sunbelt and the decline of the northeast*. Praeger

Wheat L F 1973 *Regional growth and industrial location*. DC Heath

White P E forthcoming The future course of European population change In Findlay A M, White P E *Western European population change*. Croom Helm

White R L, Watts H D 1977 The spatial evolution of an industry: the example of broiler growing, *Transactions of the Institute of British Geographers* New series **2**: 175–91

Whittington R C 1984 Regional bias in new firm formation in the UK, *Regional Studies* **18**: 253–5

Williams W V 1967 A measure of the impact of state and local taxes on industry location, *Journal of Regional Studies* **7**: 49–59

Wise M J 1949 On the evolution of the jewellery and gun quarters in Birmingham, *Transactions of the Institute of British Geographers* **15**: 57–72

Women and Geography Study Group 1984 *Geography and gender: an introduction to feminist geography*. Hutchinson

Woodward J 1965 *Industrial organisation: theory and practice*. Oxford University Press

Wright M, Coyne J, Lockley H 1984 Regional aspects of management buyouts: some evidence, *Regional Studies* **18**: 428–31

Yaseen L C 1960 *Plant location*. American Research Council.

INDEX

ability, 68–73, 174
absenteeism, 96–7
accessibility to materials, services, markets, 77,
    113–20, 171, 174, 225, 238–40
accounting frameworks *see* employment accounts
acquisitions, 31, 32, 33, 52–4, 62, 70, 122, 127, 161,
    163, 164–5, 168, 173–4, 177, 186–7, 197, 200, 203,
    237
activity locations, 185
activity rate *see* participation rate
adaptation, 72, 87, 179, 185
administrative employment *see* white-collar jobs,
    occupational structure
adoption, 72, 179
Aduddel, R., 122
advance factories, 133, 214
advice agencies, 67, 133
agglomeration economies, 136–9
    see also internal economies of scale, localisation
    economies, urbanisation economies
aggregate travel model *see* potential transport cost
airports/air transport, 26, 77
Ajao, A. J., 184
amortization *see* depreciation
areal units *see* scale, spatial
Armstrong, R. B., 227
Ashcroft, B., 217
assisted areas, 82, 90, 138, 166, 167–8, 184, 187,
    212–21
atomistic economies, 52
Averitt, R. T., 55

backward linkages *see* material linkages, service
    linkages
Bailey, S., 60
Bale, J. R., 108, 112, 123, 133
banking systems, 104
Barkley, D. L., 192, 196

Barr, B. M., 108, 133
barriers to entry, 88–9, 151, 158
base value effect, 2, 231
basing-point prices, 114
Beattie, E., 120
behavioural approach, 14
behavioural matrix, 71
Berry, C. H., 185
best-practice, 90
Birch, D. L., 189
births *see* new plants
Blackaby, F., 1
Bloomfield, G. T., 29
Bluestone, B., 1, 91, 98, 101, 132, 135, 144, 161, 191,
    192, 197, 198, 202
Boas, C. W., 40
Boddy, M., 108, 133
Bradley, J., 120
branch plants, 11, 59, 65, 70, 71–2, 73, 105–6, 110,
    131, 146, 153, 178–9, 182, 183, 184, 186, 196, 225
    closure, 191, 194, 195–6
    contribution to net change, 205–7
    definition, 142–4, 237
    location, 161–77
    regional policy, 211
Breheny, M., 84
Brewis, T. N., 214, 215
Briggs, R., 90
Britton, J. N. H., 118
brownfield site, 180, 186, 198
    see also in situ change
Brue, S. L., 187
Buchanan, R. O., 65, 96, 223
building costs, 107
buildings, 155, 156, 195, 229
    see also industrial property development, industrial
    estates, advance factories
Burgess, J., 67, 133, 134, 176